Introduction to **International** & **Global Studies**

INTRODUCTION TO

International & Global Studies

SECOND EDITION

SHAWN SMALLMAN

KIMBERLEY BROWN

The University of North Carolina Press Chapel Hill

© 2015 The University of North Carolina Press

Designed and Set in Scala and Scala Sans with Champion by Rebecca Evans.
Manufactured in the United States of America.

The paper in this book meets the guidelines for permanence and durability
of the Committee on Production Guidelines for Book Longevity of the Council
on Library Resources.

The University of North Carolina Press has been a member of the Green Press
Initiative since 2003.

Cover illustration: Visible Earth image courtesy of NASA (http://visibleearth
.nasa.gov/) and Geoeye.

Library of Congress Cataloging-in-Publication Data
Smallman, Shawn C.
Introduction to international and global studies / Shawn Smallman
and Kimberley Brown.—Second edition.
pages cm
Includes bibliographical references and index.
ISBN 978-1-4696-2165-4 (pbk : alk. paper)
ISBN 978-1-4696-2166-1 (ebook)
1. Globalization. 2. World citizenship. 3. International cooperation.
4. International relations. I. Brown, Kimberley, 1966– II. Title.
JZ1318.S597 2015 327—dc23
2014021666

19 18 17 16 15 5 4 3 2 1

To Mina, Paige, and Audrey,

with faith in your ability to make a difference

Contents

Maps, Tables, Photographs, and Figure

PHOTOGRAPHS

FIGURE

Introduction to **International** & **Global Studies**

ONE **Introduction**

Lauren grew up in a suburb of Minneapolis, Minnesota. While an undergraduate, she arranged with one of her professors to conduct an independent research project and traveled to Liberia in West Africa for a summer. Upon her return, she worked as an intern for an international nongovernmental agency and, as she completed a political science degree, made plans for a career in the areas of philanthropy and leadership. Following graduation, she joined the Peace Corps and traveled to Cape Verde, where she worked in family health. These experiences helped her choose to earn a graduate degree in public health, as well as a graduate certificate in nonprofit management. In graduate school, she met her future husband, an Indian national. She is now part of a bicultural family in which she and her husband both are working to expose their children to the plethora of cultures around the world through travel and education. She also remains deeply engaged in international philanthropy. Lauren had not initially known where her undergraduate program of study would lead her; she knew only that she thrived on making contact with individuals from other cultures, even as she came to know her own culture better.

Fekade is Ethiopian. His parents emigrated to the United States when he was eight years old. Raised bilingually and biculturally, he attended public elementary and high schools in the Pacific Northwest. His original intention was to find a way to return to Ethiopia to work in some type of international service. Following his undergraduate work in international studies, he has since decided to focus his graduate work on public health and immigrant communities in the United States. He has organized students at his university to participate in activities that focus on the United Nation's Millennium Development Goals and to try to make informed choices about everything they do. Contact with other cultures has transformed both his education choices and career choices.

The life trajectories of Lauren and Fekade (whose stories are real but whose names have been changed here) are not unusual. Many people are profoundly touched by their concern for international questions. Perhaps you will also find your life transformed by your cultural contacts and program of study. But whether or not you

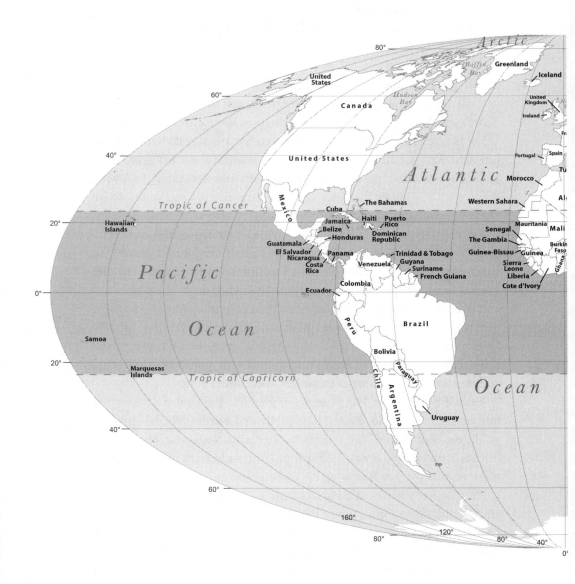

Map 1 The World (Steph Gaspers 2008)

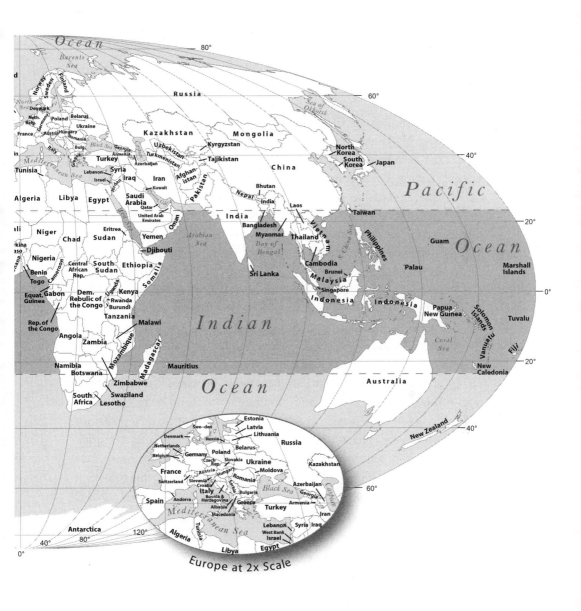

Europe at 2x Scale

choose to look for international career opportunities, your life will be affected by global trends. Some issues, such as those surrounding epidemic disease, may impact you on a deeply personal level. For example, as new strains of influenza emerge, you and your family may have to make choices about finding a vaccine. Similarly, your life is influenced by changes in the global economy. The Chinese government owns a substantial portion of the U.S. government's debt. That means that decisions made in Beijing shape the interest rate that someone in the United States pays for a student loan or their mortgage. And whether you live in Halifax, Nova Scotia, or Manchester, England, a global recession, or changes in trade patterns, may impact the company you work for by opening up new opportunities for sales or moving jobs overseas. When you purchase foods, you are making a choice that impacts people you will never see in other parts of the globe, whether you decide to buy shade-grown coffee or fair-trade chocolate. Commodity chains for other products—such as energy—also shape our daily lives. If political unrest closes the Strait of Hormuz, oil importers could see gasoline rationing. At the same time, European wind companies may invest in turbines that appear near you in Kentucky or Calgary, whether you view this positively or not. Security concerns also will impact your life, perhaps when friends or family are deployed overseas or when you encounter frustration with security measures while traveling.

With cultural globalization, our literature, art, music, trade, and technology are impacted by flows of information. You may follow a celebrity twitter in Los Angeles, Skype your grandmother in Hong Kong, and check your friend's Facebook page in London. Or you may listen to a West African fusion band that has been influenced by Celtic music. You may emigrate someday, or immigrants may shape your community. Perhaps no age has been as touched by global trends as the one you live in. For this reason, it is important for you to study international studies, the multidisciplinary field that examines major international issues.

What Is International Studies?

International studies is an increasingly common major, not only in liberal arts colleges but also in public institutions. What unites all of these programs is that they try to interpret major global trends in a manner that is multidisciplinary; that is, they draw on faculty and ways of looking at the world that come from many different areas (Ishiyama and Breuning 2004; Hey 2004). A scholar in international studies might utilize the writing of political philosophers to describe the global economy or consider how films reflect new trends in cultural globalization. This cross-pollination among multiple disciplines is central to the field. International studies programs also share certain common characteristics, such as an emphasis on language competence and various dimensions of globalization.

The related term "global studies" is preferred by some scholars because it removes the focus on the nation-state and places it instead on the transnational processes and issues that are key in an era defined by globalization. Global studies programs also often stress the importance of race, class, and gender in international affairs, as well as the importance of social responsibility. Both international studies and global studies programs share a commitment to interdisciplinary work, a focus on globalization and change, and an emphasis on how global trends impact humanity. They both also differ from international relations, an older discipline within political science that emphasizes ties between nations and topics with clear importance to nation-states, such as war, economics, and diplomacy. Finally, both international and global studies share a concern with global citizenship.

Global Citizenship

During the 2008 election campaign in the United States, then presidential candidate Barack Obama declared himself to be a "citizen of the world." Former House Speaker Newt Gingrich criticized this position as "intellectual nonsense and stunningly dangerous" (Gerzon 2009). This exchange encapsulated a debate about the nature of citizenship that stretches back to ancient Greece. The philosopher Socrates (469–399 B.C.E.) allegedly said, "I am a citizen, not of Athens or Greece, but of the world." His student Aristotle thought seriously about the meaning of citizenship, as did the Stoic philosophers. At the core of this idea of world citizenship was the idea that individuals have a duty to other people outside of their state because of their shared humanity. This debate about the nature of citizenship—and the ideal of cosmopolitanism, the belief that we need to view affairs from our perspective as global citizens—has been a thread through the writing of many scholars. It was central to the thinking of Enlightenment philosophers such as the German Immanuel Kant (1724–1804), who spoke of an individual's membership in a universal community as a basis for global peace (Kant, "Essay on Theory and Practice," in Brown, Nardin, and Rengger 2002, 441–50). It even shaped the thought of European philosophers during the Age of Empire. For example, the Italian thinker Giuseppe Mazzini (1805–72) wrote at length about an individual's duties to humanity and the fact that an individual's loyalty cannot be determined by his or her nationality alone (Mazzini, *On the Duties of Man*, in Brown, Nardin, and Rengger 2002, 476–85). Recently, Martha Nussbaum (1998) and Kwame Anthony Appiah (2006) have written influential works in defense of cosmopolitanism.

While this ideal has been enduring, it has also been contested, because global citizenship is not a legal status. Critics argue that it is a vaguely defined term that appeals to people's sentiments and emotions but has little meaning in an anarchical world—that is, in an international order that lacks a central power to impose law. This book is not the place to encapsulate this broader debate. But global citizenship remains a powerful idea, and as authors we believe it has deep meaning. As a citizen, you will face complex global issues from trade to war, commanding your attention and calling for you to make decisions. One goal of this text is to help you critically reflect on global issues and identify the contexts where your loyalty, responsibility, and connection to others will make a difference. Perhaps the notion of global citizenship seems too strong or exclusive to you. If this is so, what about the notion of being a globally minded individual?

While there are many definitions of global citizenship, one author suggests that a global citizen possesses six capacities of mind: "(1) the ability to observe oneself and the world around one; (2) the ability to make comparisons and contrasts; (3) the ability to 'see' plurally as a result; (4) the ability to understand that both 'reality' and language come in versions; (5) the ability to see power relations and understand them systemically; and (6) the ability to balance awareness of one's own realities with the realities of entities outside of the perceived self" (McIntosh 2005, 23). As you look over these capacities, you may notice some overlap between them and our descriptions of our goals for you with this text. You are living in what Pratt (1996) terms a "contact zone"; that is, your ideas come in contact with other people and other ideas all the time. In order to negotiate this space, you have to be able to "imaginatively step into the world view of the other" (Bennett 1998). In a sense, this mindset will mean that you will have a bigger "tool kit" to deal with problems. Much like the astronauts on Apollo 13, when someone is faced with a crisis, they respond best when they have more tools to work with. While you will not likely ever face such an emergency, if you have a rich, global perspective, you will be better able to take advantage of opportunities, such as the chance to work overseas or with people from different cultures. A global perspective changes not just what you think, but what you do.

The Authors and International Studies

We are both faculty members who have taught international studies for over a decade and served as director of an international studies program at a large, urban institution. Kim Brown became interested in international studies as an undergraduate while studying anthropology, French, and geography at Macalester College. During that time, she was able to coteach an international studies senior seminar with a visiting German Fulbrighter, Dr. Gotz von Houwald, whose area of specialization was Central American indigenous peoples. This experience led her to become passionate about the international learning experience. She is now a professor of applied linguistics who has expertise in world Englishes—the different forms of English spoken globally—as well as intercultural communication and education and development. She lived and worked in Iran during the late 1970s, a time of turmoil that included the 1979 Revolution, the beginning of the decade-long Iran-Iraq war, and the now-infamous takeover of the U.S. Embassy and ensuing hostage crisis. She has maintained a close cultural connection to Iran ever since.

Shawn Smallman became interested in international affairs while he was an undergraduate at Queen's University, where he became fascinated with Latin America during a history class taught by Catherine LeGrand. He is now a professor of international studies who has published books examining the history of military terror in Brazil and the evolution of the AIDS pandemic in Latin America. For the latter project, he carried out fieldwork in Brazil, Cuba, and Mexico, during which he interviewed drug traffickers, crack addicts, sex workers, transvestites, doctors, and gay leaders. More recently, he has done work on influenza and global health, with a focus on ethical issues related to pandemics in such countries as Indonesia (Smallman 2013).

We have both taught outside of our own countries (in Germany and Iran) and have traveled widely. From this background, we have the experience of crossing cultural boundaries from Rio de Janeiro to Tehran. Together, we speak or read Farsi, French, Portuguese, and Spanish. We have also served as administrators: Brown was vice provost for international affairs, while Smallman was the dean of undergraduate studies and vice provost of instruction. Currently, Smallman is the director of an international studies program. Both of us have worked to internationalize undergraduate education and have presented the results of our work at professional meetings. Our teaching, travel, disciplines, work experience, and language competence have shaped how we have written this book. Finally, we have a shared belief in the value of a liberal arts education and the importance of clear learning outcomes.

Learning Outcomes and Competing Worldviews

We want you to finish this text having achieved a number of learning outcomes: to see yourselves as members of global as well as local communities, to be aware of major world regions and the nation-states within them, to be open to intercultural contact, to place issues in historical and ideological context, and to be able to judge information about major global trends and issues. In essence, after you have read this book, we hope that you will possess the comprehensive set of skills and understandings envisioned by Howard Gardner in his exploration of what it means to be a global citizen: "(1) understanding of the global system; (2) capacity to think analytically and creatively within disciplines; (3) ability to tackle problems and issues that do not respect disciplinary boundaries; (4) knowledge of and ability to interact civilly and productively with individuals from quite different cultural backgrounds—both within one's own society and across the planet; (5) knowledge of and respect for one's own cultural tradition(s); (6) fostering of hybrid or blended identities; and (7) fostering of tolerance" (2004, 253–55). We hope that as you engage with this text, you will come to understand key global issues, the perspectives of different cultures, and the responsibilities of global citizenship. We also want you to be able to think critically about competing worldviews. This goal is critical to many disciplines, but it is particularly essential in international studies. For this reason, you will see global issues presented from different perspectives throughout this text.

In the chapters that follow, we will introduce material from all major world regions. You will see ideas and information from scholars whose ideas conflict with each other as well as from scholars whose ideas reinforce common understandings of particular issues. You will not see chapters on every global issue, although there are many key topics that might have filled entire sections, such as water, religion, and women. No comprehensive selection of chapters was possible because of the breadth of international issues. Instead, chapters 2 through 7 focus on history, globalization (economic, political, and cultural), development, and security to give you a broad understanding of the context of global issues. The second block of chapters focuses on global topics in which you may more readily see yourself as an actor who may be impacted by a commodity chain for food or energy. The subjects covered in these chapters are, in order, food, health, energy, and environment. Chapter 12 considers the many career opportunities in international fields, and the conclusion will place what you have learned in context and ask you to reflect again on the meaning of global citizenship.

References

Abdi, A., and L. Shultz. 2008. *Educating for human rights and globalization.* Albany, N.Y.: SUNY Press.

Appiah, K. A. 2006. *Cosmopolitanism: Ethics in a world of strangers.* New York: W. W. Norton.

Banks, J. A. 2001. *Cultural diversity and education: Foundations, curriculum, and teaching.* Boston: Allyn and Bacon.

Bennett, J. 1998. Transition shock: Putting culture shock in perspective. In *Basic concepts of intercultural communication,* ed. M. Bennett, 215–24. Yarmouth, Maine: Intercultural Press.

Boulding, E. 1988. *Building a civic culture: Education for an interdependent world.* Syracuse, N.Y.: Syracuse University Press.

Brown, C., T. Nardin, and N. Rengger, eds. 2002. *International relations in political thought: Texts from the ancient Greeks to the First World War.* New York: Cambridge University Press.

Carter, D., and S. Gradin. 2001. *Writing as reflective action: A reader.* New York: Longman.

Gardner, H. 2004. How education changes: Considerations of history, science, and values. In *Globalization: Culture and education in the new millennium,* ed. M. Suarez-Orozco and D. Qin-Hilliard, 235–58. Berkeley: University of California Press.

Gerzon, M. 2009. Going global: The Gingrich-Obama "global citizen" debate. June 23. http://www.ewi.info/going-global-gingrich-obama-%E2%80%9C global-citizen%E2%80%9D-debate.

Hanvey, R. 1982. An attainable global perspective. *Theory into Practice (Global Education)* 21 (3): 162–67.

Hey, J. 2004. Can international studies research be the basis for an undergraduate international studies curriculum? A response to Ishiyama and Breuning. *International Studies Perspectives* 5:395–99.

Hoopes, D. 1979. Intercultural communication concepts and the psychology of intercultural experience. In *Multicultural education: A cross-cultural training approach,* ed. M. D. Pusch, 10–38. Yarmouth, Maine: Intercultural Press.

Ishiyama, J., and M. Breuning. 2004. A survey of international studies programs at liberal arts colleges and universities in the Midwest: Characteristics and correlates. *International Studies Perspectives* 5:134–46.

McIntosh, P. 2005. Gender perspectives on educating for global awareness. In *Educating citizens for global awareness*, ed. N. Noddings, 22–39. New York: Teachers College.

Nussbaum, M. 1998. *Cultivating humanity: A classical defense of reform in liberal education*. Boston: Harvard University Press.

Pike, G. 2008. Reconstructing the legend: Educating for global citizenship. In *Educating for human rights and global citizenship*, ed. A. Abdi and L. Shultz, 223–38. Albany, N.Y.: SUNY Press.

Pratt, M. L. 1996. Arts of the contact zone. In *Resources for teaching ways of reading: An anthology for writers*, ed. D. Bartholomae and A. Petrosky, 440–60. Boston: Bedford Books.

Smallman, S. 2013. Biopiracy and vaccines: Indonesia and the World Health Organization's new pandemic influenza plan. *Journal of International and Global Studies* 4 (2): 20–36.

Stevenson, R. W. 2002. Middle path emerges in debate on Africa Aid. *New York Times*. June 9.

Suarez-Orozco, M., and D. Qin-Hilliard. 2004. *Globalization: Culture and education in the new millennium*, 1–37. Berkeley: University of California Press.

Tapias, A. 2008. Global diversity and intercultural competence development. October 3. Conference Plenary: First Annual IDI Conference, Minneapolis, Minn.

TWO **History**

> **SYNOPSIS**

Technological and military changes led to the unexpected rise of
Europe and the birth of modern imperialism beginning in the late
fifteenth century. Although the rise of nationalism ultimately destroyed European empires, nearly five centuries of European imperialism have deeply shaped our world's demography, economy, and
culture. Now the international system is defined by the nation-state,
which is increasingly challenged by the power of globalization.

> **SCAFFOLDING**

As you read through this chapter, think about how you would answer
each of the questions below.

*When you started this chapter, how much did you know about the history
of imperialism? How has the legacy of imperialism shaped our world?*

*In chapter 1, you were introduced to the idea of global citizenship, which
is not a new idea. In what ways might it have been easier for people in an
earlier era to think of themselves as global citizens?*

*Whose histories were missing from this chapter? What information could
have been added?*

> **CORE CONCEPTS**

*Why was Europe's rise unexpected? How would you describe Euro-
pean empires, and what factors led to their end?*

*What are the similarities and differences between different eras of
globalization?*

What do you think the future of the nation-state is likely to be, based on the information from this chapter? What might replace the nation-state?

Our knowledge of the world has been shaped by the stories we have been told and the contexts we have lived in. While many would say there is an absolute set of true facts regarding world events, others would argue that the lenses we put on shape both what we see and what we look for. We do not generally read an account of an event and ask "Who wrote this?," "Is something missing?," or "Are there equally compelling alternative explanations of the same phenomenon?" We learn what we are taught. In international studies, we strive to understand how local contexts and cultural issues may shape our understanding of information. Two cases, based on our own experiences with academic institutions in Brazil and Iran, illustrate how a historical context shapes the presentation of information during times of revolution and struggle.

How people understand their world is shaped by the stories they have been told and the way in which they understand their past as an individual, a family member, and a citizen. This reality became clear to me (Smallman) in the summer of 1990, when I did intensive language training in Portuguese in Brazil. At one point, I was seated on a lawn on a university campus, speaking with a group of friends who were all university students. I told them that the way that their university was laid out made no sense. They had to take a bus to travel from their residence hall to their classrooms, and then take another bus to travel to the cafeteria for lunch. Why hadn't the architects designed a space in which people could walk from one place to another throughout their day? My friends then told me that this was no accident. During military rule in Brazil (1964–85), the armed forces had feared that students could form a source of opposition to the regime. Accordingly, military officers had deliberately designed the university's layout to make it as difficult as possible for students to congregate. When I told this story to a faculty member later to learn if it was true, the professor told me that the changes the military had made during this period went much deeper than the buildings themselves. The university had also changed its curriculum, so that history classes now ended with Brazilian independence in the 1820s. The generals had not wanted university students to study more contemporary social issues. What was strange, the faculty member told me, was that since democratization in 1985, the curriculum had not changed because both faculty members and students had internalized this definition of history. When I spoke with my student friends later, they disagreed with this interpretation. They claimed that history courses ended in the early nineteenth century because anything more recent was not truly history. With time, as I researched a book on how the Brazilian military shaped historical memory to achieve its political goals, I came to understand the deep legacies that military rule had on Brazilian academia, popular memory, and society.

These issues also were relevant half a world away. In March 1979 the Ayatollah Khomeini returned to Iran. Universities were closed for a period of more than three years as the government developed a plan to Islamicize the curriculum. Students who needed fewer than nine credits to finish their degree were allowed to graduate. Others had to wait three and a half years and submit proof that they were strong Muslims who had not engaged in any antigovernment activity during the time the universities were closed or immediately preceding the closure. At the high school level, social studies textbooks were the first to undergo a rewriting process. Pictures of the shah were stripped from the front page and replaced with pictures of the Ayatollah Khomeini; photos of burning tires and demonstrations were placed within the contemporary history chapter. The shah was denounced in the textbook, and the virtues of the new Islamic Republic were laid out. At the elementary school level, all illustrations beginning with the first grade text were changed: illustrations of a family eating a meal at a table were replaced with illustrations of a family seated on a carpet with a large tablecloth spread on the floor; instead of a small girl lying in a bed with her blankets pulled up, hair askew around her face, the textbook had an image of a child lying on a pallet on the floor with a head scarf on. These changes were completed within a twelve-month period. The government was heavily invested in rewriting history and framing what was to come.

Governments care about how you understand the past because it shapes your decisions politically and your engagement in the world around you. Because multiple forces will try to shape your understanding, it is very important to learn to critically interpret the past. This chapter will focus on the surprising rise of Europe in the fifteenth century, the Age of Imperialism and its legacy, the emergence of nationalism, the roots of current globalization, and the continued importance of the nation-state. Our intent is to provide you with one perspective of world history that will allow you to frame later information in the text.

The Unexpected Rise of Europe

If a dispassionate observer had studied the globe in the fourteenth century, it would have been unlikely that he or she would have chosen Europe as the region that would dominate international affairs for the next five centuries. Nothing predestined Europe's rise. Barbara Tuchman titled her 1978 history of this period *A Distant Mirror: The Calamitous 14th Century* with good reason. The Black Death so depopulated Paris that wolves roamed its empty suburbs. The division of the papacy plunged Christendom into a prolonged political crisis, while the Hundred Years' War (1337–1453) absorbed the energies of two major states (England and France) for generations. The start of the fourteenth century saw the onset of the Little Ice Age, which perhaps explains why the Norse colonies in Greenland disappeared. Famine was a frequent challenge for European states during this period, which was so politically and socially difficult that some Europeans thought that the world might be ending. The Crusades had failed, and Europe was on the defensive.

While Europe staggered from one crisis to the next, Islam had undergone centuries of expansion during an earlier epoch of cultural and religious globalization, which had created a shared world that stretched from the Atlantic to Central Asia and from Iraq to Indonesia. The impact of this experience was enduring: "[T]he Arab conquests inaugurated a thousand-year era, lasting from the seventh to the seventeenth century, when all the major civilizations of the Old World—Greco-Roman, Irano-Semitic, Sanskritic, Malay-Javanese, and Chinese—were for the first time brought into contact with one another by and within a single overarching civilization" (Eaton 1990, 17). New cities sprang up from Baghdad to Cordova, as an urban, sophisticated civilization spread throughout the Old World (Eaton 1990, 19).

Travelers such as Ibn Battuta could travel with ease in the fourteenth century, during which he "crisscrossed North and West Africa, the Middle East, the steppes of Central Asia, India, Southeast Asia, and China, for an estimated total of 73,000 miles" (Eaton 1990, 44). For centuries, Islamic scholars had translated works from Greek, studied mathematics, and rethought agronomy. Islamic victories allowed them to experiment with new crops, including "fruits such as banana, sour orange, lemon, lime, mango, watermelon, and the coconut palm" (Eaton 1990, 23). Equally important was the diffusion of new technologies, such as paper (Eaton 1990, 22). Many Europeans feared that Christendom could not withstand Islam's waxing power. In 1453 Byzantium, which for eight centuries had shielded Europe from Islamic invasion, fell to the Turks because its famous walls could not withstand cannon fire. This defeat blocked the old spice trade to the East along the Silk Road and left Europe isolated.

At the same time that Islam was rising, China was expanding its power from Asia into the Indian Ocean. In 1421 Imperial China sent out a massive fleet—which contained many vessels that dwarfed the greatest European ships—on a nearly three-year expedition to India, East Africa, and Indonesia (Abu-Lughod 1993, 10). Chinese technology was advanced, as were its population and resources. But even for China, this fleet was so expensive that the taxes to pay for it created protests. By the time the expedition's survivors returned, China was turning inward, and the Great Fleet was disbanded. This ended an important opportunity for Chinese expansion: "Although the reasons for this reversal of policy remain shrouded in mystery and enigma, and scholars are far from agreeing on an explanation, the results were clear and disastrous for the prospects of continued Asian independence" (Abu-Lughod 1993, 16). One of the outcomes of this inward turn, both in China and Japan, was that it permitted Russia to extend its authority across Siberia to the Pacific. It also meant that expanding European empires did not face competition in India, East Africa, or Indonesia. For this reason, Janet Lippman Abu-Lughod (1993, 16) has argued that China's turn inward was fundamental to the success of European expansionism.

This expansion began in the unlikeliest of places: Portugal, a small, lightly populated nation on the edge of the Western world. When the Silk Road was closed to the West, Europeans began to wonder if they could reach the East by sea. This idea proved especially attractive to Henry the Navigator, the monarch of Portugal (1394–1460) who spent his fortune and his life encouraging scholarship in the era of navigation and ship design. Throughout the 1400s, the Portuguese expanded out into the Atlantic to the Azores (1427), the Cape Verde Islands (1455–56), and the west coast of Africa (McGhee 1991, 79). This exploration helped Europeans to develop and hone their naval skills while China was turning inward. At the same time that political divisions and other problems sapped the strength of Islamic Spain (Andalusia), the states of Christian Spain moved toward unity, especially after the marriage of Ferdinand and Isabella in 1467. With the fall of Granada—the last Islamic state in Spain—to the combined forces of Castile and Aragon in 1492, Spain was freed to direct its energies into the Atlantic.

While the new unity and naval knowledge of Iberia prompted European expansionism, an equally important force was a revolution in military affairs that made European armies vastly more powerful than their counterparts. In the fourteenth century, there had been little to distinguish European armies from those of Africa, the Islamic Empire, or China. This changed in the following three centuries. Gunpowder was a Chinese creation that the Islamic world and Europe adopted in the 1300s. At Nicopolis in September 1396, the Turks destroyed a French army, proving that European forces had no relative advantage over those of the Ottomans. A century later, however, gunpowder had brought profound changes to Europe. Mounted knights were no longer effective against foot soldiers with matchlocks. Different states began to experiment with combining pikemen with gunners. The rise of cannons made castles outmoded. With the introduction of cannons into naval warfare, even small Portuguese ships could challenge Islamic fleets in the Indian Ocean. The change took place over centuries, and the Islamic world, in particular, adopted many of the same practices and technologies. But the trend was clear: "By 1700 the disproportion between European and other styles of warfare had become pronounced and, in conjunction with parallel improvements in naval management and equipment, allowed Europeans to expand their power literally around the globe in the course of the eighteenth and nineteenth centuries" (McNeill 1989, 2). The timing of this military revolution was important, for it took place at the same moment that Europe expanded into the Atlantic and beyond.

The Americas

The New World likely had been visited by other cultures prior to Columbus. Certainly, the native populations of North America had trading relationships with their counterparts in eastern Siberia, as well as with the Norse in Greenland, which means that some archaeological finds of iron and bronze goods in northern Canada predate Columbus's arrival (Sutherland 2000, 244–47; Schledermann 2000; Pringle 2012). Archaeologists have found Norse ships in Greenland that were built of Canadian wood (Seaver 2000, 273). So the term "discovery" must be a qualified one, as flows of people and goods had taken place for thousands of years. Still, Columbus's arrival in 1492 in the Caribbean was an epoch-making event and marked the true birth of Europe's rise to global dominance. For thirty years, the Spanish expanded throughout the Caribbean, with disastrous results for local peoples. On the island of Hispaniola, the Tainos' numbers plummeted from perhaps more than 1 million to at most a few thousand in 1531. Between 1519 and 1521, Spanish troops led by Hernán Cortés overthrew the Aztec Empire; a decade later, Spanish troops under Francisco Pizarro overthrew the Incas, the greatest empire then known: "[B]igger by far than any European state, the Inca dominion extended over a staggering thirty-two degrees of latitude—as if a single power held sway from St. Petersburg to Cairo" (Mann 2006, 71). As a result, Spain gained access to the silver, gold, crops, and resources of the New World.

The reasons for the Europeans' victory were manifold, as Jared Diamond (1997), Alfred Crosby (1972, 35–63), and others have explained, and did not reflect any cultural failings of New World peoples. The Aztec and Incan Empires were masters of political organization. The Incas were an ethnic group that came to dominate the Andean region of South America in the 1400s and 1500s. They were engineers who could build roads and bridges to unite their empire from one end of the Andes Mountain chain to the other, while they constructed buildings out of stones so carefully worked that no mortar was needed. The astronomical knowledge in Meso-America may have been equal to that of Europe at the time. Anyone who has visited the Museum of Gold in Bogotá—which holds but a tiny fraction of the cultural wealth of precontact Andean peoples—must stand in awe of its riches. But none of these achievements changed the fact that New World peoples had not been exposed to smallpox and other diseases (Alchon 2003). Nor had they seen horses, steel, or gunpowder. In 542 the Byzantine Empire's efforts to reclaim the Western Roman Empire had collapsed in the face of one illness: bubonic plague (Rosen 2007, 3). The Aztecs and Incas had to deal simultaneously with smallpox, gunpowder, and cavalry. The populations of these empires underwent a stunning demographic collapse (Mann 2006, 143–44).

While the Spanish conquered the Aztec and Incan Empires, the Portuguese expanded into Africa and began the slave trade. After Vasco de Gama successfully passed the southern tip of Africa in 1498, the Portuguese gained access to the trade markets of Asia, which undercut the old spice road. In 1516 the Portuguese destroyed Islamic forces in the Arabian Sea (Abu-Lughod 1993, 9). The Islamic world was no longer the key connection of East and West. Timbuktu in West Africa was a center renowned both for its wealth and for its scholarship in the fourteenth century (Eaton 1990, 41). But that wealth depended on trade, and Portuguese galleons were more efficient than camel caravans. Portugal, which was a marginal state on the rim of Europe, controlled an empire that stretched from Goa,

India, to Mozambique, Africa. Its colony of Brazil would one day come to encompass half of South America. No longer was the Mediterranean the center of a global trading system (Abu-Lughod 1993, 18). Instead, Europeans dominated global trade—at the core of which was slavery.

The Spanish could count initially on the labor of the large indigenous populations that they had conquered in Mexico and Peru. As these populations declined, however, they turned to African slaves from Portuguese colonies in Africa. Because of the rapid decline of Caribbean populations, African slavery was always fundamental to the region's development during the colonial period. Likewise, the Portuguese—who dominated the slave trade—turned to African slaves as the main labor source in Brazil, where sugar plantations in the northeast created fabulous wealth. Similarly, the British colonies in the New World soon embraced slavery to obtain the labor that underlay an economy based on plantation agriculture. This trade enriched both the nations that controlled it and the producers in the colonies who employed it. The scale of the trade was so large that it had a demographic impact upon both the Old World and the New World while creating ideologies and inequalities that have endured until the present.

It was this period that created modern ideas of race, in which social class and standing were mapped onto skin color. This was not a long-standing tradition in European history. The Romans had not placed much importance on skin color, and while they practiced slavery, it was in no way defined by race. The demographic changes created by the slave trade brought peoples together from diverse regions of the globe. This provided a useful tool for economic elites, who could determine a person's social role by their physical appearance. The challenge, of course, was that from the start, mixing took place, and binary categories of race became complicated. Different imperial powers adopted varied approaches to this, which meant that the idea of race in Brazil was quite different from that in the United States, although both shared the brutality of slavery. But it was in this period that conceptions of race appeared that continue to shape social and political issues in North and South America and Europe. Even at the time, there were some individuals who questioned both these categories and slavery itself. But the wealth created by slavery was so central to European empires that economic interests outweighed moral concerns.

Besides the wealth created by the slave trade, the conquest of the New World also enabled Europeans to exploit new agricultural and mineral resources. After silver was discovered at Potosi, Bolivia—an old Incan mining site—in the 1540s, Spain had access to perhaps the greatest single

The same historical event can seem very different based on your cultural or national perspective. Can you identify three events or trends in this chapter that would be perceived differently by two groups?

source of mineral wealth in the world. There were also new crops that were introduced into Europe that would put an end to the cycle of famine so common in the late Middle Ages (despite counterexamples, such as the Irish potato famine of the mid-nineteenth century). Alfred Crosby (1972, 64–121) has written about the process of biological imperialism, by which European countries imported new crops to the Americas. By this term, Crosby referred to the practice by which Europeans replaced native plants and animals with crops and domestic animals from the Old World to transform the environment in a manner that suited their economic needs. There are many examples of this process. Sugar came to define Brazilian society throughout the colonial period, but important new crops—chilies, tomatoes, corn, squash, and many others—brought about an agricultural revolution in Europe. As Crosby has argued, these crops led to a demographic explosion in Europe and the Old World, as the food supply increased dramatically. This demographic change created a "surplus population" in Europe, which enabled large populations of European descent to travel and settle in the Americas (Crosby 1972, 165–207). Within Europe, the population increase, the precious metals, the slave economy, and the trade networks that came with the conquest of the New World fed rapid technological advances and the expansion of European power into new regions (Abu-Lughod 1993, 18).

Europe did not confine its ambitions to the Americas. The Dutch founded the Dutch East India Company in 1602 and came to control Indonesia; Dutch ambitions in Brazil were overcome by warfare between 1630 and 1654. In 1788 the British claimed Australia. Although they fought in the New World, the Portuguese and Dutch both expanded their holdings in Africa. In the nineteenth century, European powers competed to acquire colonies in Africa in a process in which the division of vast stretches of African territory was made in conference rooms in Europe. Even regions that had been wealthier or more technologically advanced than Europe in the fourteenth century were vulnerable. The Ottoman Empire waned, and by the early twentieth century, most of the Islamic world had come under European rule. Even China, which was once the wealthiest and most populous nation on earth, lost control of territories (Hong Kong and Macao) or had areas carved up into "Spheres of Influence." This phrase recognized the particular areas that European countries tended to dominate, even if they did not formally control them. Imperialism was the dominant political principle for much of the world in the nineteenth and early twentieth centuries. The resources of the New World helped Europe dominate much of the Old World.

The Legacy of Empire

The Age of Empire would have a profound impact upon the globe, in part because European empires proved to be surprisingly enduring. The Portuguese, who had begun this expansion in the fifteenth century, did not lose their African possessions until the 1970s. While a history of this period is far too complex to detail in this brief chapter, it marked the onset of ideas and markets that continue to shape our world. This section will focus on its legacies. One of the most important legacies is the creation of diasporas—populations outside of their homelands who still retain emotional and cultural connections to their places of origin. As this chapter has discussed, the slave trade brought millions of Africans across the Atlantic. Sections of Africa were devastated and depopulated by the trade, as one West African state after another fell to the Portuguese and other nations. The entire demography of other regions, such as the Caribbean, was remade. Of course, the slave trade was not the only great population movement during this period. The nineteenth century saw large population movements from Europe to the Americas, Australia, New Zealand, South Africa, and other colonies. While some people came looking for more opportunities, many others—such as the Irish in the aftermath of the great famine, or Russian Jews fleeing violence—sought to escape dangers in the Old World. These diasporas profoundly shaped identities and nationalities from Australia to North America.

At the same time, this period saw the creation of colonial relations, in which imperial powers established and governed the economies of their colonies to the advantage of the mother country. For example, the Caribbean islands were devoted to monocrop agriculture that created wealth for a small European population on the islands in addition to the governments of France, Spain, Holland, and England. Trade within this system was carefully controlled so as to discourage the development of manufacturing within the colonies, which might allow the periphery to compete with the center. Colonies were also only able to trade with their mother countries and not with other European powers. While imperialism came to an end with the collapse of Portuguese rule in Africa in the 1970s, many of these colonial relationships endure and have a legacy in the present. Anyone who has traveled through the vast sugar fields of Brazil or Cuba can see the enduring markets that were created during the Age of Imperialism, as well as their social legacy. The Age of Empire also gave birth to the identities that ultimately destroyed the imperial system. The inequality of colonial relations created resentments in Latin America and the United States that led to revolution. Colonial censors from Brazil to Mexico sought to limit the spread of nationalist ideals that could challenge imperial authority. But the idea of the nation-state, which was born in Europe, over time spread throughout the colonies, so that the period from 1776 to the 1970s marked the edge of Europe's expansion.

The Rise of Nationalism

In a sense, this period witnessed a struggle between two ideas. On the one hand, European imperialism had continued a process of globalization that may have stretched back to the Islamic flowering that preceded it. On the other hand, the Age of Empire also witnessed the rise of the idea of the nation-state. In 1648 the Peace of Westphalia ended the Thirty Years War in the region that would later become Germany. The key idea of the two treaties that ended this religious war was that each "prince" had the right to decide the public religion of his own people, while people who practiced other Christian beliefs could still practice their religion in private. At the same time, it was a clear principle of this understanding that states should refrain from interfering in each other's affairs, which is central to the modern idea of national sovereignty. Of course, as Europeans adopted this idea and it became an increasingly powerful tool, they did not wish to extend sovereignty to their colonies. And nation making was a violent and contradictory affair, which was often founded upon myth making and exclusion (Anderson 1983). Even the concept of nationalism is difficult to define, despite the intense hold that it gained among millions of people. Nonetheless, the concept of nationhood spread from Europe to the rest of the globe and provided the foundation for our modern international system.

The tension between the ideals of nationhood and empire first became apparent in the Americas, where the United States achieved its independence in 1783. In 1804 Haiti claimed its independence as part of the only successful slave rebellion in history. Most of Latin America achieved independence by the 1820s. In other areas, such as Canada and Australia, colonies gradually took a peaceful path to nationhood. These two contradictory processes existed side by side, so that even as much of the New World gained its independence in the nineteenth century, most of Africa and Asia witnessed the rapid expansion of European empires.

This tension between nationalist ideals and imperialist reality did not exist only on the periphery of empires. The contradiction between the two helped to lead Europe into two devastating world wars in the twentieth century. Newer nations that were late to imperial expansion sought what they argued to be their rightful place on the world stage. To mobilize their peoples, all nations—even in the staunchly antinationalist Soviet Union— turned to nationalism. Other empires, such as that of Austro-Hungary, were overwhelmed by the rising tide of nationalism and fractured into multiple nation-states. In the aftermath of the Second World War, many European nations lacked the resources or popular will to maintain an empire. Within Europe, the idea of nationalism was discredited, and sympathy grew among elites for a pan-European vision that would culminate in the creation of the European Union. In Africa, Asia, and elsewhere, the rising power of nationalism made empires increasingly untenable. In some cases, European nations gave up their empire with a minimum of resistance, as the British did in India. In other cases, such as the French in Algeria and Vietnam, European forces fought on until they were overrun or bankrupted. But the result was the same. The first great wave of nationalist movements took place in the late eighteenth and early nineteenth centuries and freed most of the Americas from European control. The second great wave, after the end of World War II in 1945, saw colonies in the Caribbean, Africa, Asia, and the Pacific gain their independence.

Within Europe itself, the continent was divided, and power passed to two external powers—a fact that demonstrates the degree to which European power was eclipsed. The United States and the Soviet Union dominated the international system. The key line between these two powers was drawn in the heart of Germany, where the Berlin wall represented the greatest division in the international order. While nations could declare their neutrality in the political, economic, and ideological struggle between these states, it proved difficult to avoid taking sides given the blandishments that each offered. The major European powers, such as England, France, and Germany, feared they could no longer define a conflict that might culminate in the destruction of Europe. The age of European dominance had passed. But the tension endured between the nation-state and global forces.

Imperialism's Collapse and the Cold War

In many respects, from the late eighteenth century onward, the Age of Empire was defined by the tension between imperialism and nationalism. In contrast, after World War II, global political affairs were dominated by the struggle between the Soviet Union and its clients and the United States and its allies. The United States depicted itself as leading an alliance of democratic countries against the totalitarian Soviet bloc. But in practice, it proved quite willing to ally itself with brutally repressive regimes in Latin America, Indonesia, and Africa—provided that they had clear anti-Communist credentials. The Soviet Union depicted itself as the standard bearer of anticolonialism, but its invasions of Hungary, Czechoslovakia, and Afghanistan showed it had much in common with the nineteenth-century Russian Empire. In theory, China and the Soviet Union were close allies as the world's great Communist powers. In practice, the two sparred over their contested borders, while in the 1970s China drew closer to the United States. Despite these contradictions, both sides sought to maintain alliances, cultivate clients, and punish those nations that aligned with the opposing side.

For more than four decades, this great contest between two global ideologies subordinated all other questions. In other words, the two Great Powers (a Great Power is a state so influential that it is able to help define the international system) viewed all international issues through the lens of the Cold War, often to the great frustration of countries—the nonaligned nations—that did not want to take part in this contest. Because this competition was viewed as a zero-sum game, a win by one side was necessarily a loss for the other. This led to terrible errors, such as the U.S. intervention in Vietnam, and near disaster, such as the Cuban Missile Crisis. But the Cold War also had positive impacts, such as freezing ethnic and nationalist struggles in Yugoslavia, despite the brutality and violence that characterized Soviet rule. The system was also predictable, and it could be assumed that both sides were rational. With time, both sides had invested so much in infrastructure, ideology, and energy in the contest that its end appeared unthinkable. Therefore, it came as a great shock when the Soviet Union collapsed with stunning speed in 1991.

One of the great tasks of the so-called post–Cold War era was formulating a new framework to understand international affairs. For a brief period, authors presented one argument after another. Some proposed that the future would be one of unstoppable democratization—which would be positive but quite boring (Fukuyama 1989). Others foresaw a future defined by clashes between major world civilizations (Huntington 1993). No one framework can capture all the tensions and movements in any historical period. With time, however, it became clear that the Cold War had obscured a contradiction between the expansion of the nation-states and the rising power of globalization. As imperialism ended, the number of nation-states climbed rapidly. At the same moment, however, the institutions that shaped globalization were founded, and the nation-state faced new challenges to its authority.

Globalization

At the broadest level, globalization refers to the rise of sociopolitical and economic networks that dominate local and regional interactions. Manfred Steger (2003, 13) refers to a "multidimensional set of social processes that create, multiply, stretch, and intensify worldwide social interdependencies and exchanges while at the same time fostering in people a growing awareness of deepening connections between the local and the distant." The strength of this definition is that it describes globalization as a process that takes place not only at the level of the state related to trade or politics but also at the level of people's daily lives, which includes culture and identity.

Globalization is not a new phenomenon, and dating its onset is difficult. As we have described already, the period of Islamic expansion (the seventh through fifteenth centuries) had witnessed a period of cultural flowering accompanied by technological, agricultural, and economic exchange that in many respects looks like an early period of globalization. Certainly, the expansion of European empires created global networks that stretched from remote Pacific Islands to West Africa. New technologies, from the development of the telegraph to the rise of steam-powered trains, have been connecting peoples since the nineteenth century. Nonetheless, the period of globalization that began after the Cold War has accelerated the manner in which the global impedes on the local to a degree unknown in earlier eras. While new technologies are important to this process, it could not have taken place without an institutional context, which was deliberately created under the leadership of the United States after World

War II. These institutions, collectively called the Bretton Woods System, are fundamental to understanding globalization. Their influence is a key factor that helps to explain why the current period of globalization differs from that of the past.

In 1944 it appeared inevitable that Germany, Japan, and their Axis counterparts would be defeated. It was also clear that Europe would be devastated and that the Soviet Union would be a Great Power. The old order was discredited by the Depression and the war, and there was an opportunity to rethink the world's financial architecture. In 1944 the United States convened a meeting in Bretton Woods, New Hampshire, which created three key institutions. The first was the International Monetary Fund (IMF). The U.S. dollar became the world's global currency, and the U.S. dollar was backed by gold. The idea was to avoid currency crises, which could bankrupt a nation's industries overnight. For example, during Mexico's financial crisis in 1994, the price of a U.S. dollar rose so quickly that Mexican corporations proved incapable of repaying their debts, while U.S. firms could not sell their goods in Mexico. The IMF was designed to address these crises, although the world no longer has a system of fixed exchange rates, and global currencies are no longer pegged to the dollar. The IMF remains a powerful financial actor. Far better known than the IMF, however, is the International Bank for Reconstruction and Development (IBRD), commonly referred to as the World Bank. Although its creators designed it to help Europe recover from World War II, its mission changed to focus on development in the 1950s. The World Bank loaned funds to developing countries at low interest rates. The idea was that the infrastructure and projects that the bank funded would prove to be so economically beneficial that the countries could use their growth to repay the costs of the loan.

The final institution in the Bretton Woods System was the General Agreement on Tariffs and Trade (GATT), which began life as a trade agreement between twenty-three nations. The original goal of this agreement was to reduce tariffs (taxes on trade) in the belief that all members of the agreement would benefit if global trade expanded. This was based on the idea of comparative advantage; that is, if each nation specialized in producing the goods to which it was most suited (so that Canada did not grow bananas, and Ghana did not produce ice wine), the total wealth of the world would increase. In order to accomplish this, member nations of GATT had to agree that if they gave a tariff break to one member, they would give the same reduction in tariffs to all. In 1995 GATT changed into a new and more powerful institution: the World Trade Organization (WTO). This body can monitor the trade in ideas as well as goods. The WTO is also extremely controversial. Like all Bretton Woods institutions, the manner in which the WTO is portrayed depends very much on how the author or speaker views globalization. Chapters 4 and 5 explore this in more detail.

In any case, all observers would agree that the Bretton Woods System created the basic architecture for globalization. The era after World War II saw the integration of the global economy in a manner that was different from earlier eras. Transnational corporations emerged that were so large they rivaled the economic scale of small nation-states. With time, some increasingly lost their identities as corporations located in particular countries. New technologies emerged that dramatically dropped the price of transportation, shipping, and communication. With these changes, global capital became increasingly mobile. People no longer invested in companies abroad but rather in indexes and commodity markets. Money moved with amazing speed. So did people.

Shifting forms of production and trade helped to create economic diasporas, ranging from Indians employed in the Gulf states to the millions of Turks living throughout the European Union. While diasporas are an ancient phenomenon, the numbers and diversity of population movements after World War II are striking, as Seyla Benhabib has suggested: "Here are some numbers. It is estimated that whereas in 1910 roughly 33 million individuals lived as migrants in countries other than their own, by the year 2000 that number had reached 175 million. Strikingly, more than half the increase of migrants from 1910 to 2000 occurred in the last three decades of the twentieth century, between 1965 and 2000" (Benhabib 2008, 45).

These demographic changes do not mean that older ideologies and inequalities have vanished. For example, many "third-party nationals" lack citizenship rights, despite the fact that they may live for decades in other nations (Benhabib 2008, 51). This is the situation, for example, for some North Africans living in France or Germany. In part, these challenges may exist because of cultural ideals created during the Age of Empire and the way these ideals are now interpreted in an era with a mass media culture, as will be discussed in the chapter on cultural globalization. Jane Rhodes argues that the global media has contributed to a backlash against these migrants, as well as the propagation of racist ideas: "The era of globalization has with it a backlash culture, in which racial ideologies allow us to keep ourselves separate and apart from those we perceive to be a threat. Global media has played a significant role in disseminating racial ideas" (Rhodes 2008, 29–30). From this perspective, globalization has not ended old ideologies that disenfranchised certain groups but rather propagated these problems, and the global media has not broken down old barriers but merely reframed old ideologies.

Other authors have argued that the global media has played a more significant and positive role than this critique might suggest. For example, the rising power of human rights as a global ideal, it can be argued, is in part the result of the proliferation of media coverage that can bring images of violence in Darfur or Kashmir into people's homes. The expansion of media outlets also enables diasporas to retain contact with their home cultures and resist assimilation by majority cultures. The impact of new cultural markets is complex. But as the forthcoming chapter on cultural globalization will illustrate, new forms of communication and expression have joined with demographic change in a manner that is equally important to political and economic globalization. This reality poses many challenges for nation-states.

The Enduring Importance of the Nation-State

Globalization now pressures the nation-state to a new degree. From the late 1940s to 1991, the Cold War limited the impact of globalization. The expansion of markets and commerce did not take place in the Soviet Union. But the Chinese adoption of capitalism in the 1980s, and the collapse of the Soviet Union in 1991, removed this constraint on globalization. With the exception of a handful of states, such as North Korea, few nations were able to reject globalization entirely. Some authors, such as Arjun Appadurai, have argued that this trend has made the nation-state increasingly irrelevant in international affairs.

> I did not begin to write this book with the crisis of the nation-state as my principal concern. But in the six years over which the chapters were written, I have come to be convinced that the nation-state, as a complex political form, is on its last legs. . . . Nation-states, for all their important differences (and only a fool would conflate Sri Lanka with Great Britain), make sense only as parts of a system. This system (even when seen as a system of differences) appears poorly equipped to deal with the interlinked diasporas of people and images that mark the here and now. Nation-states, as units in a complex interactive system, are not very likely to be the long-term arbiters of the relationship between globality and modernity. (Appadurai 1996, 19)

While globalization appears to integrate the world culturally and economically, it also may erode the authority and allegiance that nation-states have historically compelled.

There are many well-known arguments supporting this perspective. With the rise of global markets, no nation is immune from financial shocks, capital flows, and currency crises. In order to be attractive to international financial institutions, nations must accede to global norms in finance. Institutions such as the World Bank place clear expectations around loans that may limit national sovereignty. Transnational corporations may make huge investments in countries and gain great political influence as a result. Nations are no longer able to easily control information, given the rise of the Internet and social marketing platforms. The global media can bring intense pressure to bear on particular nations. The rise of global travel means that diseases can spread with unprecedented rapidity, and responses to pandemics must be coordinated to be effective. Similarly, many international problems—from drugs to nuclear proliferation—can only be addressed at the supranational level. Demographic trends, such as the aging populations of Europe and Japan, may create economic pressures to increase immigration. New peoples, however, retain old identities, which may be perceived as a challenge to the nation-state and make increased immigration politically unacceptable. The rise of the European Union and new political blocs can challenge how nations define their innate character. The global media—films, the Internet, and television—may spread a common culture among youth globally, which challenges traditional cultures.

There are many examples of nation-states in crisis. In the developing world, there are many areas that either never successfully created a strong nation-state (Somalia) or collapsed under the weight of ethnic hatreds (Syria). In truth, one of the key problems of international politics is exactly the weakness of the nation-state, as the case of Afghanistan proved. Regions in which no central government is able to monopolize violence, provide basic services, or take on the role of a state in the international arena are called "failed states." While this term dramatizes the weakness of nation-states in some poor areas of the globe, it is also true that even nation-states in developed countries are also experiencing crises (Appadurai 1996, 142–43). Belgium is currently undergoing serious tensions between its Flemish- and French-speaking populations that may cause the nation to disintegrate. Within Spain, the Basques and other cultures long suppressed by Francisco Franco—the nation's dictator from 1936 to 1975—are asserting their right to autonomy. In Canada, two referendums on sovereignty have failed, but Quebecois nationalism remains alive. In the United Kingdom, the Scottish have questioned their centuries-old relationship to the central state. These may not be isolated instances but rather examples of a larger process.

Is the nation-state increasingly irrelevant in global affairs? Our argument in this text is that the situation is more complex in that, while nation-states are engaged in a complicated interplay with new actors, they nevertheless remain powerful agents. It is true that the nation-state system faces significant challenges, but that is true of every form of political organization in any period. With globalization, supranational entities (such as the World Bank, transnational corporations, and the media) may challenge nation-states. But the idea of the nation-state remains important even in regions where the concept is the weakest, as can be illustrated with the problem of so-called failed states. This term is itself strange for several reasons, one of which is that it implies that these regions have tried in the past to become nation-states and were not able to do so because of some internal problem. In reality, many of these regions never had a coherent identity and were forged by European powers on grounds that had no basis in social reality. What is interesting is not how often these newly constructed states have failed but how often they have endured. And what is significant is how the world has responded when a region appears without a strong national government. The lesson that the global community has drawn from Somalia and Afghanistan has been that it cannot ignore statelessness in any area of the globe because other powers move to fill the vacuum; such areas then can serve as bases for terrorism, sources of refugees overseas, or sites for illicit drug production (Delpech 2007, 97).

Nation-states remain critical to understanding supranational phenomena, such as terrorism. September 11 could not have taken place without the structure of globalization, which permitted the movement of people and resources globally to make the attacks possible. The identities and alliances that the movement used also relied on an earlier period of Islamic globalization. But that does not mean that terrorism can be understood or addressed outside the context of the nation-state. Although Al-Qaida is a global organization, it needed a base in Afghanistan that was safe from attack to coordinate, train, and plan for September 11. Al-Qaida also reflects a historical moment, and the politics of nation-states in the Islamic world remain critical to its future, which is uncertain. It is for this reason and others that in many ways, Great Powers such as the United States are preoccupied with both the problem of "state making" and potential allies and

Meet with one or two other members of your class. As a group, decide what was the single most important historical question that this chapter did not cover. Why was this particular question or material critical?

enemies in the Islamic world. In all supranational issues, states are still relevant actors, despite transnational threats like terrorism.

It is also true that the old issues of international politics endure. The greatest danger to global peace is less likely to be terrorism than the competing claims of China and other East Asian nations to small islands (such as the Senkaku/Diaoyudao and Spratly Islands) in the Pacific, or Pakistan and India's standoff over Kashmir (Wiegand 2009). Russia also wishes to continue asserting its Great Power status after the trauma of the Soviet Union's collapse in 1991. In August 2008 the Russian invasion of Georgia (in response to the Georgian invasion of breakaway republics) was widely perceived as a reaction to events since 1991. Relations between the West and Russia remain difficult and contested because Russian leaders believe that they were ignored and humiliated by the West after the breakup of the Soviet Union; this drives Russia's current decisions regarding Ukraine. At the same time, many nations that are not currently Great Powers wish to improve their standing in the global system. This longing is made manifest in many issues. Some nations, such as North Korea, have been willing to take great risks to develop nuclear weapons—less to protect themselves from their enemies than to achieve the international prominence that they believe they deserve. Thérèse Delpech suggests that one reason that nations reject the current system is that they believe that it unjustly locks in the historical power of once-imperial powers: "Some countries believe that history never gave them what was rightfully theirs. The stability that European societies worship is not what such countries have in mind. . . . If New Delhi conducted nuclear tests in 1998 it was to gain greater heft in world affairs as much as to guarantee its defense" (Delpech 2007, 9–10). In politics, economics, and culture, nation-states remain powerful agents that do not just react to global trends but to some extent limit the power of globalization itself. In the economic globalization chapter that follows, we will be discussing the tension that exists between nation-states and global economic forces.

Conclusion

World history matters in international studies because without it, we cannot understand the international system—including the origins of the nation-state and globalization, two key forces in current international affairs. Ironically, European empires helped to create the nationalist sentiments that destroyed them. They united diverse peoples in the colonies, alienated this populace by ignoring their political and economic interests, provided the ideology of nationalism, and created a global structure in which nations aspired to statehood. Nation-states now dominate the international system, despite the current period of globalization. What has changed is that it is now a more complex world order, in part because there are more actors, such as international nongovernmental organizations, the Bretton Woods institutions, the United Nations, and transnational corporations. New technologies, institutions, and problems constantly emerge to challenge nation-states. But nation-states appear to be permanent. At the same time, the fundamentals of statecraft and the experience of history remain relevant to current issues.

Every global trend has its own history, and this is particularly true of economic globalization, which reflects a long series of political and international decisions. While economic globalization can challenge the authority of the nation-state, the global financial system also relies on nation-states to implement the architecture upon which economic globalization relies. In turn, how people view economic globalization often depends on their nation's history. How does the experience of a particular nation—and the memories that its people hold—affect its perspective on international questions? How does your history—both as an individual and within a state—determine what seems important to you?

➤ **VOCABULARY**

diaspora	failed state
IMF	Bretton Woods System
World Bank	national sovereignty
GATT	biological imperialism
spheres of influence	Peace of Westphalia

➤ **DISCUSSION AND REFLECTION QUESTIONS**

1 *What is the relationship between the emergence of more powerful military armaments and European expansion into the Atlantic?*

2 *What role did African slavery play in the development of North and South America and the Caribbean in the sixteenth and seventeenth centuries?*

3 *What role did New World crops and minerals play in the development of Europe?*

4 *Compare and contrast Dutch, British, and Portuguese expansion in the 1600s.*

5 *How do our present-day conceptualizations of race relate to legacies of empire?*

6 *As individuals left their homelands, new landscapes, demographics, and diasporas were created. What impact might shifting demographics have on nation-state development?*

7 *What are some of the tensions that exist between nationhood and empire?*

8 *Why did the Cold War dominate global relations for more than forty years?*

9 *What underlying frameworks for globalization were created by the development of the Bretton Woods System (World Bank, IMF, GATT)?*

10 *How do the competing forces of globalization and nationalism play out in a region you have studied or are familiar with?*

ACTIVITY 1 Prepare a timeline that begins in an era of your choosing. Make sure you cover at least 400 years of time. On the timeline, mark all critical global events that you can think of. Try and include not only wars and treaties but also other critical events that have occurred in particular regions. Once you have finished, compare your timeline with those of two other classmates. What do you notice about the events you all have chosen? Can you make any generalizations?

ACTIVITY 2 Identify one primary colonizing nation and at least five of its colonies. Research when the colonies gained their independence. What relationships still exist between the colonizing nation and its now-independent former colonies? Identify whether these relationships are economic, political, and/or cultural.

ACTIVITY 3 History affects not only nation-states and cultures but also individuals and families. Make a list of five key historical events or trends that have shaped your family's history. How did your family's experience of these events shape who you are today? How do they define what you may want for your future and for the future of your family? Then ask one family member or loved one what items would be on his or her list.

References

Abu-Lughod, J. L. 1989. *Before European hegemony: The world system, A.D. 1250–1350.* New York: Oxford University Press.
———. 1993. *The world system in the thirteenth century: Dead-end or precursor? Essays on global and comparative history.* Washington, D.C.: American Historical Association.
Alchon, S. A. 2003. *A pest in the land: New World epidemics in global perspective.* Albuquerque: University of New Mexico Press.
Anderson, B. 1983. *Imagined communities: Reflections on the origin and spread of nationalism.* London: Verso.
Appadurai, A. 1996. *Modernity at large: Cultural dimensions of globalization.* Minneapolis: University of Minnesota Press.
Benhabib, S. 2008. Global citizenship and responsibility. In *Meditations on global citizenship: Macalester Civic Forum,* ed. A. Samatar and A. Latham, 45–62. St. Paul, Minn.: Institute for Global Citizenship.
Bentley, J. H. 1996. *Shapes of world history in twentieth-century scholarship: Essays on global and comparative history.* Washington, D.C.: American Historical Association.
Crosby, A. W. 1972. *The Columbian exchange: Biological and cultural consequences of 1492.* Westport, Conn.: Greenwood Press.
Delpech, T. 2007. *Savage century: Back to barbarism.* Trans. George Holoch. Washington, D.C.: Carnegie Endowment for International Peace.
Diamond, J. 1997. *Guns, germs, and steel: The fates of human societies.* New York: W. W. Norton and Company.
———. 2005. *Collapse: How societies choose to fail or succeed.* New York: Viking Books.
Eaton, R. M. 1990. *Islamic history as global history: Essays on global and comparative history.* Washington, D.C.: American Historical Association.
Friedman, T. L. 1999. *The Lexus and the olive tree: Understanding globalization.* New York: Farrar, Straus & Giroux.
Fukuyama, F. 1989. The end of history? *National Interest* 16:3–18.
Guilmartin, J. F. 1974. *Gunpowder and galleys: Changing technology and Mediterranean warfare at sea in the sixteenth century.* Cambridge, UK: Cambridge University Press.

Huntington, S. P. 1993. The clash of civilizations? *Foreign Affairs* 72 (3): 22–49.

Lauren, P. G. 1998. *The evolution of international human rights: Visions seen.* Philadelphia: University of Pennsylvania Press.

Mann, C. C. 2006. *1491: New revelations of the Americas before Columbus.* New York: Vintage Books USA.

McGee, R. 1991. *Canada rediscovered.* Ottawa: Canadian Museum of Civilization.

McNeill, W. H. 1989. *The age of gunpowder empires, 1450–1800: Essays on global and comparative history.* Washington, D.C.: American Historical Association.

Pringle, H. 2012. Vikings and Native Americans. *National Geographic.* November. Retrieved December 26, 2013, from http://ngm.nationalgeographic.com /2012/11/vikings-and-indians/pringle-text.

Rhodes, J. 2008. Race matters. *Macalester Civic Forum* 1 (Spring): 27–33.

Rosen, W. 2007. *Justinian's flea: Plague, empire, and the birth of Europe.* New York: Viking Adult.

Schledermann, P. 2000. Ellesmere: Vikings in the far north. In *Vikings: The North Atlantic saga,* ed. W. W. Fitzhugh and E. I. Ward, 248–56. Washington, D.C.: Smithsonian Institution Press.

Seaver, K. 2000. Unanswered questions. In *Vikings: The North Atlantic saga,* ed. W. W. Fitzhugh and E. I. Ward, 270–79. Washington, D.C.: Smithsonian Institution Press.

Steger, M. 2003. *Globalization: A very short introduction.* Oxford, UK: Oxford University Press.

Sutherland, P. D. 2000. The Norse and native North Americans. In *Vikings: The North Atlantic saga,* ed. W. W. Fitzhugh and E. I. Ward, 238–47. Washington, D.C.: Smithsonian Institution Press.

Tharoor, S. 1999. Are human rights universal? *World Policy Journal* 16 (Winter): 1–6.

Tuchman, B. W. 1978. *A distant mirror: The calamitous 14th century.* New York: Ballantine Books.

Wiegand, K. 2009. China's strategy in the Senkaku/Diaoyu islands dispute: Issue linkage and coercive diplomacy. *Asian Security* 5 (2): 170–93. Retrieved December 26, 2013, from http://www.tandfonline.com/doi/full/10.1080 /14799850902886617#.UrMXfYoVgUU.

THREE Economic Globalization

➤ SYNOPSIS

Economic globalization is a dominant force in the world today. In this chapter, we explore the origins of the World Bank, the International Monetary Fund, and the World Trade Organization and the degrees to which decisions made in these organizations control the world economic scene. The development of the current neoliberal approach to economic decisions is examined through the vehicles of the Washington Consensus and the Augmented Washington Consensus. The shifting power of Brazil, Russia, India, China, and South Africa are discussed, along with power shifts for the N-11 countries. The chapter also examines financial crises from Iceland to Greece as examples of global flows of capital in both public and private sectors.

➤ SCAFFOLDING

As you read through this chapter, think about how you would answer each of the questions below.

What are three dimensions of global economics or finance that you are comfortable discussing with a friend? How likely are you to have such a discussion? Why or why not?

How can you be aware of your attitude toward fields of study that you might not know anything about in the same way that you are aware of the information you may need to learn?

Why are neoliberal economic perspectives so frequently used to determine measures of economic stability?

➤ CORE CONCEPTS

What is conditionality? What is the relationship between structural-adjustment policies, conditionality, and poverty-reduction strategies for the World Bank and IMF?

What macroeconomic functions were initially allocated to the IMF, and what microeconomic functions were allocated to the World Bank? Why have these functions and institutions in effect mixed roles?

What is financialization, and how is it affecting twenty-first-century economic flows?

Globalization means many things to many people. In *A Brief History of Globalization*, MacGillivray (2006) identifies more than 5,000 books in print with titles linked to globalization. For many, the term itself conveys images of hegemony—that is, economic and political dominance by rich nations over smaller nations. For others, the power of connectivity and information exchange cancel out any negatives that may exist in the equation. Globalization is about patterns of connectedness and patterns of inequality. Because people, goods and services, and information flow differently in the twenty-first century than in the past, landscapes have shifted (Appadurai 1996). Some authors have suggested that we now see a compression of time and space; financial transactions occur transnationally by electronic means, virtual communities are created across traditional boundaries, and information travels faster and more powerfully than ever before via the Internet (Harvey 1989). This compression is both a blessing and a curse. All over the world, citizens now expect change to occur quickly and in a similar manner in different nation-states.

In this chapter, building on information that you were introduced to in the history chapter, we explore the mobility of capital, ideas, and power. We then examine how context and localization interact with these forces. We look at the advantages and disadvantages of globalization through the lens of multiple disciplines in order to see how scholars from various perspectives have identified globalization as both a demon and a darling. The global financial meltdown of 2008 provides a practical example of how context, locale, and the regulatory abilities of key actors—such as the Economic Monetary Union (EMU) of the European Union—can lead to crisis and inequality.

What is economic globalization? For economist Paul Krugman and entrepreneur George Soros, globalization is a phenomenon intimately linked to trade among nations and various financial markets. Soros (2002) also notes the importance of multinational corporations in this picture. We see that transactions among nation-states may be superseded by transnational transactions dominated by intergovernmental organizations, global movements, or collaboration among civil-society organizations (Global Policy Forum 2008). Khanna and Rusi (2008) suggest that globalization also has a strong regional dimension. Scholte (2005, 2) sees this regional power of globalization as something that draws power away from the nation-state. Neither individual nation-states nor multinational corporations function independently in our time-space compressed world. The economic pillars of the Bretton Woods System (along with national and multinational financial institutions) work almost like a lock and dam system: nations and companies navigate waters that are determined by larger global structures.

Economic Globalization

Chapter 2 introduced you to the economic giants of globalization: the Bretton Woods System (World Bank, International Monetary Fund, General Agreement on Tariffs and Trade) and the World Trade Organization (the former General Agreement on Tariffs and Trade). We explore them in more detail here because the economic world as we know it continues to operate within the parameters shaped by these institutions. At the end of World War II, politicians tried to determine the advantages and disadvantages of a global political entity, ultimately resulting in the shift from President Woodrow Wilson's League of Nations to the charter for the United Nations. At the same time, financiers were discussing the need to create some type of global financial entity, particularly one that could assist countries with what MacGillivray (2006, 210) terms "temporary balance of payment problems."

In 1944 a meeting with representatives from forty-four nations was held at Bretton Woods, New Hampshire, in the Mount Washington Hotel. The representatives were charged with finding ways to assist global trade by helping stabilize the global economy. It was at this meeting that both the World Bank (initially the International Bank for Reconstruction and Development, or IBRD) and the International Monetary Fund (IMF) were established. The U.S. representative was Harry Dexter, and the United Kingdom representative was Lord John Maynard Keynes, who argued for a global currency called "bancor." This idea was rejected, and the U.S. dollar became the world currency for the monetary system that followed. It was intended that the two organizations would identify and implement procedures for a system of convertible currencies tied to a gold standard—set at $35.00 per ounce. At the time, 70 percent of the world's gold reserves rested in the United States, thus tying the gold standard to the dollar. As you saw in chapter 2, ultimately the currency was decoupled from gold. This is not unlike what happened in 2009 when a digital currency termed "bitcoin" was created; it, too, is decoupled from gold.

At the time of the 1944 meeting, it was clear that the Allies would win the war and soon face the challenge of rebuilding a Europe that had been burned and shattered by the conflict. Many senior U.S. officials also believed that one of the origins of the war had been the trade blocs of the 1930s and the political tensions these blocs created. For these reasons, the delegates wanted to create a global lending institution and a means to break down trade barriers. They succeeded in these two goals, but not without costs to the autonomy and social sectors of the countries receiving assistance.

The global lending institutions became the World Bank and the IMF. The solution to trade barriers emerged in the form of the General Agreement on Tariffs and Trade (GATT); this agreement became the World Trade Organization (WTO). All of these organizations are transnational, even though many argue that rich Western nations continue to dominate and drive policy formulation within them (Scholte 2005). Nation-states were and continue to be the intended recipients of decisions made by the World Bank, the IMF, and the WTO. This triumvirate of economic globalization began in response to the needs of individual nation-states to have access to the power, cash, and influence that came from collaboration with other nations. We now look in more detail at these institutions in order to better comprehend their functions.

The World Bank and the International Monetary Fund

Originally created to help Europe recover from World War II, the World Bank later turned its focus to helping the developing world (the Global South). Its original charge was to focus on microeconomic dimensions of recovery, including fiscal policy decisions. The bank makes low-interest loans to qualifying countries, which can use the money for development projects. Like the IMF, it has its headquarters in Washington, D.C. The

World Bank lends at rates lower than commercial bank rates. Its typical loans were initially designed to increase infrastructure capacity and were often for very large and visible projects such as dams, power plants, and the like. These loans came with conditions imposed on them; the actual term "conditionality" refers specifically to "the conditions that international lenders imposed in return for their assistance" (Broad 2002, 9). According to the IMF website (2008), these conditions are set in order to "restore or maintain balance of payments viability and macroeconomic stability, while setting the stage for sustained, high-quality growth." There are typically three key dimensions to these conditions: privatization, deregulation, and implementation of austerity measures that decrease the size of the government's public-sector spending on social services and education.

Examples of privatization include recommendations to privatize electricity in El Salvador and jute production in Bangladesh. Hansen-Kuhn and Hellinger (1999) suggest these have both failed: "In El Salvador, for example, the privatization of electricity distribution has resulted in increased rates, reduced access for low-income people, and a notable decline in the quality of service. In Bangladesh, the privatization of jute production—a mainstay of the country's industrial sector—was disastrous."

Deregulation removes policies that create trade barriers and competitive pricing. These policies may relate to any aspect of society. One example is from Zambia, where deregulation has redefined who can purchase property, which has not only created powerful changes to the historical governance of landholdings but also opened up the market to foreign purchasers (Brown 2000). A second example involves the crafting of waivers to permit international organizations interested in mining in Haiti to skirt restrictions. Levesque (2013) observes that private ownership of mines is prohibited in the Haitian constitution. Additionally, drilling can only occur with a signed mining convention. Yet deregulation can occur subtly and for individual corporations. For example, Levesque indicates that "U.S. Newmont mining got a 'waiver' to the current Haiti law without the approval of even the puppet Haiti legislature."

Austerity measures typically decrease the size of the government's public-sector spending on social services and education. One example is the frequent freezing of salaries of public-sector employees; this occurred routinely throughout the European Union (EU) countries of Greece, Portugal, and Spain in 2008. Yet another is legislation passed in September 2012 in Greece to allow the government to completely close a subset of universities.

The IMF was established to create stable exchange rates by pegging currencies to the U.S. dollar, which in turn was pegged to the price of gold until 1971. Roughly thirty years after the IMF's inception, though, the currency would be unfrozen from its link to gold and floated. MacGillivray (2006, 215) characterizes the shift in the following manner: "Without the pull of gold, currencies gravitated to regional or post-colonial loyalties, and attempted to peg their currency within certain limits." Stable currency exchange rates created the predictability necessary for global businesses to trade. The IMF continues to make loans to countries facing currency crises. Its primary role is intended to focus on macroeconomic issues; according to Stiglitz (2002, 14), these include a "country's budget deficit, its monetary policy, its inflation, its trade deficit [and] its borrowing from abroad." Countries that join the IMF are assigned a type of quota based on their global economic position. The balance of loans received must be repaid within five years.

The original distinction between the World Bank's focus on microeconomic policy and the IMF's focus on macroeconomic policy has gradually eroded. Stiglitz suggests that the IMF has come to dominate both microeconomic and macroeconomic decisions. Both organizations have crafted conditions for loans to be given. The conditions are sometimes termed the "Washington Consensus." Economist John Williamson coined this phrase in 1989 to characterize the recommendations made by the IMF, the World Bank, the U.S. Treasury, and other financial institutions based in Washington, D.C. At the time, the recommendations articulated were intended to help Latin America pull out of the economic crises of that decade. The phrase "Washington Consensus" has come to mean more than what Williamson originally intended, but for our purposes, it is sufficient to know this consensus refers to ten economic-policy recommendations—basically, conditions to be followed in order to qualify for loans. The Washington Consensus policies are detailed in Table 1, along with what economist Dani Rodrik calls an "Augmented Washington Consensus" (Global Trade Negotiations home page 2008).

These conditions have become part of a package called Structural Adjustment Programs (SAPs). As you can see from the table, these conditions are designed to shift economic and social structures in the countries receiving loans. Over a period of time, these SAPs have become quite controversial, as the austerity measures they have created in various nations have had very strong effects on social programs and policies therein. In 2002 the World Bank and the IMF shifted to different terminology:

Table 1 Original Washington Consensus and Augmented Washington
Consensus

Original Washington Consensus	Augmented Washington Consensus
Fiscal discipline	Corporate governance
A redirection of public expenditures toward fields offering high economic returns and potential to improve income distribution (e.g., primary health care, primary education)	Anticorruption
Tax reform	Flexible labor markets
Interest rate liberalization	WTO agreements
A competitive exchange rate	Financial codes and standards
Trade liberalization	"Prudent" capital-account opening
Liberalization of inflows of foreign direct investment	Nonintermediate exchange rate regimes
Privatization	Independent central banks and inflation targeting
Deregulation (to abolish barriers to entry and exit)	Social safety nets
Secure property rights	Targeted poverty reduction

Source: Dani Rodrik, http://www.cid.harvard.edu/search.html. Retrieved July 5, 2010.
Used with permission.

Poverty Reduction Strategy Papers (PRSPs). These PRSPs have also been
aligned with the United Nations' Millennium Development Goals, which
will be discussed in chapter 6.

General Agreement on Tariffs and Trade and the World Trade Organization

The General Agreement on Tariffs and Trade was created in 1947 to encourage countries to reduce their taxes on imports. It was the third aspect
of policy/institution development to come out of Bretton Woods. The goal
was to create an international forum based on membership that would
both promote free trade among its member nations and provide a forum

Using data from 2007 (http://bigpicture.typepad.com/comments/2007 /01/countries_gdp_a.html), we see that the gross domestic product (GDP) of Mexico is roughly equivalent to that of Illinois, and the GDP of Canada is roughly equivalent to that of Texas. How does this comparison permit you to envision exports and economic issues for Mexico and Canada, given your knowledge of Illinois and Texas?

for dispute resolution (GATT 2008). A treaty agreement and not an organization, GATT's purpose was ostensibly to reduce tariffs as well as other types of trade restrictions and subsidies favoring one nation over another. There were seven rounds of negotiations under the treaty. It is generally agreed that GATT has functioned in roughly three stages (GATT slideshow 2014). The first stage focused mostly on which commodities would be managed and recognized the tariff levels that were current at that time. This lasted until roughly 1951. The second stage attempted to reduce tariffs and functioned until roughly 1979. The seventh round of GATT talks took place in Tokyo in 1973; 102 countries participated. While some reductions in customs duties occurred, the goal of achieving agricultural reform was not met. It would take thirteen years (1986) for the next round of talks to be held in Uruguay. The last round of meetings of the GATT signatories in Uruguay occurred between 1986 and 1994. Some of the changes proposed in 1986 took almost eight years to be ratified and instituted; this happened in Marrakesh in April 1994. One of the key agreements to emerge from this round was the Agreement on Agriculture (AOA). Sylvia Ostry (2004, 246) focuses on the three main areas of the agreement—market access, export competition, and domestic support—suggesting that farmers who were members of the more powerful "developed" WTO countries managed to pressure their governments into watching out for their relatively small needs at the expense of other dimensions of multilateral agreements. Country after country, for example, bargained for the protection of their agricultural and textile products. In terms of other agreements reached at this round, Ostry characterizes the results: "The Uruguay Round concluded with what I've called a North-South Grand Bargain. It was essentially an implicit deal: the reform and liberalization of the OECD [Organization for Economic Cooperation and Development] agricultural and textile and clothing markets for the inclusion of the new issues" (Ostry 2004, 248).

Nations made substantial achievements at this last meeting. In addition to the agricultural dimensions discussed above, participants agreed to the reductions of tariffs, export subsidies, and various other import limits over the twenty-year period that followed. In addition, substantial progress was made in the area of intellectual property rights—patents, trademarks, and copyrights. Work was also begun to bring a level of enforcement of international trade law to the service sector. Finally, nations began to discuss a way to revise how disputes were settled through GATT. The last phase focused more narrowly on dimensions also central to the WTO: further elements of intellectual property rights and agriculture.

In 1995 GATT was replaced by the WTO, which is a much more powerful body in that it also covers intellectual property and services. Its membership is composed of 159 nation-states, and there are twenty-five other nations serving as "observers" (these figures are accurate as of 2013). It has assumed the functions of GATT, along with another agreement focusing on services called the General Agreement on Trade in Services (GATS). The mechanism within the WTO that allows sanctions to be leveled against particular nation-states for violating global trade rules is called the Dispute Settlement Body (DSB). Within this process, if a country is found to have violated a particular rule, there is only one way to escape the sanctions meted out: all members of the DSB must oppose the imposition of the sanctions. Ellwood (2003, 34) acknowledges the complete unlikelihood of this happening. Another somewhat slippery dimension of the DSB process is that if one country believes something it is doing within its own borders—that is, some type of domestic policy—is necessary and appropriate, any WTO member can argue that the policy could be linked to the trade process. Thus, it could be potentially linked to a dispute and sent to the DSB.

The WTO replaced GATT for all intents and purposes. Table 2 details the differences between them, while Figure 1 details the structure of the WTO. A full analysis of the WTO organizational chart is beyond the scope of this chapter, but a deeper look at a key dispute and how the DSB has resolved it to date may give you a better understanding of the ins and outs of this central arm of the WTO. Trade issues related to the marketing of particular foods are adjudicated first under regional trade organizations, but if disputes occur, they are then adjudicated by the WTO. One such dispute involved bananas.

The European Union imports bananas from both Africa and the Caribbean. The combined production of these areas is roughly 5 percent of the total global production (Millstone and Lang 2008). One reason for the EU's

Table 2 Comparison of GATT and WTO

GATT	WTO
A set of rules, a multilateral agreement • No institutional foundation • A small associated secretariat	A permanent institution with its own secretariat
GATT provisions were applied on a provisional basis	WTO commitments are full and permanent
GATT rules applied to trade in merchandise goods	WTO covers trade in services and trade-related aspects of intellectual property
Not all agreements were multilateral	Almost all agreements are multilateral and involve commitments for the entire membership
System is subject to blockages by countries	WTO disputes system is less susceptible toblockages

Sources: K. Choi, "The Roots of the WTO," retrieved November 26, 2008, from www
.econ.iastate.edu/classes/econ355/choi/wtoroots.htm; and WTO website (www.wto.org),
retrieved 2008.

choice of trading partners is an articulated commitment to assist former colonies (Koeppel 2008). Most of the U.S. banana imports come from Central and Latin America and the Far East. The combined production of these areas is roughly 95 percent of the total global production (Millstone and Lang 2008). In 1993 the European Union attempted to control the import of bananas from Central America and Latin America to protect its smaller trading partners. When this happened, American multinational Chiquita, which until that time had provided about 20 percent of Europe's market demand, had its quota halved (Koeppel 2008). Although it took some time, the United States ultimately charged that Europe was giving preferential treatment to "specific companies in what was supposed to be an open market" and took their complaint to the DSB of the WTO (Koeppel 2008, 221).

Between 1996 and 2001, while the claim was being adjudicated, the WTO gave permission to the United States to impose import duties on various European goods. Millstone and Lang suggest that these tariffs caused great damage to a number of European businesses (Millstone and Lang 2008). Ultimately, in 2001 the WTO proposed a settlement that would

All WTO members may participate in all councils, committees, etc., except Appellate Body, Dispute Settlement panels, Textiles Monitoring Body, and plurilateral committees.

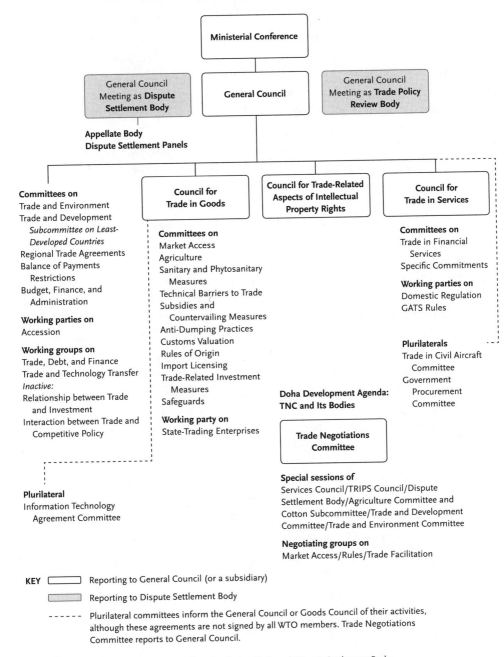

Ministerial Conference

General Council Meeting as Dispute Settlement Body

General Council

General Council Meeting as Trade Policy Review Body

Appellate Body Dispute Settlement Panels

Committees on
Trade and Environment
Trade and Development
  Subcommittee on Least-
  Developed Countries
Regional Trade Agreements
Balance of Payments
  Restrictions
Budget, Finance, and
  Administration

Working parties on
Accession

Working groups on
Trade, Debt, and Finance
Trade and Technology Transfer
Inactive:
Relationship between Trade
  and Investment
Interaction between Trade and
  Competitive Policy

Council for Trade in Goods

Committees on
Market Access
Agriculture
Sanitary and Phytosanitary
  Measures
Technical Barriers to Trade
Subsidies and
  Countervailing Measures
Anti-Dumping Practices
Customs Valuation
Rules of Origin
Import Licensing
Trade-Related Investment
  Measures
Safeguards

Working party on
State-Trading Enterprises

Council for Trade-Related Aspects of Intellectual Property Rights

Council for Trade in Services

Committees on
Trade in Financial
  Services
Specific Commitments

Working parties on
Domestic Regulation
GATS Rules

Plurilaterals
Trade in Civil Aircraft
  Committee
Government
  Procurement
  Committee

Doha Development Agenda: TNC and Its Bodies

Trade Negotiations Committee

Special sessions of
Services Council/TRIPS Council/Dispute
Settlement Body/Agriculture Committee and
Cotton Subcommittee/Trade and Development
Committee/Trade and Environment Committee

Negotiating groups on
Market Access/Rules/Trade Facilitation

Plurilateral
Information Technology
  Agreement Committee

KEY
[ ] Reporting to General Council (or a subsidiary)

[ ] Reporting to Dispute Settlement Body

- - - - - Plurilateral committees inform the General Council or Goods Council of their activities, although these agreements are not signed by all WTO members. Trade Negotiations Committee reports to General Council.

The General Council also meets as the Trade Policy Review Body and Dispute Settlement Body.

Figure 1 WTO Structure

gradually be introduced. The transition period began in 2001 and continued until 2005, when 775,000 tons of bananas per year from the Caribbean and African countries could be imported without taxes. Other suppliers from Latin America, Central America, and the Far East were taxed. By 2007 many companies began to feel the strain of the tariffs and once again approached the WTO, this time via the structure of its Compliance Panel. On November 26, 2008, an Appellate Body Report was issued in response to a charge dated February 20, 2007, in which the DSB agreed "to refer to the original Panel, if possible, the question of whether the new EC banana regime was in conformity with the DSB's recommendations and rulings" (WTO 2008, DS 27). The subsequent panel found dimensions it upheld from the original ruling as well as a number of inconsistencies. Among the dimensions it upheld was the original panel finding that "the EC Bananas Import Regime, in particular, its duty-free tariff quota reserved for ACP countries, was inconsistent with Article XIII:1 and Article XIII:2 of the GATT 1994" (WTO 2008, DS 27).

This example has given you a sense of just how prolonged and complicated both the original disputes and their settlements can be. What is important to notice is that numerous countries have been involved on both sides of the dispute. The WTO has crafted a structure to resolve these disputes. The structure is complicated but consistent. The cross-border territories of banana-producing and banana-consuming regions ultimately replace the particular countries themselves in the adjudication. The WTO has thus succeeded in the original goals of GATT: to create both a membership-based international forum that would promote free trade and a forum for dispute resolution. While the latter appears to be a neutral policy, it is clear that all free trade–based initiatives are grounded in the neoliberal perspective framed by the Washington Consensus.

The World Bank, the IMF, GATT, and the WTO are powerful multinational forces. They have served as gatekeeping devices for the mobility of capital and ideas and have imprinted the global landscape of the twenty-first century. Sadly, not all nations have been equally represented: more-powerful nations have been more successful than less-powerful nations in using these institutions to resolve disputes and plan for their economic futures. Now that you are familiar with the basic organization of the World Bank, the IMF, and GATT/WTO, we will examine how scholars with competing ideologies characterize the work of these institutions.

Perspectives on the World Bank, the IMF, and GATT/WTO

The economic policy conditions characterized above as the Washington Consensus are a set of market policies that depend on three things: privatization, liberalization, and deregulation. Within the general purview of lending policies of the World Bank and the IMF, these three dimensions can be characterized as "economism" and "marketism" (Scholte 2005). These are all part of a neoliberal economic policy. Jan Scholte, professor and director of the Centre for the Study of Globalisation and Regionalisation in the United Kingdom at the University of Warwick (2005, 8), characterizes this policy in the following way:

> Neoliberalism focuses not just on economics, but also on economics of a particular kind, namely laissez-faire market economics. In a word, from a neoliberal perspective, the global economy should be a free and open market. Production, exchange, and consumption of resources should unfold through forces of supply and demand, as they emerge from the uninhibited interactions of a multitude of firms and households in the private sector. . . . Multilateral institutions, national governments, and local authorities exist to provide regulatory frameworks that maximize the efficiency of global markets, for example, by securing property rights and enforcing legal contracts.

Scholte suggests that this dominant policy, enforced through the actions of the World Bank, the IMF, and GATT/WTO, has not truly helped arbitrate global inequality. He argues that in the areas of human security, social justice, and democracy, neoliberal economic policies have been ineffective and in fact have "increased destitution" (Scholte 2005, 11). He looks at markers of poverty in the Soviet bloc between 1989 and 1996 and describes an increase from 14 million to 147 million people living in poverty. He sees increases in global unemployment as contributing to declining global human security and also argues that when the market meets the environment, the environment loses: "[Neoliberalism] affirms—implicitly if not explicitly—that conflicts between market efficiency and ecological integrity should be settled in favour of the former" (Scholte 2005, 12).

In a paper exploring causes of poverty titled "Poverty and Activism: The Heart of Global Civil Society," coauthored with five other colleagues, Scholte states: "They lack the resources, opportunities and *participatory* avenues in collective decision making that would enable them to overcome their poverty. Their poverty is reproduced over and over again through obstacles actually constructed as a *consequence* of modernity; they are the victims not of a timeless condition of poverty but of an ongoing and renewable process of impoverishment" (2009).

In like manner, former Nobel Laureate and World Bank senior economist Joseph Stiglitz also sees the downside of these institutions and their practices. Stiglitz is unhappy with both the IMF and the World Bank. He argues quite convincingly that many of the IMF policies, in spite of their original intents, have actually contributed to instability. He describes in detail the importance of sequencing trade, capital market liberalization, and privatization and suggests that the IMF made frequent mistakes in this area. He goes on to stress the costs of ignoring or placing inadequate emphasis on particular local social contexts when decisions were made. He suggests that "forcing liberalization before safety nets were put in place, before there was an adequate regulatory framework," problematized much of the IMF's work (Stiglitz 2002, 73). Besides sequencing and the IMF, he also criticizes the inflexibility of conditionality on the part of the World Bank—"the conditions that international lenders imposed in return for their assistance" (Stiglitz 2002, 9).

Like Stiglitz, entrepreneur George Soros (2002, 13) finds specific faults with aspects of the IMF: "We can identify two major deficiencies or, more exactly, asymmetries in the way the IMF has been operating until recently. One is a disparity between crisis prevention and crisis intervention; the other is a disparity in the treatment of lenders and borrowers." He goes on to suggest that "the general principles that structural reforms in the IMF ought to follow are clear. There ought to be a better balance between crisis prevention and intervention and a better balance between offering incentives to countries that follow sound policies and penalizing those that do not. The two objectives are connected: it is only by offering incentives that the IMF can exert stronger influence on the economic policies of individual countries prior to a country turning to the IMF in a crisis" (Soros 2002, 134). He is optimistic that these are true changes that can be implemented.

Princeton philosophy professor Peter Singer has written extensively about the ethics of globalization (2002) and argues that those opposed to WTO policies and those supporting them rarely engage in functional dialogues. Those on the Left frequently point out the inattention the WTO pays on a global level to worker rights as well as the environment. Those on the far Right criticize the WTO for its attempts to reign in state sovereignty (Burgess-Jackson, 2008). Singer suggests that both sides could reach a third space in dialogue if the Left saw greater protection of people and environment through consistent global policies and the Right were to recognize that some loss of national sovereignty could be countered with an increased say in global economic decisions. Singer criticizes economists in general, even while acknowledging that some individuals have gone too far in taking the Big Three (World Bank, IMF, GATT/WTO) to task. He has also criticized the WTO street protestors.

Private financial institutions are the final pillar of economic globalization. As we will see in the case study at the end of this chapter, their activities funding trade and intellectual property development, serving direct foreign investment, and managing portfolio investments helped push the world to the fiscal ruin of 2008. Private banks have shifted approved investments and divestments in countries subject to IMF and EU monitoring. Activities that would not have been generally funded in the 1990s suddenly fell into the laps of private banks. Real estate transactions and junk-bond risks that were not originally the purview of private banks became funded activities arbitrarily approved without strategic oversight, often in countries whose cultures had not previously supported activities such as sovereign bond sales and other government borrowings. The costs of these activities are laid out in the exploration of the fiscal travails of Iceland and Greece at the end of the chapter. Before examining the fiscal crises affecting Iceland and Greece, it is useful to turn our focus toward Jamaica and a pragmatic example of competing ideological frameworks regarding economic reconstruction on the part of two Jamaican leaders: Michael Manley and Edward Seaga. By examining how strong national leaders can pull countries toward drastically different recourses to inflation, we can also see how ideology and pragmatism can arbitrarily control the experiences of individuals living in countries suffering economic hardship.

When Manley was elected prime minister of Jamaica the first time (1972–80), he crusaded on an anti-imperialist, nonaligned platform. Most would have characterized his platform as leftist, varying somewhere between neo-Marxism and dependency theory. Between 1977 and 1980, however, the economic situation in Jamaica pushed Manley to sign agreements with the World Bank that resulted in extensive SAPs, generally paralleling processes described under the Washington Consensus protocol listed above. Becoming increasingly unpopular, Manley lost the election in 1980 to Seaga, the head of the conservative Jamaica Labour Party. Seaga then served as prime minister from 1980 to 1989. During that time period, Jamaica aligned itself even more closely with World Bank and IMF fiscal policies. Handa and King (1997, 916) suggest "up until 1989, the policies were centered around fiscal and monetary management, rather than the literal structural adjustment of the economy." In spite of this, Jamaica remained an impoverished nation and was devastated during Hurricane Gilbert in 1988. As political instability increased, calls for Manley to return to leadership began. A more somber, less freewheeling Manley took up the economic reigns of his country in 1989, when he was reelected prime minister. During his second term in office, which ended in 1992, he shifted to a more centrist position, following more traditional approaches to development, capitalism, and private investment. It was during the time frame of 1989 to 1994 that trade liberalization increased along with labor market reform (Handa and King 1997).

Both Seaga and Manley had obtained higher degrees in economics, Seaga from the London School of Economics and Manley from Harvard. Both were committed to leading their nation. Their initial economic strategies conflicted with each other, as did their overall political strategies. Yet the pressure of the global market pushed them both at varying times toward neoliberal economic policies and, ultimately, agreement on fiscal austerity measures aligned with World Bank and IMF recommendations. As we will see in the development chapter, once leaders find themselves in a practical situation needing closure, many shift their ideological stances. It is doubtful that Manley would characterize his earlier leftist economic perspective as incorrect theoretically. However, from a pragmatic perspective, he had to move more to the center. This example suggests that an understanding of structural adjustment policies is insufficient to understand how political leaders are pressed into particular economic decisions.

In 2002, fifty of the top 100 global economies were companies, not countries: "The combined annual revenues of the biggest 200 corporations are greater than those of 182 nation-states that contain 80 percent of the world's populations" (Ellwood 2003, 55). In 2013 the top country economies were the United States, China, Japan, Germany, France, Brazil, the United Kingdom, Russia, Italy, and India. They are anticipated to remain in their respective positions through at least 2018 (World's Largest Economies 2013). The top multinational company economies in 2013 were Royal Dutch Shell, Walmart, Exxon Mobil, Sinopec Group, China National Petroleum, State Grid, Toyota Motor, Volkswagen, and Total (Fortune Global 500 Companies 2013). We see, then, an interweaving of nation-state economies with multinational corporate economies and nationalized company economies. How does this complicated list of players and places affect the balance of economic decisions made around the world? While a complete answer to this question is well beyond the scope of this chapter, it should be clear that it is important for you as a member of the globalized economy to reflect on these relationships.

What does all this mean in terms of our focus on economics as a pillar of globalization? First, the neoliberal policies of the Bretton Woods institutions dominate the process of economic globalization. Knowledge of these institutions is necessary, though not alone sufficient, to gain a broad understanding of the flows of capital and economic globalization. Second, globalization includes the integration of financial markets that started after the end of the Bretton Woods monetary system in 1971 and the liberalization of capital flows that followed afterward. First came the integration of financial markets among the industrialized capitalist giants of the Global North in the 1970s, followed by the entrance of emerging market economies into this picture during the 1980s and 1990s. These economies will be addressed in the next section under N-11, a term used to characterize the top eleven emerging market economies. Finally, it is important to keep in mind that transnational economic flows of capital are governed by International Finance Institutions.

BRICS and N-11

Researchers have addressed the compression of time and space that has occurred with shifts in technology (Harvey 1989; May and Thrift 2001). Brazil, Russia, India, China, and South Africa have increased their roles as resource providers and service providers because of globalization. Transactions can be managed more quickly than ever before due to technological innovation. Over the last fifteen years, four of these economic powerhouses have attracted a great deal of international attention: Brazil, Russia, India, and China. In 2010 South Africa joined these nations by mutual agreement, which created a new bloc: the BRICS. South Africa was asked to join primarily for its ability to "improve access to 1 billion consumers on the continent and mineral resources including oil and platinum" (Seria 2010). All of these economies have engaged in the types of reforms that allow them to play increasing global leadership roles. In 2007 the original four BRIC members had economies that accounted for 15 percent of the global gross domestic product (GDP). By March 2013, the five BRICS economies together accounted for 21 percent of the global GDP (Reuters, 2013). While there is diversity in the strengths of each of these nations, we can see one pattern: Brazil, Russia, and South Africa are likely to continue

as resource providers, while China and India will continue to deliver services and manufactured goods (O'Neill 2007). The ability of these economies to put pressure on the United States and various trading blocks will
increase in the next few decades. At the present time, there is no political
organization representing the interests of these four nations, nor is there
anticipation that this is likely to occur. At a July 2014 summit, they created
the New Development Bank with all five countries. Yet another dimension of these nations' economic presence is the regional role they each
will play in the next fifty years. The languages used in Russia (Russian),
India (Hindi), and China (Chinese) will be dominant regional languages
over the next fifty years (Graddol 1996). Media programming and delivery
of goods and services at a regional level will be through these languages.
South Africa remains an English-using multilingual nation. Thus language
will not be an issue for South Africa, but we can anticipate an increase in
English-language transactions throughout the southern region of Africa
in the next fifty years. How Brazil will deal with its regional power, and the
implications of Brazil's rise for the use of Portuguese versus Spanish and
English, remains to be seen. Nevertheless, the increasing regional power
of each of these countries, coupled with their global influence, means
that the rest of the world would do well to familiarize itself with their
nation-state traits.

Other nations with important roles to play in the emerging global
economy include the N-11 countries: Mexico, South Korea, Vietnam, Turkey, Bangladesh, Egypt, Indonesia, Iran, Nigeria, Pakistan, and the Philippines. Jim O'Neill of Goldman Sachs (2007) suggests that the combined
economic potential of these nations places them in a position to rival the
G-7 countries. Of all the nations listed, Mexico and Korea are most likely
to continue their growth in such a way that they may potentially rival the
BRICS countries, although O'Neill is quick to point out that both Turkey
and Vietnam have the "potential and the conditions" to do the same.

Many of these N-11 countries have both profited from and been ham-
pered by conditions imposed upon them by the World Bank and the IMF
as they have sought to grow their economies. In the long run, it appears
that the conditions imposed have ultimately contributed to their growth
potential in spite of social and environmental issues that remain unresolved. We can see, then, that the landscape of actors on the world stage
has shifted and continues to shift. The Global North will no longer have
a monopoly on determining economic policies of the future. Relationships are complicated among Global North and Global South nations

Joseph Stiglitz (2006, 285) recommends that the world consider a new global social contract in which "developed countries . . . compensate developing countries for their environmental services, both in preservation of biodiversity and contribution to global warming through carbon sequestration" (pumping CO_2 underground and capping it so that it remains out of the atmosphere). How realistic does this suggestion seem to you?

and multinational companies; among Bretton Woods institutions, other international financial institutions, and national and regional financial institutions; and among local communities interacting with all of these institutions. Some authors suggest there is a kind of continuum between the global and the local.

Global, Local, and Glocal

Thomas Friedman (2007, 422) looks at the ability of particular nations "to absorb foreign ideas and global best practices." He terms this "glocalization" and suggests that certain kinds of societies have more flexibility than others to absorb outside ideas without sacrificing the integrity of their cultures. Another way to examine this notion of glocalization is to imagine a horizontal continuum with local at one end and global at the other end. At the center of the continuum, we have glocalization. The strength of localization is its integrity in terms of context. Local customs, beliefs, and values have provided the scaffolding for the strength of societies. The strength of globalization is its flexibility to draw upon multiple modes of thinking to solve problems. The combination is a powerful tool with which to enter the twenty-first century. At the local level, we have the nation-state; at the global level, we have international organizations—fiscal, social, and technological.

Political Globalization

We began this chapter by examining economic patterns of connectedness and patterns of inequality across the globe. Having outlined the economic scaffolding of these patterns, it is now possible to explore the role that politics has played in the mobility of capital, ideas, and power. This interlinking of economics and politics is sometimes overwhelming. The next chapter explores political globalization in its own right, but the brief comments below provide a segue into the fuller discussion in chapter 4.

As you saw in the history chapter, it is generally agreed that it was after the Peace of Westphalia, a treaty-like document signed in 1648, that "the constitutional foundations for the emerging state system" were created (Cutler 2001, 134). These state systems protected citizens, negotiated bilateral agreements, and have most recently served as the recipients of international lending funds. Cutler (2001, 135) stresses the power of the nation-state: "For most of the history of modern international law, states have been regarded as the sole legitimate subjects." As we have seen throughout the text so far, though, the reach of the nation-state is decreasing in comparison to the reach of various other organizations. When this happens, social fragmentation can occur. Breakdowns in civil society occur, and the question becomes, how can globalization have a positive effect at the local level when this kind of disintegration is occurring? One answer is that regional organizations, as well as international economic agencies, can provide elements of stability to compensate. Yet some might argue that it is precisely these agencies that are maintaining the breakdowns; structural adjustment programs in particular chip away at national social budgets—including education, health, and welfare.

As states become less effective as key governing agents, other agents, such as the European Union, grow in scope; global movements of civil society organizations begin to collaborate and use technology to communicate more efficiently; and transnational corporations work around the nation-state (Global Policy Forum 2008). Within the EU in particular, we see how mobility of capital, ideas, and power have all occurred. However, political globalization does not mean political homogeneity, nor does it mean global control. It does mean movement beyond the nation-state—and collaboration when possible.

With respect to social organizations, the Global Policy Forum sees clear places in the future for global movements, such as those associated with the environment, to pull civic society organizations within particular countries together to create alliances with allies in other countries. They see the power of such movements to engage in what they term "direct lobbying," which involves "circumventing the nation-state" (Global Policy Forum 2008). Their perspective is important because they are a consultative organization to the UN with a fourfold mission that includes monitoring, advocacy, education, and activism.

Another kind of global force is the transnational corporation. These corporations have mobility of capital and power. Transnational corporations work this mobility to their advantage. One aspect of the declining power of the nation-state and the power of transnational corporations is that the transnational corporations are generally private, and as such they are neither responsible to a particular state nor subject to international organizations such as the UN. Charney (1983, 55), cited in Cutler (2001, 142), observes the benefits that transnational organizations derive from being neither fish nor fowl: "[Their] international non-status immunizes them from direct accountability to international legal norms and permits them to use sympathetic national governments to parry outside efforts to mold their behavior." This immunity allows transnational companies to move capital in ways governments are unable to do. These companies can also collaborate with other transnational entities. .

Thus political globalization involves control systems that move beyond the nation-state. In addition to the forces of transnational corporations, other systems that move beyond the nation-state include regional free-trade associations; nongovernmental organizations; and associations like the United Nations, which has a mission statement that includes peace-keeping, policy assessment and implementation regarding refugees and displaced persons, and the management of information systems through its UNESCO arm.

Roles for regional organizations loom larger than those of individual nation-states. Regional organizations may center around particular com-modities—oil, coffee, tea, even bananas. In these cases, it is not govern-ment officials who play key negotiating roles but rather business and labor representatives who make decisions, frequently independently of their government representatives (Cutler 2001). Regional organizations may also focus on general promises of trade and defense, such as NATO, Mercosur, the Asia-Pacific Economic Cooperation (APEC), and the As-sociation of Southeast Asian Nations (ASEAN). These organizations are working with both economic and political dimensions of globalization. At the regional level, in addition to organizations, particular nation-states can galvanize support for the resolution of structural problems. Australia, for example, sees itself playing a leadership role in the Pacific, collaborat-ing with "Pacific island neighbours to fight poverty in our own region" (Rudd 2008, 64). According to Kevin Rudd (2008, 64), Australia's former prime minister, "Australia also believes our commitment to giving every person a 'fair go' must extend beyond our shores." Rudd sees Pacific Rim

> The Maastricht criteria—typically termed "convergence criteria"—emerged from the 1992 negotiations and are intended to determine whether an EU member can adopt the euro. The criteria are composed of a nation's inflation rates, its government financial situation calculated as a function of annual government deficit and government debt, its currency exchange rate, and its long-term interest rates.

collaboration as central to "the best regional economic, political, and security architecture for 2020 and beyond" (2008, 64). As you will see in the next chapter, political globalization is a complicated, multilayered process. Many scholars believe that there is frequently a gap between economic and political globalization. Hopefully, this last section has demonstrated the commonalities. In the future, closing this gap will likely remain a critical task for global leaders.

We have examined the historical roots of economic globalization, linked it to political globalization, and looked at the ways various types of organizations at different levels affect how individual countries participate in the globalization process. We have seen how competing economic ideologies in Jamaica governed the election and reelection of public officials and the degree to which infrastructure changes could occur. Within the private business community, there are also competing ideologies that determine how various products are marketed, how companies link their producers and consumers, and how they make decisions about giving back to communities. It now becomes possible to look in more detail at the eurozone and how the financial crisis beginning in 2007–8 deeply affected two exemplars, Iceland and Greece, and pitted nation-states in the EU against each other. Iceland is not an EU country, but a candidate to become one. Greece is a eurozone country.

Case Study: Iceland and Greece

On February 7, 1992, a "Treaty on European Union" was passed in Maastricht, Netherlands. This treaty established both the European Union and the European Monetary Union (EMU). The EU currently has twenty-eight sovereign member states. Eighteen of these members currently use the euro as currency (Austria, Belgium, Cyprus, Estonia, Finland, France, Germany, Greece, Ireland, Italy, Latvia, Luxembourg, Malta, the Netherlands, Portugal, Slovakia, Slovenia, and Spain), while ten do not. Those who do not either "opted out" early on in the Maastricht negotiations (Denmark and the UK) or still need to meet certain "convergence criteria" (see the sidebar above). The EU official website (http://europa.eu/index_en.htm) contains a variety of position papers and clearly documents the growth and development of the Union, including current membership policies and issues (see "Economic and monetary union and the euro"). Your increasing knowledge of the fiscal stakes for the world as viewed through the lenses of both the EU and individual member nations is imperative for your understanding of both economic and political globalization.

In 2007 banks in the United States began to play different roles in the management of real estate speculation than they had earlier, which made them vulnerable to a real estate bubble. On September 15, 2008, Lehman Brothers Financial Services declared bankruptcy and AIG (at the time, the largest insurance company globally) collapsed. These two events are generally considered markers of the beginning of a global recession that still continues (Ferguson 2012).

Ferguson (2012) works backwards from this marker, describing a long period of fiscal deregulation beginning in the early 1980s in the United States. He traces how the continuation of deregulation into the 1990s resulted in the merger of a large number of multinational firms, allowing groups that were formally forbidden from collaborating to unite. In particular, the passing of the Gramm Leach Blieley Act facilitated merger processes among insurance companies, brokerage firms, and banks. Bankers were able to speculate on derivatives (see sidebar) in a manner not permitted earlier. While some see this as an example of fiscal innovation, others see it as the beginning of a "securitization food chain" (Ferguson 2012), by which derivatives became increasingly unregulated. An early proposal in

Pillar Structure of the European Union:

Common Foreign and Security Policy (governed by three supranational institutions: the Commission, the European Parliament, and the European Court of Justice)

European Community (EC)

Justice and Home Affairs (JHA)

Derivatives are "a security whose price is dependent upon or derived from one or more underlying assets. The derivative itself is merely a contract between two or more parties. Its value is determined by fluctuations in the underlying asset [such as a bond]. Futures contracts, forward contracts, options, and swaps are the most common types of derivatives." (www.investopedia.com)

May 1998 to regulate derivatives was unsuccessful, as Gramm and others pushed through legislation to exempt derivatives from such oversight. By 2000 all commodity-futures derivatives regulation was banned. Ferguson suggests then that the ultimate result was that individuals who made loans were not responsible for the success or failure of the loans. Lenders then sold mortgages to investment banks, which created collateralized debt that was sold to investors; this process is termed "credit default swap." Mortgage loans quadrupled. Credit default swaps began to increase; AIG alone accrued $5,000 billion worth of credit default swaps between 2000 and 2007 (Ferguson 2012).

The fallout from these activities affected the European Monetary Union in a drastic way. The crisis stemmed from the fact that some European countries violated the principles of the Stability and Growth Pact (SGP) (2005). Between 2008 and 2010, the economic health of Iceland, Greece, Spain, and Portugal bandied about like loose luggage in the hold of a plane: wild careens from one side to the other caused the plane to take drastic measures to stay the course. In 2011 reforms of the Stability and Growth Pact were implemented. These reforms are often called the "six-pack." They addressed gaps and weaknesses in the framework identified during the recent economic financial crisis. These reforms significantly strengthened both the fiscal surveillance and enforcement provisions of the SGP by adding an expenditure benchmark to review countries' fiscal positions, operationalizing the treaty's debt criterion, introducing an early and gradual system of financial sanctions for euro area member states, and requiring new minimum standards for national budgetary frameworks (B. Yesilada, personal communication, January 2, 2014). This case study examines what happened in Iceland and Greece between 2008 and 2010. As an EU member, Greece was directly pulled into implementing austerity measures on numerous occasions. For Iceland, the force of austerity measures came from the IMF. For both nations, Iceland in particular, private financial institutions played governing roles in both the fall and the recovery. As you read the quote below about events, try and imagine several levels of action within a matrix: multiple nation-states, multiple financial structures, public and private entities, and the general population in any given country. A principle to remember is that when austerity measures are imposed on a country to assist it in financial recovery, there are drastic differences in how particular citizens are impacted. A nation could begin to recover while individual citizens' lives remain in chaos.

This is how Costas Lapavitsas and his colleagues at the School of African and Oriental Studies at the University of London summarized the onset of the Great Recession:

> The collapse of Lehman Brothers in 2008 [in the United States]
> led to a major financial crisis that ushered in a global recession;
> the result was rising fiscal deficits for several leading countries of
> the world economy. For countries in the eurozone periphery, already
> deeply indebted after years of weakening competitiveness relative
> to the eurozone core, fiscal deficits led to restricted access to inter-
> national bond markets. Peripheral states were threatened with in-
> solvency, posing a risk to the European banks that were among the
> major lenders to the periphery. To rescue the banks, the eurozone
> had to bail out peripheral states. But bailouts were accompanied
> by austerity that induced deep recessions and rendered it hard to
> remain in the monetary unions, particularly for Greece (2012, ix).

We see above the use of the terms "eurozone core" and "eurozone pe-riphery." As will be explored in more detail in chapter 6, core nations use resources from periphery countries in ways that are frequently not sustainable to the periphery. In this case, Lapavitsas and his colleagues are suggesting that weaker EU states fiscally threatened to upend the stability of the more powerful core states. As a result, core states such as Germany took the lead in advocating austerity measures as required by the EU's Stability and Growth Pact Criteria. As we have seen in other settings with World Bank and IMF conditionality, these measures have typically taken away social programs in order to fund outside debt payment. We look now at the EU periphery states Iceland and Greece, the first a candidate and the second a member.

Iceland had begun banking deregulation in a manner similar to U.S. institutions and soon took part in the financial plunge. Even though its banks had once been known for their stability, after deregulation they had engaged in derivative speculation and international real estate speculation. In early 2000, Iceland privatized its three largest banks. KPMG, a U.S. fund-management firm, audited the banks even as they were extending derivatives, giving them an artificially high rating as late as February 2007. Index Mundi identifies the strategies Iceland was forced to adopt to begin to redress its fiscal crisis: "Since the collapse of Iceland's financial sector, government economic priorities have included: stabilizing the krona, implementing capital controls, reducing Iceland's high budget deficit, containing inflation, addressing high household debt, restructuring the financial sector, and diversifying the economy. Three new banks were established to take over the domestic assets of the collapsed banks. Two of them have foreign majority ownership, while the State holds a majority of the shares of the third." This is a type of *financialization* (defined in the sidebar below). A decade and a half after it deregulated its financial sector, Iceland is beginning a slow recovery. Lynam (2013) suggests that it is Iceland's "tenacity" that has allowed it to see growth in the past two years, calculated at approximately 2.5 percent per year. In 2010 individuals were asked to vote on the Icesave Referendum, a vote to decide whether funds should first be disbursed from the Depositors' and Investors' Guarantee Fund to Great Britain and the Netherlands as recompense to British and Dutch citizens who had invested in Icesave accounts. Iceland president Olafur Grimsson and his constituents have neither voted for nor signed the legislation. Grimsson stated, "Every Icelander was given a vote and got a new sense of self-worth: it made society stronger, this democratic thing helped give people empowerment" (Lynam 2013). This empowerment of individuals and the sort of corralling of wagon trains that has allowed Iceland to begin to rebuild its financial base has not occurred in Greece.

Greece's fiscal crisis began in 2009, when its deficit reached 15 percent, well exceeding the amount allowed under the EU's Stability and Growth Pact Criteria. Its International Debt Rating was downgraded. Index Mundi identifies three primary causes for this: "deteriorating public finances, inaccurate and misreported statistics, and consistent underperformance on

Financialization is "the increasing role of financial motives, financial markets, financial actors, and financial institutions in the operation of domestic and international economies" (Epstein 2005, 3).

reforms." Austerity measures were immediately implemented but proved inadequate for recovery. Since 2010, both the IMF and the EU have imposed three more rounds of austerity measures along with two bailouts—the first in 2010 for $147 billion and the second in October 2011 for $169 billion. Social unrest continues, with closures of schools, public television, and multiple universities, including the venerated Athens University. Routine demonstrations have done little to effect change, and Greece remains trapped in an austerity recovery program that looks to be interminable. Lapavitsas (2012) contrasts the lived experiences of people in high management positions with the experiences of common individuals, whose lives were permanently altered after multiple government and financial institutions abandoned their clients. He suggests that if peripheral economies in the EU are to survive, these non-industry individuals must be allowed to play leadership roles in the resolution of crises. He lays out an admittedly Marxist economic resolution to the problems facing Greece, calling for a three-phased solution: default, debt renegotiation, and exit. While acknowledging risks to the whole eurozone with such a solution, he states: "Peripheral countries have no obligation to accept austerity for the indefinite future in order to rescue the eurozone. Moreover, if the eurozone collapsed under the weight of its own sins, the opportunity would arise to put relations among the people of Europe on a different basis. Solidarity and equality among European people are certainly possible, but they require grassroots initiatives. The eurozone in its present form is a barrier to this development" (2012, 128).

Sets of criteria established in 2011 termed the "Euro-Plus Pact" attempt to manage deficits in particular member states, provide a level of sanctions if institutions do not meet their deficit targets, and ultimately enforce and fine countries that fail to measure up. This has led to agonizing on the part of many EU members on whether to remain in the eurozone using the euro as currency or to remain in the EU and *not* use the euro as currency. Within the next decade, other periphery eurozone nations will continue to face crises, much as Spain, Portugal, and even Ireland have. It remains to be seen whether traditional neoliberal solutions to debt will have any impact on the lives of individuals in these countries. In like manner, Marxist economic promises of greater attention to daily conditions of workers, and decisions to permit those most affected by austerity measures to have greater control over which measures are implemented, are likely to remain utopian. The European Union and all its members will play for high stakes in the economic globalization scene.

The scholars, entrepreneurs, and policy makers we have introduced to you in this chapter also have visions for our globalized world. Most have outlined roles for multinational organizations at the international or regional level to both craft and implement policy. Entrepreneur George Soros (2002, 8) calls for a complimentary organization to the WTO in order to resolve issues the WTO has been unable to resolve. He believes it is critically important to do four things: "contain the instability of financial markets; correct the built-in bias in our existing international trade and financial institutions that favors the developed countries that largely control them; complement the WTO with similarly powerful international institutions devoted to other social goals such as poverty reduction and the provision of public goods on a global scale; and improve the quality of public life in countries suffering from corrupt, repressive, or incompetent governments." Ellwood (2003, 108–36) also pushes the notion of creating another type of global financial authority, even while reforming the Bretton Woods institutions. He suggests that only by "increasing citizen participation" and "honoring the earth" will it be possible to undo some of the damage that has been caused by conditionality. In the next chapter, we continue to explore transborder flows, focusing on the history and distinguishing features of political globalization.

➤ **VOCABULARY**

Big Three privatization
liberalization
deregulation
neoliberal economic policy
Augmented Washington Consensus
neoconservative economic policy
Poverty Reduction Strategy Papers
gold standard
Dispute Settlement Body
Washington Consensus
BRICS
N-11
claim adjudication
financialization
derivatives
Stability and Growth Pact Criteria

➤ **DISCUSSION AND REFLECTION QUESTIONS**

1 *Identify three dimensions of economic aspects of globalization.*

2 *What were the initial hopes for the World Bank and the International Monetary Fund?*

3 *What are three differences between the Washington Consensus and the Augmented Washington Consensus?*

4 *What is the relationship between Structural Adjustment Programs (SAPs) and Poverty Reduction Strategy Papers (PRSPs)?*

5 *Why is it so difficult to escape sanctions meted out by the Dispute Settlement Body (DSB)?*

6 *What are some of the criticisms that have been leveled against neoliberal economic policies?*

7 *What can we expect in the future from BRICS and N-11?*

8 *If you were able to make policy recommendations to manage economic reforms at a global level and maintain social programs within a developing nation qualifying for assistance from the Bretton Woods institutions, what would two of your top priorities be?*

9 *How can you account for the kinds of intellectual and policy changes people like Michael Manley and Joseph Stiglitz have made over the course of their careers?*

10 *How has the private sector in banking along with derivative speculation changed the fiscal stability of periphery nations in the eurozone?*

ACTIVITY 1 Go online to YouTube and search for World Bank, IMF, and/or structural adjustment. Watch at least three separate clips of three to eight minutes each. Identify the perspective taken in each of the clips. Are the presenters supportive of the work of the Bretton Woods institutions? How do you know this? As you reflect on the perspectives presented in the chapter, can you begin to identify your own economic perspective on globalization?

ACTIVITY 2 Making connections. This chapter defined globalization and looked in some detail at the extended debate in the WTO and ultimately its Dispute Settlement Body regarding bananas. Go online and conduct a search to find one other major dispute currently under consideration at the WTO. Track the amount of time the dispute has been going on and its primary actors. Identify how you would resolve the dispute if the ultimate decision were in your hands.

ACTIVITY 3 Lapavitsas and colleagues (2012) suggest that acceptance of austerity principles and neoliberal recommendations on the part of many countries in the eurozone has resulted in measurable temporary fixes but long-term chaos as well. Choose one country—Iceland, Greece, Portugal, or Spain. Identify one austerity principle they were asked to follow. Then, using a newspaper database such as the *New York Times Index,* search for economic stories about that country and identify whether the austerity measures taken are addressed in the article and what the principle followed was. Can you identify the ideological stance of the author regarding these activities?

References

Appadurai, A. 1996. *Modernity at large: Cultural dimensions of globalization.* Minneapolis: University of Minnesota Press.

Appellate body issues report on banana dispute. Retrieved November 30, 2008, from http://www.wto.org/english/news_e/news_e.htm#bkmk856.

Broad, R., ed. 2002. *Global backlash: Citizen initiatives for a just world economy.* Lanham, Md.: Roman and Littlefield, Inc.

Brown, T. 2013. Contestation, confusion, and corruption: Market-based land reform in Zambia. Retrieved as pdf on December 18, 2013, from www .theidlgroup.com/.../market_based_land_reform_zambia.pdf.

Cerny, P. 1995. Globalization and the changing logic of collective action. *International Organization* 49 (4): 595–625.

Charney, J. 1983. Transnational corporations and developing public international law. *Duke Law Journal* 4 (September): 748–88.

Chin, P. 1997. Cheddi Jagan, Michael Manley, and the history of U.S. intervention in the Caribbean. April 3. Retrieved November 26, 2008, from http://www.hartford-hwp.com/archives/43/034.html.

Choi, K. 2008. The roots of the WTO. Retrieved November 26, 2008, from www.econ.iastate.edu/classes/econ355/choi/wtoroots.htm.

Conditionality. Retrieved November 26, 2008, from http://www.imf.org/external/np/exr/facts/conditio.htm.

Cox, R. 1996. A perspective on globalization. In *Globalization: Critical reflections,* ed. J. Mittelman, 22–30. Boulder, Colo.: Lynne Rienner Publishers.

Cutler, A. C. 2001. Critical reflections on the Westphalian assumptions of international law and organization: A crisis of legitimacy. *Review of International Studies* 27:133–50.

Derivatives definition. Retrieved December 20, 2013, from http://www.invest opedia.com/terms/d/derivative.asp.

Economic and monetary union and the euro. 2013. Retrieved as pdf on
    December 20, 2013, from europa.eu/pol/.../economic_and_monetary_union_
    and_the_euro_en.pdf. doi:10.2775/37006. Luxembourg: Publications Office
    of the European Union.
Ellwood, W. 2003. *The no-nonsense guide to globalization.* Toronto: New Inter-
    nationalist Publications.
Epstein, G. 2005. *Financialization and the world economy.* Northampton, Mass.:
    Edward Elgar Publishing Limited.
European Communities—regime for the importation, sale, and distribution
    of bananas. WTO dispute settlement—the disputes—DS27. Retrieved
    November 30, 2009, from http://www.wto.org/english/tratop_e/dispu_e
    /cases_e/ds27_e.htm.
European Communities—regime for the importation, sale, and distribution of
    bananas. WTO dispute settlement—the disputes—DS27. One-page summary.
    Retrieved November 30, 2009, from http://www.wto.org/english/tratop_e
    /dispu_e/cases_e/1pagesum_e/ds27sum_e.pdf.
Ferguson, C. 2012. *Inside job: The financiers who pulled off the heist of the century.*
    Oxford, UK: Oneworld Publications Limited.
Fortune Global 500 Companies 2013. Retrieved December 18, 2013 from
    http://money.cnn.com/magazines/fortune/global500/.
Friedman, T. 2007. *The world is flat: A brief history of the 21st century.* New York:
    Picador/Farrar, Straus and Giroux.
GATT. CIESIN thematic guides. Retrieved November 23, 2008, from http://
    www.Ciesin.orgTG/PI/TRADE/gatt.html.
GATT slideshow. 2014. Retrieved January 1, 2014, from http://www.wto.org
    /english/thewto_e/minist_e/min98_e/slide_e/slide_list.htm.
Global Policy Forum 2008. www.globalpolicy.org/globaliz/politics/index.htm.
Global trade negotiations home page. Retrieved January 18, 2008, from http://
    www.cid.harvard.edu/cidtrade/issues/Washington.html.[Dani Rodrik].
Graddol, D. 1996. The future of English. Retrieved December 18, 2013, from
    www.britishcouncil.org/learning-elt-future.pdf.
Greece Economic Profile. 2013. Retrieved as pdf on December 20, 2013, from
    www.indexmundi.com/greece/economy/profile.html.
Handa, S., and D. King. 1997. Structural adjustment policies, income distribu-
    tion, and poverty: A review of the Jamaican experience. *World Development* 25
    (6): 915–30.
Hansen-Kuhn, K., and A. Hellinger. 1999. SAPS link sharpens debt-relief
    debate. Retrieved as pdf on January 25, 2010, from http://www.development
    gap.org/worldbank_imf/saps_link_sharpens_debtrelief_debate.pdf (Third
    World Network; developmentgap.com).
Harvey, D. 1989. *The condition of post-modernity: An inquiry into the origins of
    culture change.* Cambridge, UK: Blackwell.
Iceland Economic Profile. 2013. Retrieved as pdf on December 20, 2013, from
    www.indexmundi.com/iceland/economy/profile.html.

IMF website. Retrieved January 17, 2009, from http://www.imf.org/external
/index.htm.

International financing institution: About the Global Fund. 2008. Retrieved
December 5, 2008, from http://www.theglobalfund.org/en/ifi/.

International networks archive: Remapping our world. Retrieved December 3,
2008, from http://www.princeton.edu/~ina/infographics/index.html.

Khanna, P., and A. Rusi. 2008. Europe's century. *The Guardian.* Retrieved
January 17, 2009, from www.globalpolicy.org/nations/sovereign/integrate
/2008/0617khanna.htm.

Koeppel, D. 2008. *Banana: The fate of the fruit that changed the world.* New York:
Hudson Street Press.

Krugman, P. 2004. *The great unraveling: Losing our way in the new century.*
London: Penguin.

Levesque, J. 2013. Haiti reconstruction: Luxury hotels, sweat shops, and
deregulation for the foreign elite. Global Research. August 16. Retrieved
December 18, 2013, from http://www.globalresearch.ca/haiti-reconstruction-
luxury-hotels-sweat-shops-and-deregulation-for-the-foreign-corporate-
elite/5344546.

Lynam, J. 2013. Iceland's "tenacity" lifts economy out of crisis. January 7.
Retrieved December 28, 2013, from http://www.bbc.co.uk/news/world-
europe-20936685.

MacGillivray, A. 2006. *A brief history of globalization.* London: Robinson.

May, J., and N. Thrift. 2001. "Introduction." *TimeSpace: Geographies of
temporality.* New York: Routledge, 1–46.

Millstone, E., and T. Lang. 2008. *The atlas of food: Who eats what, where, and why.*
Berkeley: University of California Press.

O'Neill, J. 2007. BRICS and Beyond. Retrieved as pdf on December 18, 2013,
from http://www.goldmansachs.com/our-thinking/archive/BRICs-and-
Beyond.html.

Rudd, K. 2008. Large issues and medium powers. *The World in 2009*
(*The Economist*), 64.

Scholte, J. 2005. *The sources of neoliberal globalization: Overarching concerns.*
Programme Paper Number 8 (October). United Nations Research Institute
for Social Development.

Seckinelgin, H., J. Scholte, A. Kumar, M. Kaldor, M. Glasius, and H. Anheier.
2009. Poverty and activism: The heart of global civil society. Retrieved
January 1, 2014, from http://www.opendemocracy.net/authors/jan-aart-
scholte.

Seria, N. 2010. South Africa is asked to join as a BRIC member to boost
emerging markets. December 24. Retrieved January 1, 2014, from http://
www.bloomberg.com/news/2010-12-24/south-africa-asked-to-join-bric-to-
boost-cooperation-with-emerging-markets.html.

Singer, P. 2002. *One world: The ethics of globalization.* New Haven, Conn.:
Yale University Press.

Soros, G. 2002. *On globalization.* New York: Public Affairs.

Steger, M. 2003. *Globalization: A very short introduction*. Oxford, UK: Oxford University Press.

Stiglitz, J. 2002. *Globalization and its discontents*. London: W. W. Norton and Company.

———. 2006. *Making globalization work*. New York: W. W. Norton and Company.

UN Millennium Goals. Retrieved January 17, 2009, from www.un.org/ millenniumgoals/pdf/mdg2007.pdf.

World's Largest Economies 2013. Retrieved December 18, 2013, from http:// money.cnn.com/news/economy/world_economies_gdp/

WTO DS 27. Retrieved July 6, 2010, from http://www.wto.org/english/tratop_e /dispu_e/cases_e/ds27_e.htm.

WTO Membership in brief. Retrieved December 18, 2013, from www.wto.org /english/thewto_e/acc_e/members_brief_e.doc

WTO website. Retrieved January 17, 2009, from www.wto.org.

FOUR **Political Globalization**

➤ **SYNOPSIS**

This chapter builds on the previous material regarding economic globalization by looking at the political sphere, beginning first with the League of Nations and then its successor, the United Nations. Ideological currents, such as the rise of human rights, also constrain global politics. One key trend since the 1980s has been democratization, which has made rapid progress in Asia, Eastern Europe, and Latin America. Political globalization has also been fostered by transnational alliances and multinational corporations, which constrain the power of nation-states. Similarly, states sometimes surrender power willingly to military alliances and regional associations, which may expand and change from their original formulation. While nation-states remain key actors, their actions are constrained; globalization cannot be discussed without including the political realm. The chapter concludes with a comparative look at political globalization in the polar regions, which are vital for environmental and economic interests, as well as indigenous peoples in the North.

➤ **SCAFFOLDING**

As you read through this chapter, think about how you would answer each of the questions below.

What did you already know about the League of Nations and the United Nations and the issues that surround them?

How do the institutions and trends described in this chapter relate to those discussed in the economic globalization chapter?

What other institutions or examples of political globalization might this chapter have discussed?

Why are the polar regions often ignored, and in what way are they significant in global affairs?

➤ **CORE CONCEPTS**

Because political globalization is as powerful a force as economic globalization, the two movements must be discussed together.

Despite the rise of China, an authoritarian state, democratization is arguably the most powerful trend associated with political globalization in the early twenty-first century.

Although the nation-state remains the most powerful actor in most situations, the rise of new institutions and beliefs challenges its influence. In some cases, new political organizations—such as the European Union—are even assuming aspects of sovereignty.

When people think of globalization, many of them associate it with the economic trends that are integrating the world's economies. If they think of political institutions, they likely focus on those discussed in the last chapter, which have their roots in Bretton Woods. But that only captures one aspect of the international forces that are reshaping the global order. Dramatic changes are also taking place in the realm of politics. Some political organizations have emerged that hold great power. After World War II, the founding of both the United Nations and the International Court of Justice meant that even leaders of nation-states had to fear facing justice if they committed war crimes or genocide. Other new political actors appeared that were both influential and complex, particularly when they entered into alliances with other groups to achieve their goals. For example, new transnational organizations (such as Greenpeace, Oxfam, and Amnesty International) established alliances with grassroots organizations (indigenous-rights groups or local environmental movements) to block initiatives from organizations such as the World Bank. Such coalitions have defeated powerful nation-states, including the United States. At the same time, military alliances—such as the North Atlantic Treaty Organization (NATO)—have continued not only to be relevant but also to evolve into organizations with broader identities and mandates, such as nation building and peacekeeping. Although the nation-state remains the fundamental unit in international affairs, other political actors have constrained its power. What is unusual now is not only the rising number of these challengers but also the fact that in some cases—most notably the European Union—organizations are beginning to change how we think about the nation-state's centrality to international studies. For this reason, no discussion of globalization can remain confined to the realm of economics alone.

The Legacy of World War I

The roots of political globalization, like those of economic globalization, lay in a terrible conflict. In 1914 Europe exploded into a war that probably no Great Power wanted. Historians have long debated the reasons for this war—with explanations that have emphasized imperial rivalry, rampant nationalism, and train schedules—but the origins of the conflict are so complex that this issue is still contested. For five years, millions of men fought and died in trenches that stretched across Europe on two fronts, from northern France to modern Turkey. For much of this time, the opposing sides were trapped in a stalemate, which each sought to break with weapons that ranged from mustard gas to underground tunnels that were packed with explosives and then detonated. In the end, the conflict destroyed two Great Powers—the Russian and Ottoman Empires—and the belligerents achieved nothing positive to balance the war's suffering. The complexity and devastation of the war left many shattered veterans wondering what they had fought for.

After the war, Woodrow Wilson, the American president, was determined to create a new order based on his ideals so that such a disaster could never happen again. Wilson, the founder of modern liberalism, believed that new organizations were needed to prevent wars of aggression, to permit the territories once governed by Germany and the Ottoman Empire to achieve sovereignty, and to adjudicate disputes that might lead to war. Wilson told the American people that new organizations and the rule of law—a body of international practices and rules that would resolve disputes—could control the passions and the grievances that led the Old World into conflagration. His allies—France and England—had not fought the war intending to relinquish their empires or create a new national order. But they could not ignore the United States, which had brought the manpower and the money that had tipped the balance to their side.

As a result, the first part of the Treaty of Versailles, which officially ended the war in 1919, contained language describing a new international organization called the League of Nations. Wilson himself suffered a severe stroke in 1919 in the midst of a struggle to persuade the U.S. Senate to join this new body. The United States never joined, and many historians have argued that this fact fatally weakened the league. Another challenge was that Germany was not permitted to join until 1926 (Kennedy 2006, 13). Still, during the 1920s, the League of Nations appeared to be effective, as did the Permanent Court of International Justice, which the league created in 1923. But, faced with the rising power of fascism and without U.S. participation, the league failed to confront the Japanese invasion of Manchuria in 1931 and the Italian invasion of Ethiopia in 1935 (both inspired by imperialist aims), as well as German rearmament. The league's charter contained flaws, which perhaps gave small states too much power and failed to oblige members to act (Sobel 1994, 180). Despite Wilson's vision, the League of Nations could not prevent another conflagration. The postwar period proved to be an interregnum in what came to be a single European civil war.

The United Nations

In 1939 the Second World War began and lasted six long years before the final defeat of Nazi Germany and Imperial Japan. At this point in 1945, many people believed that a new League of Nations was needed more than ever because they were determined not to repeat the mistakes that made the war possible. (For an in-depth discussion of the creation of the United Nations, see Kennedy 2006, 4–47; and Hurd 2007, 84–91.) For this reason, at the war's end, the victors extinguished the old League of Nations and created the United Nations to take its place, with the intent of learning from the league's failure. In April and June 1945, forty-six nations from around the world gathered in San Francisco to create this organization. The meetings saw heated debates, in part because the wartime alliance among the Allies was ending and the first shadows of the Cold War had crept into the meeting rooms. But there were also many serious questions to be answered. As Stephen Schlesinger (1997, 48) has argued, it is not true that the UN was "born out of a gentle, idealistic vision of a global body, a sort of immaculate conception. In fact, the U.N. Charter was a meticulously crafted, power-oriented document carefully molded by hard-nosed drafters to conform to the global realities of 1945." It divided the UN into

Traffic circle in Vietnam (Used with permission of the photographer, Christina Caponi)

two bodies. The fifteen-member Security Council addressed critical issues and had five permanent members: China, France, Great Britain, the Soviet Union, and the United States, which were the Great Powers of the time. As global power balances shifted, this choice of nations appeared increasingly anachronistic. In contrast, most nations were confined to the General Assembly, which could make recommendations to the Security Council, write reports, and approve the budget but did not address key issues of peace and security or send troops into an active war zone.

It could be argued that the UN is not democratic. But it could not have been created without the participation of the Great Powers. The United States' decision not to participate in the League of Nations had helped to doom it. If the UN was to avoid being stillborn, it needed to have the support of each of these major nations, even at the cost of inequality. This inequality might appear to be mitigated by the fact that there are fifteen members of the Security Council, of which ten are nonpermanent members from the General Assembly. But these nations soon rotate off the Security Council, and none of them has the power of veto. It was the latter power that gave the permanent members the "ability to decide on U.N. intervention, determine who leads the organization, block U.N. Charter amendments, and so forth" (Schlesinger 1997, 49; see also Hurd 2007, 93–96). While many smaller states had opposed this arrangement, they failed to overcome the position of the Great Powers. With this assurance, the U.S. Senate was willing to ratify the treaty, and the Soviet Union was willing to join.

The UN has not achieved all that was promised at its creation in 1945. There is no denying its failures. It did not stop the Rwandan genocide of 1994, and it needed U.S. leadership to be effective in Bosnia (Shawcross 2000, 124–92). In the case of Kosovo, the United States ultimately ended the fighting in 1999 without the UN. In addition, the UN has often failed to enforce its decisions. Its members were involved in a serious scandal in Iraq during the "Oil for Food" program, a system through which the Iraqi government was able to sell oil to purchase key goods such as food during the period between 1995 and 2003. It also has a long-standing reputation for being bureaucratic, ineffective, and corrupt. Reform efforts have yet to transform the institution, as a 2007 report by the U.S. General Accounting Office detailed. The wide diversity of membership within the UN has often made it difficult to reach consensus on even the most important issues, which at times has caused even the secretary general to express frustration with the organization (Anonymous 2005). The United States invaded Iraq without the support of the UN, despite UN Resolution 1441, which required Iraq to meet its obligations to disarm (Glennon 2003, 18; Hurd 2007, 124–28). As an institution, the UN has grave internal divisions regarding when the use of armed force is appropriate (Glennon 2003, 20). The UN has failed to act to end the civil war in Syria, which began as part of the Arab Spring. While its "sister organizations," such as the World Health Organization, the UN Refugee Agency, and the World Food Bank, have been recognized for their achievements, the United Nations is often condemned for the crises it has failed to avert.

Despite these failings, the UN also has a long list of major achievements, from helping to end apartheid in South Africa to moderating crises during the Cold War (Schlesinger 2007, 51). It is a cliché to say that nations do not appreciate the UN until there is a crisis. Cynics can say that the UN only resolves problems when it is in the interest of Great Powers to see them fixed. But as World War I showed, it is possible for nations to slide into war; not every conflict begins through a rational calculation of interests. The UN has provided a forum that has allowed major countries to extricate themselves from hostilities, such as the Suez Crisis in 1956. By providing nations with a face-saving means to avoid conflict, fact finders with a way of determining the truth of events, and peacekeepers with the power to separate rival forces, the UN decreases the likelihood of unintended wars. The UN also possesses moral authority. Perhaps no other power had the legitimacy, for example, to end the violence in East Timor after that nation voted for independence from Indonesia in 1999. The U.S. and NATO air campaign could defeat the Serbs militarily in Kosovo in 1999, but they then needed a UN mandate to send peacekeepers.

Through its role in peacekeeping, the UN has separated many aggrieved parties and laid the groundwork for a settlement of international disputes, despite the questions that sometimes come regarding the legitimacy of its operations (Hurd 2007, 125). The UN also plays a key role by organizing relief after international disasters. This could be clearly seen after the 2010 earthquake in Haiti, after which the UN's World Food Program began food distribution on a massive scale. Moreover, some of its components—such as the World Health Organization (WHO)—have achieved stunning successes, such as eliminating smallpox and polio. Because of its legitimacy, the WHO is able to do work in key areas that are not accessible to other organizations. The truly dangerous flaws of the UN lie less in its unending bureaucracy than in the extent to which it froze the global balance of power in 1945.

UN Reform

The Security Council is at the core of the United Nations, and its nature is defined by its history. (For a discussion of the Security Council's role, see Hurd 2007, 111–36.) At the end of World War II, there were five Great Powers, which dominated international affairs. Few scholars or diplomats foresaw that the Age of Empire had ended and that in the space of roughly two decades, both Great Britain and France would lose their empires. Both nations underwent a relative economic decline. They remained wealthy states but were no longer central to global affairs. People at the time could see that both Germany and Japan were key global powers, but the victors of World War II excluded them from the Security Council because of their responsibility for the war that had just finished. While this may have made sense at the time, did that make sense a generation later? Two generations later? Germany and Japan now have great influence on the council, but their exclusion still seems an anomaly (Hurd 2007, 118).

This problem is only likely to increase with time. If current trends continue, most of the world's economic growth over the next forty years will likely take place outside of the United States and Europe. Asia and Latin America have the most dynamic economies, while Africa will see the greatest population increase among the continents (Goldstone 2010, 33). As is common in international affairs, governance systems are created within a historical context, which pertains to that specific time and environment. These systems need the capacity to adapt if they are not to become obsolete as the context changes. But the UN charter did not create a clear process to determine the manner in which new states would be made permanent members of the Security Council. The UN charter can only be changed with the approval of the Security Council, which means that the five permanent members have veto power over any new additions to this body. This reality, and competition among neighbors, has meant that no new nation has ever become a new permanent member (Luck 2003, 15).

China is unwilling to see its old rival Japan join, a step that would dilute Chinese influence. Pakistan bitterly opposes the idea of bringing India into the Security Council. Argentina feels the same about Brazil, with discreet support from Mexico. The idea of adding South Africa to the council raises questions in Nigeria, and similar questions will doubtless cloud any other nation that emerges onto the global stage. Not only has the UN failed to add new members to the Security Council; there also have not been meaningful discussions about removing powers that no longer

Is there a mock UN on your campus, or a UN Club? Find out when they meet, what their goals are, and whether it would be useful for you to participate.

have global influence. While its role on the global stage is a key part of its identity, France might not be included if the Security Council was created today, and the same is perhaps true in the case of Great Britain. But under the current UN charter, it is impossible to remove either of these nations without their agreement, given their veto under Article 108 (Luck 2003, 3). This has led to complaints about the veto power of the Security Council's permanent members (Luck 2003, 15). Germany, the largest economy in Europe, remains excluded from the Security Council seventy years after World War II.

The danger of this situation is that the UN was created to reflect the balance of global power because, without this representation, it would not be effective—a lesson learned from the League of Nations. With each passing year, economic and demographic changes reshape the balance of power, so that the existing makeup of the Security Council seems increasingly out of date, especially in contrast to other organizations that have expanded or adapted. As nations rallied to address the economic crisis of 2009, it was the G-20 that drew media attention because the old G-8 nations no longer had the influence needed to resolve global problems (Goldstone 2010, 41). A similar evolution could not take place within the United Nations. Resolving this problem would entail revising the UN charter to create a clear process for both adding and removing powers: "International institutions will not retain their legitimacy if they exclude the world's fastest growing and most economically dynamic powers" (Goldstone 2010, 41). This problem, however, shows few signs of resolution. (For a contrary view to the above argument, see Hurd 2007, 123.) While this challenge has remained unresolved, the UN has helped to weave a new set of political ties around the globe. This can clearly be seen in the case of the International Court of Justice, which has contributed to the growing importance of international law—another concept important to Woodrow Wilson.

The International Court of Justice

While the UN has many responsibilities—including coordinating disaster relief, peacekeeping, and monitoring elections—few aspects of its work have been as important as the administration of international justice and arbitration of disputes. This was clear immediately at the end of World War II, when the victors decided to try war criminals at the Nuremberg War Trials, named for the city in Germany in which they were held. Rather than being immediately executed, those responsible for the Holocaust, ethnic cleansing, and the war were tried in a court in which they had counsel and genuine trials. The idea of international justice was to be central to the new world order. For this reason, the new International Court of Justice (ICJ), the main judicial organization of the UN, had a broad range of responsibilities. For example, countries could agree to submit boundary disputes and other arguments to the court for a binding settlement. Aggrieved parties could also take their disputes to the court for resolution. The ICJ was intended to provide judicial support to the Security Council to avoid and resolve international conflict.

The ICJ has not always succeeded. During the Cold War, the court was incapable of imposing its rulings on the superpowers. For example, in the 1980s the United States refused to recognize a court ruling that condemned it for planting sea mines in Nicaraguan ports. This substantially weakened the court. While the Soviet Union worried that the ICJ was initially weighted in favor of democracies, the United States eventually came to fear its judicial independence (Posner 2004). There has always been a tension between the ability of Great Powers to veto decisions that they oppose within the UN Security Council and their potential vulnerability within the ICJ. Justices were theoretically impartial—that is, they were not supposed to vote based on their national origin. For this reason, the United States' acceptance of the court and its authority has been conditional in a number of manners. For instance, when the United States became party to the Genocide Convention, it did so with a reservation: "[B]efore any dispute in which the United States is a party may be submitted to the jurisdiction of the International Court of Justice under this article, the specific consent of the United States is required in each case" (Jennings 1995, 495–96). In other words, the United States could only be brought to court with its own consent. On the surface, the Genocide Convention—which forbade the destruction of a people either through killing, the prevention of birth, or the removal of children—would seem uncontroversial. But the United

States was concerned about how the convention might be interpreted. For similar reasons, after the creation of the International Criminal Court in 2002, the United States made it clear that it would not ratify this document, even though it had been a signatory (Mayerfield 2003). While it is logical for any nation-state to not wish to submit itself to the authority of an outside power, states also pay a price when they do not participate in such institutions.

The power of both the United Nations and the International Court of Justice has been bound by the Great Powers. The ICJ's influence has declined in recent decades. Fewer nations submit cases to it, and the court does not always have the influence to see its judgments enacted. Moreover, the UN and regional powers have created tribunals and courts that now take on cases that once would have pertained to the ICJ for issues that range from environmental questions to the law of the sea (Dupuy 1999, 792–93). Still, the fact that Great Powers worry about the ICJ's rulings indicates that it retains influence. The court has moral authority. As Gowland Debbas (1994, 676) has noted, the ICJ also serves the role of setting the norms that are needed by the international community (see also Dupuy 1999, 793.) In other words, it has helped to codify what understandings and doctrines have the force of law. In March 2009, the court issued an arrest warrant for Sudan's president Omar Hassan Ahmad al-Bashir for crimes against humanity. Even though Sudan refused to surrender al-Bashir, international law has expanded its power and constrains states to a far greater extent than in the past, even given the realities of Great Power politics. The ICJ's role, in turn, should be considered in the context of changing legal and political norms in international affairs, as can be seen with the emerging doctrine of human rights.

The Rise of Human Rights as a Doctrine

Human rights are those claims and protections that people have because they are part of humanity, independent from their citizenship in a particular state. Historically, in Western culture, these claims came not from one's nationality but rather from one's religion; this was also the case in many other civilizations, such as the Islamic world. During the French Enlightenment of the eighteenth century, however, secular and humanist philosophers began to claim that people had the right to protection based on reason and not religion. The first great human rights battle was against slavery, which ended in the Western Hemisphere with its abolition in Cuba in 1886 and Brazil in 1888. This rights campaign was the model for many that followed. But it was the horrific events of the twentieth century, from the mass killing of Armenian civilians by Turkey during World War I to the Holocaust, that led to the creation of the UN Commission on Human Rights in 1946. Eleanor Roosevelt, the widow of U.S. president Franklin D. Roosevelt, subsequently campaigned for the UN Declaration of Human Rights, which the General Assembly passed in 1948. Some idea of its moral force can be gleaned from the fact that no nation opposed it, although Saudi Arabia, South Africa, and the Soviet Union abstained from the vote. (For a good overview of the history of human rights, see Lauren 1998.)

On the surface, it would seem that both this declaration and the UN proved to be failures because they could not prevent many of the terrible human rights tragedies of the twentieth century. Because of their political power, the Soviet Union and China were able to ignore the UN Declarations as they committed terrible human rights violations. Likewise, the United States shielded authoritarian states in Latin America and elsewhere from UN action during the Cold War. The United States did so in part because it had created many authoritarian regimes as a bulwark against Communism and to serve its business interests, as was the case with the Somoza family in Nicaragua. The United Nations also failed to act to prevent genocide in both Cambodia and Rwanda, despite clear evidence that it could have saved hundreds of thousands of lives in the latter case if it had shown the political will. Yet, the power of human rights has grown as a political ideal, and violating these norms has carried a high political and personal cost for authoritarian leaders and their governments. For example, historian John Lewis Gaddis (2005, 190–94) has argued that the Helsinki Accords, passed in 1975, were fundamental to undermining the Soviet Union's legitimacy. This agreement among almost every state in Europe, as well as Canada and the United States, committed all the signatories to respect human rights and self-determination of peoples. With the end of the Cold War, the United States withdrew its support from authoritarian governments in Latin America, which fell like dominos in part because they appeared illegitimate in the eyes of both their own people and the international community, given their terrible human rights violations. South Africa found it impossible to face sanctions and international condemnation in order to maintain apartheid, which denied rights to citizens based on race. The UN and the United States intervened to end ethnic cleansing and violence in the former Yugoslavia in the 1990s.

States can still violate human rights if they are willing to pay a political price, as nations such as Zimbabwe have shown. But those who suffer have long memories, and many authoritarian leaders must worry that in their retirement, a warrant will be issued for their arrest, and they may be brought before the International Criminal Court in the Hague. This serves as a check on behavior. The proliferation of nongovernmental organizations (NGOs), such as Amnesty International, has brought publicity to human rights violations, as has the development of global media. Nations that are willing to isolate themselves, such as North Korea and Myanmar/ Burma, are able to continue to violate human rights. But these states are so isolated that they have few allies in the event of a crisis, they pay a heavy economic cost, and no nations look to them as a model. States that violate human rights lose the moral authority to serve as international leaders. The price that the United States has paid for both the use of torture at Abu Ghraib prison in Iraq and waterboarding and other abuses at Guantanamo Bay Detention Camp in Cuba has been high in terms of its international leadership.

Still, human rights are not uncontested as a doctrine, as the work of Shashi Tharoor (1999) makes clear. Critics ask, who defines what is a human right? The idea itself, they argue, is based on an essentialist vision of human nature; that is, the idea that we are all fundamentally the same. But what an urban, Western citizen in Amsterdam may perceive to be a human right may be very different from what a rural, religious person in Indonesia believes one to be. In this circumstance, who decides? Is female genital cutting an age-old cultural practice or a human rights violation? Is it acceptable to change practices in the name of human rights if that means fundamental changes to a culture will follow? What rights are universally recognized? Those of women? Sexual minorities? How are these decisions made? If it is the West that imposes its vision of human rights upon developing nations through the World Bank or other institutions, do human rights come with a cultural and political agenda? Can they be viewed as an aspect of neocolonialism? What about human rights that are not recognized in all Western nations? Is housing or health care a human right? Clothing? Equal pay for equal work (see United Nations 1948, Articles 23:2 and 25:1)? These are not recognized as such in the United States and many European nations. Critics therefore argue that human rights is an arbitrary concept that is used by powerful Western nations to impose their cultural values on others, while they at the same time disregard those rights that they find inconvenient. The United States continues to use capital punishment, even though some other nations find this barbaric. From this perspective, Western nations focus on the rights of the individual rather than on collective right, giving too much weight to the concept of rights and not enough to the notion of responsibilities. Can the idea of human rights undermine the collective responsibilities that hold a society together?

As Tharoor (1999) notes, there are powerful counterarguments to these critiques that emphasize the involvement of developing countries in the UN Declaration of Human Rights and the fact that many different religions and philosophies share common ideals. No culture exists in a vacuum, and all change through time. Who speaks for a culture? Would not the oppressed oppose slavery and women support their own rights? Human rights are a powerful concept, one which holds intellectual rigor. It is because of this power that authoritarian states feel the need to voice critiques. But this criticism has neither weakened the idea of human rights as an international ideal nor undermined the influence of groups that advocate for them. Indeed, one of the trends of political globalization is the continuing spread of not only this intellectual construct but also that of democracy.

Democratization

At a surface level, democracy is relatively easy to define: it is a system in which the vote of the majority of the population determines the government. Yet this apparent simplicity is problematic, because the idea of democracy contains a number of tensions or questions. Is a system democratic if there is extreme economic inequality, which gives political power to a small elite? How must the will of the majority be balanced against the rights of the minority? What if a democratic state engages in imperial projects that oppress other peoples or nations, as was the case with ancient Athens? And to what extent must democracy reflect local cultures and traditions? Is true democracy procedural, or is there more to meeting the standard of being a real democracy, such as the existence of a civic culture? These contradictions and issues have become increasingly important as the twentieth century witnessed a slow but powerful trend toward the rise of democracy.

Between 1964 and 1973, one Latin American government after another fell to military rule, and such regimes were also common in Africa and Asia. But the 1980s were the "lost decade" in Latin America. A combination of factors undermined the legitimacy of military governments there, including poor economic performance, terrible human rights abuses, and the lack of a convincing ideology. Throughout the 1980s, many nations in the region returned to democracy. This trend has shown few signs of reversing. With the end of the Cold War in 1991, the United States no longer had an intellectual justification to prop up authoritarian rulers in Latin America (this was not the case in the Middle East), which likely accelerated the decline in military rule throughout the region. But this trend was not confined to Latin America. Globally, traditional authoritarian regimes in many areas lost their intellectual legitimacy and collapsed with sometimes shocking speed.

Asia witnessed an impressive trend toward democratization, as Junhan Lee (2002, 821) has described: "In this region between 1986 and 1999, Bangladesh, Indonesia, Mongolia, Nepal, Pakistan, the Philippines, South Korea, Taiwan, and Thailand all embraced genuine transitions to democracy." Obviously, these transitions have occurred in nations with widely different cultures and population sizes. Surprisingly, there seems to be little correlation between the level of these nations' economic development and their turn to democratization. Rather, a wave of mass political protests inspired the collapse of authoritarian rule among diverse nations (Lee 2002, 823–25). This was particularly clear in the Philippines in 1986, where dictator Ferdinand Marcos's attempt to steal an election failed before the nonviolent, mass mobilization of the people (Eaton 2003, 470). While this kind of mobilization has not worked in every nation—reformers in China, for example, failed in Tiananmen Square in 1989—the Philippines provided a model for how nonviolent protest could overthrow authoritarian rule in Asia and beyond. Many of these new regimes are imperfect, but democratization remains a powerful trend in the region.

A similar trend took place in Europe and the former Soviet Union after the end of the Cold War. One East European country after another, from Poland to Bulgaria, emerged as a democracy. Russia itself turned to democracy, although it still has strong authoritarian tendencies. Some former states within the former Soviet Union did turn to authoritarian rule. But these states have proved to be vulnerable to democratic currents. In 2005–2006 the "Orange Revolution" brought President Viktor Yushchenko to power in Ukraine in the nation's first free and fair elections. The promise of this revolution, however, was undermined by oligarchical power and political corruption, as well as divisions between the pro-European West and the pro-Russian East. In Russia, the success of the Orange Revolution in Ukraine was denounced as being the result of a movement funded and inspired by the West (Herd 2005, 15). Russia has also sought to reclaim territory inhabited by ethnic Russians, such as by the seizure of the Crimea from the Ukraine in the spring of 2014. President Vladimir Putin's government is increasingly intolerant of artistic, political, and social dissent, and he has sought to bolster authoritarian leaders in its zones of influence. This combination of Russian influence and internal weaknesses has challenged some newly democratic states bordering Russia, from Ukraine to Georgia.

It is also important to distinguish between these democratic revolutions from below and the effort of outside powers to impose democracy on other nations by military means. There are examples where this has succeeded, as was the case with Germany and Japan after World War II. Overall, however, the United States has a lengthy historical record of using democracy as a justification for invasions and regime change. The record in the Caribbean and Latin America—Cuba, Haiti, and Nicaragua, among many others—has shown that these regimes lack legitimacy and seldom endure. Despite this fact, the United States has used "democracy" as a basis to legitimate its interventions in Afghanistan and Iraq. It is too soon to know the long-term effects of these invasions. But the general phenomenon of democratization is quite separate from the United States' military activities, particularly in the Middle East.

In late 2010, the Arab Spring began in Tunisia, where a young man set himself on fire to protest his perceived mistreatment by a government official. These actions set off a wave of protest throughout the region, where people resented authoritarian and corrupt governments, serious economic difficulties, and a lack of opportunity for youth. In Tunisia, the government fell with little violence. In Libya, it took a civil war to overthrow Qadaffi, while in Egypt, the military has twice overthrown the nation's leadership. In Yemen, street protests and urban warfare ultimately led to a transition in government, although there was only one candidate in the February 2012 election. In Syria, protests were met with violence, which quickly escalated into a brutal ongoing civil war, which has caused massive destruction, refugee flows, and more than 100,000 deaths. Throughout the region, it has proved easier to overthrow isolated leaders than to establish meaningful democratic societies. While it is very clear what people are protesting against, the victors have often disagreed over their political agenda and the extent to which it includes democratization. Still, the overall trend seems to be against the long-standing authoritarian regimes in the region.

It is not the case that democratic revolutions succeed everywhere. Some nations, such as Zimbabwe and North Korea, have been able to resist all pressures for change. But they have little international influence and will never serve as global models. The same cannot be said for China, in which a nondemocratic regime has been able to oversee stunning growth. China will likely become the world's most economically powerful nation in the next two decades. As such, it may influence how people in some developing countries think about possible paths for their nations. While China has obtained great diplomatic influence, however, few nations aspire to follow the Chinese political model. Globally, we see the decline of the authoritarian and patrimonial state. This trend may wash over many states, including China, Iran, the Central Asian nations, and Russia, which is a quasi democracy. Much as international law has grown in power, so has the power of human rights as an ideal; democratization is the world's dominant trend in political affairs. The point to remember is that democratization's success seems heavily dependent on the process through which it arrives in a nation—that is, whether it is internally developed or externally imposed.

Local-Global Alliances and Multinational Corporations

One clear trend is that local groups, such as environmental movements or democracy campaigners, may ally with international groups, such as Greenpeace or the Soros Foundation, to challenge economic and political forces. For example, during the Orange Revolution in Ukraine, the Russian government complained that the Soros Foundation was organizing and funding the opposition. In some cases, such allegations seem exaggerated to the point of being conspiracy theories, but they reflect a real anxiety that external forces—not always tied to a particular nation—can create powerful alliances with grassroots movements. This concern is held not only by undemocratic regimes but also by democracies and major global powers. The Canadian government worried in 2011 that outside money streaming in to local environmental groups might undermine its campaign to build the Northern Gateway pipeline to British Columbia. The emergence of powerful NGOs and international organizations has enabled local movements that would otherwise have been isolated or powerless to challenge the authority of governments, the World Bank, or multinational corporations. At the same time, their foreign allies have made them vulnerable to nationalist critiques.

This can especially be seen in regard to environmental issues. The World Bank has announced plans for major programs on multiple occasions, only to be forced to modify or withdraw them in the face of local opposition allied with an international actor, which is sometimes called a "transnational coalition." This can be extremely frustrating for national governments, such as that of Brazil, which perceives itself as making decisions about national development only to find its efforts frustrated by a local-global alliance. In the case of the World Bank, the organization has responded to these critiques to such an extent that some observers have argued that it has "co-opted" outside groups, although other scholars strongly contest this characterization (Brown and Fox 1999, 1–4).

Transnational coalitions face a number of inherent challenges. One of the problems is that typically the grassroots organization is located in a developing country, while most NGOs are hosted in major Western democracies. This means that there can be power imbalances between the two parties, which may have very different interests at stake. For indigenous groups, at issue may be their land, their lives, and their identity. An NGO, however, may be focused on funding, reputation, and mission. This raises issues of authenticity: to what extent do international groups actually speak for local interests? This is a point that critics in home governments invariably raise.

After an earthquake of 7.0 magnitude destroyed much of Haiti's capital on January 12, 2010, ten American missionaries were arrested for trying to take thirty-three Haitian children over the border to the Dominican Republic. The missionaries claimed that the children were orphans and that they were being taken to an orphanage in the Dominican Republic. Reporters, however, quickly tracked down the parents of some of the children, who claimed that they had given them up to go to a center to be cared for but had not necessarily consented to adoption. The missionaries argued that it was a misunderstanding exacerbated by the breakdown of the Haitian government. Eight of them were soon freed, while two remained to face further investigation. In this case, the missionaries may have acted out of a sincere desire to help the children. But how much control did the parents have when they gave up their children, and how did power imbalances shape their choices? What is the difference between human trafficking for indentured servitude and human trafficking for the good of children?

Although there are power differentials in relationships between NGOs based in the Global North and local groups, the NGOs may be the only means for local peoples to challenge decisions that affect their lives profoundly but over which they have had little input. This can make decisions complex when national governments or the World Bank/IMF seek to form alliances with or gain feedback from these transnational coalitions. Are these actually meaningful alliances, or are the NGOs being co-opted? While such questions are difficult to answer, there is no doubt about the power of such alliances, whether they involve Brazil's battle with the United States to produce generic drugs for AIDS or environmental issues.

It is also important to note that these transnational coalitions do not always represent alliances between the North and the South, or between local actors and international NGOs. One classic example of this would be groups of indigenous peoples that come together on their own in the belief that they can better advocate for themselves and their interests as a collective rather than individually. Even in these cases, however, questions of power and authenticity can be complex. For example, the Arctic Council is an organization made up of eight nations with Arctic territories, while six indigenous communities have the status of permanent participants on the council. Such governmental/indigenous alliances have the potential to accomplish tasks that neither group could achieve on its own.

Nation-states sometimes also face challenges to their authority from multinational corporations, some of which have total revenues greater than the gross domestic product of small states. In the current era, many companies are increasingly transnational and no longer have a tight bond to an individual nation. But even now, most countries have an historical or economic tie to a particular company, whether it is an auto giant or an oil company. The history of relationships between developing nations and multinational corporations is fraught with difficulty, as is demonstrated by the cases of the United Fruit Company in Guatemala in 1954 and the Anglo-Iranian Oil Company in Iran in 1953. In both instances, the United States and Britain, respectively, overthrew national governments partly to defend the economic interests of corporations based abroad. Of course, these are two extreme historical examples. But many national leaders believe that multinational corporations are able to influence international policy against their national interests through their alliances with the governments of wealthy states or by buying political leaders. In some cases this perception may be enough to affect behavior. One example of this is the role of multinational corporations in Nigeria, where some Nigerian critics view them (accurately or not) as encouraging political corruption and ethnic division, as well as creating almost a shadow government in oil-producing regions.

Multinational corporations may appear to be an illustration of purely economic globalization. But these corporations are also political actors that are constrained by the decisions of nation-states. For example, the decision of most developing nations to rely on their own national corporations to develop their petroleum resources has meant that the major oil companies—while still extremely wealthy—control a steadily decreasing amount of the world's oil reserves. For this reason, economic globalization both influences and is shaped by political globalization. And in both examples—transnational alliances and major corporations—there is still a great power imbalance between the North and the South, although this is changing with economic development, particularly in Latin America, the Middle East, and Asia.

Regional Organizations: From Europe to Latin America

If the above examples focus on external actors that impinge on the power of the nation-state, it is also true that nations sometimes voluntarily give up some aspects of their power, either to regional organizations or military alliances. Perhaps the most dramatic example of this trend has been the rise of the European Union. In the aftermath of World War II, many Europeans blamed unrestrained nationalism for the horrible conflict. In order to create new bonds across national lines and rebuild trade among shattered economies, six nations came together to form the European Coal and Steel Community. Since that time, a series of agreements (such as the Treaty of Rome and the Merger Treaty) have steadily deepened the significance of participating in this evolving body, while it has rapidly broadened to include new members. The Maastricht Treaty of 1993 formally established the European Union, while in 2004 ten new countries—most of them in Eastern Europe—joined this body. By this point, the EU had become the world's largest economy and a political force, despite its internal divisions and political disputes.

The EU now has twenty-eight members, of which eighteen have adopted a common currency called the euro. Such monetary union requires a nation to give up a considerable amount of authority. Until 2008, the EU appeared to be a dramatic success. It had helped to ensure income equality among its members through transfers to low-income countries, which enabled nations such as Ireland to make dramatic and rapid economic progress. With the Schengen Agreement, EU citizens can travel freely across national borders without passports. There was unprecedented European labor mobility. But its successes extended beyond economics and into politics. For example, the European Union also has judicial power and has overturned national legislation that it believed violated EU law. The European Parliament sometimes inflames nationalist sentiments with regulations and directives that speak to the most daily aspects of its citizens' lives, such as the food they eat. On a more important scale, nations such as Turkey that wish to join the EU must agree to the Copenhagen criteria, which have significantly changed some countries' behavior. Most observers would agree that this union has brought major benefits. Since the EU's founding, there has never been a war between two of its members. From this perspective, it has clearly achieved the goals for which it was founded.

At the same time, the perception of the EU has changed since the financial crisis of 2008. Youth unemployment rates in southern Europe are horrific. Greece has suffered an economic depression so severe that the government is kept from collapse only by infusions of cash from the EU, which has required the financial power of Germany to implement it. For many Greeks, however, the austerity programs enacted at the EU's insistence have failed to bring prosperity. While the Germans tire of supporting Greece, Greeks resent the extreme austerity that their nation has had to bear. Of all regional associations globally, the EU is the most economically and politically integrated—a remarkable achievement in the aftermath of World War II. The crisis since 2008, however, has caused economic difficulties so severe that they have undermined the attractiveness of this model.

Outside of Europe, some leaders are seeking to use regional associations for their own ends. In the Americas, there are currently three major projects at play. The North American Free Trade Association (NAFTA) has brought together the United States, Mexico, and Canada into a free-trade area—but without much likelihood of deeper economic integration beyond trade and no plans for political integration, which likely no leader among its three members would support. Elsewhere in Latin America, two associations are currently in competition under the aegis of two nations vying for regional leadership, which is defined here as the ability to act as a political voice for a larger block of nations. Brazil is emerging as a key southern power, and it is using the South American free-trade agreement Mercosur as a means to provide access to regional markets for its businesses. Brazil also is interested in using regional bodies that can expand its efforts to ensure the political integration of the region. Brazil's project has been challenged by Venezuela's proposal for an association called Alianza Bolivariana para los Pueblos de Nuestra América (ALBA), based on ideals of social justice that reject traditional ideas of free trade. ALBA's goals are much more ambitious than those of Mercosur and include a new common currency called the sucre. Still, apart from Venezuela, ALBA's membership is relatively poor; Bolivia, Cuba, Dominica, Ecuador, Honduras, and Nicaragua are all relatively small economies. Cynics might note that they may have joined as much for the promise of Venezuela's economic gifts—such as debt forgiveness and oil—as for a belief in ALBA's structure. Since the death of Venezuelan president Hugo Chavez in 2013, ALBA seems to have lost momentum, but it remains an alternative vision for how regional economic associations might be structured.

Antarctica and the Arctic

The potentials and pitfalls of globalization may be most clearly seen in the polar regions. In both the North and the South, political globalization has the potential to limit or avoid international conflict over resources. In the first half of the twentieth century, various nations made competing claims to territory in Antarctica. Indeed, such claims continue to be made. Britain, for example, renamed a region of Antarctica "Queen Elizabeth's Land" in December 2012 to honor the Queen's diamond jubilee. This step predictably outraged Argentina, which has conflicting claims to territory with Britain, not only in Antarctica but also in the Falkland Islands/Malvinas. But this was also a moot point. While Argentina, Australia, Chile, France, New Zealand, and the United Kingdom all have made claims to Antarctica (many of which overlap), the Antarctic Treaty of 1959 froze all of these claims (Myhre 1986, 7). The United States had played a leading role in the formation of this treaty, in part because it feared that these territorial disputes would tear apart the Western alliance against the Soviet Union (Myhre 1986, 2). The inhospitable environment of Antarctica made it easier to reach an understanding, because the territory is unsuitable for permanent habitation: "It is the coldest and highest continent with winter winds commonly exceeding 100 kilometers an hour. An ice-sheet averaging over a mile thick covers about 95 percent of Antarctica, and the ice extends into the adjacent sea" (Myhre 1986, 1). The oceans surrounding Antarctica also have the highest winds and largest waves on the planet and are famous among mariners as being the most dangerous waters on Earth. For all of these reasons, nations were able to collaborate to create the Antarctic Treaty System—a series of further diplomatic agreements following the original 1959 treaty—that has prevented waste dumping, resource extraction, and territorial disputes while fostering scientific research and environmental preservation (Gillian 2011). States still spend funds in Antarctic research for political motives, which perhaps explains why China has made significant investments in its Antarctic program (Brady 2010; see also Child 1988). The Antarctic Treaty System also has weaknesses, particularly in the area of fishing. Nonetheless, these treaties perhaps represent a model that can now be applied to the Arctic, where global warming and energy demands are creating an international rivalry.

Global warming is increasing tensions in the Arctic, where the polar cap may disappear during the summer by as early as 2020 (Borgerson 2013, 76). In a recent article in *Foreign Affairs*, Scott Borgerson argues that this change may be positive:

> No matter what one thinks should be done about global warming, the fact is, it's happening. And it's not all bad. In the Arctic, it is turning what has traditionally been an impassible body of water ringed by remote wilderness into something dramatically different: an emerging epicenter of industry and trade akin to the Mediterranean Sea. The region's melting ice and thawing frontier are yielding access to troves of natural resources, including nearly a quarter of the world's estimated undiscovered oil and gas and massive deposits of valuable minerals. Since summertime Arctic sea routes save thousands of miles between the Pacific Ocean and the Atlantic Ocean, the Arctic also stands to become a central passageway for global maritime transportation, just as it already is for aviation. (Borgerson 2013, 77)

Overall, the tone of Borgerson's article is that the losses from global warming will be more than outweighed by economic growth in the Arctic: "While equatorial microstates may soon disappear into the rising sea, Greenland might well become the first country born from climate change" (Borgerson 2013, 85). Borgerson's article also contained a map entitled "Economic Opportunity in the Arctic," which shows areas likely to have large supplies of oil.

One challenge created by the disappearing Arctic ice cap—besides the risks to sea life, indigenous peoples, and planetary climate—is that this situation also is increasing interstate disputes, sometimes between unexpected partners. Canada considers the waters through its Arctic archipelago to be within its national territory, while the United States holds them to be international waters. When supertankers of oil begin to thread through northern islands, this situation could lead to tension. If one of the supertankers ruptures, or if there is a release of oil comparable to the Deepwater Horizon spill by BP in the Gulf of Mexico in 2010, the countries impacted may not be those extracting the oil wealth. The peoples of the Arctic, who are already disproportionately impacted by climate change, would face the environmental costs without commensurate benefits. Lastly, despite some progress, national boundaries in the Arctic are not all defined, which has led to tension between even such unlikely opponents as Denmark and Canada, which have disputed the ownership of tiny Hans Island. This context of interstate border disputes and potential environmental damage seems not unlike the situation in the Antarctic in the 1950s. It may make sense to look to the Antarctic Treaty System as a model to be applied to the other polar region while there is still time. In this respect, political globalization may be a necessary means to mitigate the damage caused by global warming.

Conclusion

Although the nation-state remains the most powerful factor in global affairs, economic and political globalization are both restraining states' power to act in an autonomous fashion. In some cases, states willingly surrender some aspects of their power through membership in regional blocs like the European Union. In all such cases, states give up some of their political control—such as the decision to engage in military action, economic authority, or the right to a separate currency—as part of their participation in a political and economic body. In other cases, states are compelled to face challenges to their power from international actors, whether it is through international law, transnational alliances, or multinational corporations. While states can sometimes decide to fight such groups, they cannot choose to ignore them without paying a price. For this reason, globalization cannot be thought of as a purely economic phenomenon. Instead, economic, political, and cultural trends all form part of the common phenomenon called globalization. In the next chapter, we continue our exploration of transboundary flows, this time with a focus on cultural aspects of globalization.

➤ **VOCABULARY**

Great Powers
League of Nations
NATO
Mercosur
Security Council
General Assembly

Helsinki Accords
democratization
International Court of Justice
transnational coalitions
ALBA

➤ **DISCUSSION AND REFLECTION QUESTIONS**

1 *What three global events did the League of Nations fail to confront?*

2 *Identify a critical difference between the structure of the UN Security Council and the UN General Assembly.*

3 *What are some criticisms that have been leveled against the UN?*

4 *The International Court of Justice is part of the UN. What is its primary charge, and what are some weaknesses of the court vis-à-vis its authority and the authority of individual nation-states?*

5 *Although it is possible for nation-states to violate human rights, globalization has allowed checks on leaders' behavior as never before. What are some examples of these checks?*

6 *How does culture impact our understanding of human rights? Are certain human rights universal?*

7 *What twentieth-century phenomena have contributed to democratization processes around the globe? How does the general phenomenon of democratization differ from the U.S. approach to democratization?*

8 *Why is the dimension of authenticity important for transnational coalitions?*

9 *What are some examples of regional political organizations? What are some of their strengths and weaknesses?*

10 *What new roles are emerging in the polar regions as sites of globalization due to global warming?*

ACTIVITY 1 Go to the main UNICEF website (http://www.unicef.org/ crc/index_framework.html) and examine one of the following pdf documents listed there. Choose one dimension of the document and, in a one-page reflection, discuss how it is linked to a global issue that is important to you.

1   Universal Declaration of Human Rights

2   International Covenant on Civil and Political Rights

3   International Covenant on Economic, Social, and Cultural Rights

4   Convention on the Rights of the Child

5   Convention on the Elimination of All Forms of Discrimination against Women

6   Convention on the Elimination of All Forms of Racial Discrimination

7   Convention against Torture and Other Cruel, Inhuman, or Degrading Treatment or Punishment

ACTIVITY 2   In February 2010, the East African Community, a bloc composed of the nations of Uganda, Kenya, Tanzania, Rwanda, and Burundi, met to reinforce joint military commitments to each other and to explore food and other joint security issues. Go online to investigate the status of their work at this time. Identify two issues these countries may have in common in terms of security interests.

ACTIVITY 3   Mercosur is the Southern Common Market and the largest trading bloc in South America. Investigate which countries make up Mercosur's sovereign member states and identify their working languages and current leaders. What do you imagine three critical issues to be for this organization and its members?

References

Angie, A. 2002. Colonialism and the birth of international institutions: Sovereignty, economy, and the mandate system of the League of Nations. *International Law and Politics* 34:513–633.

Anonymous. 2001. NATO's purpose after the Cold War. Retrieved February 11, 2010, from www.brookings.edu/fp/projects/nato/reportch1.pdf.

Anonymous. 2005. Better than nothing: United Nations reform. *The Economist* 376 (September): 54.

Bauer, T. G. 2001. *Tourism in the Antarctic: Opportunities, constraints, and future prospects.* New York: Hospitality.

Brady, A. M. 2010. China's rise in Antarctica? *Asian Survey* 50 (4): 759–85.

Borgerson, S. 2013. The coming Arctic boom. *Foreign Affairs* 92 (July/August): 76–89.

Breuss, F. 2010. Globalization, EU enlargement, and income distribution. *International Journal of Public Policy* 6 (1): 16–34.

Brown, D., and J. Fox. 1999. Transnational civil society coalitions and the World Bank: Lessons from project and policy influence campaigns. Boston: The Hauser Center for Nonprofit Organizations and the Kennedy School of Government, Harvard University.

Carr, E. H. 2001; originally published, 1939. *The twenty years' crisis.* Introduction by Michael Carr. New York: Palgrave.

Child, J. 1988. *Antarctica and South American geopolitics: Frozen lebensraum.* Westport, Conn.: Praeger.

Dupuy, P. M. 1999. The danger of fragmentation or unification of the international legal system and the international court of justice. *International Law and Politics* 31:791–807.

Eaton, K. 2003. Restoration or transformation: "Trapos" versus NGOs in the democratization of the Philippines. *Journal of Asian Studies* 62 (2): 469–96.

Gaddis, J. L. 2005. *The Cold War: A new history.* New York: Penguin.

Gillian, T. 2011. Antarctica: A possible case of snow blindness. *New Zealand International Review* 32 (4): 39–49.

Glennon, M. J. 2003. Why the security council failed. *Foreign Affairs* 82 (3): 16–35.

Goldstone, J. 2010. The new population bomb: The four megatrends that will change our world. *Foreign Affairs* 89 (1): 31–43.

Goodritch, L. M. 1947. League of Nations to United Nations. *International Organization* 1 (1): 3–21.

Gowland Debbas, V. 1994. The relationship between the International Court of Justice and the Security Council in the light of the Lockerbie case. *American Journal of International Law* 88 (4): 843–67.

Herd, G. P. 2005. Russia and the Orange Revolution: Response, rhetoric, reality? *Quarterly Journal* (Summer): 15–28.

Hurd, I. 2007. *After anarchy: Legitimacy and power in the United Nations' Security Council.* Princeton, N.J.: Princeton University Press.

Jennings, R. 1995. The International Court of Justice after fifty years. *American Journal of International Law* 89 (3): 493–505.

Kennedy, P. 2006. *The parliament of man: The past, present, and future of the United Nations.* New York: Vintage.

Lauren, P. G. 1998. *The evolution of international human rights: Visions seen.* Philadelphia: University of Pennsylvania Press.

Lee, J. 2002. Primary causes of Asian democratization: Dispelling conventional myths. *Asian Survey* 42 (6): 821–37.

Luck, E. 2003. Reforming the United Nations: Lessons from a history in progress. Ed. J. Krasno. United Nations Occasional Papers.

Mayerfield, J. 2003. Who shall be judge? The United States, the International Criminal Court, and the global enforcement of human rights. *Human Rights Quarterly* 25:93–129.

Myhre, J. 1986. *The Antarctic treaty system: Politics, law and diplomacy.* Boulder, Colo.: Westview Press, Inc.

Orbie, J., and L. Tortell, eds. 2008. *The European Union and the social dimension of globalization: How the EU influences the world.* New York: Routledge.

Posner, E. 2004. The decline of the International Court of Justice. December. John M. Olin Economics and Working Paper Series.

Schlesinger, S. 1997. Can the United Nations reform? *World Policy Journal* 14 (3): 47–52.

Shawcross, W. 2000. *Deliver us from evil: Peacekeepers, warlords, and a world of endless conflict.* New York: Simon & Schuster.

Sobel, R. 1994. The League of Nations Covenant and the United Nations Charter. *Constitutional Political Economy* 5 (2): 173–92.

Tharoor, S. 1999. Are human rights universal? *World Policy Journal* 16 (4): 1–6. Retrieved January 25, 2010, from http://www.worldpolicy.org/journal/tharoor.html.

United Nations. 1948. Universal Declaration of Human Rights. Retrieved January 25, 2010, from http://www.un.org/en/documents/udhr/.

U.S. General Accounting Office. 2007. United Nations: Progress on management reform has varied. Report to the permanent subcommittee on investigations, committee on homeland security and government affairs, U.S. Senate.

Way, L. 2009. Debating the color revolutions: A reply to my critics. *Journal of Democracy* 20 (1): 90–97.

Weiss, T. G., D. Forsythe, R. Coate, and K. Pease. 2007. *The United Nations and changing world politics.* 5th ed. Boulder, Colo.: Westview Press.

Yesilada, B., and D. Wood. 2010. *The Emerging European Union.* 5th ed. New York: Longman.

FIVE Cultural Globalization

> **SYNOPSIS**

This chapter examines flows of people and information in the age of globalization. Voluntary and involuntary movements of individuals account for shifting demographics within countries; refugees and even international students dramatically shift economic and social bases of the new places they call home. Technology and media have created fusions of information and art that move far beyond the nation-state. Political activism on the part of citizens and scholars in particular nations is both aided and suppressed by emerging technologies.

> **SCAFFOLDING**

As you read through this chapter, think about how you would answer each of the questions below.

How old were you when you began using a computer? How much of your work was school supervised and how much was independent? What other technologies are critically important to you?

Can you compare what is important to you with what may be important to individuals living in another country—in particular, a university student, a government official, and a young child attending elementary school in a rural area?

What are the advantages and disadvantages of calculating the fiscal contributions that international students make to a state or province's economy?

Do you foresee changes in how nations regard the inflow of refugees, undocumented workers, and international students?

Why do you think the fine arts are sometimes forgotten in studies of globalization?

➤ **CORE CONCEPTS**

What is the relationship among technology, ideology, people, and finance in a globalizing world?

What flows of people may be important to track in the future?

How can access to the Internet, television, and radio broadcasts impact how people move forward in their lives?

In the previous chapters, we focused on the economics and politics of globalization. However, the patterns of change that have come with greater financial connectedness have also deeply affected societies and individuals throughout the world. Cultural globalization is just as critical a component of the globalization phenomenon as economic and political globalization. People have left their homelands voluntarily and involuntarily, for brief periods of time or forever. They have transformed the landscapes they have joined even as many of them have attempted to remain connected to their homelands via media, the Internet, and other electronic and social-networking technologies. In this chapter, we explore how shifts in demography have ultimately affected cultures and created wholly new social landscapes. Nation-states and individuals have been transformed by these changes.

We begin by focusing on the elements and processes that explain, provide gatekeeping for, and promote movement across national boundaries. These cultural flows involve "contacts between people and their cultures—their ideals, their values, their way of life—[all of which] have been growing and deepening in unprecedented ways" (*UN Human Development Report* 1999, 30). At the same time, we continue with the notion that the nation-state is no longer the sole base for relations. Instead, we return to the global-local continuum, described by MacGillivray (2006, 9) as "a tense dynamic between local identity and global ambition, whether in religion, art, film, music, or football." Attending to cultural globalization is central for Thomas Friedman. In his popular tome *The World Is Flat*, Friedman faults globalization chroniclers for their omission of culture: "One answer is culture. To reduce a country's economic performance to culture alone is ridiculous, but to analyze a country's economic performance without reference to culture is equally ridiculous, although that is what many economists and political scientists want to do. This subject is highly controversial and is viewed as politically incorrect to introduce. So it is often the elephant in the living room" (2007, 420). It is also central to our study here. In this chapter, we look at how individuals move within real spaces and virtual spaces, how their identities shift, and how the spaces they inhabit shift. We do so in order for you to recognize how these shifting communities and landscapes affect your own spaces—literal and virtual—by asking: what do global citizens need to know about transcultural flows? We will answer this by looking at "the ways in which cultural forms move, change, and are re-used to fashion new identities in diverse contexts" (Pennycook 2007, 6).

In this millennium, flows of people and information are changing the landscape of our world at a pace exponentially greater than that of past centuries. When confronting difference, it is important to identify these shifts as a means to avoid lapsing into a state of fear. As individual members of our communities, we cannot control the flow of people and information across nation-states. A far more productive response is to take full advantage of the richness of cross-cultural mobility by recognizing the natural forces that push people out of one country or region and into another. In looking at flows of people and information, one can get a more organic sense of how these flows work together by imagining a multidimensional figure with a number of facets. This knowledge, in turn, allows a deeper analysis and understanding of how globalization has remastered the earth's landscape. In a now-classic text on globalization titled *Modernity at Large: Cultural Dimensions of Globalization* (1996), anthropologist Arjun Appadurai offers a way to explore the transcultural flows that have contributed to the fragmentation of people and information by examining relationships among what he defines as ethnoscapes, mediascapes, technoscapes, financescapes, and ideoscapes. Imagine a kaleidoscope in which a slight turn of the lens changes the entire picture seen. As you will see from the descriptions that follow each of these "scapes," a number of forces are shaping how we engage with each other in ways that are more complicated than ever before.

Ethnoscapes identify "the landscape of persons" that represent flow and movement among various groups—refugees, tourists, and exiles—and the change that occurs in locations because of who is there and who isn't there (Appadurai 1996, 33). An example would be how international capital shifts in relation to production and technology needs. Tapias (2008) describes the complexities of immigration within the European Union. With Romania's entry into the EU, Romanian workers have been leaving Romania to work for higher pay in Spain, resulting in a worker shortage in

Romania that attracts new workers from China. In turn, China has drawn upon Africa to replenish its workforce.

Technoscapes are global flows determined by particular technology needs. Appadurai observes that the nation-state, fiscal flows, and "market rationality" no longer frame the shape of technoscapes. Instead, they are controlled by "increasingly complex relationships among money flows, political possibilities, and the availability of both un- and highly skilled labor" (1996, 34). Examples of technoscapes include outsourcing and the movement of companies from one country to a free-trade zone in another country.

Financescapes are the "very complex fiscal and investment flows that link [various] economies through a global grid of currency speculation and capital transfer" (Appadurai 1996, 34). An example is the current financial crisis in the United States, where there is speculation that the next wave of investments from other countries will not be in treasury bonds but rather in real estate (Gopal 2008). It is the complex and rapid flows of information, people, and money that shift in a manner that Tapias describes as a "global tsunami" (2008).

Mediascapes are "the distribution of the electronic capabilities to produce and disseminate information (newspapers, magazines, television stations, and film-production studios), which are now available to a growing number of private and public interests throughout the world, and to the images of the world created by these media" (Appadurai 1996, 35). Pepper (2008) paints a deeply contrasting picture in Myanmar (Burma) over a three-year period that attests to the instability and fluidity of mediascapes:

Two years ago—eleven months before the monk's rebellion [Saffron Rebellion]—I sat in one of the few cramped Internet cafes in Yangon, the former capital, and glanced at my neighbors' screens—all soft porn and foreign news Web sites. When I returned this summer, I found the cafes had become diverse and diffuse, packed with young people gabbing away on G-talk, checking out the social networking sites Orkut, hi5, and Friendster. Signs posted openly, even in small towns, explained how to circumvent government censors through proxy servers hosted at www.yoyahoo.com and www.bypassany.com. (2008, O-5)

This example demonstrates changes in access to information, changes in gatekeeping, and the creativity of a young generation of digital natives determined to use media in formats that are expanded in comparison to those of the past decade.

Ideoscapes are "concatenations of images . . . often directly political and frequently [having to do] with the ideologies of states and the counter-ideologies of movements explicitly oriented to capturing state power or a piece of it" (Appadurai 1996, 36). Ideoscapes are composed of elements of the Enlightenment worldview (discussed in chapter 2), which consists of "a chain of ideas, terms, and images, including freedom, religion, welfare, rights, sovereignty, representation, and the master term democracy" (Appadurai 1996, 36). Appadurai looks at how cultural context affects interpretations of particular terms and how these are incorporated into a nation-state's landscape. An example might be the phrase "loyal citizen." Its meaning would vary greatly from country to country, and behaviors seen as tolerable in one context might be seen as threatening government security in another.

Appadurai also suggests that there are "disjunctures" among the various scapes. In contrast to the smooth framing of contrasting flecks of color within one turn of the kaleidoscope lens, Appadurai acknowledges that when one scape comes in contact with another, it is not necessarily smooth. Tapias (2008) goes further, arguing that the "global demographic tsunami caused by tectonic shifts in labor" we experienced in the last century will reappear in new and unpredictable ways. Just as a prism or a kaleidoscope never shows the same picture twice, the elaborate interaction of flows of people and information that shape these scapes will create constantly shifting realities for all of us living in the twenty-first century. As members of the global community, we need to become familiar with who and what has accounted for this tsunami. The economic and political forces explored in the previous chapters have focused on empire, colonialism, and industrialization. Policies and procedures enacted at the international, regional, and local levels all cause movement.

Flows of People

The shifting demographics of the world's population occur both intentionally and unintentionally. Many individuals choose to move from one place to another, crossing borders intentionally. These individuals fall into two categories: immigrants and sojourners. Immigrants are individuals who have willingly and legally left their home countries to work and live in a new country, either for an extended period of time or permanently. Unlike

"Justice for Migrants" wall mural, Oaxaca, Mexico (Used with permission of the photographer, Margaret Everett)

refugees, who face a documented fear of persecution or even death if they remain in their home countries, immigrants most often move for economic or family-reunification purposes. They arrive in their new countries with travel documents that indicate they have come legally. In some cases, they must possess a certain amount of money or a certain skill set. This is often the case if the receiving country has granted them immigrant status in order to receive an infusion of monetary investment in the private financial infrastructure or to make up for a shortage of skilled workers, particularly skilled scientists or engineers.

Some international students remain in the country in which they have gone to school. Most, however, return to their home country, or perhaps settle in a third country. Students who temporarily live in a place to receive an education are part of a group of individuals known as sojourners. International students have been the subject of much study and speculation, but they form an almost invisible presence in the globalization kaleidoscope. They are in classes next to you, yet perhaps you have never thought of the role your fellow students are playing in Tapias's "global tsunami." Heynemann (2003) notes that in many countries, international-education flow can actually be tabulated like other commodities. This includes not only students going from one country to another but also students studying in a virtual environment, paying one country to take courses online while living in another country. In addition, the export of textbooks and materials, as well as tests such as the Test of English as a Foreign Language (TOEFL) or International English Language Testing System (IELTS), often involves the exchange of currency across borders.

During the 2011–12 school year, the countries that sent the most students to the United States were China, India, South Korea, Saudi Arabia, and Canada. In 2011, 764,495 students chose the United States as their academic study destination. In 2012 this number increased to 819,644 (Project Atlas 2013). The landscapes of the campuses that they came to have shifted substantially from past years. In some cases, more than 10 percent of the student body is composed of international students. Presence of international students, however, does not necessarily guarantee a globalized education experience for anyone. Milton Bennett (2002) argues that simply being in a new country or being in a contact zone with someone from another place is no guarantee of any substantial intercultural contact taking place. We also know, however, that without contact, there is no possibility for personal change. By extension, shifting the demographics of the people within your place of study increases the probability that your college experience will be different from that of your peers on campuses with fewer international students. Additionally, your international connections may extend into your life after graduation. For example, "the probability of an Indian student in the United States marrying a U.S. citizen is almost 200 times that of a resident of India" (Rosenzweig 2006, 78).

In his vision of European higher education, Figel (2008) suggests "it should be the norm—rather than the exception—for university students to undertake a period of study or a work placement in another country of the European Union." Academic institutions outside Europe, Figel hopes, would emulate European outcomes for their own educational planning: "There is a lot of interest from outside Europe for the European Qualifications Framework, which could inspire policy makers across the globe" (2008).

In Canada, international students play a key role in the national economy. Le-Ba (2007) cites trade statistics indicating "that international students contribute over C\$4 billion (US\$4.2 billion) annually to the Canadian economy." As in the United States, students who remain and become permanent residents are seen as individuals who can contribute quickly and efficiently to the growth of the economy. Sadly, not all international students who remain in the country where they were educated will find employment. Le-Ba (2007) suggests that there is often a mismatch between immigrant jobs and their skill set: "Foreign-educated immigrants earned C\$2.4 billion less annually than native-born Canadians with comparable skills, because they work in occupations below their skill levels [ultimately costing] the Canadian economy between C\$3.5 and C\$5 billion a year." Many Canadian immigrants lack Canadian work experience, and their credentials are often not recognized (Le-Ba 2007).

There is no question, though, that these immigrants are becoming in-

Recent terms used to describe circular migrants (those who come and go from one place to another and back) include "astronaut fathers" and "parachute children" (Yu 2009). Astronaut fathers work in a distant place but come to visit their family throughout the year. Parachute children are under the age of eighteen and live in their adopted countries without either one of their parents living permanently with them. Investigate these two terms with respect to either the United States or Canada. See if you can find a strong example of each term.

creasingly important to the international economy, to the extent that they are impacting the evolution of the English language globally. One example can be found with the approximately 10 percent of international students who become permanent residents and remain in the United States as immigrants after their studies (Rosenzweig 2006). Southeast Asian students graduating in fields such as engineering have suddenly found themselves listening to the English spoken by their Indian engineering colleagues in a U.S. setting. Korean, Chinese, or Japanese students often have little experience listening to Indian English accents, and, in like manner, they have little experience adjusting their accents to be more understandable to their Indian colleagues. Globally, interactions in English between individuals whose first language is not English will continue to become more prevalent than interactions between individuals whose first language is English (Hahn-Steichen 2008).

While the flows of international students are an important international force, they are also impacted by political and natural situations. For example, in the late 1970s, Iranian students were the largest international student population in U.S. universities. Soon after the Iranian Islamic Revolution in 1979, Nigerian students dominated the U.S. higher education population. At the present time, in both the United States and Canada, students from Asian and South Asian countries like China, Korea, Japan, Taiwan, Indonesia, and India dominate the landscape. However, a recent U.S. initiative has begun to bring Saudi and Libyan students into the United States at a rate not seen for over a decade. Typically, support from their home governments requires students to return home to serve their countries after completing their degrees. With the advent of the Islamic Revolution, many Iranian students were unable or did not choose to go home, and the anticipated return on the home country's investment did not occur. In the mid-1980s, the Malaysian government sent thousands of students to English-speaking nations as part of a human-development campaign, most of them going to the United States. If this initiative had taken place in 2010, many fewer Malaysians would have come to the United States because it would be much easier to get them into Great Britain and Australia than wade through Homeland Security paperwork, which has extended the time required to apply for a student visa by six months or more.

These pressures can create difficulties for universities that welcome large numbers of international students. When global-health scares occur, student flows change. With the advent of the SARS virus in 2002–2003, for example, three American universities—the University of California, Berkeley; the University of Minnesota; and Syracuse University—closed their campus-based, intensive English programs due to a lack of students—specifically, Chinese students, who had represented the bulk of those enrolling in these programs but were banned from entering the United States. Though not a light decision, programs that had been in existence for decades ceased. In the summer of 2009, numerous overseas programs prevented U.S. students from going to their expected destinations due to fears of the H1N1 (Swine Flu) virus. Those that did let students travel frequently found them quarantined in hotels in places like Korea and China instead of experiencing a season of tourist explorations.

Traditionally, study abroad is promoted as both a long- and short-term investment for the growth of students and the communities they interact with. When student flows change drastically in the short term, we need to expect long-term consequences. Certainly, no treaties are signed, but overseas study is often a first contact, and from such contacts, later contacts emerge. It is these later contacts that can permanently shift landscapes within and across borders. This is not to say that landscapes (and Appadurai's other scapes) are not changed by temporary flows, but permanent shifts occur more frequently with involuntary flows of people. We turn now to these involuntary flows, looking at the example of refugees and internally displaced peoples.

People who do not choose to move from one place to another, particularly from a homeland to a new space, include refugees and internally displaced persons. The United Nations High Commissioner for Refugees (UNHCR) crafted a convention in 1951 that is still in place. Article I defines a refugee as "a person who is outside his or her country of nationality or habitual residence who has a well-founded fear of persecution because of his or her race, religion, nationality, membership of a particular social group or political opinion; and is unable or unwilling to avail himself or herself of the protection of that country, or to return there, for fear of persecution" (UNHCR Self-Study Module 2 2005).

As of December 31, 2012, the UNHCR placed the total number of refugees worldwide at 10.5 million. The top receiving nations were the United States, Germany, France, Sweden, the United Kingdom, and Northern Ireland. Three nations—Syria, Pakistan, and the Republic of Macedonia—accounted for an increase of 22,600 claims for asylum in industrialized nations. In addition, while the UNHCR Convention does not cover internally displaced peoples, the organization estimated their number to be over 17.7 million in 2012. These individuals have been displaced most frequently by domestic and international wars, insurrections, and natural disasters. Internally displaced peoples have fewer resources to draw upon than those identified as refugees, in spite of danger and sordid conditions that occur in many of the refugee camps that are set up. Refugees are forced to create new lives and, to varying degrees, new identities. Because many of them remain for extended periods of time in refugee camps, they are literally caught in a kind of third space, neither here nor there. Turner (1967) refers to this state as one of liminality. A liminal person is usually in a less-than-defined space for a temporary period of time, frequently in a socially created transition, between the teens and adulthood in age, and between civilian status and full enlisted status in the military. Remaining in a liminal space for an extended length of time stresses the body, soul, and, ultimately, the social bonds that have created community. Refugees and immigrants do not expect to return; they are expected to shift their identities in some fashion to better accommodate a new culture for the long term and frequently must use the private sector as the space to maintain home language and home-culture attitudes, behaviors, and beliefs. In some cases, these individuals develop a strong, grounded, bicultural or multicultural identity. In other instances, they develop what Peter Adler (1998) terms a "multiphrenic" identity, shape-shifting in a manner that causes long-term stress and potential disability.

Another group of individuals, temporary asylumees, are those who intended to stay in a new place for a brief period of time due to something like a natural disaster but are subsequently unable to return home. This would include people displaced by hurricanes or tsunamis who expect to return home after a period of rebuilding, only to find that their homes have been completely destroyed. In some cases, they are assigned "temporary asylum status" or "temporary protected status" by the UN and allowed to settle for an indeterminate but not indefinite period of time in a country that agrees to temporarily accept them. In 2007, for example, Reuters reported that 962 out of 1,020 temporary asylum applications in Russia were from Afghanistan (UNHCR struggles to find solutions for Afghan asylum seekers in Russia, 2008).

These individuals do not possess equal status with members of the dominant culture that they come in contact with. When they move from their home space to another, they rarely exist in equal situations of power with the dominant culture. When wars, genocides, and incursions occur, people move from their homes (and often homelands) to other spaces, where they are typically treated differently from the general population. In

Climate refugees (ecological immigrants) are individuals who are forced to relocate because of climate-induced changes to their homelands. Their numbers are anticipated to double from 25 million (2010) to 50 million in less than five years. Investigate this phenomenon further. What Arctic and Pacific regions may be particularly affected?

some cases, the movements are temporary, isolating them not only from their countrymen but also from their new hosts. Many refugee camps are walled off or sealed by barbed wire to prevent culture contact between those in the camps and those outside the camps.

The UNHCR and a variety of global organizations track in detail the global situation of refugees and internally displaced persons. Videos are available on YouTube, officially posted by the UNHCR. Reuters has an Alert Net (www.alertnet.org) with working pages detailing country profiles, offering ways that individuals can help, and providing research tools for practitioners, much as the UNHCR site does. Because this is such a large and dramatic problem, it is difficult to summarize information on refugees into a concise form. What is central to our discussion at this point is the knowledge that the number of refugees and displaced peoples is not likely to decline in the near future. Wahlbeck (1998, 8) reminds us "undoubtedly, the process of globalization has a profound impact on the social relations of refugees and migrants in the contemporary world." The responsible resettlement of these individuals will continue to fall within the purview of international organizations, national governments, and private aid organizations.

Diasporas and culture mixing have profoundly shifted our landscapes, both real and imagined. Ten percent of the population growth in Europe is driven by migration (Tapias 2008). In 1950, 90 percent of the U.S. population was white, but by 2040, only 50 percent of the population will be. The United States is at the halfway point: 40 percent of U.S. citizens age ten years or younger are racial minorities. As various authors look at the power of migration to cause these shifts in peoplescapes, many focus on the stress that exists between former systems and patterns and newer systems and patterns. May (1999, 154) looks at what he terms "nomadic identities," suggesting that the "large-scale displacement of people from the rural to the urban or across nations has heightened the precariousness of arbitrary boundaries while fueling the contemporary identifications with ossified national identities."

In other words, the mixing of the various types of individuals described above into what were formerly not panethnic spaces is changing who interacts with whom and for what purposes. Appadurai's ethnoscapes are changing. Just as the kaleidoscope picture shifts with a twist of the wrist, linkages between people change. Many strive to recreate a narrowly defined ethnic community in the new locations that they have migrated to. Others use global flows of information, discussed below, to stay in touch with their former homelands. Still others use the intercultural contact to fuse new identities and new friendships and, ultimately, to establish more connections with more kinds of people in more places than ever before. In all cases, there is often stress in change—whether at the personal level or the societal level. Globalization, for all its positive aspects, takes a toll. In the next section of the chapter, we explore how various kinds of information assist individuals and societies in making connections—again, for better or for worse.

Flows of Information

At one point in time, only smoke, drums, and carrier pigeons could cross borders without control. Over time, radio and television waves were included. Now we have information flows via fiber-optic cables and wireless Internet. In the future, there will be forms of communication that we cannot now imagine. Appadurai's mediascapes will change just as ethnoscapes have changed. Pennycook (2007, 25) reminds us that all media serve as vehicles "enabling immense and complex flows of people, signs, sounds, images across multiple borders in multiple directions." Much of the information is regulated, but much is also pirated. Films cross borders without permission; pirated versions of DVDs are available at a fraction of the real non-pirated cost. Identities are brokered and maintained via these technological connections. In this section, we explore the forces responsible for these flows.

Music

Pennycook (2007) draws on work by Connell and Gibson (2003, 271), who suggest that "music nourishes imagined communities, traces links to distant and past places, and emphasizes that all human cultures have musical traditions, however differently these have been valued." Individuals who are no longer physically at home can recreate their sense of space through links to their traditional music via electronic sources or gatherings of individuals in new spaces. In addition, global connections have allowed people around the world easy access to the musical traditions of those in other areas. A brief review of just one music catalog by Putamayo reveals scores of albums showcasing music from around the world, as well as "third culture" or "fusion" music, made when musicians from different contexts come in contact with each other to create completely new forms. Afropop is an example of such a fusion form.

At the same time, local languages have been used to produce new types of music. One example is Sami rap. If you are a Sami in Lapland, the rap music you write in your own language and distribute over the Internet may be enjoyed by many music lovers, but within a short span of years, no one will be able to understand it because your language is dying out (Boevers 2006). By recording rap music on the Internet in Sami, it is possible to not only maintain a living record of the language but also creatively preserve Sami identity even as the language is dying.

This transcultural flow of information has accomplished three things: individuals in the diaspora have been able to remain connected to the music of their own culture; new music has been created as a function of contact; and local and sometimes dying languages have emerged in new music forms and are thus maintained. Connell and Gibson (2003, 270) reflect on the ability of music to play an active role in how people interpret the world around them, going so far as to suggest that music can even play a role in flattening diversity insofar as it becomes omnipresent.

In the U.S. presidential election of 2008, hip-hop music became a political tool for reaching out to young people and drawing them not only into national politics but also into an international political party. Rosa Clemente, vice presidential candidate for the Green Party, represented the hip-hop community, crafting a platform clearly linking music with political activism and, ultimately, national and international concerns. Clemente, a scholar-activist, explained in her acceptance speech: "Well, I am from the Hip-Hop generation, and we can remix anything. . . . We can lead the nation with a microphone. Hip-Hop has always been that mic, but now the green can be the power that turns up the volume of that microphone" (www.rosaclemente.com).

Pennycook (2007, 5) sees hip-hop as a way for the global to shape the local and vice versa. As he suggests, "If English can be used to express local cultural practices, can such practices include more recently localized forms such as hip-hop?" The transcultural flow of hip-hop allows it to move among and beyond nations. For example, hip-hop is very popular in Japan. Pennycook examines the Japanese site Nip Hop and its characterization of the hybridity that occurs when a language and hip-hop enter a singular contact zone: "Hip-hop is a culture without a nation. Hip-hop culture is international. Each country has its own spin on hip-hop. . . . Japanese Hip-Hop has its own culture but a culture that has many similar aspects of Hip-Hop around the world. These aspects include the DJ, MC, dancers, and urban artists (taggers, spray paint art)" (2007).

Dance, Theater, and Sports

As with music, other embodied art forms pull us into contact zones. Dance is perhaps the most embodied form of transcultural flows. McIntosh (2005, 24) characterizes the physical and behavioral in cross-cultural movement: "I further associate global citizenship with related capacities of the physical body. . . . The global citizen knows his or her body not as a tool for mastery or beauty, but as a body in the body of the world." One example of this is Pascual Alvarez's (2008) description of the visit of the Dutch hip-hop group Ish to the Children's Theatre Company in Minneapolis, Minnesota, in which he notes the paradoxical nature of a U.S. dance form being successfully appropriated by another international dance company.

Theater is a close second to dance in terms of embodied forms of transcultural flows. Pascual Alvarez, a young Columbian international student at a small, private, liberal arts college in the Midwest United States, explores how a novel written in West Africa roughly twenty years ago can make its way to a Minneapolis children's theater. Describing the staging of Amina Sow Fall's *The Beggar's Daughter*, Pascual Alvarez (2008) observes the nature of global flows that have brought the issues of begging, tourism, and religion to the United States, suggesting that there is something particularly powerful in theater's ability to move across nations and bring the world to a local audience. Pascual Alvarez (2008, 129) also cites Peter Brook's idea that the "complete human truth is global, and the theatre is the place in which the jigsaw can be pieced together." Clearly, there are many more examples that could be explored, but what has been demonstrated here is that theater plays a central role in creating hybridity, allowing local context to shape a universal theme. When young theater patrons are introduced to global themes and global pieces of writing, they "are given a window into world society and are empowered to enact change" (Pascual Alvarez 2008, 146).

Sports are not necessarily considered art forms. However, the transcultural flow of athletes accounts for average individuals becoming familiar with the rest of the world through their local sports. When European soccer superstar David Beckham moved to Los Angeles, ticket sales for the Los Angeles Galaxy games tripled. When the NBA All-Star basketball player Yao Ming lifted a young Chinese earthquake hero onto his shoulders at the 2008 Summer Olympics, spectators typically uninterested in global affairs thought not only about sports but about the devastating effects of an earthquake and the leadership demonstrated by individuals to ensure the safety of their fellow citizens. Sometimes, sports are used for international political purposes. If not a global citizen, Ming can at least be seen as a global icon. While apartheid was still in effect in South Africa, poet Dennis Brutus organized artists to use international sports schedules as a vehicle of protest, creating boycotts and actually interrupting the transglobal flows of athletes—disrupting everything from cricket schedules to the Olympic Games. As Appadurai (1996, 61) points out: "All lives have something in common with international athletic spectacle[s]." Moving from the three-dimensional planes of theater, dance, and sport, we now explore how information flows through fiber-optic cables and radio waves.

The Internet and Radio

Perhaps the two key changes in terms of mediascapes that have occurred in the past decade are the ways the Internet and radio have, first, created sociopolitical venues for information to leave countries cracking down on dissidents and attempting to severely restrict access to information and, second, established powerful virtual connections for diasporic communities. Lisa Taraki (2007, 529) cites what she terms "the excessive charms of the Internet." Taraki argues that, at least in the Middle East, "Internet-based resources vastly expand individuals' abilities to access greater social information, for example, the importance of blogs . . . from which we can presumably better understand the subjectivities of middle-class intellectuals and other cultural workers or identify the burning public issues as seen by citizens of the region. . . . The same applies to the veritable explosion of Internet sites featuring videos, fatwa forums, celebrity gossip, and myriad other issues of the day." Blogging has become an essential way for citizens in various countries to express themselves in forums safer than face-to-face speech; it serves a key role in freedom of expression and civil society. The degree of government control of electronic communication also affects language.

Iran currently has one of the highest numbers of bloggers in the world. Alavi (2005, 1) indicates "Farsi is the fourth most frequently used language for keeping on-line journals. There are more Iranian blogs than there are Spanish, German, Italian, Chinese, or Russian." Yet Iranian bloggers cannot count on being able to access their sites in a reliable manner. Many bloggers have had to leave the country due to persecution. Others have had their sites closed and have had to set them up over and over with new names and URLs. This has become such a problem that Western political pressure is being used to protect bloggers throughout the Middle East via a project known as the Voice Initiative (Ephron 2007). Ephron reports on the difficulties endured by Syrian blogger Ammar Abdulhamid. In spite of being the son of a famous musician, he cannot escape governmental scrutiny when he blogs about negative aspects of his homeland. Michael Totten and others decry the travails of an Egyptian blogger with the moniker "Sandmonkey" who was actually forced to close down his blog in a situation similar to that of the Iranians discussed by Alavi (Totten 2009). In addition to blogging, more recent social-networking sites such as Facebook and Twitter have played critically important roles in providing information to the world during events such as the protests preceding and following the elections in the Islamic Republic of Iran in the summer of 2009.

Taraki notes two other dimensions of the Internet that are related to knowledge exchange. One is that academic scholarship can go on in spite of problems such as mail strikes. The second is that the Internet permits a "vastly enhanced ability of . . . scholars to act as public intellectuals, that is to invoke their scholarly responsibility and/or authority to express themselves on issues of public concern" (Taraki 2007, 528). For many of us

Explore the coverage of a recent international event—for example, the Olympics, the World Cup, the Global Climate Forum, or G-20 summits. Referring back to Appadurai's notion of "mediascapes," identify the degree to which the event you have tracked demonstrates the true interdisciplinary nature of media.

who live in less censored or more stable societies, it is difficult to imagine what it is like to work as a scholar but not have the freedom to interact with colleagues around the world. For most scholars in the West, speaking out entails less risk than in many other places. In terms of leadership on these "issues of public concern," Kuttab (2007, 535) further comments on the role that Internet-streamed radio has played in allowing traditional radio to thrive while also subverting national restrictions on print media: "Perhaps the most important lesson on the AmmanNet experience is that the creation and success of an Internet radio station in a country [Jordan] of state-run monopolies offers a major forum for activists, liberal politicians, and government officials as they help their press reform and push to allow terrestrial radio to broadcast with freedom." This dimension links mediascapes with ideoscapes.

Returning again to the link between ethnoscapes and mediascapes, we see that Internet-streamed radio allows individuals around the world to access local programs in a variety of languages. As with satellite dishes, this ability to connect in a specific language with a particular radio station halfway around the world is often very empowering. Globalization in this case has pulled together the best of what is local and what is global. Non-Internet, community radio programming in various languages allows members of the diaspora to remain connected to their languages and culture. In the future, we can expect these various forms of social networking to continue to create and maintain transcultural flows and to provide voices for dissidence as well.

Film, Television, and Satellite Programming

Film, television, and satellite programming provide another means to cross borders virtually. As competing sites such as the famed Bollywood in India have given Hollywood a run for its money, we can see shifts in financescapes. Again, the kaleidoscope lens has shifted. Films have long been understood to be carriers of culture and to provide opportunities for outside individuals to come to know and understand more about the values, attitudes, and beliefs of the home culture of a particular film. In some cases, particularly those films exported by the United States and other English-speaking nations, there is some question as to how the power of the visual pulls viewers into either a love or hate relationship with what Braj Kachru (1988) terms "Inner Circle" English and culture and what is perceived as its hegemony. Inner Circle countries are those where English is spoken as a native language, including the United States, Canada, Great Britain, Australia, and New Zealand. Kachru argues in all of his work that English can belong to all who use it and that the distribution of English-language films moving throughout the world does not necessarily imply an overt or covert agenda of cultural imperialism (1988). Films invite viewers into an imagined contact zone. They provide one set of lenses from which to view the human condition. But it is context and the interaction of particular viewers with particular films that is the true determinant of cultural flows. Perhaps one of the most powerful aspects of general film distribution all over the world is the degree to which films can be viewed multilingually, particularly in DVD formats.

Television broadcasting reaches around the globe. In places like the United States, Great Britain, and Italy, viewers watch an average of 27–28 hours of television per week (NationMaster Media Statistics 2008). In many situations, individuals who are no longer living in their native countries access television in their home languages, either via local programming or satellite programming. For example, Panagakos (2003, 210) found that in the Greek immigrant population in Calgary, Canada, that she surveyed, "viewing Greek television from satellite dishes was strongly favored by the first generation. . . . [O]ver 54% of first-generation [Greek] immigrants were viewers." She goes on to characterize the power of the activity: "Watching satellite television is a prestige-generating activity and has the ability to intensify preexisting or generate new discourses on homeland activities."

Karim (1998, 8) looks at the economic power of broadcasting to and for ethnic communities: "The growing ethnic-based commercial broadcasting infrastructure is integral to the increasingly global ethnic economy." Numerous scholars routinely examine the effects of satellite programming in various languages around the world, noting how both diasporic populations and local populations are affected (see Panagakos 2003; Georgiou 2006; Jeffres 2000; and Karim 1998). Media studies throughout the world introduce students to the role of global television programming and the power of digital satellite broadcasting (DSB) systems. Panagakos (2003, 203) sees the power of both media and information technologies in the maintenance and negotiation of identity building on the part of immigrants. She states that mass "computer-mediated technologies can create new spaces for identity formation." She goes on to characterize these technologies as a "forum for expressing and cultivating [ethnicities in the

Satellite antennas in Morocco (Used with permission of the photographer, Aomar Boum)

diaspora]" (Panagakos 2003, 207). In like manner, indigenous groups have been able to use various media sources to maintain local language and identity (Couldry 2003).

The Written Word

Poetry and fiction provide yet another glimpse into transcultural flows of information. What does it mean to be comfortable writing in a language other than one's own? In most of the previous chapters, we have drawn primarily on various social science and environmental science disciplines to present information. Here, we see the power of literature to capture feelings of displacement in a manner accessible to those of us who have not been displaced. Olaoluwa (2007, 223) suggests that the theme of exile "occupies a conspicuous place in poetic exploration in particular and literary expression in general." Iranian American A. Naderpoor looks at longing and exile in his poem "Shards of Memories" (2010):

> Oh land of my birth
> Oh land whose shards hold memories for me
> I'm caught in thoughts of you
> absent and homesick
> A homesickness like a candle, burning from the inside.
> My homeland, I can't deny you
> for you are the truth and undeniable
> Tossed into the fire of my heavy heart.

Olaoluwa (2007) sees the poet as a medium, able to capture the experiences of those described in the section above on flows of people. The descriptions describe states of mind, behavior, and, most important, emotions, something less frequently captured in the other disciplines we have drawn from throughout this text. In like manner, poets who have not left their homelands can capture historical pain experienced by ancestors. Korean-American poet S. K. Kim, in her 2003 collection *Notes from a Divided Country*, includes a poem titled "Borderlands." In the poem, dedicated to her Korean grandmother who lived in Korea at the time of the Japanese occupation, Kim creates a painful landscape: "We tried to escape across the frozen Yalu, to Ch'ientao or Harbin / I saw the Japanese soldiers shoot" (Kim 2003). The poet goes on to create a question in her grandmother's mind as to why she survived.

Individuals who indicate they have multiethnic identities draw frequently on their own personal border crossings around the world (compare Japanese American poet David Mura and Chinese Singaporean Edwin Thumboo). The anguish of transferring from writing in one's mother tongue to writing in a second tongue also poignantly reflects the affective dimensions of border crossings (Li 2007; Jin 2008). In addition, comparative perspectives on universal processes such as attending school; interacting with members of new groups; discovering oneself; and even encountering war, racism, and prejudice provide us with ways of comparing border crossings (Adiele and Frosch, 2007).

The genre of fiction provides yet another dimension of border crossing. There is a plethora of writing from contact zones—immigrants as protagonists in numerous novels socialized into new lives, trying to retain shards of the old while exploring the new. One large volume of such fiction focuses on Pakistani, Sri Lankan, and Indian immigrants settling in the United States and Great Britain. Writers include individuals such as Jumpha Lahiri, B. Mukerjee, and Bharti Kirchner, among others. While some of these stories might question exactly how a homeland long abandoned or never seen must look, others see the power of multicultural individuals able to evoke imagined communities all over the globe.

How does this information connect to the other parts of the chapter that have been exploring flows of information in a less personal way? First, the field of international studies has room for scholars of the heart—those who explore affective dimensions of crossing borders. Second, work in identity theory, critical theory, and diaspora studies is often centered in scholarship in humanities—literature, film studies, and culture studies. Examinations of positive and negative dimensions of globalization as discussed in chapters 3 and 4 frequently find their way into literature. Authors such as Nigerians Ken Saro Wiwa and Chinua Achebe draw on globalization and colonialism themes. As you begin to work your way around the map of international studies, literature and culture studies may become part of your program choices.

Conclusion

In this chapter, we have examined flows of people and information in ways that transcend traditional border crossings. We have examined how changes in places cause deep identity shifts for individuals. At the same time, landscapes at the local and national levels have shifted, changing

the ways schools deliver education and community governments deal eq-
uitably (or not) with individuals who speak different languages and do
not resemble their neighbors physically. The lives of individuals who have
involuntarily left their homelands are infinitely more stressful than the
lives of those who have left voluntarily (Berry 2006). Like a kaleidoscope,
the frames painted by the intersections of these individuals with those
who have never left home or even encountered people different from
them are complicated. Cross-cultural communication scholars suggest
that intercultural competence is an integral component of successful interactions in contact zones. These zones will continue to increase—in real
time and space as well as virtually. In like manner, media and technology have framed new relations for students, scholars, and others seeking
connection.

Communities are formed by individuals. With increasing person-to-
person contact around the globe comes an increasing responsibility to
connect in an ethical manner. While what Hammer (2009) terms "mono-
cultural mindsets" are quite functional for individuals who will never
leave their home cultures, they are not functional for those who interact
face-to-face or virtually with individuals from other cultures. Some level
of intercultural competence is necessary for these individuals. Hammer
(2008) defines intercultural competence as "the capability to shift cultural
perspective and adapt behavior to cultural differences and commonality."
Unless we are able to walk in the shoes of people who are different from
those who live in our immediate neighborhood or our country of origin,
or who communicate with us from afar via technology, we will experience
fear, a lack of safety, and an unwillingness to engage in making connections. Without the warp and woof of these connections, our world as we
know it will unravel. As global citizens, we can keep this fabric from unraveling, serving as edge walkers, gatekeepers, and the thread that joins
various human and technological forces together. Your ability to perceive
differences in perspectives, to be curious about what accounts for successful movement in and out of particular cultures, and to tolerate the
ambiguity that arises when individuals with strong differences come in
contact with each other will allow you to play a facilitative role in how
people relate to one another. The following chapter on development will
revisit economic, political, and cultural dimensions of globalization as they
relate to particular nation-states and provide a more extended description
of one setting in India where shifts in culturescapes and financescapes
have caused more harm than good.

➤ **VOCABULARY**

sojourner	immigrant
liminal person	multiphrenic identity
nomadic identity	digital satellite broadcasting
diaspora	(DSB)
UNHCR	

➤ **DISCUSSION AND REFLECTION QUESTIONS**

1 *What do you understand about Appadurai's terms "ethnoscapes, media-scapes, technoscapes, financescapes, and ideoscapes"? How do these compare to the notion of "landscapes," and why might they be important to understanding transcultural flows?*

2 *What has your personal experience been with shifting demographic trends?*

3 *How could someone acquire a "nomadic identity," and how does this compare with a traditional identity?*

4 *What role can music genres such as hip-hop play when they are imported into local languages?*

5 *What do you think Connell and Gibson meant when they said "popular music has the ability to mediate social knowledge, reinforce (or challenge) ideological constructions of contemporary (or past) life, and be an agent of hegemony"?*

6 *Explain this statement by Peter Brook (1988) in your own words: "The complete human truth is global, and the theatre is the place in which the jigsaw can be pieced together."*

7 *How do new technologies change the ways people develop their notions of "homeland"?*

8 *How can new technologies create new spaces for identity formation?*

9 *How can literature help us to understand refugee and immigrant feelings of exile and displacement?*

10 *What is intercultural competence?*

ACTIVITY 1 Find a community radio station that is broadcasting in your city or town. Examine its program guide. Are there various programs broadcasting in different languages? If so, try listening briefly to one or two of them. Can you hear English mixed with the other language? In linguistics, this can be one of three processes: language borrowing, language (or code) mixing, or code switching. Language borrowing is a word or short phrase from English entering into the other language; language mixing is the introduction of longer, complete phrases from English into the other language; and finally, code switching involves including whole clauses or sentences from English into the other languages. In all of these cases, we see evidence of contact. As we have seen over and over in this chapter, new kinds of scapes, both imagined and real, are being created with the assistance of various media. At the same time, these media allow for maintenance of the local landscape as well.

ACTIVITY 2 Identify one of the larger immigrant populations in your community and investigate one of the neighborhoods in your city with a high immigrant population. Document the linguistic landscape with a camera or smartphone. Choose one or two retail streets in the community and take pictures of a bilingual sign. Identify whether both languages are presented equally on the sign or whether English or the other language appears dominant.

References

Adiele, F., and M. Frosch. 2007. *Coming of age around the world: A multicultural anthology.* New York: The New Press.

Adler, P. 1998. Beyond cultural identity: Reflections on multiculturalism. In *Basic concepts of intercultural communication*, ed. M. Bennett, 225–46. Yarmouth, Maine: Intercultural Press.

Alavi, N. 2005. *We are Iran.* London: Portobello Books.

Appadurai, A. 1996. *Modernity at large: Cultural dimensions of globalization.* Minneapolis: University of Minnesota Press.

Benhabib, S. 2004. *The rights of others: Aliens, residents, and citizens.* Cambridge, UK: Cambridge University Press.

Bennett, M. 2002. Personal communication.

Berry, J. K. 2006. Acculturative stress. In *Handbook of multicultural perspectives on stress and coping*, ed. P. Wong and L. Wong, 287–98. New York: Springer.

Boevers, P. 2006. The Sami languages: Surviving the odds. Unpublished manuscript submitted in fulfillment of course requirement, International Studies Senior Seminar, Portland State University.

Brook, P. 1988. *The shifting point: Forty years of theatrical exploration, 1946–87.* London: Methuen.

Castells, M. 2000. The rise of the network society. Vol. 1 of *The information age: Economy, society, and culture.* 2nd ed. Oxford, UK: Blackwell.

Connell, J., and C. Gibson. 2003. *SoundTracks: Popular music, identity, and place.* London: Routledge.

Couldry, N. 2003. *Media rituals: A critical approach.* London: Routledge.

Ephron, D. 2007. Arab bloggers face unwanted attention: Government clampdown. *Newsweek*, 33. June 11.

Figel, J. 2008. Promoting understanding and dialogue. NAFSA Conference session: International student and scholar mobility: Programs, trends, challenges and impact. Washington, D.C. May 27. Retrieved October 18, 2008, from www.eurunion.org/en/index2.php?option=com_content and task.

Fall, A. 1981. *The beggar's strike.* Trans. Dorothy S. Blair. Essex, England: Longman.

Friedman, T. 2007. *The world is flat: A brief history of the 21st century.* New York: Picador/Farrar, Straus and Giroux.

Georgiou, M. 2006. Diasporic communities on-line: A bottom-up experience of transnationalism. *Hommes et Migrations* 1240 (November).

Giddens, A. 1999. *Runaway world: How globalisation is reshaping our lives.* London: Profile Books.

Gopal, P. 2008. Foreign investors love U.S. real estate. Retrieved July 5, 2010, from http://www.businessweek.com/the_thread/hotproperty/archives/2008/ol/foreign_investors_love_us_real_estate.html.

Hahn-Steichen, H. 2008. Speaking and listening exercises for high-tech work environments. Unpublished master's project, Portland State University.

Hammer, M. 2008. IDI guided development: Building intercultural competence. Conference Plenary: First Annual IDI Conference. October 3. Minneapolis, Minn.

———. 2009. Personal communication. October 10.

Heynemann, S. 2000. Educational qualifications: The economic and trade issues. *Assessment in Education* 7 (3): 417–38.

———. 2003. International education: A retrospective. *Peabody Journal of Education* 78 (1): 33–53. Retrieved November 2, 2008.

Hoopes, D. 1979. Intercultural communication concepts and the psychology of intercultural experience. In *Multicultural education: A cross-cultural training approach*, ed. M. D. Pusch, 10–38. Yarmouth, Maine: Intercultural Press.

Hutnyk, I. 2000. *Critique of exotica: Music, politics, and the culture industry.* London: Pluto Press.

Jeffres, L. 2000. Ethnicity and ethnic media use. *Communication Research* 27 (9): 496–535.

Jin, H. 2008. *The writer as migrant.* Chicago: University of Chicago Press.

Kachru, B. 1988. Teaching world Englishes. *ERIC/CLL News Bulletin* 12 (1): 1–8.

Karim, K. 1998. From ethnic media to global media: Transnational communication networks among diasporic communities. Paper Presented to the International Comparative Research Group: Strategic Research and Analysis/ Canadian Heritage. June. Retrieved as a pdf file on December 20, 2008.

Kim, S. K. Borderlands: For my grandmother. Retrieved July 17, 2010, from http://www.griffinpoetryprize.com/see_hear_poetry.php?t=26.

————. 2003. *Notes from the divided country: Poems*. Baton Rouge, La.: LSU Press.

Kuttab, D. 2007. Pensée 3: New media in the Arab world. *International Journal of Middle East Studies* 39 (4): 534–35.

Le-Ba, S. 2007. Profiling international students in Canada within the global context. Retrieved from *World Education News and Reviews* October 18, 2008, from www.wes.org/ewent/PF/07oct/pfpractical.htm.

Li, J. G. 2007. Subterranean geography: A learner's experience of searching for identity and voice through poetic language. Unpublished M.A. thesis, Portland State University.

MacGillivray, A. 2006. *A brief history of globalization*. London: Robinson.

Massachusetts Institute of Technology. The human cost of the war in Iraq. Retrieved December 20, 2008, from mit.edu/humancostiraq/.

May, J. 1999. *Nomadic identities: The performance of citizenship*. Minneapolis: University of Minnesota Press.

McIntosh, P. 2005. Gender perspectives on educating for global citizenship. In *Educating citizens for global awareness*, ed. N. Noddings, 22–39. New York: Teachers College Press.

Michelfelder, D. 2008. Global citizenship and responsibility. In *Meditations on global citizenship*, ed. A. Samatar. *Macalester Civic Forum* 1 (Spring): 19–26.

Naderpoor, A. 2010. Shards of memories. Trans. K. Brown. Unpublished poem. Reprinted with permission of the author.

NationMaster Media Statistics. Retrieved December 21, 2008, from www .nationmaster.com/graph/med_tel_vie-media-television-viewing.

Nip Hop. 2004. Retrieved November 10, 2008, from http://www.gijigaijin .dreamstation.com/Introduction.html.

Olaoluwa, S. 2007. From the local to the global: A critical survey of exile experience in recent African poetry. *Nebula* 4 (2): 223–50.

Panagakos, A. 2003. Downloading new identities: Ethnicity, technology, and media in the global Greek village. *Identities* 10 (2): 201–19.

Pascual Alvarez, H. 2008. World society onstage: The globalization of theatre for young audiences in the United States and the Netherlands. *Macalester/ Maastricht Essays. Macalester International* 20 (Winter): 129–50.

Pennycook, A. 2007. *Global Englishes and transcultural flows*. London: Routledge.

Pepper, D. 2008. Aftermath of a revolt: Myanmar's lost year. *New York Times*, O-5. October 5.

Pratt, M. 1992. *Imperial eyes: Travel writing and transculturation*. London: Routledge.

Project Atlas [Institute for International Education]. Retrieved November 27, 2013, from http://www.iie.org/Research-and-Publications/Project-Atlas.

Rosenzweig, M. 2006. Global wage differences and international student flows. Retrieved October 18, 2008, from http://muse.jhu.edu/journals/brookings_ trade_forum/v2006/2006.1r.

Samatar, A., ed. 2008a. Meditations on global citizenship. *Macalester Civic Forum* 1 (Spring).

————, ed. 2008b. The musical imagination in the epoch of globalization. *Macalester International* 21 (Summer).

Savicki, V., ed. 2008. *Developing intercultural competence and transformation.* Sterling, Va.: Stylus.

Tapias, A. 2008. Global diversity and intercultural competence development. Conference Plenary: First Annual IDI Conference. October 3. Minneapolis, Minn.

Taraki, L. 2007. The excessive charms of the Internet. *International Journal of Middle East Studies* 39:528–30.

Textor, R. 2003. Honoring excellence in anticipatory anthropology. *Futures* 35 (5): 521–27.

Totten, M. 2009. Sandmonkey shut down. Retrieved January 26, 2009, from www.michaeltotten.com/archives/001420.html.

Turner, V. 1967. Betwixt and between: The liminal period in rites de passage. In *The forest of symbols: Aspects of Ndembau ritual,* 93–111. Ithaca, N.Y.: Cornell University Press.

UNHCR. 2012. Displacement: The new 21st century challenge. UNHCR Global Trends 2012. Retrieved November 30, 2013, from http://www.unhcr.org/cgi-bin/texis/vtx/home/opendocPDFViewer.html?docid=51bacbof9&query=2012%20number%20of%20refugees%20worldwide.

UNHCR Self-Study Module 2. 2005. Refugee status determination: Identifying who is a refugee. Legal Publications. September 1. Retrieved September 6, 2009, from http://www.unhcr.org/cgi-bin/texis/vtx/search?page=search&docid=4314.

UNHCR struggles to find solutions for Afghan asylum seekers in Russia. Retrieved December 21, 2008, from http://www.alertnet.org/thenews/newsdesk/UNHCR/3f794231487ec6d67485b8bf144f455e.htm.

UN Human Development Report. 1999. New York: Oxford University Press.

VandeBerg, M., R. M. Paige, and J. Connor-Linton. 2009. The Georgetown Consortium Project: Interventions for student learning abroad. *Frontiers: The Interdisciplinary Journal of Study Abroad* 18 (Fall): 18–75.

Wahlbeck, O. 1998. Transnationalism and diasporas: The Kurdish example. Paper presented at the International Sociological Association XIV World Congress of Sociology, July 26–August 1, Montreal, Canada (Research Committee 31, Sociology of Migration).

Yu, H. 2009. Global migrants and the new Pacific Canada. *International Journal* 64 (4): 1011–28.

Zuberi, N. 2001. *Sounds English: Transnational popular music.* Urbana: University of Illinois Press.

SIX **Development**

➤ **SYNOPSIS**

This chapter explores the historical origins of development strategies, as well as the ideological underpinnings of competing frameworks. The UN Millennium Development Goals are presented in tandem with sample development projects from a nongovernmental agency. Global debt and Jubilee 2000, a debt-reduction program, are examined, as are microfinance strategies first introduced in Bangladesh by Nobel Prize winner Muhammad Yunus. A case study from Ladakh, a key province in India that borders China, is presented to illustrate the costs and benefits of moving from a self-sustaining model to a more globalized model that impacts traditional patterns of family and community.

➤ **SCAFFOLDING**

As you read through this chapter, think about how you would answer each of the questions below.

What terms have you typically used to distinguish the countries of the Global North from those of the Global South?

Can you think of advantages or disadvantages to using particular terms?

How might the past three chapters on globalization relate to the concept of development?

What academic or intellectual barriers may prevent you as a reader from accessing information about both development theories and practices around the world?

➤ **CORE CONCEPTS**

How do the concepts of modernity and industrialization represent targets of development?

How do either dependency theory or world-systems theory compare and contrast with modernization theory?

How can local context promote the creation of development theories that represent powerful alternatives to theories brought in from the outside?

The focus of this chapter is development, which can be thought of as a partner of, or bookend to, globalization. Just as positive and negative aspects of globalization underlie much current work in international studies, the relationship between "those who have" and "those who have significantly less" has captured the attention of social scientists since the late 1940s, particularly in the fields of economics, political science, sociology, geography, and anthropology. Now, however, researchers argue that this arbitrary split does not adequately account for context and local situations. In the twentieth and twenty-first centuries, disciplines such as ecology, environmental studies, and education have joined the debates. In this chapter, we examine various definitions of development and look historically at how the interactions of individual nation-states in relation to development have become intertwined with those of nongovernmental organizations (NGOs) and multinational organizations.

What Is Development?

Black (2002) suggests that U.S. president Harry Truman first introduced the present-day vision of development in his 1949 inaugural address. Within Truman's concept of the "Fair Deal" was an obligation to share new industrial and scientific achievements with less-privileged regions. At its earliest, then, the term "development" incorporated a kind of dichotomizing, a dimension of "othering" that created poles or ideological camps: "developed" was contrasted with "underdeveloped," or sometimes "undeveloped." Later on, the labeling branched into "developed" versus "less developed." In each of these cases, the positive anchor "developed" was the starting point for defining its opposite; in other words, the notions

Boy at irrigation line in Morocco (Used with permission of the photographer, Aomar Boum)

of undeveloped, underdeveloped, and less developed could only exist in relationship to developed. Later on, the dichotomies became less transparent, such as in the terms "First World" and "Third World." The invisibility of countries behind the Iron Curtain, the so-called Second World countries, was a product of the West's relationship to these countries following World War II. Eventually, weaknesses in the bipolar framework caused us to create a Fourth World category. In the early 1970s, West German chancellor Willy Brandt proposed the terms "Global North" and "Global South." In a type of magic that still puzzles the best cartographers, the Global North includes Australia and New Zealand. In fact, we have yet to find expressive yet neutral terms to describe "those who have" and "those who have less." In the same way, we have been unable to find ways to characterize certain areas that do not force a comparison with other areas. In his much-cited TED talk (2009), Hans Rosling explores the importance of using actual data to move beyond dichotomies, stating: "We cannot look upon the world as divided." As he examines convergences among nations due to improvements in social services, he affirms the importance of not overgeneralizing. In breaking out data sets by year and country, he establishes parallels between nations once classified on other sides of the "developed"/"developing" divide: the United States, China, and Mexico. He also cautions against generalizing: with respect to AIDS and the continent of Africa, he states: "[D]on't make it Africa. Don't make it a race issue. Make it a local issue. And do prevention at each place."

For more than half a century, various scholars have searched for necessary and sufficient measures of development to create a type of index, while others have criticized the inflexibility of such an approach in accommodating particular contexts. The initial measures chosen were tied to economic indicators: national gross domestic product (GDP) and per capita income. Later measures have included literacy rates, maternal and infant death rates, life expectancy, and now even HIV-infection rates. As we will see later in the chapter, certain scholars have pushed practitioners hard to establish measures that are more holistic and include the actual quality of life. Subsequent development projects throughout the world have been tied to these indices. Table 3 shows eighteen categories of active development projects undertaken by Mercy Corps, an international NGO. As you read through the list, identify what you believe to be the five most important development issues.

Having seen how one NGO characterizes their development efforts,

Table 3 Mercy Corps Development Priorities 2008

Agriculture	Emergencies	Civil society	Climate/ Environment	Women	Education
Health	Children	Sports	Peaceful change	Hunger/ Nutrition	Social entre-preneurship
Micro-finance	Tsunamis	Silent disasters	HIV/AIDS	Economic development	Water

we now examine the UN Millennium Development Goals. In a resolution adopted by the UN General Assembly on September 8, 2000, eight broad-based development goals were proposed:

1 Eradicate extreme poverty and hunger.

2 Achieve universal primary education.

3 Promote gender equality and empower women.

4 Reduce child mortality.

5 Improve maternal health.

6 Combat HIV/AIDS, malaria, and other diseases.

7 Ensure environmental sustainability.

8 Develop a global partnership for development.

Since 2000, *Millennium Development Reports* documenting the progress made in achieving these eight goals have been issued annually by the UN. Evident in these goals, the original resolution, and the subsequent annual reports is a broad-based and contextualized focus on holistic dimensions of development. Attention to indexes of development is clearly evident. Look at the Mercy Corps chart once again and find the overlap between their projects and the UN goals. These descriptors are what might be termed a "view from the ground"—that is, real measures and real projects tied to someone's view of what is necessary to help less-developed nations reach the UN goals. We also need a "view from the air"—broader philosophical and ideological considerations about development. What follows is a historical examination of development theories.

Economic and Political Theories of Development from a Historical Perspective

World War II and the rapid industrialization that followed it shaped how early economists framed the development dilemma. The issues that scholars and policy makers saw as important ranged from identifying deep-seated roots of economic and political development to linking these roots to social change, self-governance, and the degree to which governments need to craft individual development opportunities for all their citizens. These areas of focus drew on the nation-state as the unit of analysis. However, it was both bilateral assistance programs like the Marshall Plan and multilateral and multiorganizational assistance plans that were being developed (Bryant and White 1982, 3). Western economists and economic planners conceived these recovery plans; the ideologies they drew from came out of their own cultural frameworks and the intellectual ideas that were dominant from the 1930s into the 1950s. One powerful theory that emerged during this time and fully evolved between 1950 and 1970 was modernization theory.

Modernization Theory

Modernization theory—also known as modernity theory—traces its roots back to the economic perspective of Walter Rostow (1916–2003). Rostow proposed a now-classic model of economic growth in which a society moves through five distinct stages: (1) traditional society; (2) preconditions for takeoff; (3) takeoff; (4) drive to maturity; and (5) age of high mass consumption. His description of how a nation-state becomes modern was first anchored in economics. However, Western political scientists, sociologists, and even education policy planners educated in the era when this theory was most prevalent adapted it to their own fields. Modernization theory is a neoevolutionary theory in that it supposes that all nation-states will follow through from one stage to the next in a linear fashion. It is a somewhat inflexible model that cannot be adjusted for particular contexts. If we were to look within the United States into disadvantaged areas of our urban cores, for example, we would find situations not unlike those in a variety of Third World countries in terms of death rates, literacy rates, and economic status. Yet the United States is centered only in Rostow's fifth stage—that of high mass consumption.

Rostow's five-stage theory was clearly tied to an assumption that "West was best," and his ideas had a deep impact on development scholars in the 1960s and 1970s. One of the early architects was sociologist Alex Inkeles, who, with coauthor David Horton Smith, wrote *Becoming Modern: Individual Change in Six Developing Countries* (1974), an exploration of the economic, political, and social dimensions of modernity. In the book, Inkeles and Smith offer a profile of a modern society as one that assumes a level of social organization above that of tribes and is inhabited by individuals who "can keep to fixed schedules, observe abstract rules, [and] make judgments on the basis of objective evidence" (Inkeles and Smith 1974, 4). Inkeles and Smith's language defines modern society as the industrialized society of the West. The indices of modern economic development are posited as factors indicating the status of societal development. Actual quality of life and dimensions of equality among citizens are not discussed. In addition to measures outlined above, these indices include productivity per person, level of literacy, level of nutrition, and breadth of infrastructure (Rogers 1976).

Inkeles looked both at modern society and the modern person, suggesting that modernity may take on somewhat different forms because of "local conditions, the history of a given culture, and the period when it was introduced" (Inkeles and Smith 1974, 16). This focus on individual aspects of development singles out the work of Inkeles from that of his contemporaries, among them Samuel Huntington. Although the next chapter will focus on Huntington's broader conceptualizations of security challenges, his earliest work and that which first brought him prominence was in the field of development.

As economists were making their mark in planning for modern societies, the discipline of political economics began to emerge. Political economists urged the inclusion of "the context of political reality" (Bryant and White 1982, 10) and recommended that growth be separated from development. The subfield of development economics also emerged. Central to development economics is the notion that "distributional issues and the necessity for structural change in society" are paramount to any attempt to redistribute wealth (Bryant and White 1982, 11).

The modernization model is sometimes called the developmental model or the "benign" model. It posits that education makes a direct contribution to both economic output and social stability. Critics of the model, such as Martin Carnoy (1974), suggest that this same education is also used as a means to institutionalize control, maintain income structure, and socialize the dependence of one class on another. An outgrowth of this work is the acculturation view, in which societies that adopt the markers of development begin to more closely resemble model industrialized nations (Frank 1970; Frank 2002). Frequently, an investment in human capital characterizes the impetus for these changes. Harbison and Myers (1964; 1965) suggest that human-resource development is the first step in raising the GDP of a country and that an investment in education for all will shift the speed and efficacy of development.

In the 1980s, examples of the acculturation view, or human-capital approach, could be seen throughout the world. The Malaysian government began a massive higher education investment that sent hundreds of students out of the country to the United States, the United Kingdom, and Australia for undergraduate and graduate education. Students received full scholarships but were obliged to repay them with a minimum of ten years of government service or through a repayment of the monetary investment. Majors were determined before students left Malaysia. Malaysian students of Indian or Chinese origin were not offered these scholarships, which were reserved for the bumiputra, or "children of the soil" (native Malays), and other indigenous groups.

Following the work of these early modernity theorists, scholars began writing about the human costs of development as defined by the West. Bryant and White (1982) call this focus on human and ethical dimensions "Humanist Views." These views move between dependency theory and, ultimately, world-systems theory. A chief architect in this arena is philosopher Denis Goulet, who argues that all development policy "contains an implicit ethical strategy" (1971, 118). He goes on to identify three core values: "life sustenance for all, optimum esteem, and freedom" (Goulet 1971, 118). Policy recommendations made by scholars and practitioners with a humanist perspective frequently looked at broad-based human rights alongside traditional markers of development.

Modern-day development theorists and activists remain committed to an awareness of these ethical dimensions. Helena Norberg-Hodge is one of these activists. Her work in Ladakh, India, is profiled in a case study at the end of this chapter. As she reviews the changes that took place in Ladakh after 1974, the year that the region was opened to tourism, Norberg-Hodge argues that "the shift from lama to engineer represents a shift from ethical values that encourage an empathetic and compassionate relationship with all that lives toward a value-free 'objectivity' that has no ethical foundation" (1991, 109).

In the late 1980s, many scholars of development moved into systems theory. While it is beyond the scope of this chapter to expand on the notions of this theory in detail, what you need to remember is that systems theorists identify lists of dimensions, principles, and other elements; model how one element is connected to another; and provide elaborate discussions of how elements function together within a system.

Systems theory continues to be important for certain scholars, including Maturana and Varela, whose *Tree of Knowledge: The Biological Roots of Human Understanding* (1987) has profoundly influenced the work of numerous social scientists, who draw from their creation of constructivist epistemology. What is remarkable about Maturana and Varela's work is that both scholars trained initially in biology and medicine and then moved to philosophy. Their exploration of human development at the social level is grounded in a scientific exploration of neurology and biology. Like modernization theory, systems theory was refined by Western scholars in developed nations who explored applications to less-developed nations. The grounding principles provided by modernization theory are still evident in systems theory. They include the following:

1 Modernization is possible; there is optimism that change can come about.

2 A particular region could change rapidly with the right incentives and inputs.

3 Some level of abandoning traditional social and political institutions is necessary.

4 Structures successful in modern nations should be adopted by modernizing nations.

5 Foreign expertise will be required to help implement change.

6 Foreign investment is uniformly positive and should be accepted without restriction.

The last three principles imply a uniform recipe for development no matter what the context. They suggest that a developing nation will be unsuccessful if it does not adapt Western recommendations based on ideologies developed at Bretton Woods. Outside assistance is deemed paramount. These three principles, in particular, greatly disturbed anthropologists and other social scientists working in Latin America. Dependency theory was developed as a direct rejoinder to modernization theory.

Dependency Theory

Even as American and European social scientists attached themselves to indices of development, a group of anthropologists in Latin America were refining quite another set of theories they had been working on for decades. However, it was not until the early 1980s that their works on dependency theory were translated into English. Raul Prebisch, Andre Gunter Frank, and Fernando Cardoso, among others, have all actively contributed to theory building in this arena. For the dependency theorists, a dependency on the West—and in particular on "core" countries—keeps nations from developing to their true potential. These scholars termed developing nations "periphery" countries, which provide raw goods and services to their core partners but remain in a state of dependency (and most often, poverty). The terms "core" and "periphery" are replaced by some dependency theorists by "metropolitan" and "satellite." External factors determine the degree to which a country can develop. These factors can be multinational corporations, as well as development agents like the World Bank, the International Monetary Fund (IMF), and even international commodity markets, as we saw in chapter 3.

Infrastructure and other internal elements were rarely identified as items that prevented development. Within the dependency-theory model, educational systems based on Western, capitalist models fostered continuation of a status quo in which elites in the periphery countries carried out the management functions of companies in the host countries. The language of dependency theorists often reflects a focus on class and strong criticism of capitalism.

Dos Santos (1991, 144), a key architect of dependency theory, identifies a clear set of parameters in his often-quoted definition: "A situation in which the economy of certain countries is conditioned by the development and expansion of another economy to which the former is subjected. The relation of interdependence between two or more economies, and between these and world trade, assumes the form of dependence when some countries (the dominant ones) can expand and can be self-starting, while other countries (the dependent ones) can do this only as a reflection of that expansion, which can have either a positive or negative effect on their immediate development." Thus the origins of the term "dependency" become clear.

We see that dependency theorists wish to redress the inequality among nations and find remedies to increase the ability of less powerful nations to make decisions that are not dependent on First World nations. The basic tenets of dependency theory are:

1   Developing nations must follow their own paths to industrialization; their history and context prevent them from industrializing in an identical manner to the United States and Europe.

2   The state must play a key role in development, particularly with respect to key industries like steel and petroleum.

3   The state must enact large tariffs.

4   The state must protect domestic industries from foreign competition until they are stable.

5   Foreign investments must be severely restricted.

6   Any development plans enacted must be clearly in the national interest.

7   Investment in agriculture, particularly as a monocrop export, should be discouraged.

8   The core/periphery relationship must shift to a more equal relationship.

Reflected in all of these principles is a grounding within the nation-state. Dependency theorists do not believe that assistance can only come from outside the country. They find that dependence on external, powerful nations keeps countries from truly developing. They are supportive of nationalizing energy and mineral-exploration companies. Early attempts in Iran in the 1950s to nationalize the oil industry, as well as the policies of late Venezuelan president Hugo Chavez, are examples of development decisions that fall more closely within the parameters of dependency theory.

Bryant and White (1982, 12) suggest that "dependency theorists insist upon going behind events and leaders to determine the use and abuse of power, whose interests are being served, and what alternatives exist." Many of these scholars grounded their early work in classic Marxism (as distinguished from Marxist-Leninism), drawing in particular on explanations of scarcity. Bryant and White make it quite clear, however, that there is disagreement among Marxist scholars over the role of scarcity in preventing development. A good introduction to some of the tenets of classic Marxism can be found in Edmund Wilson's *To the Finland Station* (1972). Whether these ideas of dependency appeal to you or not, one dimension is relevant for further study: Hamnett, Porter, Singh, and Kumar (1984) explore general social science and how a dependence on the Global North to generate theories that are used around the world is a present-day extension of dependency theory.

Critics of dependency theory often focus on the degree to which external, core countries are given all the blame for a lack of development and suggest that this outward focus should also have an internal component. They argue it is somewhat simplistic to assume there are no internal conditions that, by themselves, prevent development. We even see evidence of attempts to include a broad range of factors by one of dependency theory's earliest architects, Fernando Cardoso, the former president of Brazil. Cardoso, writing with colleagues Carnoy, Castells, and Cohen, called for a redefinition of dependency: "Therefore, whether with a utopian vision or with a plan for preserving well-being already attained, the 'new socialism'—or more properly social democracy—must address the North-South relationship in a new spirit" (Carnoy, Castells, Cohen, and Cardoso 1993, 159). Like Inkeles, Cardoso acknowledges that local context may determine how to resolve dependency issues; for example, one country may need to renegotiate debt, while another may simply need an infusion of resources into the human sector.

Like Michael Manley in Jamaica, Cardoso shifted ideologies drastically. Following his work as a chief architect of dependency theory, Cardoso became president of Brazil in 1995 and bowed to conservative fiscal measures to help Brazil work its way out of debt. His accounting of this perceived ideological switch is quite pragmatic:

> I would contend that, even as I settled into my new job [as president], I was still a sociologist at heart. My goals were mostly the same, even if my sense of how best to accomplish them had evolved. I still tried to see Brazil's problems with the same detached objectivity of the young professor in the white lab coat who had marched through the favelas of southern Brazil forty years earlier. Before making a decision, I struggled to collect all the relevant information and understand all points of view, as my old mentor from [the Universidade de São Paulo], Florestan Fernandes, had taught me. Methodology, more than ideology, was the true legacy of my academic career. (Cardoso and Winter 2006, 207)

Cardoso has recently published his memoirs, addressing to some degree how leadership demands flexibility (Cardoso and Winter 2006). In describing current Latin American leaders, he suggests there is a difference between their rhetoric and their actual behavior. While the rhetoric of these leaders often suggests they are at odds with neoliberal economic reforms, Cardoso believes they are primarily working within the system.

It is important to understand that dependency theory is one of only a handful of development theories that were created outside of the Global North, and that there are scholars today who continue to use this theory to account for inequality. For those interested in the study of language as a commodity—assessing, for example, how language can be used as a "carrot" or a "stick" in development—Robert Phillipson, in *Linguistic Imperialism* (1992), uses dependency theory to provide a fascinating account of how the British Council manipulated English as a commodity throughout Asia.

World-Systems Theory

Immanuel Wallerstein is the chief architect of the world-systems theory. His most seminal work in this area occurred between 1974 and 1976. World-systems theory focuses on the nature of inequality but does not use the nation-state as the primary locus of control; nor does it hold up highly industrialized nations as markers of development. This theory outlines the role of labor movements and social democratic movements in redressing inequality. Wallerstein's theory was characterized by Chirot and Hall (1982, 81) "as a direct attack against Modernization theory." Van Rossem (1996) sees it as a powerful theory that can be used to compare development as it occurs in different places. Many scholars characterize world-systems theory as a subset of dependency theory, but others emphasize the depth of its links to not only Marxist economics but also the social analysis of the French Annales school. Scholar Fernand Braudel distinguishes it from dependency theory. One contribution that is clearly Wallerstein's alone is the concept of "semi-periphery" countries. He suggests the term is critically important and should be used along with the "core" and "periphery" standards of dependency theory explored above. What is perhaps most significant about the world-systems theory is that current political, economic, and social researchers have been able to adapt many of its tenets to contemporary analysis—both quantitative and qualitative—and avoid many of the commonly denounced weaknesses of dependency theory.

The Present

Since the 1990s, there has been no dominant development paradigm. At the macro level, neoliberal economic policies have governed the allocation of funding for many projects. Former World Bank chief economist Joseph Stiglitz (2003, 74) terms this "market fundamentalism." These policies are those characterized as Washington Consensus policies and described in chapter 3. In a later volume, Stiglitz (2007, 27) summarizes the five key elements of the Washington Consensus strategies for development as "minimizing the role of government, emphasizing privatization, trade and capital market liberalization, and deregulation." Neoliberal prescriptions for development adhere to the five principles listed above, as well as the following: strong promotion of private initiatives for investment and management; privatization of government-owned monopolies for increased efficiency; and adoption of structural adjustment programs. Stiglitz argues that in general, Washington Consensus views and neoliberal views do not adequately emphasize equity, nor do they watch out for the interests of the poorest members of a nation-state. An alternative view would "put more emphasis on employment, social justice, and non-materialistic values such as the preservation of the environment than do those who advocate a minimalist role for government" (Stiglitz 2007, 28).

In summary, the theories of development that have been proposed so far have cracks that prevent them all—even the best-formulated ones—from performing completely as desired. There have been dominant development paradigms over the years, but no individual theory has yet found a corner on the truth. All development strategies are linked to their ideological underpinnings. Modernization theory presumes that all nations must develop in the same manner. Dependency theory presumes that the root causes of underdevelopment are primarily brought about by external forces and that most private fiscal initiatives are problematic. Human-capital theory presumes that there is room at the top of the economic ladder for all who wish to get there. Neoliberal theory presumes that the free market and fiscal austerity will help any nation out of poverty. Your task is to recognize the underpinnings of any development strategies that are proposed. If you find yourself in disagreement with a particular project, ask yourself what underlying tenets have led to it and consider the degree to which you agree with these tenets and why.

Sustainable development has not yet emerged from any of these theories. Yet the UN Millennium Goals and recent statements by UN leaders

Watch the TED talk presented by Hans Rosling available at this website: http://www.ted.com/talks/hans_rosling_reveals_new_insights_on_ poverty.html. In his nineteen-minute speech, titled "New Insights on Poverty," Rosling uses UN demographic predictions to explore what may happen in the next fifty years in terms of generational change. Once you have finished watching the speech, identify what personal links you can make to the patterns Rosling discusses and write a one-page reflection on it.

demonstrate an ongoing search for principles, policies, and actions that promote sustainability. On December 17, 2007, in an address to the UN in honor of United Nations Day for South-South Cooperation, Secretary General Ban Ki-moon underscored the importance of sustainable development and urged nations to step up to the task of truly meeting the Millennium Goals. He stated: "The international community must reinvigorate efforts to meet its commitments. Countries of the South must use their growing surpluses to reach development goals, including funding public goods, creating and distributing vaccines, supporting agricultural research and development, establishing social insurance systems, enhancing access to credit for the poor, and improving transportation and communications structures" (UN press release 2007).

We see strong evidence for adherence to these goals in the administration of microloans such as those crafted by the Grameen Bank and discussed in the following section. Having focused briefly on common development frameworks, we can now move to a more practical exploration of development. We first explore the relationship of debt to development. We then look at the role of microfinance in development and conclude with a case study from northern India.

Relationship of Debt to Development

As discussed in chapter 3, structural adjustment programs (SAPs) proposed by the World Bank and the IMF are frequent linchpins in restructuring debt and repayment plans. Such plans generally call for a decrease in spending on the social sector, an increase in foreign investment, and shifts in subsidies. Since the 1980s—generally agreed to be the starting point of the debt crisis—SAPs have dominated perspectives on debt management. James Hayes-Bohanan (2007) profiles plans in the 1980s by U.S. Treasury secretaries James Baker and Nicolas Brady to manage debt. In 1985 Baker proposed a plan to extend loans to countries that agreed to three conditions: privatization of state enterprise, shifts in subsidies, and opening to foreign investment. Roughly 80 percent of the largest debtor nations complied with the plan. In 1989 Brady proposed that private banks reduce their claims against many less-developed nations and that the IMF and World Bank use new funding to multilateralize the debt. Hayes-Bohanan (2007) reiterates that the neoliberal approach discussed by Stiglitz is still another type of structural adjustment. He goes on to explore ways of relieving debt, including debt-equity swaps and debt-for-nature swaps. A very readable discussion of these elements is available at http://webhost.bridgew.edu/jhayesboh/debt.htm. It is generally agreed that in spite of strong commitments to and calls for extra aid from the IMF and discussions at various G-8 meetings—and while individual nations such as Tanzania, Uganda, Mozambique, and Guyana have made impressive steps in decreasing their debt—there is still a need for sweeping reform that is not completely controlled by SAPs.

One forum that attracted a great deal of attention was Jubilee 2000, a program to forgive or cancel debt among the world's poorest nations. For example, at the G-8 meeting in Gleneagle, Scotland, in 2005, a decision was made to grant debt relief to eighteen of the poorest nations in the world: Benin, Bolivia, Burkina Faso, Ethiopia, Ghana, Guyana, Honduras, Madagascar, Mali, Mauritania, Mozambique, Nicaragua, Niger, Rwanda, Senegal, Tanzania, Uganda, and Zambia (Stiglitz 2007, 227, 347). While there have been additional calls to extend this type of debt forgiveness, much of the impetus behind Jubilee 2000 has subsided. A review of their website (http://www.jubileeusa.org) details current efforts and activities. A European perspective on debt is available from EURODAD (http://www.eurodad.org), the European network on debt and development. This site is managed by a network of NGOs and provides news articles, reports, and action alerts.

Microfinance

While country-level policies were being designed and implemented at the macro level, solutions to poverty were also being proposed and implemented at local levels. The best known of these is a microfinance model

Irrigation catchment basin in Morocco (Used with permission of the photographer, Aomar Boum)

designed by Muhammad Yunus, a Bangladeshi economist honored with the Nobel Peace Prize in 2006 for his design of the Grameen Bank. Yunus opened the Grameen Bank, the first microfinance bank, in Bangladesh in 1983. It was designed to assist poverty-stricken individuals without collateral to acquire very small loans that were typically too small for ordinary banks to deal with. The ordinance that allowed the bank's creation was ratified by the Bangladeshi parliament and stipulated that "the Bank shall provide credit with or without collateral security in cash or in kind, for such term and subject to such conditions as may be prescribed, to landless persons for all types of economic activity, including housing" (Dowla and Barua 2006, 17). Borrowers were able to take out a loan for one year and were required to make weekly payments, typically after the Friday prayer, when they were assembled in a group. The group formation became a key dimension of the Grameen Bank; groups of five individuals with comparable incomes and trust in each other formed the backbone of the lending scheme. These groups went through a training process, elected officers, and remained committed to a social charter that specified Sixteen Decisions they would abide by. These "decisions" covered dimensions of health, housing, agriculture, and even marriage contracts, all subsumed under four principles: discipline, unity, courage, and hard work (Dowla and Barua 2006, 55). This microfinance model has been successfully duplicated in hundreds of settings around the world. It provides a development model that is sensitive to local context and the needs of the poorest people. Over the span of one decade, the Grameen Bank's percentage of borrowers moving out of poverty increased roughly 5 percent each year. In 1997 only 15.1 percent of borrowers had moved above the poverty line one year after receiving a loan, while by 2005, 58.5 percent of borrowers were above the poverty line (Dowla and Barua 2006, 43).

The Grameen Bank uses ten measures to determine changes in poverty levels of its borrowers. These measures are very functional measures of development and correspond to a large number of the UN Millennium Development Goals (Dowla and Barua 2006, 42).

> Todaro (1989) suggests that three elements are critical to a development strategy: "life sustenance," "self-esteem," and "freedom from servitude." Think about which one of these three seems the most important to you and why.

- The members and their families are living in a tin-roofed house or in a house worth at least 25,000 [Bangladeshi] takas, and the family members sleep on cots or a bedstead instead of the floor.

- The members drink pure water from tube wells, boiled water, or arsenic-free water purified by the use of alum, purifying tablets, or pitcher filters.

- All of the members' children who are physically and mentally fit and are above the age of six either attend or have finished primary school.

- The member's minimum weekly installment is 200 takas.

- All family members use a hygienic and sanitary latrine.

- The family members have sufficient clothing to meet daily needs. Further, the family has winter clothes such as kanthas (light wraps made out of used clothing), wrappers, sweaters, quilts, and blankets to protect them from the cold, and they also have nets to protect them from mosquito bites.

- The family has additional sources of income, such as a vegetable garden or a fruit-bearing tree, to fall back on when they need additional income.

- The borrower maintains an average annual balance of 5,000 takas in her saving account.

- The borrower has the ability to feed her family members three square meals a day throughout the year; essentially, the family faces no food insecurity.

- All family members are conscious of their health. They have the ability to take immediate action for proper treatment and can pay medical expenses in the event of illness of any member of the family.

The success of the Grameen Bank model all over the world has provided the impetus to launch a model termed Grameen II. We do not examine Grameen II here, but it is important to note that changes implemented in the bank all have pragmatic roots and continue to focus on streamlining procedures and on improving borrowers' abilities to save for the future.

Throughout the world, microfinance programs based on the original Grameen model are changing the lives of individuals in small rural communities and urban neighborhoods. There is now competition among NGOs and various government banks in many places to extend this type of credit. Even Dannon Yogurt and Intel have collaborated with the Grameen

Bank. In the first case, Group Danone created both a manufacturing and marketing partnership to sell yogurt in Bangladesh. In the second case, Intel collaborates via its Intel World Ahead Program with Grameen Solutions to strengthen technological access in education (Intel press release 2008). Details of these projects can be found in Yunus's volume *Creating a World without Poverty* (2008). Microloans have allowed many individuals to climb out of poverty. Their individual success has not necessarily changed the overall poverty level of their countries, but microlending strategies remain powerful tools in the development puzzle.

We now turn to a case study of one region in India, where traditional development strategies and tourism have torn apart a sustainable society. Because of its unique history, its location, and the efforts of strong-minded local and nonlocal leaders, Ladakh is managing its current development in a manner that combines the best of traditional and nontraditional development strategies.

Case Study: Ladakh

Ladakh is a geographic region situated in northern India and wedged between Pakistan, China, and Tibet. It holds strategic importance because of its geopolitical location. It is within the Indian state of Jammu and Kashmir but holds special autonomous status, at least for the time being. Ladakh is one of the administrative regions in this state. Because of the unique role local sustainability has played in its path to development, and because it was not opened to tourism until 1974, Ladakh provides us with rich case-study data.

History

Until 1974 few tourists came to this area of Jammu and Kashmir. Due to its high altitude (3,534 meters), scarce water supply, and dramatic ecology, fragile environmental conditions determine the lifestyle of its inhabitants. Only about 0.2 percent of the area is inhabited (Wiley 1997; Mann 1986). Misri (n.d.) states: "The total area of Ladakh is 95,876 km², of which twenty-eight percent is cultivable (this area is confined to lower valleys where irrigation from adjoining streams and rivers is available)." Numerous volumes characterize Ladakh's area prior to 1974 as "a finely tuned and harmonious equilibrium between population, culture, and environment. . . . [T]raditional lifeways of the population of Ladakh have been

Map 2 Ladakh, India (From J. Fox, N. Chering, S. Bhatt, and A. Chandola. 1994. Wildlife conservation and land-use changes in the Trans-Himalayan region of Ladakh, India. *Mountain Research and Development* 14 [1]: 39–60. Reprinted with permission.)

hailed as superbly adapted to a natural environment in which numerous stresses are present" (Wiley 1997, 274).

Helena Norberg-Hodge—a linguist who has since gone on to a distinguished career as a chronicler of Ladakh's struggles to link past and present development traditions—describes Ladakh in the early 1970s as a sustainable, mostly self-sufficient area: "Ladakhis traditionally have recycled everything. There is literally no waste. With only scarce resources at their disposal, farmers have managed to attain almost complete self-reliance, dependent on the outside world only for salt, tea, and a few metals for cooking utensils and tools" (Norberg-Hodge 1991, 26).

Norberg-Hodge and others describe a democratically run village structure with individual landholdings. At critical times of harvesting and sowing, neighbors routinely assist each other. Norberg-Hodge characterizes the position of women in traditional Ladakhi society as very strong. Ladakh was originally a polyandrous society in which one woman could have several husbands. By most accounts, this was one mechanism for regulating population against scarce resources. Even though the Indian government declared polyandry illegal in 1942, the system remained largely in place, along with both monogamous and polygamous relationships, until the shift in development in the early 1980s. Norberg-Hodge describes the wide variety of skills acquired by many individuals and contrasts this level of generalization with specialization that occurs in societies moving along traditional industrial paths to development. Elders participate in all aspects of the community: "[F]or the elderly in Ladakh, there are no years of staring into space, unwanted and alone; they are important members of the community until the day they die" (Norberg-Hodge 1991, 67). She describes the influence of Tibetan Buddhism on Ladakhi culture, focusing on the importance of meditation and the degree to which individuals find themselves in semimeditative spaces throughout their days as they walk and work. She characterizes their worldview as one that is highly contextualized and holistic.

In 1974, however, the government not only opened Ladakh to tourism but began to implement more-traditional development plans. The balanced, sustainable place where Norberg-Hodge began her research would soon turn into an area struggling with all the issues outlined at the beginning of this chapter. The strengths of Ladakh as an independent region were challenged by the perceived need to develop in a manner consistent with the rest of the world. Norberg-Hodge (1991, 93) characterizes this foray into tourism—which has impacted not only the material culture but also people's minds—as "wide-ranging and disturbing."

Once plans were in place to develop the infrastructure, numerous roads were built. Less-sustainable buildings were constructed at tremendous costs with materials hauled in from other areas. Water—already scarce—suddenly became a commodity that was marketed and delivered to those who could pay, ultimately disrupting the elaborate cooperative system. Norberg-Hodge has only harsh words for the pressures brought on by this new development. She argues that farmers can no longer afford to farm. In the past, there was no exchange of money for the collaboration engaged in by all. With a move to a more market-oriented economy, farmers actually have to pay wages to those helping them. She suggests that food sustainability is giving way to planting cash crops.

Technology, formerly governed by local context and available materials, has shifted to what we have come to understand as high-tech and one system for all. Norberg-Hodge is perhaps most stressed at the likelihood

Kristof and WuDunn (2009, 122) refer to an estimate of $9 billion per year to "provide all effective interventions for maternal and newborn health to 95% of the world's population." What do you imagine to be some of the key impediments in the allocation of such an amount of money? See if you can find cost estimates for other comparable financial outlays. Why is it harder or easier to allocate funds for these things than for maternal and infant health?

that future generations are losing the pride, self-esteem, and centeredness that marked their parents' lives. While she acknowledges the advantages that come with literacy and numeracy and a greater connectedness to the outside world, she argues that these same forces have "divided Ladakhis from each other and the land and put them on the lowest rung of the global economic ladder" (Norberg-Hodge 1991, 114).

Norberg-Hodge describes the introduction of asbestos as a product used to bake bread; the introduction of pesticides—banned or severely restricted in other areas—to control nonexistent pests; the abandonment of traditional building materials for cement that must be hauled great distances; and an ultimate weakening of family ties, as young people relocate to the city to work and no longer maintain the traditions that once bound them to their families. In spite of all these problems, a dedicated group of individuals tried early on to bring in development tools that would "build on ancient foundations, rather than tearing them down" (Norberg-Hodge 1991, 140). These tools have primarily been threefold: education, technology, and media. As early as 1978, Norberg-Hodge began meeting with the Indian Planning Commission to develop solar technology. She formed the Ladakh Project, which has since come to be known as the International Society for Ecology and Culture (http://www.isec.org.uk/pages/ladakh.html).

The goals envisioned by Norberg-Hodge seem to be in evidence in Ladakh. She described the Ladakh Project's vision as follows: "We seek to encourage a revisioning of progress toward more ecological and community-based ways of living. We stress the urgent need to counter political and economic centralization, while encouraging a truly international perspective through increased cultural exchange. We also feel that a shift from ever more narrow specialization toward a broad systemic perspective—an approach that emphasizes relationship and context rather than isolated phenomena—is essential to prevent further social and environ-mental destruction" (Norberg-Hodge 1991, 171, 172).

In 1986 Norberg-Hodge and the Ladakh Ecological Development Group were awarded the Right Livelihood Award, which is sometimes known as the alternative Nobel Prize. For a rich description of the award and indi-viduals who have been honored, consult the website of the Right Livelihood Award (http://www.rightlivelihood.org).

The International Society for Ecology and Culture lists current develop-ment projects on its website. Its achievements regarding Ladakh include:

> [N]etworking with farmers' groups elsewhere in the [Global] South; tours of sustainable farms in the West for Ladakhi farmers' repre-sentatives; an ongoing campaign about the hazards of pesticides, fungicides, and chemical fertilizers; a wide range of meetings, from "hands-on" village workshops to international conferences; the intro-duction and demonstration of solar greenhouses, enabling villagers to grow vegetables the year round (there are now thousands throughout the entire region); and a seed-saving programme to promote the culti-vation and protection of local varieties of grains and legumes.

An examination of these activities demonstrates both a commitment to local, sustainable community building and a commitment to letting the rest of the world see what types of projects are working.

An additional project, the Students' Educational and Cultural Movement of Ladakh (SECMOL), was founded in 1988. The goal of its creators was to reform Ladakh's educational system. A review of their website (http:www.secmol.org/index.php) reveals a number of local sustainable initiatives, including a solar-heated campus that serves students from isolated villages and numerous outreach and publication activities. Youth camps that re-inforce traditional language and culture, in addition to English and sports, are offered throughout the year. Radio and television are used to promote ecodevelopment.

In Ladakh today, there is a movement to counter traditional develop-ment with a dynamic set of alternatives. It is a small region, but one that consciously strives not to abandon the best of its culture in the face of encroaching development. Ladakh is one of the few communities in the world that has been studied extensively because of its former sustainabil-ity and the degree to which lessons from its past are continually used to identify paths to its future. Unfortunately, while Ladakh can be studied as an isolated region, it is not really isolated. It is located at the confluence of political and economic tensions between India and China. A *Wall Street Journal* article in September 2009 captures the stakes involved for both China and India in a border dispute related to territory termed Arunachal Pradesh and, within it, a disputed road. Arunachal Pradesh is adjacent to Ladakh (Wonacott 2009). India believes that the territory belongs to it and has for centuries, while China claims it as its own. Wonacott suggests the border dispute is symbolic of rising trade tensions between China and India. Ostensibly, arguments over something as simple as a road are actually arguments over the future of a geopolitically strategic, contested borderland. It is important to recognize the success of particular projects, but it is also necessary to avoid romanticizing them. As much as sustainability projects in Ladakh are inspiring to read about, it is incumbent on you as a student of development policy to look beyond the local and investigate the regional and the international.

Conclusion

This chapter has introduced you to various perspectives on what it means for a country to develop and to be developed. We have seen the strengths and weaknesses of most of the models that have captured the attention of the West and have suggested that indicators of development vary from one ideology to the next. In our earlier chapters on globalization, we looked at policies and institutions that both promote change and sometimes increase inequality between nations. In the case of the development dichotomy, we have suggested that no country or policy has a corner on the truth. It is in the interconnections that Norberg-Hodge discusses that we will find the best way to coexist in our various contact zones. It is evident how even the smallest loans can make major differences in the lives of the most impoverished people throughout the world, especially when their dignity is maintained and they are recognized for their strengths. We are connected to everyone around us. Pause now to think of sustainable dimensions of your life in the context of your neighborhood.

➤ **VOCABULARY**

Jubilee 2000	Right Livelihood Award
microfinance	Sixteen Decisions
Grameen Bank	core, periphery, and semi-
Ladakh Project	periphery countries

➤ DISCUSSION AND REFLECTION QUESTIONS

1 *How would you define the following pairs of terms: developed/underdeveloped; developed/developing; First World/Third World; and Global North/Global South? Which set of terms do you think best describes the world? Why?*

2 *What are three of the five key questions about development framed by early economists?*

3 *What are Rostow's five stages of modernization?*

4 *What are two positive and two negative dimensions of the modernization questions that early theorists posed?*

5 *Why do you think neoliberal economic principles played such a key role in the global economy and, ultimately, in development practices in the decade of the 1990s?*

6 *What is the significance of the Sixteen Decisions of the Grameen Bank?*

7 *Why is Ladakh a unique case in development?*

8 *Why is it important to consider ethical dimensions of development decisions?*

9 *How do you perceive the relationship between globalization and development?*

10 *What is the relationship between personal development and community development?*

ACTIVITY 1 Examine the UN Millennium Development Goals as described on the UN Web page (www.un.org/millenniumgoals/). Now look at the United Nations Development Programme Web page (http://www.undp.org/content/undp/en/home.html). You can track the success of particular goals in particular countries. Choose two of the goals that most appeal to you and track their success in three countries. In a brief paragraph, compare what has happened in the three countries regarding each of the two goals. What do you believe accounts for any differences in the outcomes among the three countries?

ACTIVITY 2 You have been introduced to the notion of microfinance in this chapter. The website Kiva (http://www.kiva.org/) is an interactive site that links potential lenders with entrepreneurs via the Internet. Go to this site and work your way through the introduction and description of its activities. Identify a country and entrepreneur you could imagine yourself partnering with. Identify the amount of money you are willing and able to invest. Now imagine that it is six months after your investment. Write a two-paragraph letter to the individual you have partnered with. Identify three things you would like to know about how their project has progressed. Include a message of hope and success for the partner.

References

Bigelow, B., and B. Peterson. 2002. *Rethinking globalization: Teaching for justice in an unjust world*. Milwaukee, Wisc.: Rethinking Schools Press.

Black, M. 2002. *The no-nonsense guide to development*. Oxford, UK: New Internationalist Publications.

Bryant, C., and L. White. 1982. *Managing development in the Third World*. Boulder, Colo.: Westview Press.

Cardoso, F. H., and B. Winter. 2006. *The accidental president of Brazil: A memoir*. New York: Public Affairs.

Carnoy, M. 1974. *Education as cultural imperialism*. Boston: D. McKay.

Carnoy, M., M. Castells, S. Cohen, and F. Cardoso. 1993. *The new economy in the information age*. University Park, Pa.: Penn State University Press.

Chirot, D., and T. Hall. 1982. World-systems theory. *Annual Review of Sociology* 8:81–106.

Dadzie, K. K. S. 1980. Economic development. *Scientific American* (0036-8733) 243:58.

Dos Santos, T. 1991. The structure of dependence. In *The theoretical evolution of international political economy*, ed. G. Crane and A. Amawi, 144–52. New York: Oxford University Press.

Dowla, A., and D. Barua. 2006. *The poor always pay back: The Grameen II story*. Sterling, Va.: Kumarian Press.

Fox, J., N. Chering, S. Bhatt, and A. Chandola. 1994. Wildlife conservation and land-use changes in the Trans-Himalayan region of Ladakh, India. *Mountain Research and Development* 14 (1): 39–60.

Frank, A. G. 1970. *Latin America: Underdevelopment or revolution*. New York: Monthly Review Press.

———. 2002. *World accumulation, 1492–1789*. New York: Algora Publishing.

Friedman, T. 2007. *The world is flat: A brief history of the twenty-first century*. New York: Picador/Farrar, Straus and Giroux.

Goulet, D. 1971. *The cruel choice*. New York: Atheneum.

Hamnett, M., D. Porter, A. Singh, and K. Kumar. 1984. *Ethics, politics, and international social science research: From critique to praxis*. Honolulu: University of Hawaii Press.

Harbison, F. H., and C. A. Myers. 1964. *Education, manpower, and economic growth*. New York: McGraw-Hill.

————. 1965. *Manpower and education: Country studies in economic development.* New York: McGraw-Hill.

Hayes-Bohanan, J. 2007. International debt relief. Web page and PowerPoint presentation revised January 2007 from the Earth Sciences and Geography Club Lecture Series presentation "Global recession and the future of debt relief," February 2002. Retrieved July 17, 2010, from http://webhost.bridgew .edu/jhayesboh/debt.htm.

Inkeles, A., and D. H. Smith. 1974. *Becoming modern: Individual change in six developing countries.* Cambridge, Mass.: Harvard University Press.

Intel press release. 2008. Intel, Grameen announce joint business venture to fund social and economic development opportunities empowered by technology. May 19. Retrieved May 16, 2014, from http://www.intel.com/pressroom /archive/releases/2008/20080518corp.htm.

Jubilee USA Network. Retrieved November 30, 2007, from http:www.jubileeusa .org/nc/home/front-page-news.html?print=1.

Kristof, N., and S. WuDunn. 2009. *Half the sky: Turning oppression into opportunity for women worldwide.* New York: Alfred A. Knopf.

Ladakh. Retrieved December 12, 2007, from http://en.wikipedia.org/w/index .php?title=Ladakhand printable=yes.

Ladakh Non-Governmental Organizations. Retrieved December 12, 2007, from http://www.reachladakh.com/Non_Governmental_Organisations.htm.

Mann, R. 1986. *The Ladakhi: A study in ethnography and change.* Calcutta: Anthropological Survey of India.

Maturana, H., and F. Varela. 1987. *Tree of knowledge: The biological roots of human understanding.* Boston: Shambhala.

Mercy Corps. Retrieved December 12, 2007, from http://www.mercycorps.org.

Michaud, J. 1996. A historical account of modern social change in Ladakh (Indian Kashmir) with special attention paid to tourism. *International Journal of Comparative Sociology* (Brill) 37 (3/4) : 286–300.

Millennium Development Goals Report. 2007. Retrieved November 11, 2007, from http://www.un.org/milleniumgoals/.

Misri, B. Variability in alfalfa of Ladakh. Retrieved January 21, 2009, from http:// www.fao.org/AF/agp/agpc/doc/Bulletin/ladakh.htm.

Norberg-Hodge, H. 1991. *Ancient futures: Learning from Ladakh.* New Delhi: Oxford University Press.

Paulston, R. 1976. *Conflicting theories of social and educational change: A typological review.* Pittsburgh: University of Pittsburgh Center for International Studies. (ERIC Document Reproduction Service # ED 130921).

Rogers, E. M. 1974. Communication in development. *Annals of the American Academy of Political and Social Science* 412:44–54. DOI: 10.1177/ 000271627441200106.

————. 1976. Communication and development: The passing of the dominant paradigm. *Communication Research* 3 (2): 213–40. DOI: 10.1177/009365027600300207.

Rosling, H. 2009. Let my dataset change your mindset [posted August]. TED Talk. Retrieved December 31, 2013, from http://www.ted.com/talks/hans_rosling_at_state.html.

SECMOL: The Students' Educational and Cultural Movement of Ladakh. Retrieved December 12, 2007, from http:www.secmol.org/edurefroms/index.php.

Stiglitz, J. 2003. *Globalization and its discontents*. New York: W. W. Norton and Company.

———. 2007. *Making globalization work*. New York: W. W. Norton and Company.

Todaro, M. 1989. *Economic development in the Third World*. New York: Longman.

United Nations Millennium Development Goals. Retrieved November 30, 2007, from www.un.org/millenniumgoals/.

UN press release. Cooperation among developing countries central to global anti-poverty efforts, says secretary general, in International Day message. Retrieved December 12, 2007, from http://www.un.org/News/Press/docs/2007/sgsm11341.doc.htm.

Van Rossem, R. 1996. The world-system paradigm as general theory of development: A cross-national text. *American Sociological Review* 61 (3): 508–27.

Wade, L. 2009. Are there really two kinds of countries: Developed and undeveloped? April 28. Blog post. Retrieved December 31, 2013, from http://thesocietypages.org/socimages/2009/04/28/questioning-the-developed developing-binary/.

Wiley, A. 1997. A role for biology in the cultural ecology of Ladakh. *Human Ecology* 25 (2): 273–95.

Wonacott, S. 2009. China, India stoke 21st-century rivalry. *Wall Street Journal*, A-18. October 26.

World Bank. 2003. *World development report: Making services work for poor people*.

Yunus, M. 2008. *Creating a world without poverty*. New York: Public Affairs.

SEVEN Security

> **SYNOPSIS**

How policy makers and citizens define security depends upon how they perceive particular threats, the historical context in which they live, and whether they focus on dangers to the nation-state or the individual. As such, our understanding of the notion of security is framed by our membership in particular communities and ideologies. Some twentieth-century scholars have been particularly influential in determining how Western nations define their security. Flash points around the world may cause individual nation-states and global organizations to respond in particular ways to fears of terrorism, nuclear proliferation, and biological warfare. At the same time, technology is changing security issues, forcing societies to make judgments about privacy, intelligence gathering, and drone strikes.

> **SCAFFOLDING**

As you read through this chapter, think about how you would answer each of the questions below.

Are you familiar with the terms "Realism" or "human security"? In what context did you learn about them?

What do you remember about the development of the nation-state from chapter 2 ("History")?

Why has this chapter incorporated perspectives about the U.S. war with Iraq from Middle East sources? Where would you go to find European, Latin American, Asian, or African perspectives on this issue?

Are you willing to trade your privacy online or during phone calls in return for greater security?

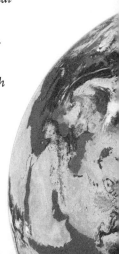

➤ CORE CONCEPTS

How do differing perspectives on the ways nation-states and international governing bodies can keep individuals safe affect policy decisions in times of terror or insecurity?

What are five "flash points," or geographic areas of conflict, that may dominate security discussions in the next five years?

How have new technologies and globalization changed the threats we face?

How do we balance the need for security against the right to privacy?

The first task of every government is to ensure the security of its citizens from outside threats. Any government that fails in this task faces not only the risk of external takeover but also the loss of legitimacy among its people. But which threats are so important that they are security issues? In France in 1938 or Kuwait in the 1990s, it was easy to define the threat. In other periods, however, nations might define the danger differently. People in Angola might be extremely concerned about the threat of land mines laid decades before, while someone in Caracas, Venezuela, might be frightened of street crime. Europeans might worry that the National Security Agency of the United States is monitoring their phone calls or e-mail. A Pakistani might be simultaneously worried about violence of the Taliban and U.S. drone strikes that undermine Pakistan's sovereignty. A pandemic might endanger a nation with losses larger than those likely in any conventional conflict. For people in a small Pacific island, the greatest threat to national security might be a rising sea level. For other nations, it might be the threat of climate refugees fleeing from environmental change. How people define security is defined by the historical and national context. At the current moment, the key U.S. security threat is terrorism, not only because of the attacks of September 11, 2001, and the real threat the country continues to face but also because there is no peer military competitor that could challenge the nation by conventional means. Ultimately, what people fear determines how they define security, and a number of related issues follow from this axiom. Where do citizens look to obtain security? How has the definition of security changed through time? And how do you balance the reality of threats against the importance of human rights?

Security from the Emergence of the Nation-State to Realism

Some scholars would argue that security represents the most basic international issue. It was the central theme of the Greek historian Thucydides, who sought to understand the Peloponnesian War, the greatest conflict of his era. He argued that the war began because of the rising power of Athens, which caused Sparta to act before it could be overwhelmed. His account shaped Western interpretations of international relations for 2,400 years (Monten 2006). In the millennia that followed, a series of thinkers, such as Niccolò di Bernardo dei Machiavelli and Thomas Hobbes, wrestled with the same issues, and their work continues to underpin modern scholarship on international affairs (Sobek 2005). When Renaissance and Enlightenment thinkers in Europe tried to understand the origins of the state, they concluded that its most fundamental reason for existence was to provide security for its citizens from outside threats. People came together and gave up certain freedoms in order to have security from both internal threats, such as criminals, and external threats, such as invasion (Hobbes 1982). At the same time, these European thinkers lived in a world in which the nation-state system was relatively new. Their work represented an effort to understand an emerging kind of state.

Security was not always defined solely in terms of threats to the nation-state and its sovereignty. In the Middle Ages, political units were defined by dynasties, which meant that people's allegiances could change with a royal marriage. Whether in Angevin England or medieval Italy, political boundaries often did not align with ethnic groups. Authority was frequently fractured or divided. Under the feudal system, a powerful leader could be bound to more than one overlord. People owed political allegiance to their king (or kings), but moral and religious authority was bestowed in a pope. Additionally, there was an ideal of chivalry in which the bond of knighthood appeared more important than those of language or homeland. An English knight probably believed that he had more in common with a Spanish lord than an English peasant. Nationhood did not determine political authority or the role of the state (Rapley 2006, 96–99; see also Ganshof 1971).

This reality began to change in 1648. In that year, the Peace of Westphalia ended the Thirty Years War while giving rise to the modern nation-state. As Enlightenment authors sought to explain this new state of affairs, they established ideas that have shaped much subsequent writing on security, which has focused both on the nation-state and issues relevant to the developed world. There are good reasons for this fact. The nation-state system

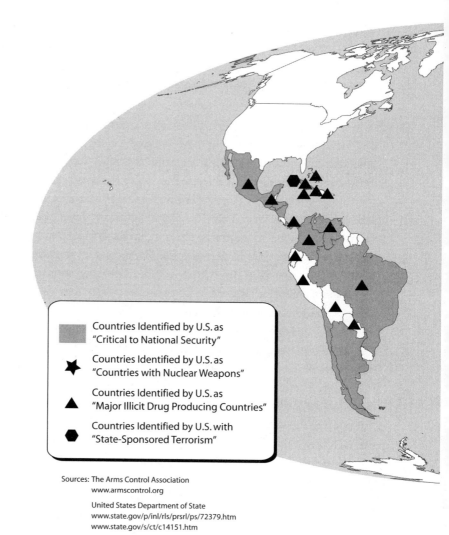

Map 3 Countries Critical to U.S. Security (Steph Gaspers 2008)

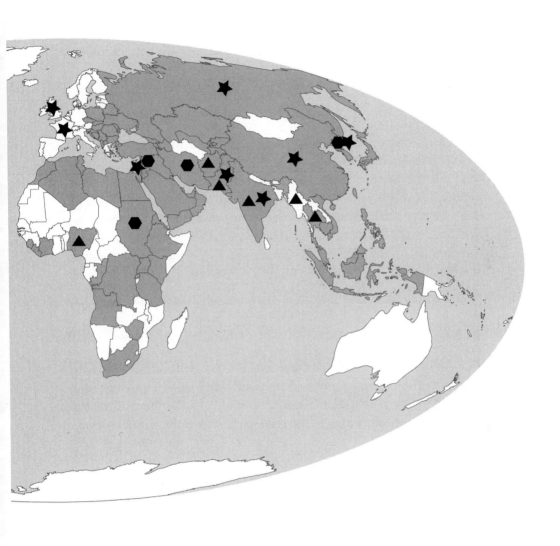

has proven to be an enormously successful construct. As formal empires waned after World War II (1939–45), all newly freed regions adopted the nation-state system. For this reason, security was defined in terms of the survival of the nation-state, and its ability to maintain its sovereignty, rather than the security of its people from violence or death. Internal conflicts and economic issues consequently received little attention as security issues because they rarely threatened the nation-state at the systemic level.

Europe was also the center of global political power for the latter half of the millennium, which meant that security was perceived through the lens of the Great Power competitions, with a focus on armed conflict. When power shifted to the United States and the Soviet Union with the onset of the Cold War, the two parties viewed all security issues in terms of their contest. Because even local conflicts could draw in either power (Vietnam, Afghanistan) and potentially escalate to nuclear war, Great Power competition remained the key issue. Security continued to be thought of as a question defined by relationships between states. Scholarship in the field was dominated by a theory called Realism, which reflected this context and remains the dominant paradigm in the field.

Realism

Realism is a complex and rich theoretical perspective that traces its roots back to the work of Thucydides, Machiavelli, and Hobbes (Jackson and Sorenson 1999, 72–76). But the British author E. H. Carr first articulated the theory in the twentieth century, as he sought to explain why Europe was again sliding into a world war in his book *The Twenty Years' Crisis* (Jackson and Sorenson 1999, 41–42). Because of the complexity and depth of this literature, it is difficult to briefly summarize the meaning of Realism, which has developed and evolved over time. Despite its many interpretations, however, Realism as a worldview generally has certain characteristics (Jackson and Sorenson 1999, 68–70). Its proponents typically view security as the key issue in international affairs. They often share a pessimistic view of both human nature and the inevitability of war. Within this theoretical framework, the key factor in international politics is the state. And one of the axioms of Realism is that the international system is anarchic, in the sense that there is no superior power to which an aggrieved nation can appeal. Realists tend to doubt the power of international law or the international community to limit conflict. Although nations may cloak their actions in moral rhetoric, they act based on their national interests, and it is unrealistic to expect them to do otherwise. Realists argue that states therefore have no choice but to engage in the strategies of realpolitik, such as alliance formation and power balancing. Any state that fails to do so may be moral, but it may not survive. (For a brief description of Realism, see Sheehan 2005, 5–23.) This theory has evolved considerably through the work of such authors as Hans Morgenthau and Kenneth Waltz, but most of its key ideas have remained intact (Morgenthau 1948; Waltz 1959; Jackson and Sorenson 1999, 51–53, 76–80, 84–89).

This doctrine had been challenged by other theories, such as liberalism, which stresses the importance of international institutions and international law in shaping behavior. This more optimistic vision argues that organizations such as the United Nations could create a new global framework to avoid the devastating warfare of the twentieth century. Progress is possible (Jackson and Sorenson 1999, 108–11). Constructivists, in contrast, argue that the international order is defined by identities that result from history and experience. The international order is not given but rather historically contingent; that is, it could change (Jackson and Sorenson 1999, 238–40). Both theories are more complex than this thumbnail sketch can capture. But they each seek to mount a challenge to Realism, which they argue focuses excessively on conflict and oversimplifies a complex reality.

Other political scientists—such as Robert Keohane and Joseph Nye— have mounted sophisticated critiques of Realism as a doctrine because actors other than states are important in international affairs, nations are interdependent in complex ways, and military force is not always the key factor in international relations (Keohane and Nye 2001, 20–32). But during the Cold War, most policy makers drew heavily on Realism because its emphasis on Great Power politics—the balance of power, alliances, and military strategy—seemed to accord with an era defined by global tension (Sheehan 2005, 6, 23). Then, almost overnight, the Soviet Union collapsed. Some scholars argued that in an era defined by globalization, the meaning of security needed to be rethought. It is not clear, however, that Realism has been superseded as a doctrine.

The End of the Cold War

In the early 1980s, it was difficult to imagine that the Cold War might end. As Philip Gordon notes, the Reagan administration had warned that the United States and its allies were falling behind in the military competition with the Soviets and that vast resources were needed to keep up (Gordon

2007, 56). Even after the fact, many people could not believe that the Cold War had actually ended (Gordon 2007, 56). The collapse of the Soviet Union brought a period of euphoria in the West. Because global security threats had been viewed in this context, it seemed that the end of this period would eliminate not only the risk of nuclear annihilation but also many of the conflicts between client states. During this time, there was also a wave of democratization, as military regimes collapsed throughout Latin America—in part because the United States no longer bolstered authoritarian governments based on their anti-Communism. But there was also a larger process of democratization taking place, as South Africa ended apartheid and Eastern Europe adopted democracy, as did the Philippines. All of these factors, combined with the rise of the European Union, created a sense of optimism. Francis Fukuyama wrote a much-cited article entitled "The End of History?," which proposed that the era of global competition was over, as no great ideological questions remained to be addressed: "We may be witnessing the end of history as such: that is, the endpoint of mankind's ideological evolution and the universalization of Western liberal democracy as the final form of human government" (Fukuyama 1989, 4). There was a great deal of discussion of the peace dividend. Military spending fell across the globe.

There was no theoretical framework in place to shape how policy makers interpreted this new era. A new mood of isolationism washed over the United States and, to a lesser extent, Canada and Europe. While developed countries appeared to be transitioning into a more stable future, this was not the case for nations in the Global South, some of which seemed to be sliding into anarchy. There was little concern in rich countries about this, however, because it appeared that Western nations had the security to disengage from poor regions of the world, which might be chaotic or dangerous. In the future, it seemed that the world might divide into two areas, which Singer and Wildavsky have called "zones of peace" and "zones of turmoil" (1993, 8). In practice, these zones were defined by their wealth. In the developed world, few ideological questions divided the Great Powers, and ties of democracy mitigated conflict. Political scientists spoke of the democratic peace hypothesis, which states that democracies are less likely to go to war; that if they do go to war, they are less likely to fight other democracies; and that a world with more democracies likely would see less conflict (paraphrasing Mitchell, McLaughlin, Gates, and Hegre 1999, 771–72; see also Gleditsch and Ward 2000; O'Neal and Russett 1999; and Sheehan 2005, 32–42). In contrast, in the developing world, there

appeared to be frequent conflicts over ethnic, nationalist, and resource issues, which had little meaning to key global actors: "While Europe enjoyed
what John Gaddis (1986) termed the 'long peace' (the longest period in
the post-Westphalia era without a major war among the major powers),
conflicts in the Third World inflicted all but 176,000 of the 22 million
battle deaths that occurred between 1945 and 1989" (Mason 2003, 19). In
the developed world, there was a sense that combat in these areas might
entail moral issues but no longer security questions.

The term "failed states" emerged as a common term to describe regions
in which a clear nation-state (with a monopoly on violence and the ability
to assert its sovereignty) did not exist. The term was also politicized, as outside powers were able to define which states had "failed" according to their
national interests. Still, the term endured because it provided a means to
understand common patterns of violence in the developing world. For the
most part, these failed states, such as Haiti or Somalia, were too distant and
too weak to impact U.S. security interests during the 1990s (Sloan 2005,
127; for a broader discussion of failed states, see Gros 1996 and Helman
and Ratner 1992–93). People seemed to turn in despair from the fighting
that washed over many poor nations, such as the tragic history of the Lord's
Resistance Army in Uganda. Places such as Afghanistan, which had been
at the center of international media coverage in the 1980s, were forgotten.

The Challenge of Terrorism

Western nations, however, were not impervious to turmoil or violence. In
conventional military terms, wealthy nations were untouchable, but rational opponents would not choose to launch a conventional attack. With new
technologies such as the Internet, distance seemed to provide less security
than in the past (Verton 2003). The rise of globalization was fracturing
the power of the state and empowering small substate actors—from Aum
Shinrikyo, a Japanese cult that launched the Sarin nerve-gas attacks in
Tokyo's subway, to Middle Eastern groups such as Al-Qaida and Hezbollah.
While no state was likely to attack the United States, terrorists and other
groups were not deterred. Throughout the 1990s, a series of attacks by
terrorists foreshadowed the threat to the United States and Europe.

The list of attacks is too long to detail here, but a few key events give a
sense of the scale of the challenge. In 1992 a failed effort to destroy the
World Trade Center in New York City with a car bomb injured more than
1,000 people in the building. Shortly afterward, the police and intelligence

services halted a planned attack by Islamic radicals targeting New York landmarks. In 1995 authorities found a laptop computer in the Philippines that detailed a plan by Ramzi Yousef to destroy ten airliners at the same time. In 1996 suicide bombers exploded a truck at the Khobar Towers complex in Saudi Arabia; nineteen Americans and 300 other people died in the attack. In 1997 Islamic radicals in Luxor, Egypt, opened fire on visiting tourists, killing over sixty people (British Broadcasting Corporation 1997). In 1998 the U.S. embassies in Kenya and Tanzania were bombed. Mostly local people died in the attacks, which left more than 4,000 people injured (U.S. Department of State Bureau of International Information Programs 2006). In 1999 Ahmed Ressam was arrested in Port Angeles, Washington, after an alert border guard noticed his nervousness. He confessed to being part of a plan to carry out a major bombing at the Los Angeles airport (Bernton, Carter, Heath, and Neff 2002; U.S. District Court 2001). In 2000 the USS *Cole* was bombed off the coast of Yemen. Seventeen sailors died in the attack, and the ship required extensive rebuilding. Many similar but smaller strikes were carried out during the 1990s, while several large-scale attacks were intercepted before they could be launched (9/11 Commission 2004, 59–73, 145–60).

The U.S. government responded to these strikes by using the legal apparatus, working with its partners in the developed world, and launching cruise missiles against terrorist training sites (9/11 Commission, 73–86, 108–43; for why the United States turned from using a legal approach to dealing with terrorism militarily after September 11, see Shapiro 2007, 10–14). The legal approach was sometimes effective in leading to the arrest and imprisonment of the people who carried out the attack. But the perpetrators were often willing to sacrifice their lives, and the people who planned, financed, and supported the attacks often remained free overseas. The cruise missile strikes destroyed buildings but did little to dismantle terrorist networks. The second attack on New York's World Trade Center took place less than a decade after the first. The United States and other Western nations might have overwhelming military power, but that alone did not isolate them from violence.

Samuel Huntington

Faced with this problem, people sought to find a new intellectual framework to understand international politics and account for this rising tide of violence. Even before September 11, international terrorism—and a wave

of ethnic conflict—had helped fuel an intellectual backlash against Fukuyama's optimism. A political scientist, Samuel Huntington, emerged as
the leading spokesperson for this point of view, and his arguments would
influence many neoconservative thinkers. Neoconservatism is a United
States–based intellectual movement that emphasizes the centrality of security issues in foreign affairs and the need for the United States to adopt
an interventionist foreign policy. Although Huntington would likely have
disavowed many of their arguments—particularly because he opposed
interventionism—neoconservatives used his framework to advance their
arguments.

Huntington's key work was *The Clash of Civilizations and the Remaking of World Order*, which first saw light as an article in *Foreign Affairs* in
1993. His core thesis held that conflicts between civilizations have replaced
struggles between nations and ideologies as the greatest threat to peace.
Most conflicts, he argued, took place along the "fault lines" between civilizations. Wars can take place within a civilization (such as the struggle
in the Congo), but these do not threaten wider conflict. In contrast, conflicts between two civilizations—such as the West and Islam—have far
greater potential for violence (Huntington 1996, 254–65). Huntington
(1996, 209–10, 217, 220) argued that the contest between the West and
the Soviet Union was a historical aberration that was less important than
what he depicted as a 1,400-year struggle between the West and Islam.
U.S. policy increased the risk of conflict between civilizations because the
United States preached the universality of its values, despite the reality that
not all nations wanted to be liberal democracies or multiethnic societies
(Huntington 1996, 21). Much as Paul Kennedy's work reflected the thought
of his time, Huntington's work reflected the mood of pessimism, the trend
toward isolationism, and the concern about terrorism that marked the late
1990s. Huntington's work also attracted widespread attention because it
seemed to explain the growing importance of ethnic conflict.

Huntington's argument also attracted broad criticism (Bottici and Challand 2006; Gerges 1999; Kupchan 2002; Russett, O'Neal, and Cox 2000).
Huntington (1996, 305–7) seemed to depict all cross-cultural contact as
being dangerous and multiculturalism as a threat to Western identity—a
strange argument in a nation of immigrants. This argument appeared
xenophobic; that is, it represents an irrational fear of foreigners. Perhaps
this was an inevitable result of his approach, which did not incorporate
multiethnic societies, which have dominated most of human history.
Huntington's model also seemed to be arbitrary in its definition of "civi-

lization," with one continent in particular failing to gain this label: Africa (Huntington 1996, 47; see also Said 2001). In some respects, Huntington's argument seemed to recreate the Cold War. The world system was still defined by conflict, only now the enemy was Islam. But Bottici and Challand (2006) and other authors argued that this perspective in itself was dangerous because it could become a self-fulfilling prophecy (see Fukuyama 2006, 20). If the West viewed Islam as a monolith, did that mean that Western nations would not ally with Islamic nations that were also threatened by terrorism? Did not the West share common interests in this struggle with key Islamic states? While Huntington's argument was powerful rhetorically, he presented little quantitative data to support his thesis. When data was produced, it did not seem to back his work. Even an author who generally supported Huntington's argument, such as Andrej Tusicisny (2004, 485, 496), found that there did not seem to be a correlation between the duration of conflicts and whether they take place between civilizations; nor did conflicts between the West and Islam define warfare in the post–Cold War world. Similarly, Russett, O'Neal, and Cox (2000) found that civilizations were as likely to fight within themselves as against each other. Other criteria seem to be as effective as "civilization" in explaining conflict. For example, Gerges (1999) suggested that interests, not culture, shaped international politics, an argument echoed by other authors, such as Kupchan (2002). Huntington's work was important because it refocused attention on both religion and culture, two topics that were strangely absent from most writing on international affairs during the Cold War period. But as a new framework for understanding issues in international security, it has not dominated recent scholarship.

Human Security

At the same time that Huntington was making his argument, the intellectual groundwork for another vision of security was being laid. At the core of this approach was a new answer to the question "What is security?" The traditional response had been that security came from the nation-state, which held a monopoly of violence that it used not only to maintain internal order but also to protect its citizens from external threats. In this respect, security threats needed to be dealt with through the traditional tools of statecraft, such as alliances, deterrence, and war. But this argument appeared outdated to some scholars, who advanced an ideal called "human security" by arguing that threats should be defined by what endangers not only the state but also the individual. An example might be pandemic flu. It could not threaten the state, which would survive even the most devastating pandemic imaginable, but it could take the lives of hundreds of millions of people globally. It needed to be treated with the same seriousness as a potential bioterrorism attack. This represented a different way of looking at international security and how thinkers since the Enlightenment have defined it.

Although its intellectual roots may be traced to before the Cold War, human security first came to prominence after the UN released a 1994 document entitled the *Human Development Report* (United Nations Development Programme 1994; Paris 2001, 89; MacFarlane and Khong 2006, 23–142). The document reflected the end of the Cold War and a new international environment in which the rising power of globalization seemed to decrease the importance of nation-states while also increasing the threat posed by nonstate actors such as Al-Qaida (Ripsman and Paul 2004). The growing importance of failed states, organized crime, environmental problems, and infectious disease also led to a reassessment of the security environment (Newman 2001; Axworthy 2004, 348). By shifting the focus from the state to the individual, a new perspective could focus resources on the threats killing the most people.

This argument gained traction in part because many small states were dissatisfied with the traditional military approach to security problems. These nations seized upon the idea of human security as a means to not only alleviate human suffering but also create an alternative political order. Their patronage gave great impetus to this new approach: "Among the most vocal promoters of human security are the governments of Canada and Norway, which have taken the lead in establishing a 'human security network' of states and nongovernmental organizations (NGOs) that endorse the concept" (Paris 2001, 87; Owen 2004, 378). Policy makers in these nations (as well as in Japan, Australia, and other Scandinavian nations) often felt that social and economic issues, especially poverty, underlay conflict (Thomas 2001; Kacowicz 2005, 123). An approach that only dealt with crises when they reached the level of open conflict was doomed to a reactive response; it could never take the initiative to prevent emergencies by resolving ethnic disputes, ending political grievances, or preventing economic conflicts (Monaghan 2008, B-9).

Proponents of this approach also argued that traditional Realism was irrelevant to the kind of violence faced by many people living in developing countries. For example, since 1945, most global conflicts had been civil wars, which accounted for most of the world's combat deaths (Mason 2003, 19). Yet traditional Realism gave little thought at all to civil wars or the state's role as an agent of internal violence (Owen 2004, 375). There seemed to be a split between the widespread violence in the developing world and the focus on Great Power contests. From this perspective, Realism ignored key issues in developing nations, such as land mines, which represented both a security threat and an economic cost in many countries. For this reason, scholars began to question the utility of Realism: "To many, there is little doubt that (in and of itself) the traditional state-based security paradigm is failing in its primary objective—to protect people. Millions a year are killed by communicable disease, civil war, environmental disasters, and famine, none of which fall under the mandate of current security thinking" (Owen 2004, 374). By the 1990s, the idea of human security emerged as a major challenge to Realism.

This new framework did not go unchallenged by Realist authors, who argued that globalization had not fundamentally changed security issues and that states remained the key actors in security affairs (Ripsman and Paul 2004). Scholars such as Barry Buzan (2004, 369–70) suggested that the term "human security" was so broad that the phrase had little meaning and practically made every issue a security issue. Roland Paris similarly argued that the term was too vague to be useful to policy makers facing competing demands: "Human security is like 'sustainable development'— everyone is for it, but few people have a clear idea what it means" (Paris 2001, 88). He further suggested that the very vagueness of the concept allows it to unite people with widely different ideas: "The term, in short, appears to be slippery by design" (Paris 2001, 88; for an overview of the field, see Newman 2001).

Critics argued that this vagueness could be dangerous. For example, AIDS has been depicted as a security threat because it tends to undermine African militaries (which have high rates of HIV infection), which could lead to failed states (Elbe 2006, 121–2). This argument may have been intended to persuade the U.S. government to act by suggesting that this health question had security implications. But this hypothesis also presented a danger, according to Stefan Elbe: if HIV/AIDS became viewed as a military threat, it could then be fought according to the extent the disease impacted U.S. interests (Elbe 2006, 119, 120, 128; see also Peterson, 2002–2003). This might warp the response to HIV, so that only those aspects of the pandemic that influenced "security" issues would receive attention and funding. What Elbe suggested is that HIV was a serious moral issue in itself, regardless of how it impacted the United States. Recently, former U.S. surgeon general Richard H. Carmona argued that obesity in the United States was a security issue because it decreased the number of men available for military service (Gosik 2007).

Critics argue that human security needs boundaries, without which all issues could become securitized (Shapiro 2007, 113; Owen 2004, 379). Human security scholars are working now to develop responses to this critique, in part by drawing on work from the insurance industry that looks at degrees at risk. But critics are also concerned that if poverty and development come to be defined as security issues, then militaries from developed nations will become involved in addressing them, which would expand their role in developing countries. There is some evidence to suggest that this is a realistic worry regarding U.S. foreign policy: "Refugees International released statistics showing that the percentage of development assistance controlled by the Defense Department had grown to nearly 22 percent from 3.5 percent over the past 10 years, while the percentage controlled by the Agency for International Development dropped to 40 percent from 65 percent" (Shanker 2008, 14). If failed or failing states foster terrorism, should the armed forces of developed nations help with state making, or do other agencies have more expertise?

Partly for this reason, the perception of human security has been mixed within developing countries. Some leaders have welcomed a reframing of global priorities to give greater weight to their concerns and justify their requests for more resources. In other nations, leaders have worried that this framework might give European and North American nations the means to involve themselves in issues of national sovereignty: "Even some intended beneficiaries of the approach are skeptical of it. The Group of 77—the coalition of developing countries at the United Nations—'tend to be deeply suspicious of human security, seeing it as part of a "West against the rest" ideological push by countries of the North to impose alien values on the developing world'" (Monaghan 2008, B-11). Human security is a concept that is viewed by some developing countries as a potential means of neocolonialism—that is, the maintenance of colonial relations after formal connections are severed.

Despite these criticisms, human security has been an innovative area that has led to fresh work on security issues. For example, the Canadian government sponsored a study on urban issues in the developing world from this perspective (Foreign Affairs Canada). Many scholars are working to address these critiques and to bring greater rigor to the field (Owen

2004, 380, 382–83). It is also true that all emerging fields tend to face such ideological debates. Human security continues to attract attention because of rising concerns about organized crime, infectious disease, and the environment. But like every approach at the moment, it is being judged based on its ability to describe a period in which security issues are mainly defined by terrorism.

September 11 and Its Aftermath

These debates about the nature of security became critical after September 11. The idea that the United States found itself in a clash of civilizations was as widely debated as it was troubling. How should the United States understand the motivation of the people who attacked it? One study found that "55 percent of Jordanians and 65 percent of Pakistanis held favorable views of Bin Laden" (Shore 2006, 5, citing material from the Pew Global Attitudes Project; see also 9/11 Commission 2004, 375). This perspective confused many Americans. Was the United States' position in the Arab-Israeli conflict the determining factor in how it was perceived abroad? Or did people lash out because the United States supported authoritarian leaders in the Middle East, while the Central Intelligence Agency (CIA) had a sad history that included the overthrow of Iran's prime minister Moham-med Mosaddeq in 1953? Did Islamic extremists associate the United States with globalization, Western secularism, and modernity, which they viewed as threatening? (For the association between the United States and global-ization, see Keohane and Nye 2001, 234–35, 250.) Every author seemed to have a different opinion. At root was the question of whether it was U.S. actions or U.S. values that caused hostility toward the United States (Holsti 2008, 64). It was critical for U.S. citizens to understand how their nation was viewed in the Middle East.

A careful study of attitudes in the Muslim world did shed some light on these questions. It found that people in Islamic countries tended to be almost equally split in their opinion on the United States. The main reason that people gave for disliking the United States (57 percent of respondents) was the country's support for Israel, while other respondents (41 percent) pointed to the United States' economic power or overall American hege-mony (41 percent). Neither U.S. support for authoritarian regimes nor the power of American multinational companies seemed to be a key factor. While people might be split on their view of the United States, 73 percent agreed that it was good for the United States to be vulnerable. At the same time, 58 percent reported that they felt sympathy for Americans in this time of crisis (Pew Global Attitudes Project 2001). In sum, people seemed to fear the power of the U.S. government, particularly in the region, while liking Americans themselves.

At root, much of the polling data reflected the complexity of the Islamic world. There is no monolithic view of the United States in the region, even though polls show that people in Islamic nations have concerns about the spread of American values and lack of religiosity (Holsti 2008, 74–81). Overall, what is striking in much of the polling data is the diversity among Islamic countries. In a 2007 poll, more Jordanians than Canadians reported that they liked the United States' way of doing business (Holsti 2008, 80). The United States has historically had a very positive image in the world's largest Muslim country, Indonesia. The view of the United States tended to vary based on the historical experience of these nations with the U.S. government. In this respect, the Islamic world resembles other major world regions, which also have complex attitudes toward the United States. Globally, polls show that Americans tend to be perceived much more positively than their government (Holsti 2008, 64–66).

In the aftermath of September 11, Americans struggled to understand their nation's image in the Muslim world and the motivations for the attacks upon the United States by extremists based in the region. But there was consensus in the West that the main base of Al-Qaida in Afghanistan had to be eliminated. Al-Qaida had found safety under the rule of the Taliban, a fundamentalist movement that had begun among students who promised to end the violence that followed the Soviet-Afghan war. The Taliban sheltered Osama Bin Laden and refused to give him up as the United States demanded in September 2001. In response, the United States allied with the Northern Alliance, whose leader, Ahmed Shah Massoud, had been assassinated by a suicide bomber on September 9, 2001, as Al-Qaida prepared to attack the United States. With support from both British and U.S. airpower, the Northern Alliance had overrun Taliban forces by December 2001, although Osama Bin Laden escaped U.S. and Afghan troops at the Battle of Tora Bora that same month.

This invasion was widely seen as legitimate both in the United States and in many European nations (Holsti 2008, 48). The Netherlands, Canada, Germany, and other NATO powers contributed troops to the International Security Assistance force (Shanker and Myers 2007). The Canadians in particular took the lead in some of the fiercest fighting. The role of these U.S. partners was key, because if Australia, Britain, Canada, or the Netherlands had withdrawn from Afghanistan before planned pullout dates, the mission would likely have collapsed, not only from a lack of force but also from a lack of legitimacy. It is difficult to address the security challenge of Afghanistan within a framework defined by one nation-state, even one with as much military power as the United States. For example, the very real possibility exists that ethnic tensions could lead Afghanistan into a civil war, despite the U.S. presence within the country.

After this invasion, there was a larger debate within the United States about the best means to respond to terrorism. One argument favored a defensive strategy, the broad outlines of which were articulated by the September 11 commission (9/11 Commission 2004, 380–98; for a summary of the offensive/defensive debate, see Sloan 2005, 6–12). Ian Shapiro (2007), for example, argued that the West should adopt the same strategy of containment that it had followed during the Cold War. Countless authors have written that the "war on terror" is not winnable in a conventional sense. But as Philip Gordon (2007, 54) notes, terrorism will not last forever. He suggested investing resources into strengthening the nation's defenses, much as we did against the Soviet Union. By securing their ports, tightening airport security, rebuilding public-health infrastructure, and improving intelligence, Western nations could address this threat. The funds needed would be a fraction of what the United States spent on the Iraq invasion: "As one analyst noted in *Mother Jones*, delayed security upgrades for subway and commuter rail systems could be paid for by twenty days' worth of Iraq war spending. Missing explosives screening for all U.S. passenger airlines could be covered by ten days' worth. Overdue security upgrades for 361 American airports could be covered by four days' worth" (Shapiro 2007, 58). The United States and its allies also needed to ensure that the focus on security neither bankrupted the nation nor caused the West to abandon its fundamental values (Shapiro 2007, 120).

The counterargument to this position came from neoconservatives such as David Frum (who wrote President George W. Bush's 2002 speech that coined the term "Axis of Evil") and Richard Perle (2003), as expressed in their book *An End to Evil: How to Win the War on Terror*. It is important to note that the arguments of the neoconservatives were diverse, as there were many different strands within this movement. But some key ideas stand out. The United States was the world's main military power, and conventional force still mattered. The United States needed to use this advantage to change the culture of the Middle East and to foster democracy in the region. At a time of extraordinary threats, neoconservatives suggested, the

United States could not be bound by conventional rules. The government could not know when an attack with weapons of mass destruction (WMDs) was imminent (Frum and Perle 2003, 34). Old ideas of security did not apply (see Vice President Dick Cheney's comments in Shapiro 2007, 16). Failed states could not be ignored: "There are places where law truly has collapsed and evil has moved to exploit the void: Yemen, Somalia, Sierra Leone" (Frum and Perle 2003, 118). It was better to fight the terrorists abroad rather than face them in the United States' own territory. (For a critique of the "Bush Doctrine," see Shapiro 2007, 15–31.) The key was not to try to win an ideological contest but rather to promote democracy—except in places where "Islamists" might win, as in Algeria in 1995 (Frum and Perle 2003, 158–63). Terrorists could not survive without the support of states (Frum and Perle 2003, 231). From this perspective, the war on terror entailed a war on states. And it had to be fought, even if it angered the United Nations or caused the United States to lose support among naive allies (Frum and Perle 2003, 243–50, 270–71). Neoconservative arguments shaped the U.S. government's decision to attack Iraq in the face of widespread international opposition. (For neoconservative arguments regarding Iraq, see Bollyn 2004; Project for the New American Century 1998.)

The U.S. invasion of Iraq took place without either a UN mandate or the support of the majority of the population of its traditional allies. For example, even though Britain sent troops to fight alongside U.S. soldiers, most British people opposed their country's involvement. Before the invasion, more than 1 million people turned out for an antiwar rally in London (British Broadcasting Corporation 2003). And two contemporaneous polls found, first, that only 9 percent of the Britons polled favored invading Iraq without a supporting UN resolution; and second, that no more than 29 percent of respondents favored the invasion even with UN support (ICM Research 2003a and 2003b). These numbers would probably have been lower in almost any other European country and not dissimilar in many key U.S. ally nations in Asia and the Pacific. The outcome of the war was a disaster. Although the U.S. quickly overthrew Saddam Hussein, it found no WMDs, and Iraqi society fractured into ethnic conflict. Even after U.S. forces withdrew, this violence did not end, and Al-Qaida now has a greater presence in Iraq than it did before the invasion. Equally serious, America's popularity plummeted in the Muslim world. One poll in 2003 found that 99 percent of Jordanians had a negative view of the United States (Pew Global Attitudes Project 2003; see also Pew Global Attitudes Project 2002). If the struggle against Al-Qaida required Muslim partners, that effort was endangered. In the end, the war of Afghanistan also dragged on, with the entire might of the U.S. military incapable of overcoming a force of thousands of guerrilla troops armed with technologically basic weapons. Because of the failure of traditional military forces to operate effectively, the United States has moved to the increasing use of new technologies, from a reliance on drone strikes to kill its opponents to the use of technology to monitor global communications. But these also raise human rights issues.

Human Rights

After 9/11, an intense debate began about the balance between human rights and security. Bush officials defended the use of "waterboarding," which they argued was not torture. There was some popular support for this position. Polls show that "57 percent of white evangelicals in the South believe torture can be justified. By comparison, an earlier poll by the Pew Research Center finds just 48 percent of the general public in support of torture" (Krattenmaker 2008, E-2). Support and opposition to the implementation of torture seemed to break down on the lines of political parties: "Nearly two-thirds of Republicans in this survey supported torture, in contrast with just 42 percent of Democrats" (Krattenmaker 2008, E-2). The American use of waterboarding and other forms of "extreme interrogation" raised concerns that the United States had violated the Geneva Convention by using torture, which not only was a moral crime but also might encourage other nations to use torture.

At the same time, deep concerns about personal-privacy issues began to emerge. Modern technology has made it possible to monitor almost all aspects of a person's life. While most people are familiar with the CIA, until recently, far fewer Americans were aware of the National Security Agency (NSA), even though its budget is larger (Todd and Bloch 2003, 75). This organization is charged with monitoring communication and electronic surveillance. The scope of its activities is impressive, as Paul Todd and Jonathan Bloch describe. International e-mails are routinely monitored (Todd and Bloch 2003, 43). But this is only the tip of the iceberg. Through a system called Echelon, the United States and its allies "intercept nonencrypted e-mail, fax, and telephone calls carried over the world's telecommunication systems" (Todd and Bloch 2003, 44). Software designed in the United States allegedly contains openings that permit intelligence services to view the contents of computers (Todd and Bloch 2003, 52).

Major American corporations have worked so closely with the NSA that the Bush administration lobbied for legislation to protect them from lawsuits for supporting these efforts (Lichtblau and Risen 2007). It is no surprise that thousands of Americans' phone calls to Latin America are tracked to "detect narcotics trafficking" (Lichtblau and Risen 2007). But some requests have worried telecommunications companies because of potential liability issues: "Executives at a Denver phone carrier, Qwest, refused in early 2001 to give the agency access to their most localized communications switches, which primarily carry domestic calls, according to people aware of the request, which has not been previously reported. They say the arrangement could have permitted neighborhood by neighborhood surveillance of phone traffic without a court order, which alarmed them" (Lichtblau and Risen 2007). Technological changes have been matched by legislative changes, increasing concerns about electronic surveillance. With the passage of the Patriot Act, critics worry that the firewalls between intelligence agencies directed abroad, such as the CIA, and domestic agencies, such as the Federal Bureau of Investigation, have eroded. Nor should these issues be thought of as a purely U.S. problem. Other Western powers, such as Britain, undertake similar activities (Todd and Bloch 2003, 63).

All of these issues came to a head after Edward Snowden, a contractor for the American corporation Booz Allen Hamilton who had worked for the NSA, leaked information on U.S. intelligence activities in 2013. In particular, Snowden revealed information about the NSA's monitoring of both telephone calls and Internet traffic. Snowden contacted England's *Guardian* newspaper late in 2012 and continued leaking information through his departure from his job in May 2013. When the revelations became public, they created a media firestorm, and Snowden fled abroad to Hong Kong seeking political shelter. He ultimately received asylum in Russia, where he now works as a security official for a Russian social media company. Throughout his extended fight to seek asylum, Snowdon found support from the organization Wikileaks. Publicly, Snowden has said that he did not seek to conceal his identity after acting, even though he knew the costs he would bear. He has made reference to the U.S. Constitution in order to justify his actions. For the United States, this was a diplomatic disaster, as Germany was infuriated that President Angela Merkel's phone was monitored, while Brazil was equally angry about the tapping of President Djilma Rousseff's calls. One of the disturbing aspects about Snowden's revelations was the extent to which people in the private sector have acquired security clearances that allow them access to critical information, seemingly with little oversight. Allegedly, Snowden had misinformation on his résumé, but Booz Allen Hamilton decided to hire him regardless (Reuters 2013). The fact that Snowden, a high school dropout who later acquired a GED, was able to obtain this level of access raised red flags (Reuters 2013). Who else was able to acquire information without proper vetting? To what extent has the privatization of security operations undermined the firewall protection of people's personal information? His experience also points to the power of nonstate organizations such as Wikileaks, which challenge states' ability to conceal security information. Ultimately, public opinion on Snowden has been divided; a German organization awarded him a "whistleblower" prize, while some Americans viewed him as a traitor. What is clear is that Snowden has changed the conversation about the balance between security and privatization.

Traditional Security Concerns

Although the war on terror currently shapes most scholarly discussions concerning the meaning of security, traditional security issues have not disappeared. Indeed, it is not clear that Al-Qaida is the main security threat to the Western nations. As Thérèse Delpech (2007, 111–75) has outlined, there are multiple flash points around the world and several security threats to world order. A renascent China now threatens to invade Taiwan should the island nation officially declare its independence, a step that would likely lead China into conflict with both the United States and Japan. Recently, China has come into conflict with a number of Southeast Asian states as well as Japan over land claims and sea-rights issues in Pacific waters. In South Asia, India and Pakistan continue their standoff over Kashmir, which brought the two nuclear powers to the brink of conflict in 2001 and 2002 (see Margolis 2002). Finally, there are a number of "rogue states," which are generally thought of as being countries that fail to adhere to certain key international standards of behavior, of which the most important is probably nuclear nonproliferation (Nincic 2005, 56–58).

The nightmare scenario is that a fragile nuclear state will collapse into anarchy, or that a faction within the state may sell nuclear technology. Both fears are particularly acute in the case of Pakistan, where the "father of the Pakistani bomb," A. Q. Khan, was later revealed to have been selling the technology to create nuclear weapons to the highest bidder, including Libya. The United States and Europe viewed Libya as a "rogue state" after the 1988 Lockerbie bombing of Pan Am Flight 103. Successful diplomacy by both Britain and the United States persuaded Libya in December 2003 to state that it would exchange its nuclear program (which was literally flown out of the country) for an end to its diplomatic isolation (Graham 2004, 13–14, 135; Naím 2005, 38–45). This effort succeeded and led to the unraveling of Khan's network—in particular the work of Swiss engineer Friedrich Tinner and his sons, who gave Pakistani weapons designs to Libya, Iran, and North Korea, according to the president of Switzerland (Broad and Sanger 2008). If Pakistan should collapse in revolution, people fear that its nuclear weapons could fall into the wrong hands. In this region, Realism retains both power and relevance as a framework.

Another major security concern is North Korea, which is the nation most commonly perceived as a rogue country largely because it appears to ignore international law and accords. In October 2006 North Korea also declared that it had successfully tested a nuclear weapon. It seems to have received support from Khan's network, in exchange for which it provided missile technology to Pakistan; clearly, Khan's network acted with support from the highest level of the Pakistani state (Graham 2004, 57, 139–40, 142).

North Korea's nuclear test threatened to destabilize the entire region, as South Korea, Japan, and even Taiwan could react to this threat by developing their own nuclear capabilities if North Korea's nuclear program continued to develop. The United States and Asian countries have engaged in a frustrating dialogue with the North Korean state but have had few successes. North Korea has faced both an economic crisis and a mass famine in the mid-1990s that likely killed "between 600,000 and 1 million" people (Goodkind and West 2001, 220). In such circumstances, North Korea has found its nuclear weapons and arms sales to be key means to ensure the resources that the nation needs to survive. From the North Korean perspective, Libya made a mistake by giving up its nuclear weapons program, which led to the downfall of the regime. Other nations—such as Iran—are also the focus of attention because of concerns about their nuclear programs. People in the Middle East ask why Western powers worry so much about regional states acquiring nuclear weapons and so little about Israel's nuclear stockpile.

Although these traditional security concerns ensure that Realism retains its power as an analytical framework, technology also has changed security issues in ways that challenge this older paradigm. One of the most likely means for an outside enemy to attack the United States would be an online hacking of critical infrastructure, such as the energy grid. Military forces may not be the best way to address this challenge. The United

States worries about its ability to keep critical information secure against the threat of hacking by both outside states and nonstate organizations such as Wikileaks. In Iraq and Afghanistan, the immense military power of the United States was unable to obtain many of the nation's goals. As a result, the United States is increasingly relying on drone strikes to pursue the leadership of Al-Qaida and the Taliban. It's also possible that Western allies hacked Iranian computers in order to destroy centrifuges critical to the Iranian nuclear effort. Such cyberattacks entail a different infrastructure than traditional military forces. This shift changes the dynamics of military encounters in a way that older paradigms do not address. How do we think of security in traditional terms when the enemy uses software as a means of attack, or our military personnel are stationed in Nevada while carrying out an attack in western Pakistan?

All security issues ultimately raise the question of fear. On the one hand, there are serious threats to global security, and people are right to be afraid. But how dangerous are these threats to individuals in comparison to the other dangers of daily life? Are security fears manipulated for political ends? And how do we weigh our fear of possible enemy attacks against concerns that we may lose our liberties? It is true that technology is making the development of horrific weapons possible, particularly biological agents. The potential devastation is so severe that it might justify extreme security measures. But some authors, such as Philipp Sarasin, the author of *Anthrax: Bioterror as Fact and Fantasy* (2006), have argued that the risks are overblown. If the threat is truly so great, why has the United States refused to support an international treaty to constrain the development of biological weapons (Sarasin 2006, 130–31; Graham 2004, 124)? Other authors argue that it may be far more difficult for terrorists to obtain nuclear weapons than is generally believed (Shapiro 2007, 65). This position is controversial (Sloan 2005, 26–27; Graham 2004, 15, 125–32; Falkenrath, Newman, and Thayer 1998). Still, the fears of a nuclear or biological attack must be weighed against the human-rights costs of surveillance (9/11 Commission 2004, 393–95).

In part, your vision of how you choose to view security will depend on the extent to which you believe new technologies and globalizations have changed the threats that we face. The September 11 attacks could not have taken place without globalization, which permitted the flow of money, people, and ideologies that underpinned the attack. Similarly, new technologies, some argue, have put unprecedented power into the hands of small groups rather than states. From this perspective, the war against

terrorism is the defining security issue of our age. But if you look globally at the security threats that we face, you might argue that the greatest
danger remains traditional military conflict between states. In this case, it
may be that the older theory of Realism still represents the best framework
to understand global affairs. In contrast, proponents of human security
might argue that their theory represents the best lens through which to
view a multiplicity of security issues, given the complexity of current world
affairs. But both of these approaches will need to address how technology
is reshaping security issues.

Demography and Conflict

In addition to these theories, other disciplines also speak to issues involving security. Of these, the most important is probably demography, which
is the academic study of populations by mathematical means. Because
changes in human populations have major effects on the demand for resources and the power of states, demographic trends within nations and
regions are of broad interest. But the relationship between security and
demography is complex. In the 1970s, many authors—influenced by the
nineteenth-century British thinker Thomas Malthus—looked at the rapid
increase in the global population and predicted disaster. It would be impossible to feed 6 billion people by the end of the century. They predicted
that governments would break down as hunger became widespread, and
conflicts would sweep the globe. This did not happen (Urdal 2005, 418).
But after 2000, other scholars began to argue again that population growth
and resource scarcity would herald a new period of conflict as governments
faced internal unrest. Careful studies have failed to find any statistical evidence of this effect, which is reassuring. Indeed, in some circumstances,
rapid population growth seems to correlate with a decreased risk of conflict (Urdal 2005, 420, 430). However, this does not mean that population
changes do not impact security questions but only that context is everything. (For a look at demography and conflict as an emerging field, see
Brunborg and Tabeau 2005.)

Research has found that population growth does not lead to conflict in
cases in which there is commensurate economic growth or the presence
of a strong and legitimate state. Environmental destruction also does not
increase the risk of conflict in and of itself, whether in cases were there is
a shortage of arable land or a lack of water. But other demographic changes
can increase the risk of conflict, such as "rapid growth in the labor force

in slow-growing economies, a rapid increase in educated youth aspiring to elite positions when such positions are scarce, unequal population growth rates between different ethnic groups, urbanization that exceeds employment growth, and migrations that change the local balance among major ethnic groups" (Goldstone 2002, 5). These findings are important because the world will undergo rapid population growth over the next half century and understanding these trends may help to predict those areas that will be placed under the greatest strain. And some of the effects can be quite dramatic, as in one study that found that "the risk of political crisis nearly doubled in countries with above-average levels of urbanization but below-average levels of GDP/capita" (Goldstone 2002, 10). This research also highlights factors that mitigate conflict. For example, migration often serves as a key safety valve to prevent conflict, which appears to have been the case with many Pacific island nations (Ware 2005). With sea-level rise, some populations will become climate refugees. In July 2014 Kiribati purchased eight square miles of higher land from Figi, 1,200 miles away, as a hedge. How will climate refugees create security issues for Australia or New Zealand as Pacific islands are flooded? Will migration still provide a release valve for nations if their landmass is shrinking?

Of all these demographic trends, two are of particular importance. First, due to sex selection during pregnancy, many Asian nations—in particular, China, India, Pakistan, and Taiwan—have a surfeit of males. In other words, parents abort female daughters to ensure that their families will have sons in large numbers of cases. The result is that the sex ratio in these nations is widely skewed, which means that many young men have little hope of finding marriage partners, particularly when they are at the bottom of the socioeconomic scale. Because the dearth of women is so large—certainly tens of millions, and perhaps 100 million—this is a broad social problem. Historically, societies in which this has been the case have been particularly prone to violence, both because these men are more prone to rebellion and because governments may view conflicts as a useful means to free the state from these dangerous individuals (Hudson and Den Boer 2002) For this reason, the skewed demography of some major Asian states leads to concerns about Asia's future, both in terms of the maintenance of democracy and the potential for security crises.

A second demographic trend that merits interest is the rapid population decline in many nations that were key powers in the mid-twentieth century. This is particularly the case in Japan, which has seen a dramatic decline in fertility rates since 1973. The reasons for this are complex—more women in the workplace, a greater age at marriage, and the high financial cost of children—and the government has tried to address these questions, even going so far as to subsidize dating services. But these actions have not changed the trend. Japan's population will decline by 14 percent by 2050 (Retherford and Ogawa 2005, 25). The government could address this challenge with immigration, but this is politically unlikely because of the scale of the changes it would entail. If the current fertility rate were to "continue for a long time into the future, [it] would result in a population decline of approximately 38 percent per generation, which is approximately every 30 years. Were that gap to be filled with immigration, a large majority of Japan's population would be foreign-born after only two generations, and Japan would be a very different nation from what it is today" (Retherford and Ogawa 2005, 35). As a result, not only will Japan's population be shrinking, but it will also be aging. This will result in an inverted population period in which there are more elderly people than children. Japan now sells more diapers for adults than for children.

Japan's example is more extreme than most other nations, but it is not unique. Other countries, such as Italy and Russia, are facing a similar demographic decline. This will inevitably lead to a decline in their relative power, as they have less manpower for the military and little funds left over from the demands for pensions and elder care. On the other side of the demographic equation, nations such as Nigeria are facing a spectacular rise in population. It is true that population growth in and of itself does not lead to conflict. But these demographic trends will shift power away from Europe and Japan to Asia and Africa, and to a lesser extent to Latin America. This context already informs policy debates, from how the United Nations should be structured to which world regions may be vulnerable to conflict. How scholars view the likely impact of these trends depends not only on the particular view of security that they hold but also upon an understanding of demography.

Conclusion

Debates about security may seem abstract or distant from your life. This chapter may seem less accessible than later chapters in this book, in that it is harder to make an emotional connection to this topic. There is a "psychic numbing" that comes with security concerns (Lifton 1993, 82, 208). The threats seem so large, the possibilities so horrific, and the danger so beyond the capacity of ordinary people to absorb that there is a tendency to tune these questions out. This may be difficult to do for someone of Middle Eastern descent, who may be reminded of security issues every time she or he passes through the security line at a U.S. airport. But this issue affects everyone, from people who choose not to fly because they are always selected for a search to citizens making judgments about their government's policies during elections.

In times of fear, people turn to the state to protect them. Who defines security issues? Who decides how to respond and how to balance legitimate security needs against human rights? What threats are real, and what responses are excessive? The United States began to use torture (such as waterboarding) on non-American prisoners after 9/11 (Sanos 2009). The United States also has used rendition to deliver prisoners to its allies for torture, which has created a globalized network of terror. We often associate torture with nondemocratic and premodern states, but it is now linked to the world's richest democratic country. But there is no legislative framework to define the United States' use of state terror and extrajudicial killing, such as through drone strikes in Middle Eastern countries. Many other Western states have greatly increased the resources and power of their intelligence agencies since 9/11, from New Zealand to Britain. Some Western nations tolerate other countries spying on their own citizens because by sharing information with one another, countries can gain intelligence on domestic targets that their own national intelligence services would be prohibited from targeting. New technologies allow the NSA and equivalent intelligence services to monitor entire populations' texting, Facebook usage, e-mail, and phone calls to create comprehensive information (metadata) on a nation's electronic activities. The United States is not unique in this surveillance.

Countries ceded these powers to their intelligence services—and created a globalized network of intelligence sharing—because there is a real threat from terrorism, as events both before and after 9/11 demonstrated. And terrorism is not the only threat that people face, a fact used by countries to justify such intelligence gathering. For example, technology allows states or criminals to launch cyberattacks on everything from the cloud to financial systems. Of course, people in developing countries might fear other threats. As a citizen, it is important for you to be informed and to be aware of the government's actions. Otherwise, we are only working with the government's definition of security and hoping that it will always make the best choices for us. Every security decision entails high-stakes ethical choices that are so complex that security has remained the most difficult international and moral issue since the time of Thucydides. As such, we all need to be informed about security issues and to think about how these questions affect us. What are you afraid of? How do you want your government to make you more secure? What liberties are you willing to trade in order to have more security? You may or may not agree with the perspective presented in this chapter. How do you think about security in a way that reflects your own values? And how do some approaches to security—such as Realism and human security—highlight or conceal certain issues?

➤ VOCABULARY

psychic numbing	Realism
NSA	human security
rogue states	constructivism
NGOs	realpolitik
WMDs	failed states
liberalism	zones of peace and zones
neoconservatism	of turmoil
pandemic	

➤ DISCUSSION AND REFLECTION QUESTIONS

1 *How would you define Realism, the theory that dominated security scholarship from the 1940s until 1991?*

2 *What is a failed state?*

3 *What is political scientist Samuel Huntington's core thesis?*

4 *What do some members of the humanitarian-relief community fear will happen if foreign aid is allocated according to security issues?*

5 *What are two central tenets of neoconservative views on the United States and the world?*

6 *What is the relationship between electronic surveillance, human rights, and security?*

7 *What does Delpech mean when she uses the phrase "multiple flash points" regarding threats to world order?*

8 *Why does demography matter when discussing security issues? What demographic trends will shape security issues in the future?*

ACTIVITY 1 Examine the security map at the beginning of the chapter. What general observation can you make about countries deemed critical to U.S. national security? Are there any patterns you can identify? What countries have been identified as major illicit drug-producing countries? How are these nation-states linked to national security?

ACTIVITY 2 Use the following questions as prompts to help you begin to articulate your personal views on security. What are you afraid of? How do you want your government to make you more secure? What security issues matter most to you? How have you come to hold these beliefs? Write for about twenty minutes, answering each of the four questions.

ACTIVITY 3 Think about contrasts between Realism and human security perspectives. Identify one aspect of each. Stephen Legomsky (2005) suggests that recent U.S. security strategies have increasingly targeted or singled out aliens—immigrants or undocumented workers—through the process of profiling. Does this process strike you as being linked more to the Realism perspective or the human security perspective? Why?

References

Anderson, B. 2006. *Imagined communities: Reflections on the origin and spread of nationalism.* London: Verso.

Axworthy, L. 2004. A new scientific field and policy lens. *Security Dialogue* 35:348–49.

Bapat, N. A., D. Ertley, C. Hall, and M. Lancaster. 2007. Perfect allies? The case of Iraq and Al-Quaeda. *International Studies Perspectives* 8:272–86.

Bawer, B. 2006. *While Europe slept: How radical Islam is destroying the West from within.* New York: Doubleday.

Bernton, H., M. Carter, D. Heath, and J. Neff. 2002. The terrorist within. *Seattle Times,* A-6. July 22.

Bollyn, C. 2004. America "Pearl Harbored." Retrieved January 26, 2008, from http://www.americanfreepress.net/12_24_02/America_Pearl_Harbored/america_pearl_harbored.html.

Bottici, C., and B. Challand. 2006. Rethinking political myth: The clash of civilizations as a self-fulfilling prophecy. *European Journal of Social Theory* 9:315–36.

British Broadcasting Corporation. 1997. Tourists massacred at temple. Retrieved January 8, 2008, from http://news.bbc.co.uk/2/hi/32179.stm.

————. 2003. Anti-war rally leaves its mark. Retrieved December 24, 2007, from http://news.bbc.co.uk/2/hi/uk_news/2767761.stm.

Broad, W. J., and D. Sanger. 2008. In nuclear net's undoing, a web of shadowy deals. *New York Times.* August 25.

Brown, M. E., ed. 2003. *Grave new world: Security challenges in the 21st century.* Washington, D.C.: Georgetown University Press.

Brunborg, H., and E. Tabeau. 2005. Demography of conflict and violence: an emerging field. *European Journal of Population* 21 (2/3): 131–44.

Bueno de Mesquita, B., R. M. Siverson, and G. Woller. 1992. War and the fate of regimes: A comparative analysis. *American Political Science Review* 86 (3): 638–46.

Burkeman, O., and J. Borger. 2003. War critics astonished as U.S. hawk admits invasion was illegal. *The Guardian.* November 20. Retrieved January 26, 2008, from http://www.guardian.co.uk/Iraq/Story/0,2763,1089158,00.html.

Buzan, B. 2004. A reductionist, idealistic notion that adds little analytical value. *Security Dialogue* 35:369–70.

Carr, E. H. 2001; originally published, 1939. *The twenty years' crisis.* Introduction by Michael Carr. New York: Palgrave.

Delpech, T. 2007. *Savage century: Back to barbarism.* Trans. George Holoch. Washington, D.C.: Carnegie Endowment for International Peace.

Elbe, S. 2006. Should HIV/AIDS be securitized? The ethical dilemmas of linking HIV/AIDS and security. *International Studies Quarterly* 50 (1): 119–45.

Falkenrath, R., R. D. Newman, and B. A. Thayer. 1998. *America's Achilles' heel: Nuclear, biological, and chemical terrorism and covert attack.* Cambridge, Mass.: MIT Press.

Farley, M. 2007. Watchdog tells Iran it must do more to assuage nuclear fears. *Oregonian,* A-17. November 23.

Foreign Affairs Canada. 2006. *Human security for an urban century: Local challenges, global perspectives.* Ottawa: Foreign Affairs Canada. Available at: www.humansecurity-cities.org/page119.htm.

Frum, D., and R. Perle. 2003. *An end to evil: How to win the war on terror.* New York: Random House.

Fukuyama, F. 1989. The end of history? *National Interest* 16:3–18.

————. 2006. *America at the crossroads: Democracy, power, and the neoconservative legacy.* New Haven, Conn.: Yale University Press.

Ganshof, F. L. 1971. *The middle ages: A history of international relations.* Trans. Remy Inglis Hall. New York: Harper and Row.

Gerges, F. A. 1999. *America and political Islam: Clash of cultures or clash of interests?* Cambridge, UK: Cambridge University Press.

Gleditsch, K. S., and M. D. Ward. 2000. War and peace in space and time: The role of democratization. *International Studies Quarterly* 44 (1): 1–29.

Goldstone, J. A. 2002. Population and security: How demographic change can lead to violent conflict. *Journal of International Affairs* 56 (1): 3–20.

Goodkind, D., and L. West. 2001. The North Korean famine and its demographic impact. *Population and Development Review* 27 (2): 219–38.

Gordon, P. H. 2007. Can the war on terror be won? *Foreign Affairs* 86 (6): 53–66.

Gosik, A. 2007. Obesity in kids called a security risk for US. *Oregonian*, A-8. November 4.

Graham, T., Jr. 2004. *Common sense on weapons of mass destruction*. Seattle: University of Washington Press.

Gros, J. G. 1996. Towards a taxonomy of failed states in the new world order: Decaying Somalia, Liberia, Rwanda, and Haiti. *Third World Quarterly* 17 (3): 455–71.

Helman, G. B., and S. R. Ratner. 1992–93. Saving failed states. *Foreign Policy* 89 (Winter): 3–20.

Hobbes, T. 1982. *Leviathan*. Oxford: Blackwell.

Holsti, O. R. 2008. *To see ourselves as others see us: How publics abroad view the United States after 9/11*. Ann Arbor: University of Michigan Press.

Hudson, V. M., and A. Den Boer. 2002. A surplus of men, a deficit of peace: Security and sex ratios in Asia's largest states. *International Security* 26 (4): 5–38.

Huntington, S. P. 1993. The clash of civilizations? *Foreign Affairs* 72 (3): 22–49.

———. 1996. *The clash of civilizations and the remaking of world order*. New York: Touchstone.

ICM Research. 2003a. Iraq poll, 1. Retrieved December 24, 2007, from http://www.icmresearch.co.uk/pdfs/2003_february_iraq_britain_decides_iraq_poll.pdf.

———. 2003b. *Guardian* opinion poll, 9. Retrieved December 24, 2007, from http://www.icmresearch.co.uk/pdfs/2003_february_guardian_february_poll.pdf.

———. 2006. Opinion poll, 4–5. Retrieved December 24, 2007, from http://www.icmresearch.co.uk/pdfs/2006_july_guardian_july_poll.pdf.

Jackson, R., and G. Sorenson. 1999. *Introduction to international relations*. New York: Oxford University Press.

Kacowicz, A. M. 2005. Globalization and poverty: Possible links, different explanations. *Whitehead Journal of Diplomacy and International Relations* 6 (2): 111–27.

Kennedy, P. 1989. *The rise and fall of the great powers*. New York: Vintage.

Keohane, R. O., and J. S. Nye. 2001. *Power and interdependence*. 3rd ed. New York: Longman.

Krattenmaker, T. 2008. Faith takes back seat to power and politics. *Oregonian*, E-1. October 19.

Kupchan, C. A. 2002. *The end of the American era: U.S. foreign policy and the geopolitics of the twenty-first century*. New York: Random House.

Lake, D. A. 1992. Powerful pacifists: Democratic states and war. *American Political Science Review* 86 (March): 24–37.

Legomsky, S. 2005. The ethnic and religious profiling of non-citizens: National security and international human rights. *Boston College Third World Law Journal* 25 (1): 1–36.

Lichtblau, E., and J. Risen. 2007. NSA relies deeply on businesses. *Oregonian*, A-4. December 16.

Lifton, R. J. 1993. *The protean self: Human resilience in an age of fragmentation.* New York: Basic Books.

Lucassen, L. 2005. *The immigrant threat: The integration of old and new migrants in Western Europe since 1850.* Urbana: University of Illinois Press.

MacFarlane, S. N., and Y. F. Khong. 2006. *Human security and the UN: A critical history.* Bloomington: Indiana University Press.

Margolis, E. 2002. *War at the top of the world: The struggle for Afghanistan, Kashmir, and Tibet.* New York: Routledge.

Mason, T. D. 2003. Globalization, democratization, and the prospects for civil war in the new millennium. *International Studies Review* 5:19–35.

McRae, R. G., and D. Hubert. 2001. *Human security and the new diplomacy: Protecting people, promoting peace.* Montreal: McGill-Queen's University Press.

Mitchell, S., S. McLaughlin, S. Gates, and H. Hegre. 1999. Evolution in democracy-war dynamics. *Journal of Conflict Resolution* 43 (6): 771–92.

Monaghan, P. 2008. Beyond bullets and borders: "Human security" advocates call for a different approach to global problems. *Chronicle of Higher Education* 54 (42): B-8. June 27.

Monten, J. 2006. Thucydides and modern realism. *International Studies Quarterly* 50 (March): 3–26.

Morgenthau, H. J. 1948. *Politics among nations: The struggle for power and peace.* New York: Knopf.

Morris, B. 2008. Using bombs to stave off war. *New York Times*, A-19. July 18.

Naím, M. 2005. *Illicit: How smugglers, traffickers, and copycats are hijacking the global economy.* New York: Doubleday.

Newman, E. 2001. Visions of international studies: Human security and constructivism. *International Studies Perspectives* 2 (3): 239–51.

Nincic, M. 2005. *Renegade regimes: Confronting deviant behavior in world politics.* New York: Columbia University Press.

9/11 Commission. 2004. *The 9/11 commission report.* New York: W. W. Norton & Company.

Nowosielski, R. 2006. *911: Press for truth.* Documentary film. New York: Banded Artists/Standard Issue Films.

Nye, J. S., Jr., and J. D. Donahue, eds. 2000. *Governance in a globalizing world.* Washington, D.C.: Brookings Institute Press.

O'Neal, J. R., and B. Russett. 1999. The Kantian peace: The pacific benefits of democracy, interdependence, and international organizations, 1885–1992. *World Politics* 52:1–37.

Owen, T. 2004. Human security: Conflict, critique, and consensus; Colloquium remarks and proposal for a threshold-based definition. *Security Dialogue* 35:373–87.

Paris, R. 2001. Human security: Paradigm shift or hot air. *International Security* 26 (Fall): 87–102.

Peterson, S. 2002–2003. Epidemic disease and national security. *Security Studies* 12:43–81.

Pew Global Attitudes Project. 2001. America admired, yet its new vulnerability seen as good thing, say opinion leaders. Retrieved January 9, 2008, from http://pewglobal.org/reports/print.php?PageID=62.

———. 2002. What the world thinks in 2002: How global publics view: Their lives, their countries, the world, America. Retrieved January 9, 2008, from http://pewglobal.org/reports/display.php?ReportID=165.

———. 2003. Views of a changing world 2003: War with Iraq further divides global politics. Retrieved January 24, 2008, from http://pewglobal.org /reports/display.php?ReportID=185.

———. 2005. U.S. image up slightly, but still negative: American character gets mixed review. June 23. Retrieved March 21, 2010, from http://pewglobal.org /reports/display.php?ReportID=247.

———. 2006. Muslims in Europe: Economic worries top concerns about religious and cultural identity. Retrieved January 25, 2008, from http:// pewglobal.org/reports/display.php?ReportID=254.

Project for the New American Century. 1998. Letter to president Clinton on Iraq. Retrieved January 26, 2008, from http://www.newamericancentury.org /iraqclintonletter.htm.

Rapley, J. 2006. The new middle ages: Gangsters' paradise. *Foreign Affairs* 85 (May/June): 95–104.

Retherford, R., and N. Ogawa. 2005. Japan's baby bust: Causes, implications, and policy responses. East-West Center Working Paper. Population and Health Series 118, 1–44.

Reuters. 2013. Booz Allen hired Snowden despite discrepancies in his résumé. *South China Morning Post.* Retrieved June 22, 2013, from http://www.scmp .com/news/world/article/1266209/booz-allen-hired-snowden-despite-discrepancies-his-resume.

Ripsman, N. M., and T. V. Paul. 2004. Globalization and the national security state: A framework for analysis. *International Studies Review* 7:199–227.

Rummel, R. J. 1983. Libertarianism and international violence. *Journal of Conflict Resolution* 27:27–71.

———. 1991. *The conflict helix: Principles and practices of interpersonal, social, and international conflict and cooperation.* New Brunswick, N.J.: Transaction Publishers.

Russett, B. M., J. R. O'Neal, and M. Cox. 2000. Clash of civilizations, or realism and liberalism déjà vu? Some evidence. *Journal of Peace Research* 37 (5): 583–608.

Said, E. W. 2001. The clash of ignorance. *Nation*, www.thenation.com/doc /20011022/said. October 22.

Sanos, P. 2009. *Torture team: Rumsfeld's memo and the betrayal of American values.* New York: Palgrave.

Sarasin, P. 2006. *Anthrax: Bioterror as fact and fantasy.* Trans. Giselle Weiss. Cambridge, Mass.: Harvard University Press.

Shanker, T. 2008. Command for Africa established by Pentagon. *New York Times,* A-5. October 5.

Shanker, T., and S. Myers. 2007. Reassessments reflect fear of Taliban Rise. *Oregonian,* A-2. December 16.

Shapiro, I. 2007. *Containment: Rebuilding a strategy against global terror.* Princeton, N.J.: Princeton University Press.

Sheehan, M. 2005. *International security: An analytical survey.* Boulder, Colo.: Lynn Reiner.

Shore, Z. 2006. *Breeding Bin Ladens: America, Islam, and the future of Europe.* Baltimore: Johns Hopkins University Press.

Shuster, M. 2008. Missile defense aimed at potential threats. National Public Radio. September 22. Retrieved December 4, 2008, from www.npr.org/templates/story/story.php?storyID=94838546.

Singer, M., and A. Wildavsky. 1993. *The real world order: Zones of peace, zones of turmoil.* Chatham, N.J.: Chatham House.

Sloan, E. C. 2005. *Security and defense in the terrorist era: Canada and North America.* Montreal: McGill-Queen's University Press.

Sobek, D. 2005. Machiavelli's legacy: Domestic politics and international conflict. *International Studies Quarterly* 49:179–204.

Thomas, C. 2001. Global governance, development, and human security. *Third World Quarterly* 22 (January): 159–75.

Thucydides. 1972. *History of the Peloponnesian War.* Trans. R. Warner. Harmondsworth, UK: Penguin.

Todd, P., and J. Bloch. 2003. *Global intelligence: The world's secret services today.* New York: Zed Books.

Tusicisny, A. 2004. Civilizational conflicts: More frequent, longer, and bloodier. *Journal of Peace Research* 41 (4): 485–98.

United Nations Development Programme. 1994. *Human development report.* Oxford: Oxford University Press.

U.S. Department of State Bureau of International Information Programs. 2006. U.S. embassy bombings. Retrieved January 8, 2008, from http://usinfo.state.gov/is/international_security/terrorism/embassy_bombings.html.

U.S. District Court, Southern District of New York. 2001. *United States v. Mokhtar Haouari,* no. S4 00 Cr. 15, 573.

Urdal, H. 2005. People vs. Malthus: Population pressure, environmental degradation, and armed conflict. *Journal of Peace Research* 42 (4): 417–34.

Verton, D. 2003. *Black ice: The invisible threat of cyberterrorism.* Toronto: McGraw-Hill.

Waltz, K. N. 1959. *Man, the state, and war.* New York: Columbia University Press.

Ware, H. 2005. Demography, migration, and conflict in the Pacific. *Journal of Peace Research* 42 (4): 435–54.

Woods, D. 2003. Bringing geography back in: Civilizations, wealth, and poverty. *International Studies Review* 5 (3): 343–54.

Wright, Robin. 2008. Tape links North Korea to Syrian reactor. *Oregonian*, A-9. April 24.

Youde, Jeremy. 2005. Enter the fourth horseman: Health security and international relations theory. *Whitehead Journal of Diplomacy and International Relations* 6 (Winter–Spring): 193–208.

EIGHT **Food**

➤ **SYNOPSIS**

Following a broad introduction to multiple global issues linked to
food, this chapter traces historical origins, current concerns, and
critical issues associated specifically with chocolate, coffee, and sugar.
Child labor, fair trade, genetic modification of crops, industry monitoring, monocropping, worker migration, biopiracy, and slavery are
examined. The chapter also discusses various partnerships for the
export and marketing of particular products.

➤ **SCAFFOLDING**

As you read through this chapter, think about how you would answer
each of the questions below.

How often do you think about the food choices you make?

Do you know the origins of the food you eat on a regular basis?

*How do terms like commodity speculation, biopiracy, and slavery relate
to food, values, and agriculture?*

*As you read descriptions about causes of food-related issues, think about
how the information is presented and supported. Does it seem sufficient?*

➤ **CORE CONCEPTS**

*How does a globalized food economy change the types of food people
consume?*

What is a food commodity chain?

*How do the products of chocolate, coffee, and sugar provide a way
to understand the broader implications of globalization?*

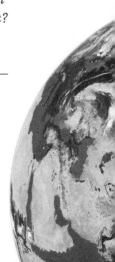

*How can context-specific agriculture education systems such as the Field
School Method allow farmers to spend less money to manage their crops?*

*How does your ability to make informed food choices affect farmers around
the globe?*

Everyone has to eat. Our connections to our daily bread, rice, tortillas,
or chapatis reflect a complicated chain from producer to consumer.
Heintzman and Solomon (2004, 6) remind us: "[F]ood lies at the cross-
road where global issues meet personal choice, where we all quite literally taste the world around us. Every bit of food connects us, however
unconsciously, to systems and debate about fat and famine, mad cows
and GMOs [genetically modified organisms], global trade regulations and
subsidies, pesticides and collapsing food stocks." Scientists now believe
that climate change will deeply affect the food we consume and crop yields.
The United Nation's Intergovernmental Panel on Climate Change recently
published a study suggesting that heat waves may harm sensitive crops,
and that crop production will be reduced by roughly 2 percent per decade,
resulting in about a 20 percent reduction by the end of the twenty-first
century (Gillis 2013). Typically, there is an inequality between what the
Global North produces and consumes and what the Global South produces
and consumes. This leads to more challenges for some than for others. In
the Global North, the middle class generally has access to sufficient food
to avoid problems of starvation and malnutrition, but for others in the
United States today, economic pressures—including shifting gas prices
and a lingering recession—have contributed to an increased dependency
on local food banks and government support.

Such dependency, however, comes nowhere close to the food issues affecting people in the Global South. In 2007 people all over the world paid
40 percent more for food than in the previous year (Millstone and Lang
2008, 160). In places like Rwanda and Tajikistan, close to three-quarters
of each family's income went toward food expenses during this same
time period (Millstone and Lang 2008, 18). There is also a clear pattern of
inequality between where food is produced and where the population is
most dense. Millstone and Lang (2008, 20) indicate that "chronic under-
nutrition is not a consequence of overall scarcity, but of unequal access
to land, technology and employment opportunities, coupled with a whole
range of socioeconomic and environmental factors." Some of these factors

include inequality in food distribution as described above, competition between biofuel needs and human-consumption needs, availability of water, food security, and food contamination. Other structural factors include a shift from producing food locally for local needs to producing export crops for the global market. Pollan (2008, 14) describes a global food economy based on inexpensive fuel:

> More recently, cheap energy has underwritten a globalized food economy in which it makes (or rather, made) economic sense to catch salmon in Alaska, ship it to China to be filleted, and ship the fillets back to California to be eaten; or one in which California and Mexico can profitably swap tomatoes back and forth across the border; or Denmark and the United States can trade sugar cookies across the Atlantic. About that particular swap the economist Herman Daly once quipped, "Exchanging recipes would surely be more efficient."

If we move to identify the actual cost of producing and marketing food products, it is necessary to look at the carbon and water cost: planting, harvesting, transportation, shipping, and distribution. Another dimension of true cost identification is to look at how a product has been subsidized. In many developed countries, agricultural dimensions of the GATT/TRIPS (Agreement on Trade-Related Aspects of Intellectual Property Rights) provisions allow for heavy subsidizing of foodstuffs. World Bank and IMF conditionality provisions do not permit countries receiving assistance to provide these same subsidies to their own farmers.

This chapter will not explicitly address more than an introduction to the issue of potable water for consumption and agriculture. No agricultural issue can be understood without knowledge of the role of water in production and how access to water is a local, regional, and global issue. The UN chose not to make "water" one of its individual development goals in its *Millennium Report*. The reason for this is that water underlies all of the goals and issues addressed.

In 2004 Rwandans spent an average of 72 percent of their disposable consumer income on food. In the United States that year, consumers spent only 14 percent of their disposable income on food (Millstone and Lange, 2008, 18, 19). Can you estimate what percentage of your disposable income you spend on food?

In a recent article, Lester Brown (2013) made the argument that the real threat to our future is "peak water." Brown suggests that this topic should gain as much attention as "Peak Oil" (see chapter 10) because globally, people have extracted water from aquifers more rapidly than it has been possible for them to replenish it, which is causing a major environmental crisis. Saudi Arabia, in particular, has drawn down its water reserves rapidly: "After being self-sufficient in wheat for over 20 years, the Saudis announced in early 2008 that, with their aquifers largely depleted, they would reduce wheat planting by one-eighth each year until 2016, when production would end. By then, Saudi Arabia projects it will be importing some 15m tonnes [metric tons] of wheat, rice, corn, and barley to feed its 30 million people. It is the first country to publicly project how aquifer depletion will shrink its grain harvest" (Brown 2013). Brown makes the point that water depletion is also a major problem in China, India, and the United States. Still, it is in the Middle East that the change is happening most quickly. In Yemen, for example, some aquifers are falling six feet a year, and "grain production has fallen by nearly half over the last 40 years." While the Saudis are reducing grain production as part of a plan, Yemen is doing so simply because the water is no longer available. There is no global infrastructure in place to redress these imbalances, nor is there any indication that individual nation-states will do so.

Water raises larger issues of social equity and the ability of people to meet this basic need. Unfortunately, as we will see in the section of this chapter focusing on the food commodity chains of coffee, chocolate, and sugar, we are not yet moving toward greater equality in access to foodstuffs, nor are we making sustainable plans for how to harvest and market food crops. Forced labor in both the chocolate and sugar industries remains a little-known fact to most consumers. Our ability to redress imbalances due to our global interconnectedness is fueling greater food safety and security issues than ever before.

Before examining any of these products, it is necessary to clarify what is meant by the term "commodity chain." Commodity chains, first defined by Hopkins and Wallerstein in 1977, are analyzed by "tak[ing] an ultimate consumable item and trac[ing] back the set of inputs that culminated in this item—the prior transformations, the raw materials, the transportation mechanisms, the labor input into each of the material processes, the food inputs into the labor. This linked set of processes we call a commodity chain" (128). With respect to food products, the commodity chain would

Table 4 Global Food Issues

	In This Chapter			On Your Own		
	Cacao/Cocoa	Coffee	Sugar	Quinoa	Rice	Bananas
Commodity speculation, global supply and demand		•		•	•	•
Monoculture crops for export	•	•		•		•
Fair labor practices, human trafficking, child labor	•	•	•			
Industry monitoring (private companies, regional cartels)	•	•				
Fair trade	•	•		•		•
Niche marketing	•	•		•		
Sustainable practices	•	•		•		
Worker migration issues			•			
Biopiracy					•	
Shifting consumption patterns			•	•	•	•
Genetic modification issues			•	•	•	•
Private/public/NGO partnerships	•	•		•		
Global/local continuum issues				•		

begin with the acquisition of seeds and, potentially, fertilizers and chemicals, then move through to harvesting, marketing, and distribution phases.

Through the lenses of what are no doubt some of your favorite foods, it is possible to explore some of the most pressing global issues of the twenty-first century. In each case, we begin with a historical overview of connections between peoples and products looking at both producers and consumers. We look at critical issues with respect to these products, challenging you as a reader to identify your own thoughts about them. Table 4 shows the myriad of issues interconnected with the food products discussed in this chapter. Many of the terms you will see are probably not familiar to you. We hope that, by the end of the chapter, this will no longer be the case.

Health claims have been made about the "magic elixir" properties of chocolate and coffee for more than 400 years. While consumers of chocolate and coffee are found all over the world, the central producing region for these products is a belt around the Equator. The next forty years of climate change will determine whether this pattern changes.

Chocolate

History

Throughout Mexico and Central America, archaeologists have found ancient remains of cacao trees, as well as vessels with cacao seeds in them. The cacao beans served both as a source for a chocolate beverage believed to have healing properties and as a form of currency. Excavated sites suggest a long link between both consumption and trade use of cacao on the part of cultures such as the Maya and the Olmecs. Lopez (2002) cites historical data confirming cacao trade routes between Costa Rica, Nicaragua, and Mexico that even Columbus was familiar with. Archaeologists also have discovered traces of cacao in sites in El Salvador (590 A.D.), Honduras (2000 B.C.–1000 A.D.), and Guatemala (500 A.D.) (Lopez 2002, 30–45).

In Mexico, legend has it that cacao was a gift from the god Quetzalcaotl. When the explorer Hernán Cortés arrived in Mexico in the early 1500s, some Aztecs may have believed him to be a reincarnation of Qeutzalcaotl. In spite of attempts on the part of the indigenous peoples to welcome him, Cortez was ultimately responsible for the political demise of the Aztec chief Montezuma. In approximately 1528, Cortez returned to Spain, bringing with him Europe's first taste of cocoa, which was reserved for royalty alone. Weatherford (1989) argues that this is one of the earliest cases of gifts from the indigenous peoples of the New World to Europe. At the time that the cacao beans made their way to Spain to be processed into cocoa, there were no trade and tariff protections. As we will soon see, the bean's most recent travels now fall under such protections.

By the 1700s, European leaders and members of the Catholic Church were weighing in on the benefits of chocolate. While the Jesuits were much in favor of the product, Lopez suggests the Dominicans strongly criticized its consumption. In London, purveyors of chocolate began to appear. As would later be true in the tea industry, the British government played a role in importing cacao beans by controlling supplies through high tariffs. By the early 1800s, chocolate consumption reached all of England's classes, and by the mid-1800s, recipes for sweet milk chocolate had been developed by the Swiss.

While cacao beans went first from the New World to the Old World, it was Spain that ultimately shipped cacao beans *back* to the Caribbean and South America to become the primary crop of plantations, ultimately staffed by slave labor. While the Spanish went west and the French joined them on the Caribbean islands of Martinique and St. Lucia, the Dutch moved into Indonesia. The British tried briefly to produce cacao in Jamaica, but after an expensive six-year investment, disease killed off almost the entire crop. The British also brought cacao to Sri Lanka (then named Ceylon) to substitute for coffee beans ravaged by disease. Ultimately, however, it was tea that replaced cacao in Sri Lanka. For 250 years, ending around 1850, the plantation system supplied chocolate to consumers throughout Europe and the United States.

It will come as no surprise that the opportunity to consume chocolate was virtually nonexistent for individuals farming the cacao beans. The beans were strictly for export and for the consumption of the nonindigenous people heading up the plantations. Economic control of the plantations was never in the hands of anyone other than colonizers. For 400 years, single crops, or monocultures, have continued to flourish under the plantation system. However, the failure to maintain a diversity of local food sources along with crops for export comes at an enormous cost, leaving nations without a hedge against disease and major price fluctuations. Time and again, we see the problems that arise when a nation has only one major crop to export—or when a critical crop for domestic consumption, such as quinoa, suddenly becomes an export darling and the center of health-food niche marketing.

The Present

There are four primary areas where cacao beans are grown today: the Caribbean, Latin America, West Africa, and Indonesia (Map 4). While there are

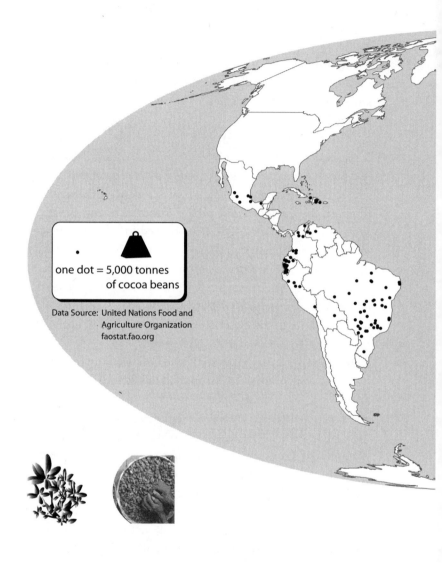

one dot = 5,000 tonnes
of cocoa beans

Data Source: United Nations Food and
Agriculture Organization
faostat.fao.org

Map 4 World Cocoa Production (Steph Gaspers 2008)

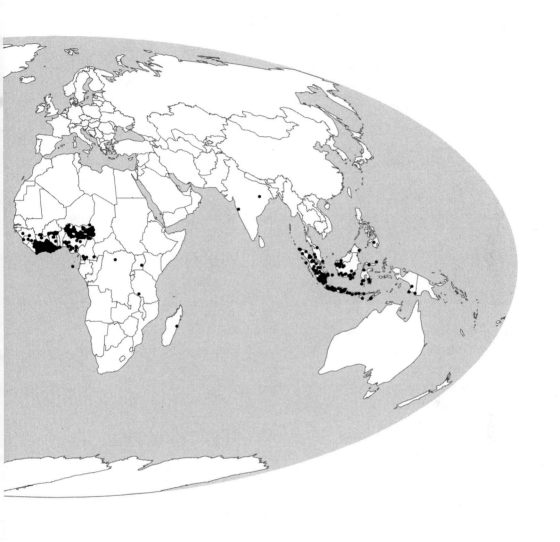

large production areas of cacao plantations in countries like Côte d'Ivoire (Ivory Coast), in general, cacao trees are part of mixed-culture plantings generally grown on small family farms. In 2007 there were more than 5 million family farms producing over 3 million tons of cacao beans; Côte d'Ivoire was the largest producer, followed by Ghana and Indonesia. In 2012 the World Cocoa Foundation indicated "total production has increased in absolute terms from 3.66 million metric tones in 2007–2008 to 3.98 million metric tones in 2011–2012." Change in production has not been linear, however; it has fluctuated in various patterns among the different regions. Africa is projected to remain the principal cocoa producer, with a 73 percent market share in 2012. Table 5, drawn from multiple sources, is available from the World Cocoa Foundation and details production over a sample five-year period.

Cacao plays a key role in the economies of a number of West African countries. In the case of nations like Côte d'Ivoire, almost a third of their economy is based on cocoa exports (Chanthavong 2002). The fragile nature of global prices of this commodity contributes to what Chanthavong terms "pull" factors supportive of conditions promoting indentured servitude. They cannot afford to risk potential market loss and thus are ready to do anything necessary to guarantee appropriate market shares.

Predicting prices and export volumes are part of futures forecasting. Forecasting is key to all commodity production. Weather, internal politics, international politics, and international agreements all affect production. As we will see in later discussions of coffee, there frequently exist alternative explanations for the apparently arbitrary rise and fall of prices. For example, from 2007 to 2012, there was a 43.5 percent net drop in cocoa production in Malaysia (World Cocoa Foundation 2012). Agricultural decisions to increase land devoted to palm oil production account for much of this change. Although it is not apparent in Table 5, Vietnam is an up-and-coming player in the cocoa market. The country anticipates an increase from 5,500 tons in 2011 to 52,000 tons by 2020. Additionally, Vietnam plans to produce what is termed "clean cocoa"—cocoa that is UTZ certified (www.saigongp.daily), which means that it is in compliance with a 2002 global sustainability protocol for production and product labeling. Eighty percent of cocoa production in Vietnam is owned by the private U.S. company Cargill. Cargill is in negotiations to purchase Archer Daniels Midland's cocoa business. During the summer of 2013, Callebaut chocolates (Switzerland) "became the world's largest cocoa processor" (Khan 2013) when it purchased the cocoa division of Petra Food. Khan reports that

Table 5 World Cocoa Foundation Statistics 2012 (in Thousands of Tons)

	2007–2008	2008–2009	2009–2010	2010–2011	2011–2012	2007–2008 to 2011–2012 Total Percent Change
WORLD TOTAL PRODUCTION	3,667	3,507	3,569	4,197	3,987	8.73%
Percent change from previous year	7.2%	−4.4%	1.8%	17.6%	−5.0%	
AFRICA TOTAL PRODUCTION	2,603	2,451	2,428	3,076	2,801	7.61%
Percent change from previous year	9.5%	−5.8%	−0.9%	26.7%	−8.8%	
Cameroon	188	210	205	230	220	17.02%
Cote d'Ivoire	1,431	1,234	1,184	1,668	1,400	−2.16%
Ghana	730	730	740	860	870	19.18%
Nigeria	200	210	230	240	230	15.00%
Other Africa	55	67	69	78	81	47.27%
ASIA/OCEANIA TOTAL PRODUCTION	614	596	642	563	623	1.47%
Percent change from previous year	−3.3%	−2.9%	7.7%	−12.3%	10.7%	
Indonesia	500	490	530	450	500	0.00%
Malaysia	32	25	20	18	18	−43.75%
Other Asian countries	82	81	92	95	105	28.05%
AMERICAS TOTAL PRODUCTION	450	459	499	558	563	25.11%
Percent change from previous year	10.7%	2.1%	8.5%	12.0%	.8%	
Brazil	170	155	159	197	185	8.82%
Ecuador	115	130	150	160	170	47.83%
Other Latin American countries	165	174	189	201	208	26.06%

this means two companies now control more than 60 percent of global cocoa processing. Given the example from Vietnam, we can see that full control of production to processing of a significant percentage of cocoa now lies in the hands of large, multinational agribusiness firms. Fears for the livelihood of small farmers and niche-marketing chocolatiers are increasing (Khan 2013). Most of the Latin American and Caribbean beans are exported to the U.S. market, while the West African and Indonesian beans are exported to Europe. In all cases, there are large auction houses that sell the beans. Because of the speed and volume of sales, it is sometimes difficult to keep an eye on the origin of the beans, which is important when attempting to guarantee that no forced child labor has been involved in their harvesting and marketing.

Nestlé, Mars, Hershey, and Kraft are the largest manufacturers and marketers of chocolate in the world. As we will see with the other products profiled in this chapter, these companies are all members of the International Cocoa Initiative and wield a great deal of power in terms of production and marketing policy. In the United States, Hershey and Mars control between two-thirds and three-fourths of the market, while in Europe, Cadbury (now Kraft), Nestlé, and Mars account for a similar market share. In January 2009 a bidding war to acquire Cadbury began between U.S. food giants Hershey and Kraft. As of this writing, Kraft won the war; Hershey, meanwhile, has gone on to acquire organic chocolate company Dagoba.

Critical Issues

Perhaps the most troubling issue in cacao production is that of child labor. In 2000 the BBC produced an investigative report documenting how tens of thousands of children were taken from countries such as Mali, Burkina Faso, and Togo to work as indentured laborers for ten to fourteen hours per day on cacao farms. Parents were unaware of their children's perilous lives; some thought their children were working as legitimate laborers under controlled conditions, while others thought they were being groomed to head to Europe as sports stars. A 2000 U.S. State Department report estimated that at least 15,000 children from Mali were working on cocoa plantations in Côte d'Ivoire. The price of purchase was US$40 per child. The children worked twelve-hour days for less than US$200 per year (Off 2006, 133). In 2002 similar numbers were reported, and the children on these cocoa farms were characterized as slaves (Save the Children Canada 2005). A powerful, richly descriptive account of this servitude is presented

In January 2010 the European Union approved the acquisition of British chocolate giant Cadbury by Kraft Foods. It ruled that in both Poland and Romania, Kraft needed to divest its Cadbury division due to fears of too great a market share. If you have traveled or worked in Europe, try and remember which brands of chocolate were the most popular. If you have not traveled or worked in Europe, think about what brands of chocolate have been most prominent around your school. What do you imagine has happened as a result of this acquisition?

in Carol Off's *Bitter Chocolate: Investigating the Dark Side of the World's Most Seductive Sweet* (2006).

The issue of child indentured labor was so critical that beginning in the late 1990s, the Chocolate Manufacturers' Association joined together with a variety of domestic and international organizations to survey labor practices in West Africa. On October 1, 2001, the Harkin-Engel Act, co-sponsored by U.S. senator Tom Harkin and U.S. congressman Eliot Engel, went into effect. The protocol was designed to ensure that by 2005, there would be no child slavery or indentured servitude used in the production of chocolate. Unfortunately, this goal was not achieved. In 2005 Tulane University in Louisiana was appointed as a third party to monitor activities related to the protocol. In a report issued in 2011, Tulane indicated that in the 2008–2009 growing season, the number of children aged five to seventeen working in the worst forms of child labor in the cocoa sector totaled approximately 820,000 in Côte d'Ivoire and 997,000 in Ghana (Harkin press release 2011). The recommendations made in the Tulane report can be found at http://childlabor-payson.org/.

In 2002 the cocoa industry set up the International Cocoa Initiative with the intention of creating an advisory board to attend to these child-labor issues. It was a collaborative initiative between industry giants like the Big Four described above, an advisory council, and nonindustry members such as the Global March Against Child Labor and Free the Slaves. While some question the ultimate effectiveness of the partnership, there is now a national plan of action in Côte d'Ivoire with protocols for protection and local-level collaborations designed to gradually eliminate problematic actions in the production and sale of cocoa. This is an ongoing process.

Off (2006, 201) argues that the pilot plans in Côte d'Ivoire, as well as in Ghana, are simply window dressing: "Shortly before the July 2005 deadline for the Harkin-Engel protocol, the cocoa companies . . . announced a small pilot project [Côte d'Ivoire and Ghana]: Ghana had no identifiable issue with abusive child labour on cocoa farms and Oume, in Côte d'Ivoire, was never cited as a problem area. As the congressmen had hinted in the Valentine's Day address, Big Cocoa was offering up these small pursuits as tokens of their good intentions but little more." Clearly, there are multiple perspectives on what types of measures are being effectively implemented—and by whom—to change abusive labor practices.

The chocolate bar you eat to fend off hunger pangs may have been created from labor you would not approve of. How can you tell? For the most part, particularly in the United States, this is very difficult because in the fast-moving auction houses throughout the world, beans from all over the globe frequently get mixed together. One possible choice is to buy organic chocolate. Because no organic cocoa beans come from areas like Côte d'Ivoire—a key site of indentured labor—you can be reasonably sure that by buying organically, you are not supporting an unjust labor practice. Among the companies able to document that no slave labor has been involved in the production of cacao beans in their products are Clif Bar, Cloud Nine, Dagoba Organic Chocolate, Denman Island Chocolate, Gardners Candies, Green and Black's, Kailua Candy Company, Koppers Chocolate, L.A. Burdick Chocolates, Montezuma's Chocolates, Newman's Own Organics, Omanhene Cocoa Bean Company, Rapunzel Pure Organics, and the Endangered Species Chocolate Company (Stop chocolate slavery 2014). An even more active choice is to participate in campaigns to change child-labor practices. Equal Exchange is an example of an organization that makes use of a range of strategies from school-based campaigns to petition drives, and its efforts are detailed on its website.

In addition to the question of whether indentured labor has been used in the harvesting of cacao is whether fair prices have been paid to the cocoa farmers. Luttinger and Dicum (1999, 195) characterize fair trade as a "market-driven model that redefines the dynamics of the trading system to achieve [the goal of fair trade]. Fair trade relationships are simplified; exploitative middlemen are bypassed as farmer co-ops trade directly with importers in consuming countries. And, crucially, power across the value chain is equalized as growers have access to better market information and credit on fairer terms." Pettigrew (1997, 46) further addresses advantages of fair trade in her discussion of the tea trade (as do Luttinger and Dicum 1999 in their discussion of coffee), reminding her readers that when a fair trade system is put in place, more money is invested in bettering the

lives of workers through "pension funds, alternative training opportunities, environmental improvements, and welfare and medical programs."

A third critical issue is that of agricultural sustainability. The Alliance
for Sustainability provides the following definition: "A sustainable agriculture is ecologically sound, economically viable, socially just and humane.
For different regions and contexts the exact meaning may vary—in some
cases no chemicals are used—in others, a much smaller amount than in
conventional agriculture without costs to the ecosystem." Sustainability
practices can increase crop yields and decrease the amounts of fertilizers
and pesticides used.

An illustrative case study comes from the Indonesian region of Sulawesi, a key coffee-producing area where cocoa is also produced that was
hit hard by the tsunami of 2005. Cacao in Indonesia is largely grown by
small farmers; as of 2002, there were more than 400,000 of them (*Renewing Hope for Cocoa Farmers in Sulawesi* 2002). Many of the farmers
do not engage in sustainable farming. However, we do have present-day
collaborative models of nongovernmental agencies working closely with
farmer cooperatives and government initiatives in areas such as Indonesia
to prevent the bug- and blight-related disasters that have more than once
brought down the cacao industry, causing the country's cocoa farmers to
go in and out of cocoa production. For Indonesia, the world's third-largest
exporter of cacao beans, this is quite dangerous for the domestic economy.
When Indonesia was still a colony of the Netherlands, a pest called the
cocoa pod borer (CPB) killed off the flourishing cacao business. It was not
until the early 1980s that farmers again began to plant cacao trees (*Renewing Hope for Cocoa Farmers in Sulawesi* 2002).

An example of a collaborative, sustainable approach between nation-
state departments of agriculture, international organizations like the UN's
Food and Agriculture Organization (FAO), and small NGOs committed to
a bottom-up approach to development can be found in Indonesia (profiled
in the film cited above). In the late 1990s, the CPB returned. This pest literally bores into the cacao fruit and deposits its eggs, which hatch inside the
fruit and feed off of it, destroying the cocoa pod. Hundreds of thousands of
small farmers' holdings were at risk. Through the collaborative efforts of a
set of NGOs from the United States, the United Kingdom, and Indonesia,
whose shared goal was to derive a nonpesticide response to the CPB, the
Field School Method evolved. Local farmers came together in a laboratory
on a designated farm and learned to engage in four steps: frequent harvesting, pruning, sanitation, and fertilizer application. Using outside advice

but focusing on local solutions to local problems, these farmers developed a sustainable method for ridding their farms of a pest that could potentially have reduced their incomes by a full 90 percent.

A training program like the Field School Method is termed a "participatory training approach." Generally, such programs are more successful than top-down programs because farmers teach each other. In this case, the program goals focus on sustainable agriculture methods that require less chemical intervention and are generally less expensive to the farmers. Field School Methods have also been pioneered in West Africa, reaching more than 15,000 farmers in 2003–2004 alone. Efforts are also being made to provide vocational education in villages with large numbers of cocoa farmers. These efforts match those occurring in coffee-producing areas and will be discussed later.

Chocolate: Summary

This section has profiled the history of and current conditions in the trade of cacao beans for the production of cocoa and, ultimately, chocolate. Critical issues such as indentured labor, fair trade, and sustainability dominate the discussion. At the present time, niche marketing has allowed for a broad increase in the numbers and types of chocolate bars sold around the world. Recent health advertisements for dark chocolate's antioxidant properties have drawn in a broad base of consumers beyond chocoholics and children. While an examination of health benefits is well beyond this chapter, it is clear that chocolate is here to stay. We turn next to coffee.

Coffee

History

Two accessible publications detail the role of coffee in our lives. Tom Standage (2005) captures coffee's role in relation to five other beverages in his lively romp through the centuries, *A History of the World in Six Glasses*; while Nina Luttinger and Gregory Dicum (2006) provide a more comprehensive account in *The Coffee Book: Anatomy of an Industry from Crop to the Last Drop*, which includes a rich timeline detailing events from 1000 A.D. to the present. For our purposes, the following events are of note. History suggests that Avicenna of Bukhara (located in present-day Uzbekistan) was writing about coffee's health benefits in 1000 A.D. Some time between 1470 and 1499, coffee made its way to Mecca and Medina (Saudi Arabia) from Yemen. Wile (2004) details this—in contrast to descriptions of coffee as first appearing in Ethiopia, which has been proposed in other histories. The first appearance of coffee in Europe seems to have been in Holland around 1616. By the late 1600s, it was the subject of futures speculations in auctions throughout Europe.

As trading and speculation escalated, coffeehouses sprouted up in Venice and England. Fears arose on the part of government officials in England about the role these coffeehouses were playing in promoting opinions that differed from those of the government. Seeking a place to produce coffee that belonged to the empire, the British began coffee cultivation in Sri Lanka around 1658. Europeans strove to gain control of the plants themselves, sending Javanese coffee beans to Holland's botanical gardens in 1706. Some might term this one of the earliest instances of "biopiracy" or "industrial espionage." Biopiracy "refers to the appropriation of the knowledge and genetic resources of farming and indigenous communities by individuals or institutions who seek exclusive monopoly control (patents or intellectual property) over these resources and knowledge" (Biopiracy 2009).

In 1723 France sent coffee seedlings to its colony of Martinique in the Caribbean. In like manner, in 1727 coffee seedlings from French Guyana made their way to Brazil. In 1730 the British joined in, sending seeds from England to Jamaica. Over a ten-year period in Sri Lanka, coffee plants had been slowly dying from hemileia vastatrix, a disease commonly called coffee rust. By 1869 the volume of acreage killed off by coffee rust decimated coffee production and provoked a switch from coffee to tea production, a decision accounting for the first planting of tea seeds in 1867 (Pettigrew 1997).

Between 1727 and 1800, the coffee industry developed to such a degree that Brazil was able to export the product. Its ability to do so was enhanced by two years of abject destruction of coffee plantations and estates in Haiti during the 1791–93 uprisings by the nearly 500,000 African slaves on the island. This caused Haiti to fall from its top position, and it no longer delivered half of the world's coffee supply (Dicum and Luttinger 1999). Over the next thirty-five years, Brazil secured its position as a producer of somewhere between half and three-quarters of the global supply of coffee. This success allowed it to "replicate the policies of the original coffee exporters and began a series of initiatives to create a coffee cartel on a scale that dwarfed anything the Arabs were able to accomplish at the dawn of

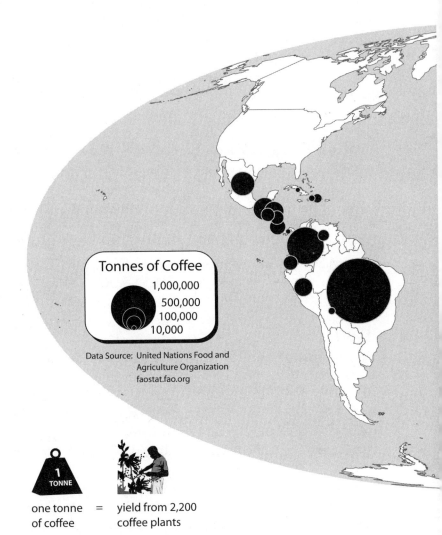

Tonnes of Coffee

1,000,000
500,000
100,000
10,000

Data Source: United Nations Food and
Agriculture Organization
faostat.fao.org

one tonne   =   yield from 2,200
of coffee   coffee plants

Countries that produce under 5,000 tonnes
(in order from least to greatest): Guyana,
Gabon, Comoros, Belize, Cambodia, Dominica,
Mozambique, Malawi, Congo, Angola, Myanmar,
Paraguay, Jamaica, Central African Republic,
Liberia, Zimbabwe, Zambia, Nigeria

Map 5 World Coffee Production (Steph Gaspers 2008)

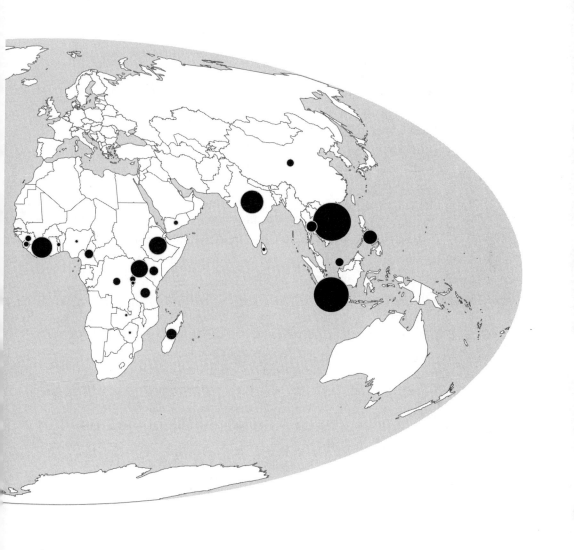

the original coffee era" (Luttinger and Dicum 2006, 30). By 1906 Brazil was powerful enough to control the global supply and price of coffee in a process termed "valorization," government price control of a commodity. An organization begun first by the growers and later taken over by the government, the Brazilian Instituto de Café was one example of a developing nation crafting a leadership role in commodity control.

Inspired by its neighbor Brazil, Colombia was struck with coffee fever. As thousands of coffee farms began in Colombia, a domestic organization called the Federacion Nacional de Cafeteros (FNC) was created. Luttinger and Dicum (2006, 75–76) contrast the two organizations, characterizing the Colombian FNC as a group that "promoted unrestrained and aggressively expansionist trade in coffee. While the [Brazilian] instituto was inward-looking and more concerned with domestic control of supply to established markets, the FNC was resolutely cosmopolitan and sought to stimulate demand—particularly demand for Colombian coffee."

The contrasting approaches of the two organizations came together briefly in 1936, when Brazil and Colombia finally decided to work together to keep the prices of their coffees consistent on the world market. This effort fell apart by June 1937, however, as the FNC once again separated itself from the Colombian government and continued a sort of cowboy-style expansionism. Brazil then dumped much of its coffee supply on the market, and the resultant glut caused the complete collapse of the world market. Luttinger and Dicum (2006, 79) characterize the resulting move by Colombia, Brazil, and the United States to create a trilateral agreement as one of the earliest examples of a combined economic and political policy: "The Inter-American Coffee Agreement (IACA) was a major break with established trade policy that generally favored free international markets. The United States entered into it to support friendly nations in its hemisphere, thereby securing their resistance to Axis overtures during this time of global war."

Between 1937 and 1962, international players shifted a bit. Instant coffee became important. Central America and Africa joined the playing field. In the years after World War II, the era of the Cold War, the United States was hypervigilant in attempting to keep Communism from crossing into Latin America. The trade relationships with Colombia and Brazil were instrumental in this effort and eventually provided the scaffolding for the creation in 1962 of an International Coffee Agreement (ICA). Like OPEC (the Organization of Petroleum-Exporting Countries) today, the ICA was designed to set quotas for production and maintenance of market prices. The stability of this organization invited Central America, Africa, and Indonesia to step up their roles in production. Organizations like the World Bank and the IMF provided start-up monies. However, since the ICA was designed primarily to assist giant producers like Brazil and Colombia, these other geographic areas were forced to sell their beans to countries that were not part of the ICA. For roughly ten years, this "us" and "them" system continued. The types of beans planted in the smaller countries were not carefully monitored by the ICA.

The Present

By 1994 the ICA shifted from an agency that designed and enforced policy to one that provided and maintained a database of coffee information to disseminate for trade and marketing purposes. The lack of global policing via an association again put pressure on individual nation-states and multinationals to develop production and marketing plans, often in isolation. For example, in 1997, Vietnam stepped in as a key player, with production rising from zero to more than 1.8 billion pounds in 1997. In spite of unevenness in quality, Vietnamese coffee continued to flood the market, which ultimately impacted global pricing. Luttinger and Dicum (2006) argue convincingly that the role of Structural Adjustment Programs imposed by the World Bank and the IMF essentially rendered ineffective the national coffee boards in Africa, Indonesia, and even Mexico. In terms of patterns, we see the push and pull between independent development and product marketing and large-scale international governmental and multinational corporations. We have looked at costs and benefits of individual nation-states controlling the destiny of their GNP through the single commodity export of cacao; we see this same situation with coffee.

By 1999, a global coffee crisis was triggered by a glut in production and a drop in prices. The year 2001 brought the lowest adjusted prices per pound in the history of coffee production (Luttinger and Dicum 2006). In *The Coffee Book*, Luttinger and Dicum present a list of the world's most coffee-dependent countries in terms of export for 2003. Several of the countries at or near the top of the list, including East Timor, Burundi, Ethiopia, and Rwanda, have also experienced some of the worst political and human-rights crises in recent history. These authors argue that "worldwide, the regime of careless capitalism contributed to one national tragedy after another" (Luttinger and Dicum 2006, 104). Coupled with corruption, these gluts in production and price fluctuations played central roles in the destabilization of these countries.

At this point, it becomes useful to revisit the notion of ideologies within arguments, which we first introduced in chapter 1. The information presented to you in this chapter is ultimately a set of facts, woven together with arguments designed by your authors. Perhaps you agree with us; perhaps you disagree with us. Whether or not you agree is not as important as whether you can identify how we have built up rationales for the perspectives presented in this chapter and elsewhere in the book.

Read through the three numbered paragraphs below. They present the perspectives of different authors on the causes of the massive genocide in the East African nation of Rwanda within the three-month period of April to July 1994. More than 800,000 people were killed, including both Tutsi and Hutu sympathizers. Some estimates range as high as 1 million victims (see www.gendercide.org. Two of the paragraphs suggest that the drastic fall in coffee prices played a major role in destabilizing Rwanda, while the third sees it as simply one small factor in a labyrinth of more complicated factors. Some of the authors seek a purely economic, structural argument for primary causes of the genocide, while some examine a broader base of historical factors, including relations among the key ethnic groups, Hutu and Tutsi, as well as gender (www.gendercide.org). Luttinger and Dicum and Shiva (1997) are adamant in their attribution of instability and, ultimately, genocide to the rise and fall in commodity links, while Diamond (2005) suggests that factors other than globalization are primary causes of the civic instability. Trace the arguments laid out in each passage below. Can you see how each follows a logical link from one sentence to the next, ultimately resulting in different sets of conclusions? Is there sufficient information to keep your attention as a reader? Why does the argument seem sufficient or insufficient?

1. Luttinger and Dicum (2006, 107):

Eighty percent of [Rwanda's] export earnings had been from coffee, with the overwhelming majority of citizens growing at least some of the crop. This economic body blow, combined with political instability and World Bank structural adjustment demand (which included an end to the Equalization Fund with which the government bought coffee from growers, an end to agricultural supports, and currency devaluation), helped push the country over the brink into the bloody meltdown of 1994. Half a million people were slaughtered and a quarter of the population became refugees.

2. Shiva (1997, 116–17):

The Rwandan genocide had similar links to the globalization processes of structural adjustment. In 1989, the International Coffee Agreement reached a deadlock, and worldwide coffee prices plunged by more than 50 percent. Rwanda's export earning from coffee declined by 50 percent between 1987 and 1991. In November 1990, a 50 percent devaluation of the Rwandan Franc was carried out under the World Bank–IMF adjustment program. The balance of payments situation deteriorated dramatically, and the outstanding external debt, which had already doubled since 1985, increased by another 34 percent between 1989 and 1992. In June 1992, another devaluation was ordered, leading to a 25 percent decrease in coffee production. . . . Everywhere, globalization leads to the destruction of local economies and social organizations, pushing people into insecurity, fear, and civil strife. The violence against people's livelihoods builds up into the violence of war.

3. Diamond (2005, 326–28):

As Gerard Prunier, a French scholar of East Africa, put it, "The decision to kill was of course made by politicians, for political reasons. But at least part of the reason why it was carried out so thoroughly by the ordinary rank-and-file peasant in their ingo [family compound] was feeling that there were too many people on too little land, and that with a reduction in their numbers, there would be more for the survivors." Other factors did contribute [to the genocide]. Just to reiterate, regardless of the order of their importance, those other factors include Rwanda's history of Tutsi domination of Hutu, Tutsi large-scale killings of Hutu in Burundi and small-scale ones in Rwanda, Tutsi invasion of Rwanda, Rwanda's economic crisis and its exacerbation by drought and world factors (specially falling coffee prices and World Bank austerity measures), hundreds of thousands of desperate young Rwandan men displaced as refugees into settlement camps and ripe for recruitment by militias, and competition among Rwanda's rival political groups willing to stoop to anything to retain power. Population pressure joined with those other factors. . . . I conclude that population pressure was one of the important factors behind the Rwandan genocide, that Malthus's worst-case scenario may sometimes be realized, and that Rwanda may be a distressing model of that scenario in operation. [Thomas Robert Malthus was an eighteenth-century British scholar who forecast the dangers of population growth in settings of limited resources.]

Whether changes in coffee prices were the ultimate reason for political instability in Rwanda or not, the instability of commodity pricing continues. Since 1999, we have seen chaotic ups and downs of coffee prices. The period from 2001 to 2003 saw the spread of the crisis of 1999, almost exclusively targeting small farmers throughout the world. The recovery process has focused on the promotion of specialty coffee, which now accounts for roughly half of the U.S. coffee market (Luttinger and Dicum 1999, 7). Internet sales and a move toward coffee marketed as both organic and sustainable mark current trends. The following Starbucks case study walks you through some of these events.

Case Study: Starbucks

Starbucks is clearly a key player in economic globalization. In 2004 it was listed fourth among effective global brands, just behind Apple (1), Google (2), and Ikea (3) (Clark 2007, 94). It is a company "whose signature innovation in the world of marketing [is] its invention of an entire proprietary language for its products" (Clark 2007, 97). It is also one of two companies (along with McDonald's) that "act as global hubs that connect some of the world's poorest, most remote countries with some of the wealthiest." By Starbucks's own account, "since 1971, [it] has been committed to ethically sourcing and roasting the highest quality Arabica coffee in the world. Today, with stores around the globe, the company is the premier roaster and retailer of specialty coffee in the world." It has committed itself to 100 percent ethical sourcing by 2015. In 2012, 93 percent of its coffee was ethically sourced (www.Starbucks.com/responsibility/sourcing/coffee).

In 2006 Starbucks's gross revenue was US$7.786 billion, with a stated gross profit of $1.92 billion. By November 10, 2008, the company was reporting a 97 percent drop in net income (Stone 2008c). In the fall of 2007, it had net profits of roughly $158.5 million (21 cents per share); by the next fall, its profit had dropped to roughly $5.4 million (one cent per share) (Stone 2008c). Within the four-month time period ending on September 28, 2008, what the company terms "same-store sales" declined by 9 percent, according to the Starbucks chief financial officer (Shepherd 2008). Starbucks's fiscal future resembles the fiscal ebbs and tides of many countries: local and global events affect its sales, and local and global links play off each other—sometimes in supportive ways and sometimes in competitive ways. Its total sales per year are comparable to the GDP of a number of countries. By July 2013 it was reporting a 25 percent profit, with estimated growth reaching roughly 8 percent outside the United States and 9 percent within the United States (Choi 2013). Coffee is one of our more prominent commodity chains, connecting producers with marketers and consumers around the world. Clark (2007, 181) describes this connection the following way: "In the 2005–2006 crop year, the globe's coffee plantations generated 14.3 billion pounds of coffee beans. . . . Tropical developing nations supplied almost all of it, while temperate, industrialized nations consumed 80 percent of it. To put it bluntly, poor countries grow coffee for rich ones." Yet Starbucks has only been a global player since the late 1980s. Initially focused on coffee, the institution has since expanded into the arts and the global service area, crossing into cultural globalization as well. In the section that follows, we explore a bit of Starbucks's history and look at what insiders and outsiders have to say about the organization.

Starbucks was founded in 1971 in Seattle, Washington. In 1982 Howard Schultz, the current chairman and CEO of Starbucks, joined the company. By 1985 he had created a concept coffee bar called Il Giornale with financial support from the original Starbucks partners. In 1987 Shultz was given the opportunity to purchase Starbucks from its owners, Jerry Baldwin and Gordon Bowker. When this happened, Il Giornale acquired Starbucks's assets and purchased rights to the original name. From 1987 to 1992, Starbucks was a privately owned and held company. On June 26, 1992, Starbucks held its initial public offering (IPO) of stock and became listed on the NASDAQ. With its humble beginnings of four stores well behind it, Starbucks now has more than 13,000 stores worldwide. Its ambitious initial expansion plan of six new stores per day did not come to pass. However, analysts expect the international sector to see continued expansion, even as stores in Canada and the United States have closed; in January 2013 Starbucks revealed a plan to add 1,500 new stores outside the United States ("Venti"-size expansion 2013). We do not know what its global imprint will be even five years from now. Is Starbucks an icon, a quintessential brand, or a multinational corporation hell-bent on forcing the independent coffeehouse out of existence?

In an interview with journalist Garrick Utley, then president of the Levin

Institute at the State University of New York, Schultz himself refers to Starbucks as the "quintessential experiential brand." In his memoir, *Pour Your Heart into It* (1997), Shultz clearly distances himself from images of early twentieth-century business barons and goes to great lengths to separate Starbucks from McDonald's and Walmart on a variety of levels. In spite of current economic problems and restructuring operations, most business analysts are positive about the changes introduced and optimistic about the company's future. Shepherd (2008) reports that "the company is following the right strategy in dealing with its competitors." Schultz himself indicates that without a doubt, Starbucks can coexist with mom-and-pop operations. His goals for the company link profitability with a social conscience. He suggests over and over again that Starbucks wishes to be a good neighbor, a third space, and a company that can "make a difference and give back." He states clearly that it is not the intention of Starbucks to put mom-and-pop coffeehouses out of business.

Joseph Michelli, a business trainer and consultant who interviewed a wide variety of Starbucks executives and baristas over a two-year period, came away with much the same impression, gathering his results in *The Starbucks Experience: Five Principles for Turning Ordinary into Extraordinary* (2007). Michelli refers to the blog www.starbucksgossip.com as an example of a company-sanctioned space for Starbucks employees to comment on aspects of the business even as they gather daily updates on the company. Michelli (2007, 120) explores how Starbucks functions in both local and globalizing manners, citing John Simmons from brandchannel.com: "As long as the core product stays true to its quality and principles, other elements of the offer can adapt to local market needs. Go to a Starbucks in China, Japan, France, Greece, or Kuwait, and you will drink the same espresso but the food will have a local flavor. . . . [W]here adaptation is needed to fit cultures, Starbucks adapts." Michelli looks at examples, such as the introduction in Japan of gelatin coffee cubes ("Coffee Jelly Frappuccino Blended Beverage"), and contrasts the fact that in China, Starbucks stores are set up to deliver 80 percent of their drinks "to stay," while in the United States, they are set up to deliver 80 percent of their drinks "to go."

Even as Starbucks adapts to certain local conditions for product delivery and sales, critics accuse it of failing to sufficiently invest in coffee growers in producing countries. As a result, and also due to its ubiquity, the company is an easy target for protests calling for shifts in inequality. Clark (2007, 194) is unequivocal in his negative characterization of the company's forays into avoiding the middleman and helping change working conditions for growers: "I want to be perfectly clear about one thing: Starbucks has never voluntarily done much to help struggling coffee growers. On the rare occasion when the company has taken steps to better the lives of farmers, it has generally only done so because a consumer group was planning a protest or a boycott." Clark (2007, 177) characterizes coffee's relationship to Latin American in the following way: "Coffee is both the hand that feeds Latin America and the noose around its neck." In this quote, we see the dimensions of globalization that we have explored in the earlier part of the chapter; each connection costs something.

Starbucks provides 2 percent of the world's coffee (Clark 2007). In spite of the uncomplimentary observation made above, Clark also points out that Starbucks has worked more directly with its growers than have the companies that provide 60 percent of U.S. coffee: Nestlé, Proctor and Gamble, Phillip Morris, and Massimo Zanetti. While its marketing practices may garner only lukewarm praise, its philanthropic profile is rising. A global commitment to service has resulted in consistent support at the local level of particular causes.

Starbucks is a global player with a conscience and a passion for looking toward the future, evidenced in its trademarked Shared Planet Commitment. One of its global projects focuses on delivery and maintenance of safe water systems. Profits from Ethos water-bottle sales support this initiative. In October 2008, as part of both its Shared Planet Commitment and its business plan, Starbucks committed to doubling the amount of fair trade coffee that it purchased. From November 2008 through March 2012, it partnered with RED, a program whose "primary objective is to engage the private sector in raising awareness and funds for the Global Fund, to help eliminate AIDS in Africa" (Starbucks press release 2008a). The Global Fund was created in 2002; its focus is on the delivery of medical assistance around the world to fight AIDS, tuberculosis, and malaria. It was initially working under the World Health Organization's auspices with an Administrative Services Agreement. On January 1, 2009, it became administratively autonomous, allowing it to make independent choices in terms of how to deliver its products and "find ways of working that are more appropriate and efficient for a Geneva-based international financing institution" (Starbucks press release 2008b). This fund represents strong alliances between the private business sector and the private/NGO sector. Starbucks later diversified its local and global charitable contributions, no longer serving as a key retail sponsor of RED. Its partnership model within an international NGO may be seen by some as an example of "Brand Aid"

(Richey and Ponte 2011), but for others it may reinforce their appreciation of Starbucks, not only for its coffee but for much more.

Starbucks has also moved into the twenty-first century by diversifying its products and services. It has entered the food market via Starbucks Ice Cream (in collaboration with Breyers), Evolution juices, and La Boulange bakery products. It has entered the music industry via the CDs it sells in its stores and even the motion-picture industry through its underwriting of films such as *Akeelah and the Bee* (2006).

Alas, by some accounts, Starbucks has also reached the stagnant domains of maturity and middle age, and its diversification may or may not be enough to help it survive and thrive. Santarris and Gunderson (2008, D-2) recommend that, even as former CEO Howard Schultz has stepped back in to handle the daily reins of his company, Starbucks should "take a breather from wildfire growth, take stock, take measures to retool and refocus—in short . . . undertake the whole midlife, belt-tightening regimen." Schultz remains optimistic that his choice to bring back Arthur Rubinfield as president of global development allowed it to regain its stride. Schultz stated: "When we have been doing our best work, it has been because people have seen Starbucks for more than a cup of coffee" (Stone 2008b).

You may be a young student who works as a barista at Starbucks and, even as a part-time employee, qualifies for health benefits. Or you may be an avid local "foodie" committed to the slow-foods movement and coffee—which you believe should be ground, roasted, and consumed within a 100-mile radius. You may be a member of a coffee cooperative in Guatemala who is unable to secure a multiyear contract with Starbucks—or Green Mountain, for that matter. Clearly, each of you would view this corporation with different eyes. Is there one true Starbucks, or are there many versions of Starbucks that are all equally true? The business community continues to be enchanted with Starbucks. Those benefiting from environmental and health initiatives throughout the world in programs administered by global NGOs—from CARE and Mercy Corps all the way down to local development providers—see Starbucks in a generally positive light. But

Brand Aid is a term that refers to the combination of a social cause, such as global health relief, a retail brand, and a well-known "aid celebrity" working together to raise awareness and funds for the cause. (See https://brandaidworld.wordpress.com/.)

to young protesters at the World Trade Organization meetings in Seattle in 1999, Starbucks epitomized the megagiant corporation, eating up all those around it. There are no easy answers, but only complicated questions. If you frame a debate in simplistic terms, it is easy to find villains and Robin Hoods.

Critical Issues

Niche marketing of coffee, tea, and chocolate has increased dramatically. Terms like "organic," "fairly traded," and "80 percent cacao content" help consumers distinguish products that have not been on the market for very long. Nations traditionally seen as key market players are being challenged by newcomers, often with the support of global entities such as the World Bank. Coffee cooperatives in Central and Latin America are now competing for the attention of organizations like Green Mountain Coffee to ensure their continuing existence. Farmers on many of these cooperatives have never actually tasted the coffee produced from the beans they have grown. As some cooperatives live and others die, the World Bank is providing incentives to Vietnam to strengthen its place in the global coffee market. These man-made shifts are not dissimilar to the natural shifts that have occurred over time. Personal choices we make can affect whether a cooperative thrives or dies.

Coffee: Summary

With the products profiled in this chapter so far, we have visited the notions of sustainability, fair trade, and fair labor practices. In addition to these issues—all of which are linked to the growth and consumption of coffee—we have seen a tighter framing of the relationship between producing and consuming countries. Many authors who examine the commodity of coffee throughout the world today have scrutinized how much money from the sale of a single cup of coffee actually reaches anyone in the producing country. Clearly, the consumer countries have a stronger grip on aspects of the profit margin—from roasting the beans all the way to marketing and sales. Some authors have suggested that a more equitable balance of profit between the bean-producing countries and all others is in order. This brings us back to the issue of commodity and value chains. As with other luxury products such as chocolate, daily choices you make will trickle back to the land of origin. Is your impact positive, negative, or neutral? More important, can you begin to see yourself as a member of a broad global community? The relationship between producing and consuming nations affects the overall health of our planet.

Sugar

We move now to an exploration of the final product of this chapter, the carbohydrate darling of our daily consumption: sugar. Before proceeding, examine Map 6 showing world sugar production and see if you can recognize any patterns that are similar to or different from the cocoa and coffee maps. Mintz (1985, 192) suggests that humans have always centered our diets around a major carbohydrate: "Since the invention of agriculture [our diets] ha[ve] centered upon a core complex carbohydrate 'fringed' with contrasting tastes and textures to stimulate appetite." As in the other sections, we begin with a brief historical overview, followed by a description of present-day market statistics and a discussion of the most critical issues.

Just as with the plantation practices for cocoa and coffee, slave labor ended on sugar plantations in the mid-1800s, but the commodity chains that were developed early on still remain. Because of sugar's link to other products, such as tea and milk chocolate, it is sometimes difficult to see its role in fostering or restricting development. Nevertheless, sugar is clearly at the center of development issues discussed in this and earlier chapters. Most important is the connection to human servitude: of all the industries profiled here, the sugar industry has enslaved more human beings than any other and accounted for the indentured servitude of hundreds of thousands of others. Additionally, the use of sugarcane for biofuel production and the degree to which sugar beets, which account for roughly half of the sugar produced globally, are genetically modified remain as other critical issues.

History

While people have been consuming sweet beverages from time immemorial, the earliest documentation of actual production of sugar comes in 500 A.D. (Mintz 1985). After 700 A.D. but before 1000 A.D., sugar made its way to Europe, starting with Spain. As Mintz (1985, 23) describes it: with the Arab conquest of Spain came "sugarcane, its cultivation, the art of sugar making, and a taste for this different sweetness." The introduction of sugar to Europe followed the earlier pattern of its introduction throughout Persia, India, and the Arab Mediterranean, where both sugar and the secrets of its production followed the Arab conquest of each area.

People in Western Europe first joined the sugar commodity chain as consumers. However, Mintz describes their subsequent development as controllers of sugar after the Crusades. Both Mintz and J. H. Galloway suggest that declines in population due to the Black Death caused places like Crete and Cyprus to withdraw as sugar producers. Mintz (1985, 28–32) describes the roles that Sicily, Spain, and Morocco played in producing sugar in the 1400s and suggests in no uncertain terms that the links between sugar and slavery began at this time. Citing Galloway, he states that "it was the expanded use of slave labor to compensate for plague-connected mortality that initiated the strange and enduring relationship between sugar and slavery" (Mintz 1985, 29).

In the New World, as early as the fifteenth century, African slaves were brought to Brazil to work sugarcane fields: "Between 1450 and 1600 the Portuguese shipped 175,000 slaves from West Africa, transforming what had been a series of regional slave markets into a transatlantic trade where the tickets were one-way" (MacGillivray 2006, 148). Brazil's primary trading partner was Lisbon. Mintz (1985, 33) characterizes the sixteenth century as "the Brazilian century for sugar." The following centuries drew in both British and French colonies in the Caribbean with at least 3.5 million slaves (MacGillivray 2006, 149). In Haiti alone, more than half a million Africans were enslaved as sugar plantation laborers in the late 1700s (West 2007). In the Guianas in 1595, attempts were made to grow sugarcane. Both sugarcane and slaves were brought to Jamestown in the early 1600s, but the cane did not take (Mintz 1985). In 1627, however, Barbados was settled by the British, and within thirty years, noticeable exports of sugar were making their way to Great Britain. Mintz suggests that this seamless link between centers of production and centers of consumption enabled England to be its own commodity chain. In all the settings described above, with the exception of Jamestown, it was slave labor that fueled the successful plantation economies. In like manner, slave labor fueled rum production. West (2007) details what was termed the Triangle Trade: "Sugar stands at the center of the Triangle Trade; it was the engine that drove the African Diaspora. Slaves of the Caribbean sugar plantations produced molasses that was transported to New England for distillation into rum that was shipped to Africa in exchange for the slaves who would endure the

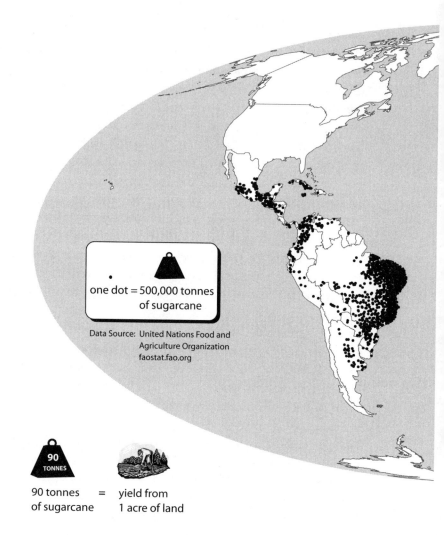

one dot = 500,000 tonnes
of sugarcane

Data Source: United Nations Food and
Agriculture Organization
faostat.fao.org

90
TONNES

90 tonnes   =   yield from
of sugarcane   1 acre of land

Map 6 World Sugar Production (Steph Gaspers 2008)

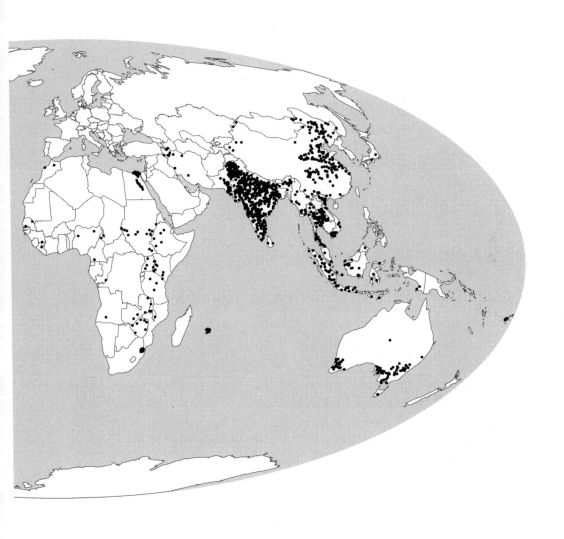

Table 6 Global Sugar Production (2011–2012 Estimate)

Country	Production (Million Tons)	Exports (Million Tons)	Export Ranking	Population (Millions)	Per Capita Consumption (Kg/Person)
Brazil	39.014	27.590	1	203	61
India	27.837	2.911	4	1,263	19
European Union	18.549	2.174	5	499	35
China	12.184	–	–	1,383	10
Thailand	11.347	8.520	2	70	38
United States	7.257	–	–	321	30
Mexico	5.467	1.000	8	113	34
Southern African Development Community	5.435	1.960	6	263	13
Australia	5.167	3.061	3	22	49
Pakistan	5.109	–	–	196	21

Source: Czarnikow Sugar. Reprinted with permission.

final leg of the triangle, the horrific Middle Passage to the sugar islands."
These plantation economies "would foster the beginnings of the largest
trafficking in human souls the world had seen" (Hohenegger 2006, 102).

Although the slave trade ended in 1807, it was not until thirty to forty
years later that slavery was abolished—1838 for the English and 1848 for
the French (Mintz 1985, 53). In Haiti, a successful slave rebellion in 1791
led to the country's independence in 1804. In the Caribbean, slave labor
shifted to indentured labor (in French, *engagés*). While the title changed,
sugar was still being harvested on the backs of nonpaid or ill-paid workers
unable to leave workplaces of their own free will. MacGillivray (2006, 151)
argues that the "reliance on cheap sugar . . . created an ethical callousness
on the part of consumers towards distant producers that continued long
after the abolition of slavery." This is the same point made by Off (2006)
regarding cocoa harvesting in West Africa: when we are geographically
separated from the sources of production, it is easy to anesthetize ourselves
and ignore the dehumanizing aspects of conditions of harvest and production. Keeping the core countries and their behavior "clean" while restricting "dirty" behavior to the periphery countries allows the core countries to

maintain an aura of innocence. For postcolonial theorists, the issue with sugar and other commodities is part of a larger system of neocolonial relationships that define the global structure of power (Fischer-Tene 2010).

According to the Illovo Sugar website (Czarnikow Sugar), close to 80 percent of the world's sugar production comes from the top ten producers. Sugar is clearly embedded in the food chains of consumers around the world. However, it cannot be called primarily an export crop because roughly 70 percent of sugar produced in any area is sold within its country of origin. Table 6 details the world's primary producers.

Critical Issues

Critical issues linked to sugar production remain safety, sourcing, work conditions, and genetic modification. Regarding the potential use of genetically modified sugar beets in products such as candy and other food products, Dr. Edward Group (2008) suggests in his blog that there has been a lack of transparency on the part of the National Confectioners Association regarding when and where GMO sugar beets have been used:

> At the start of this year, American Crystal Sugar Company bragged about breaking their company records for having the best 2 years of harvesting in 2006 and 2007. They projected similar possibilities for the 2008 sugar producing crops because of their plans to use Monsanto's new Roundup Ready XBeet in conjunction with new pesticides and improved fungicides.
>
> Here's the thing: in 2001, American Crystal Sugar Company along with M&M/Mars and Hershey's agreed to use natural sugar instead of the sugar from genetically engineered sugar beets. They have deceived us all and are breaking their promises—I guess they thought people would forget. Not only have people not forgotten, but they're not happy about it.

The National Confectioners Association (NCA) has a much more neutral presentation of this issue:

> At the present time, approximately 50 percent of the corn and more than 80 percent of the soybean acreage in the U.S. is planted with seeds that have been improved through agricultural biotechnology. About a third of the sugar beet acreage in 2008 also will be planted using seeds that were enhanced to improve weed control. Standard

practice by intermediaries between the farm and food manufacturers is to combine conventionally derived and genetically modified crops with similar functional traits rather than market them separately. However, it is important to remember that any ingredients derived through agricultural biotechnology have been thoroughly evaluated by the FDA and the scientific community to ensure their safety. Regarding cocoa, there are no genetically modified cocoa plants or trees in field tests or in production anywhere in the world, to our knowledge. There are no products containing cocoa from genetically modified trees.

As a consumer using their website, you would be hard-pressed to see the problem articulated above by Group. In returning to our questions of ideology and information, the website itself has no articles or postings that directly address the issue of GMO sugar beets.

The Global Alliance for Sugar Trade Reform and Liberalisation (2009) has pushed strongly for the removal of sugar subsidies on the part of the more powerful WTO members. The United States is unlikely to support this; there are serious current concerns about NAFTA and Mexican sugar production. Kraus (2009) notes that due to NAFTA, for any given sugar harvest, Mexico could theoretically sell its sugar in the United States at a high price and then purchase lower-priced sugar on the world market for domestic consumption.

With respect to indentured servitude, general work conditions, and civil society, various NGOs and alliances continue to present information at world meetings. Even the popular press routinely notes issues related to worker conditions and debt. *Brazzil Magazine*'s archives reveal dozens of articles with titles linking slavery and debt to sugar production in Brazil. One of the most recent is "For Brazil's Sugar Cane Workers the Day Starts at 4:30 A.M. and Debts Never End." World meetings and local workshops will not change the severity of these conditions without permanent structural changes to the politics and economics of sugar consumption.

Conclusion

Food connects us all on physical, emotional, and economic levels. The commodity chains we have explored in this chapter reflect common relationships between developed and developing nations. We have seen clear examples of the power differentials between multinational corporations, international organizations, and small family farms and cooperatives. From the examples you've read, you should now have a sense of the fragile nature of food on the global commodities market; politics, economics, and weather can wreak havoc on the GNP of smaller nations in a very short period of time.

Perhaps you can now catch a glimpse of the wider world in your coffee cup or in the next chocolate bar you eat. As sustainability becomes more important to everyone, we see that even large, multinational companies are making changes in the way they do business. For example, Burger King now purchases a percentage of its pork from suppliers that engage in humane practices, such as not using sow gestation crates (Newswire reports 2007). Burger King also plans to increase to around 4 percent its use of eggs that have not come from hens in battery cages. Burgerville, a fast-food chain in the Pacific Northwest, uses only eggs that have been sustainably produced. Even Costco, the large discount chain that sells in bulk, has begun to seek out eggs laid by cage-free hens. We have seen that sustainably produced items may have less of a negative impact on our agricultural future than those produced in a more technological setting.

At the same time, we have observed the complexity of producer/consumer relations over time and the impact of export and import commodities from year to year. Historical patterns of relationship can maintain dependency between exporting and importing nations. In addition, new actors have arrived on the scene, and products once consumed in single areas are being brought to new markets to satisfy newly acquired consumer tastes. Land productivity issues and bilateral relations are also very important. China has been purchasing land in East Africa. Many characterize their purchases as "land grabs," a type of neocolonialism that will never benefit small landholders and may ultimately pull arable land out of availability to its citizens. Hypothetically, China could become a core country, using Ethiopia as its breadbasket at the expense of both Ethiopia's sovereignty and food security.

The largest repository of agricultural seeds in the world is located in an area of the Arctic owned by Norway. Why do you think the Svalbard Global Seed Vault exists when there are 1,400 seed banks located in other parts of the world?

We have looked primarily at connections between countries but have not examined in detail connections between individuals. Nevertheless, it is important to be aware of the impact our individual choices have on the environment and to notice how global trends in consumption and marketing affect us all. Global issues such as world hunger have clearly been beyond the scope of this chapter. A key point to remember as you consider this chapter is that perhaps the problem of global hunger is due less to production than to food availability in particular areas.

On Your Own

One product not profiled in this chapter is rice. Yet all of the issues we have discussed so far are relevant to the current global production of this foodstuff. On your own, we invite you to explore the links between rice—particularly the jasmine and basmati varieties—and issues such as biopiracy, seed banks, genetically modified foods, and agrobusinesses. A great deal has been written about these topics. One issue you may want to consider is whether biopiracy is always one-sided; that is, are developed countries spiriting resources out of developing countries without proper compensation? Scholar Wade Davis suggests that China benefited from the adoption of both New World and European crops. The Green Revolution of the 1960s substantially changed producers and consumers forever. Nations such as Iran, once self-sufficient in rice production, became rice importers. High-yield hybrid varieties of rice, complete with their own compatible pesticides, became varieties of choice in numerous Asian nations. Some multinational corporations applied for patents on staples such as basmati and jasmine rice, varieties grown in India and Thailand for centuries. Charges of biopiracy were filed. Cases have been taken to court. Promoters of sustainable agricultural practices go head-to-head on the local level with marketers of less-traditional practices. See what you can discover on your own online and through other resources. As you reflect on foods in your daily life, it is important to recognize the role that food security will play throughout the globe in the coming decades. In early 2009 a UN-sponsored meeting that focused on the global food crisis was held. It centered on food security and unequal distribution of food. In spite of a commitment on the part of members of the UN Food and Agriculture Organization (FAO) to try and reduce global hunger levels by 2015, it is believed that at the present rate, it will be 2150 or later until that goal is achieved (Call for New Focus 2009).

> **VOCABULARY**

monoculture crops	Big Four—chocolate
fair trade	niche marketing
valorization	sustainable agriculture
seed banks	food security
Field School Method	genetically modified (GMO) food

> **DISCUSSION AND REFLECTION QUESTIONS**

1 *How would you characterize the relationship between food production and population density in the world today?*

2 *What is the relationship between food production, biofuels, and water?*

3 *How do fuel prices—both high and low—contribute to our globalized food economy?*

4 *How does a fragile commodities market for cacao promote human trafficking and indentured servitude?*

5 *What factors make it difficult to keep track of the origins of cacao beans, and what relationship do these factors have to the use of child labor?*

6 *What recent examples of niche marketing in either cacao/cocoa or coffee are you familiar with?*

7 *How did the IMF and the World Bank shift the world map in terms of coffee production, and how did the activities of these organizations impact national coffee boards around the globe?*

8 *In what ways might the General Agreement on Trade in Services (GATS) and the protection of intellectual property rights enter into the world of food production and consumption?*

9 *How do you believe production and marketing of the products described in this chapter relate to the issue of food security discussed at the beginning of the chapter?*

10 *How will water rights, intellectual property rights, and changing climate patterns affect food security in the next ten years?*

ACTIVITY 1 *Information to Activism*

Choose one of the issues raised in this chapter and think about the information you now have. Look at the continuum below and identify where you are on this spectrum.

1	2	3	4	5	6	7
Identify local/global problems associated with one food issue.	Gather information.	Compare/ contrast what you knew initially and what you know now.	How does this relate to your current program of study?	How might you engage in a level of stewardship or activism while in school?	What could you do to parlay your interest into a local or global internship?	What could you do to parlay your internship into a paid position in this arena?

ACTIVITY 2 Look again at Table 4 and focus on the columns for quinoa, rice, and bananas, crops not discussed in this chapter. See if you can find details about any of the areas on the matrix that are marked with a •.

ACTIVITY 3 *Resources and Information about Local → Global Hunger*

Examine the facts in the table below regarding hunger in the United States, Canada, and the world. See if you can find information from your local community or state regarding hunger.

Hunger in Your Community or State/Province	Hunger in the United States	Hunger in Canada	Hunger in the World
	35.5 million Americans were food insecure in 2006.	1.1 million Canadian households experienced food insecurity in 2004.	There are 59 million schoolchildren worldwide who are hungry.
	12.6 million children lived in food insecure households in 2006.	9 percent of adult Canadians experienced hunger in 2004.	1 billion people worldwide are food insecure.
	96 billion pounds of food are wasted each year in the U.S.	5.2 percent of children experienced hunger in 2004.	
	http://www.feedingamerica.org	http://www.ncbi.nlm.nih.gov/pubmed	http://www.wfp.org/hunger
	Feeding America (formerly Second Harvest)	Canadian Medical Association	World Food Programme

ACTIVITY 4 Buy a product discussed in this chapter. Using the packaging information, identify where the product was produced, where it was packaged, and where the packaging came from. How far did the product travel from its harvesting to your door?

ACTIVITY 5 Quinoa, a nongluten grain with high protein content, is the newest darling of niche marketers in North America and Europe. Grown in a variety of Latin American countries and central to the diet of indigenous peoples in these countries, quinoa has become a dominant export crop. Go to a local food store that carries a variety of natural products and go to a store that is part of a national chain. Count the number of quinoa products available in each. Note the degree to which these products are marked as ethically sourced and sustainable. See if you can find the companies that own and distribute these products in North America. Try and determine whether small-scale farmers are part of this commodity chain or not.

References

Alliance for Sustainability. Retrieved March 29, 2007, from http://www.mnt.org /iasa/susafdef.htm.

Biopiracy. Retrieved January 24, 2009, from http://www.etcgroup.org/en/issues /biopiracy.html.

Brown, L. 2013. The real threat to our future is peak water. *The Guardian*. July 6. Retrieved October 31, 2013, from http://www.theguardian.com/global-development/2013/jul/06/water-supplies-shrinking-threat-to-food.

Call for new focus on food security ahead of Madrid meeting. 2009. AFP. Retrieved January 24, 2009, from http://www.google.com/hostednews/afp /article/ALeqM5jHrLboZQ.

Chanthavong, S. 2002. Chocolate and slavery. TED Case Studies 664. Retrieved January 24, 2009, from www.american.edu/ted/chocolate-slave.htm.

Chocolate Manufacturer's Association (Chocolate Council of the National Confectioners Association). Retrieved January 24, 2009, from http://www .chocolateusa.org/About-Us/.

Choi, C. 2013. Starbucks' profit rises 25 percent. *Oregonian*, C-5. July 26.

Clark, T. 2007. *Starbucked: A double tall tale of caffeine, commerce, and culture*. New York: Little, Brown and Company.

Cocoa Market Update. Retrieved August 30, 2013, from http://www.chocolateusa .org/About-Us/.

Cocoa production under control of foreign companies. 2013. *Saigon GP Daily English* edition, March 13. Retrieved May 5, 2013, from http://www.saigon-gpdaily.com.vn/Business/2013/3/104360/.

Diamond, J. 2005. *Collapse: How societies choose to fail or succeed.* New York: Penguin.

Dicum, D., and N. Luttinger. 1999. *The coffee book: Anatomy of an industry from crop to the last drop.* New York: The New Press.

Ethical Sugar. 2009. Retrieved September 9, 2009, from http://www.sucre ethique.org/Brazilian-seminar-Ethical-Sugar.html.

Fischer-Tene, H. 2010. EGO: European History Online: Postcolonial Studies. Retrieved November 20, 2013, from http://www.ieg-ego.eu/en/threads /europe-and-the-world/postcolonial-studies/harald-fischer-tine-postcolonial-studies.

Gillis, J. 2013. Climate change seen posing risk to food supplies. *New York Times.* Retrieved November 12, 2013, from http://www.nytimes.com/2011/06/05 /science/earth/05harvest.html?_r=0&pagewanted=print.

Global Alliance for Sugar Trade Reform and Liberalisation. Retrieved September 9, 2009, from http://www.globalsugaralliance.org/resources.php? action=displayResources&requestType=News.

Group, E. 2008. Do you know what's in your candy? September 8. Retrieved September 9, 2009, from http://www.globalhealingcenter.com/natural health/do-you-know-whats-in-your-candy/.

Harkin, Engel final report shows that work must continue to eradicate child labor in the cocoa supply chain. 2011. April 4. Retrieved August 30, 2013, from Tom Harkin press release, http://www.harkin.senate.gov/press/release .cfm?i=332330.

Heintzman, A., and E. Solomon, eds. 2004. *Feeding the future: From fat to famine, how to solve the world's food crisis.* Toronto: House of Anansi Press, Inc.

Hohenegger, B. 2006. *Liquid jade: The story of tea from East to West.* New York: St. Martin's Press.

Hopkins, T., and I. Wallerstein. 1977. Patterns of development in the modern world system. *Review* 1 (Fall): 111–45.

Illovo Sugar. Retrieved October 10, 2013, from http://www.illovosugar.com /worldofsugar/internationalSugarStats.htm.

Khan, L. 2013. Big bite of the chocolate market. *Oregonian,* D-10. November 17.

Kraus, S. 2009. Mexican sugar imports a concern for U.S. Agriculture Weekly. September 8. Retrieved September 9, 2009, from http://www.agweekly.com /articles/2009/09/08/news/ag_news/news95.txt.

Luttinger, N., and G. Dicum. 2006. *The coffee book: Anatomy of an industry from crop to the last drop.* New York: The New Press.

Lopez, R. 2002. *Chocolate: The nature of indulgence.* New York: Harry N. Abrams.

MacGillivray, A. 2006. *A brief history of globalization.* London: Robinson.

Michelli, J. 2007. *The Starbucks experience: Five principles for turning ordinary into extraordinary.* New York: McGraw-Hill.

Millstone, E., and T. Lang. 2008. *The atlas of food: Who eats what, where, and why.* Los Angeles: University of California Press.

Mintz, S. 1985. *Sweetness and power: The place of sugar in modern history.* New York: Viking/Penguin.

NCA statement on biotechnology. 2008. August 5. Retrieved September 9, 2009, from http://www.candyusa.com/News/PublicPolicyDetail.cfm?Item Number=835.

Newswire reports. 2007. *Oregonian*. March 29.

Off, C. 2006. *Bitter chocolate: Investigating the dark side of the world's most seductive sweet*. Toronto: Random House Canada.

Pereira de Almeida, J. L. 1996. Witches' broom disease of cacao in Bahia: Attempts at eradication and containment. *Crop Protection* 15 (8): 743–52.

Pettigrew, J. 1997. *The tea companion: A connoisseur's guide*. New York: Macmillan USA.

Pollan, M. 2008. The food issue: Farmer in chief. *New York Times*. October 12. Retrieved October 24, 2008, from http://www.nytimes.com/2008/10/12/magazine/12policy-t.html.

Renewing hope for cocoa farmers in Sulawesi. 2002. Film. Chocolate Manufacturers Association/World Cocoa Foundation.

Richey L., and S. Ponte. 2011. *Brand Aid: Shopping well to save the world*. Minneapolis: University of Minnesota Press.

Rojas databank: The Robinson Rojas archive—Notes on agribusiness. Retrieved January 24, 2009, from www.rrojasdatabank.info/agribi.htm.

Santarris, B., and L. Gunderson. 2008. A mid-life sea change: Starbucks, the coffee standard has grown up—and it's OK. *Oregonian*, D-1. January 13.

Save the Children Canada. 2005. Expert forum. Child protection in raw agricultural commodities trade: The case of cocoa. Retrieved January 24, 2009, from http://www.savethechildren.ca/canada/what_we_do/advocate/cocoa.

Shepherd, L. 2008. Starbucks warns profit will miss its mark. *Oregonian*, B-2. December 5.

Shiva, V. 1997. *Biopiracy: The plunder of nature and knowledge*. Boston: South End Press.

Standage, T. 2005. *A history of the world in six glasses*. New York: Walker and Company.

Starbucks gross revenue. Retrieved September 30, 2007, from www.google.com/finance.

Starbucks press release. 2008a. Starbucks holiday beverages turn (RED)^{TM}. November 27 [November 26]. Retrieved December 3, 2008, from http://markets.on.nytimes.com/research/soocks/news/press release.

———. 2008b. Starbucks takes next step in putting money back to loyal customers' wallets. Retrieved December 3, 2008, from http://markets.on.nytimes.com/research/stocks/news/press release.

Stone, B. 2008a. Original team tries to revive Starbucks. *New York Times*. October 30. Retrieved May 5, 2014, from http://www.nytimes.com/2008/10/30/business/30starbucks.html.

———. 2008b. Starbucks profit plunges 97 percent. *New York Times*. November 11. Retrieved November 27, 2013, from http://www.nytimes.com/2008/11/11/business/worldbusiness/11iht-sbux.1.17713420.html.

————. 2008c. Starbucks profit down sharply on restructuring costs. *New York Times*. November 11. Retrieved May 5, 2014, from http://www.nytimes.com/2008/11/11/business/11abux.html.

Stop chocolate slavery. Retrieved May 5, 2014, from http://vision.ucsd.edu/~kbranson/stopchocolateslavery/main.html.

"Venti"-size expansion. 2013. *Oregonian*. January 20.

Weatherford, J. 1989. *Indian givers*. New York: Crown Publishers.

West, J. Slavery in America. Retrieved May 1, 2007, from http://www.slaveryinamerica.org/history/hs_es_sugar.htm.

Wile, A. 2004. *Coffee: A dark history*. New York: W. W. Norton and Company.

World cacao production forecast. Retrieved January 24, 2009, from http://www.worldcocoafoundation.org/info-center/statistics.asp.

NINE **Health**

➤ **SYNOPSIS**

This chapter examines the role of health issues in a globalizing world. It explores tensions between science and policy, focusing in depth on AIDS, tuberculosis, and malaria. The chapter also discusses the link between health and other aspects of society, such as food production and environmental conditions. In some cases, diseases are caused by the medical system itself. It also presents country-specific responses to global pandemics and considers ethical issues related to the control and production of vaccines and medications. As we have seen in prior chapters, nation-states may deal with their own internal health issues very differently from how they address these same issues in a global context.

➤ **SCAFFOLDING**

As you read through this chapter, think about how you would answer each of the questions below.

How have you viewed global health issues prior to reading this chapter?

How did the 2009 H1N1 influenza outbreak affect your daily life or your family's daily life?

What food production and consumption issues seem intimately linked to global health?

Why do you suppose indigenous health knowledge is often presented as less effective and less appropriate than scientifically developed medicines?

> ➤ **CORE CONCEPTS**

How do nation-states decide how to take care of their citizens in terms of providing health care for both regular and infectious diseases?

What kinds of factors have contributed to the resurgence of infectious diseases?

What are some potential links between global health, development, demographics, and global organizations such as the World Health Organization?

Why may the next field for bioterrorism be our food supply?

Chile, Costa Rica, Cyprus, Guadalupe, Hong Kong, Israel, Macau, Malta, Martinique, Singapore, and the United Arab Emirates are a diverse set of nations and territories. Yet they all have one fact in common: their citizens live longer than those of the United States, as do the citizens of many developed countries (United Nations 2006). This truth is unexpected, given the wide gap between the wealth, power, and technology of these countries and that of the United States. But health inevitably becomes linked to broader issues of politics and policy. This may appear strange, given that in Western culture, our perception of health is defined by medicine, which entails a rigorous process of scientific training for people entering that profession. But health cannot be discussed outside of a social context. While Costa Rica, for example, does not have the United States' wealth or technology, it has found a way to address health issues so as to give its citizens a greater lifespan than its northern neighbor. Health is such a broad topic that it touches most global issues, such as food production, public policy, global equity, and economic growth. Like security, health issues can also be defined in different ways. In the United States and some Latin American nations, illicit drug usage is seen as a security issue that is best fought through the national security apparatus. In other countries, such as the Netherlands, it is thought of mainly as a public-health issue. Both approaches have unintended consequences and problems. How nations perceive health issues depends on their cultural background. These perceptions have profound impacts, in turn, on how governments ensure their citizens' health.

In some sense, the story of medicine and health in the last three decades has been one in which Western medicine has come to understand its limits

(Garrett 1994, 30–52). It is important to examine this in order to understand the current challenges to global health. Only a few decades ago, it seemed that technological change could manage most health challenges, and the future would bring steady progress. The remaining diseases that threatened health would be eliminated, while developing countries would gradually follow the path of Europe and the United States. This vision of health placed great emphasis on medical technology and the ability of the medical profession alone to manage disease. Trends in both infectious and chronic disease now have created a more complex and chaotic vision of the future.

In the 1960s it seemed clear that infectious diseases were on the decline: "In 1969, the U.S. surgeon general, Dr. William H. Stewart, told the nation that it had already seen most of the frontiers in the field of contagious disease. Epidemiology seemed destined to become a scientific backwater" (Karlen 1995, 3). People gradually stopped studying infectious diseases in medical schools because it was perceived to be a dead end, as the famous virologist C. J. Peters described: "For at least twenty years I have heard that the discipline I work in is a dying field and there is no career track. . . . In spite of our optimism (which may be the optimism of the brontosaurus) and deep belief in the need to continue, the number of gray heads around the conference tables is disproportionate" (Peters and Olshaker 1997, ix). Across the developed world, governments made a renewed commitment to fight chronic diseases, which they believed to be the new frontier in medicine (Karlen 1995, 3).

By the late 1980s, it became clear that this belief needed to be qualified, as a host of new diseases emerged to infect humanity. (For a partial but nonetheless impressive list, see Karlen 1995, 6; Miller 1989, 509; and Ryan 1997, 383–90.) Far from a backwater of medicine, the rise of AIDS and other illnesses pushed infectious disease into the newspaper headlines. By the 1990s, a plethora of books (Garrett 1994; Karlen 1995; Peters and Olshaker 1997; Ryan 1997) dealt with the threat that emerged. After the terrorist acts of September 11, 2001, and the anthrax attacks that followed, people worried about the threat posed by bioterrorism. Ken Alibek's revelations about the secret Soviet bioweapons program, combined with the penury of many Russian scientists in the post-Soviet era, magnified these fears (Alibek and Handelman 1999; see also Garrett 2000, 481–545). By 2005 there was global concern about the emergence of a lethal strain of bird flu (H5N1) that had emerged in South Asia. Government authorities warned that sufficient stockpiles of antivirals did not exist, and that in

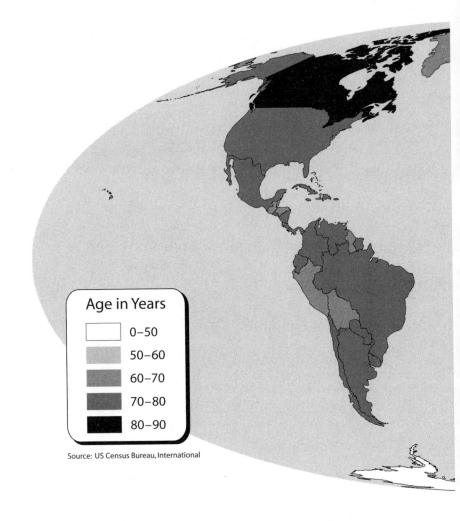

Age in Years

- 0–50
- 50–60
- 60–70
- 70–80
- 80–90

Source: US Census Bureau, International

Map 7 World Life Expectancy (Steph Gaspers 2008)

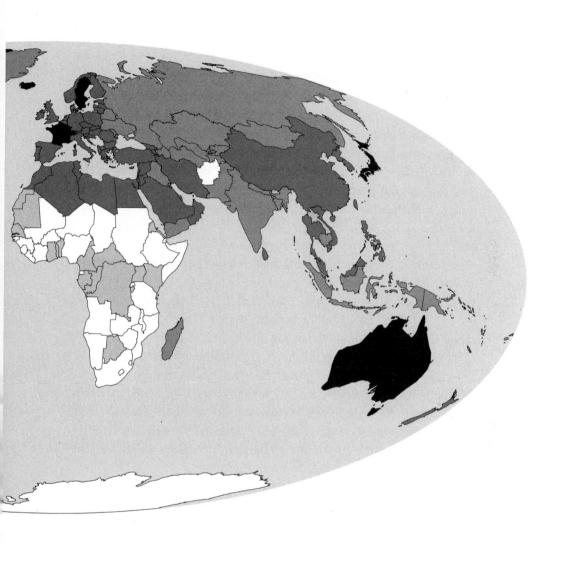

the event of a pandemic, it would take a least six months to create enough medications for North Americans, Europeans, and Japanese. In most of the world, neither medications nor drugs would be available. In 2009 the emergence of novel H1N1 (swine flu) showed that even though much work had been done, it would be months before a vaccine against pandemic influenza could be developed. By 2013 global health experts worried about the simultaneous emergence of H7N1 in China and MERS-COV in Saudi Arabia. How could infectious diseases, which had seemed to be fading into a nightmarish past, have returned to pose such a threat?

There were multiple reasons for their revival (Karlen 1995, 215–30). Health conditions are related to food, and some emerging diseases sprang from agricultural practices. For example, a new illness—bovine spongiform encephalopathy (BSE), or mad cow disease—first appeared in Britain in the mid-1980s (Ryan 1997, 330–32). The appearance of this terrible disease that attacked the brain—a disease that was always fatal and for which there was no known treatment—was a mystery. The only known outbreak of a similar disorder (called kuru) had been among the Fore people of New Guinea, who had acquired it in ritual cannibalism when they consumed the brains of their dead (Schwartz 2003, 58–72). The disease had a devastating effect on the Fore in the 1950s: "In some Fore clans, 5 to 10 percent of the population was affected, and half the deaths over the preceding five years had been attributed to kuru. The total number of kuru deaths was several thousand. To those already high figures had to be added the deaths of sorcerers in revenge killings—*tukabu*—and of young children of women who died of the disease" (Schwartz 2003, 66). As these authors describe, the outbreak finally vanished when Australian authorities suppressed cannibalism among the Fore people (Karlen 1995, 198).

While tragic, the travails of the Fore seemed far from the experience of industrialized Western nations. And yet in both Britain and New Guinea, cannibalism was apparently the key to the emergence of the disease. The current thinking is that BSE is spread by a prion, a mutant protein that contains no DNA. The disease agent was most likely spread throughout European herds because slaughtered animals were being processed into feed: "Once a number of other hypotheses had been eliminated, the conclusion remained that the cattle had been infected by scrapie agent in feed additives. Among those additives were meat and bone meals (MBMs) made from slaughterhouse and processing plant waste" (Schwartz 2003, 144). The animals did not like to eat this waste, as one nineteenth-century author described: "Dairy cows and beef cattle, which are initially reluctant to eat it, soon come to accept it when it is taken in small quantities and thoroughly mixed with the rest of their feed—it is possible to go as high as 1.5 kilograms per day" (Schwartz 2003, 147). In other words, it was by making cattle into involuntary cannibals that this epidemic became possible. The images on British television of drooling, mad, quivering cattle being dragged to their slaughter created panic in Europe. Everyone wondered if the beef they were eating had been contaminated.

Other aspects of modern agriculture may also facilitate the spread of disease. Massive quantities of antibiotics are fed to livestock and chickens, which increases the problem of antibiotic resistance. A new respiratory illness called SARS emerged in southern China in November 2002. The outbreak likely began in the wild game markets of Guandong province, where civet cats were housed in small cages in open-air markets and buyers would come to purchase them as food for meals (Murray 2006, 23; M. Davis 2005, 75–76). Corporations raise chickens in dense populations of tens of thousands of birds to a building, which has led to devastating scenes of destruction when bird flu has arrived in places as varied as the Netherlands and Canada's Fraser valley. Of course, these issues are complex. The poultry industry, for example, points out that small backyard producers have seen the most cases of bird-to-human transmission of flu in Indonesia and Vietnam (M. Davis 2005, 80–114). The point is that the same food-production methods that have allowed countries to feed ever-growing populations also pose health threats. The widespread adoption of high-fructose corn syrup in the 1970s was a key step in the ever-widening global diabetes epidemic. Illness and food production are linked.

Diseases such as mad cow have also illustrated the risks posed by iatrogenic disease—that is, diseases created by modern medicine itself (Karlen 1995, 223–24). The first victims of BSE in Europe were the recipients of growth hormone for pituitary dwarfism (Schwartz 2003, 128–41). Ultimately, more than 100 people were infected in this manner. Yet there are more important iatrogenic illnesses, which might even include Human Immunodeficiency Virus (HIV). HIV is a retrovirus, which is spread through sex, blood, birth, and breast-feeding and is characterized by a long latency period. Although the syndrome that this virus creates, AIDS (Acquired Immune Deficiency Syndrome), was first described in 1981, we know that the virus dates back decades before that. The first blood sample to contain HIV was drawn in 1959 in Zaire, Africa, while molecular geneticists have suggested that the epidemic first began in the 1930s (Hooper 1999, 29, 869–70). The virus itself is a clear descendent of Simian Immunodeficiency Virus (SIV), a disease that infects primates. This virus of primates has been found in many people who were infected by bites from monkeys or from nicks on their hands while butchering primates for food. Yet SIV never seems to have converted to a form that readily spread from human to human. Then something changed, most likely between 1880 and 1930.

There have been many debates about what caused SIV in humans to transform to a pathogenic form, but the probable explanation may be that its rapid transmission by contaminated needles during mass vaccination campaigns created profound changes to the virus. It may also have been transformed through blood transfusions. (For an introduction to the debate around HIV's origins, see Smallman 2007, 10–11.) Tens of millions of people have died of HIV/AIDS, and many millions more are infected. There is now hope with the development of treatments to manage the infection, which are also able to reduce the transmission of the virus. But the irony is that modern medicine itself may have also unleashed this pandemic, although the people responsible acted only with the best of intentions.

Infectious diseases also emerged for natural reasons, the most basic of which is evolution. Antibiotics seemed extremely effective for a decade, but with misuse and time, resistant strains of bacteria began to appear. The routine use of antibiotics in agriculture to promote the rapid growth of livestock has been a serious concern (McKenna 2010, 140–57). The same thing took place in the case of parasitic diseases such as malaria. Human behavior, such as saving leftover medications to self-treat other illnesses, also likely exacerbated this problem. As Laurie Garrett (1994, 411–56) has described, this situation has created a frightening situation in which diseases that most modern doctors have never seen are now reemerging. Without question, the most worrying example is tuberculosis (TB), which the HIV/AIDS epidemic accelerates. In some countries of southern Africa, the HIV prevalence is terrifying; in Botswana and Swaziland, it now infects over 40 percent of adults. People with HIV are especially vulnerable to TB and therefore often transmit it to others.

At the same time, inadequate medical infrastructure has created environments in which people often receive only partial treatment for TB, which has led to a catastrophic rise in the proportion of the disease's strains that are now multidrug resistant. In South Africa, where over 5 million people are HIV positive, this has created a situation in which a new epidemic of drug-resistant TB threatens the country with disaster:

The form of TB, known as XDR for extensively drug-resistant, cannot be effectively treated with most first- and second-line tuberculosis drugs, and some doctors consider it incurable. Since it was first detected last year in KwaZulu-Natal Province, bordering the Indian Ocean, additional cases have been found at 39 hospitals in South Africa's other eight provinces. In interviews on Friday, several epidemiologists and TB experts said the disease had probably moved into Lesotho, Swaziland, and Mozambique. (Wines 2007)

This form of tuberculosis has since been found in other nations, such as India and China. As the work of Paul Farmer (2004) has shown, this problem can be addressed through improved policy decisions, even in the slums of Lima or the prisons of Siberia. Yet this task takes a concerted effort at the international level that until now has been lacking.

New diseases also continue to emerge because of ongoing changes to the earth's environment, many of which have been caused by humans. One such disease is Kyasanur Forest Disease (KFD), which emerged in South India in the late 1950s. As Mark Nichter has described, by the early 1980s, the disease had become a true epidemic in rural India. As researchers studied the disease, they learned that it was a form of tick-borne encephalitis. Changes in forest cover had led to the outbreak; the first instance of the epidemic followed the construction of a cashew plantation. Because monkeys could no longer inhabit the natural forest, they spent more time on the ground, where they "became increasingly exposed to the vector. The virus proved highly virulent among monkeys and ultimately humans, who also proved to be suitable hosts" (Nichter 1987, 407). There are parallels to other diseases (Ryan 1997, 329). KFD was not unique. Indeed, in the 1990s, authors such as Garrett (1994, 550–91) and Frank Ryan (1997, 318–42) argued that global environmental changes were key factors driving the emergence of dangerous new diseases.

Writing from this perspective, authors portrayed diseases as the emissaries of a wounded Mother Nature, who was reacting against the human populations that harmed her: "It could be argued that viruses have, through the empirics of evolution, become unwitting knights of nature, armed by evolution for furious genomic attack against her transgressors. Although not primarily designed to attack humanity, human exploitation and invasion of every ecological sphere has directed that aggression our way" (Ryan 1997, 320; see also Miller 1989). These authors used multiple examples to support their arguments, from the emergence of a hemorrhagic fever in Argentina that was associated with wheat production (Garrett 1994, 27–28) to the rise of the Oropouche virus on cacao plantations in the Amazon (Ryan 1997, 327). The emergence of new diseases, they suggested, can be viewed as an environmental response to the damage inflicted by people: "It is significant in this sense that Ebola, Marburg, and HIV all derived from the African rain forest or its hinterland, savannah. When scientists map the epicenters of origin of newly emerging virus infections on the global map, it is clear that interference with the rain forests, and deforestation in particular, is the most dangerous activity with regard to the emergence of epidemic viruses" (Ryan 1997, 321–22). There is almost a religious rhetoric to this argument, though instead of a plague being God's wrath for sin, now nature is defending itself against humanity. Arno Karlen (1995, 10) has pointed out how arbitrary these attributions of blame for disease creation are: "Some call AIDS a divine chastisement. So far, at least, they have not similarly blamed Lassa fever, Lyme disease, and legionellosis on the sins of Nigerians, suburbanites, and aging veterans."

Another perspective is that all environments change, which means that new niches are endlessly created for diseases. This can happen in unexpected ways. For example, although both Garrett (1994, 550–52) and Ryan (1997, 330) depicted new diseases as emerging because of the environmental damage humans caused in the tropics, both also discussed the emergence of Lyme disease, a tick-borne disorder that expanded in New England as agricultural land reverted to forest. The extent of the environmental change in the region is striking. Moose have settled regions they had abandoned for hundreds of years. Moises Velasquez-Manoff (2007) has reported that more than a thousand moose inhabit Massachusetts, the "third most densely populated state in the nation, according to the U.S. Census (after New Jersey and Rhode Island)." There are black bears in Connecticut. The change has been striking and positive, but it has also created new opportunities for a disease vector to infect humans with a terrible microbe, as large numbers of deer spread the tick that carries this disease (Karlen 1995, 179; Karlen 2000, 134–44).

The point is that viruses and bacteria are not merely a problem to be conquered; they are an integral part of our environment, from the canopy of the rain forest to the planet's oceans, where they swarm in stunning abundance (Ryan 1997, 338–41). They cannot be eliminated, and no technological fix will ever free us from them. The same agricultural and medical technologies that have improved our lives have also created new op-

Medication package inserts vary from country to country, even for an identical drug. The advised dosage, contraindications, and description of the drug's purpose in these inserts may differ. How can you guarantee that you have accurate information for your health purposes when you travel outside of your home country? (Hint: find out what the *Physicians' Desk Reference* is and how it is used.)

portunities for viruses and bacteria. Equally important, humans also form part of the planet's ecosystem, one characterized by increasingly dense populations. As Karlen's work (1995) has made clear from a historical perspective, the emergence of "crowd" diseases has been intimately connected to the emergence of cities, the appearance of new trade routes, and changing levels of human population. Viruses such as measles could only spread once viruses had reached critical densities, associated with the rise of urban living (Karlen 1995, 47–63). Diseases cannot be understood apart from a social and global context. This means that diseases are a particular concern in the era of globalization.

As chapter 2 suggested, there is a major debate over when the modern era of globalization began. Some authors suggest that this process truly originated with the European expansion around the globe in the fifteenth century. From this perspective, globalization is a process intimately linked with the spread of disease. The inhabitants of the Americas had no immunity to New World diseases, from smallpox to yellow fever. Tens of millions died; entire peoples disappeared (Alchon 2003; Karlen 1995, 93–110). The process was repeated countless times in North America as Europeans spread to the North and West (Boyd 1999; Hackett 2002). Many times, the disease arrived before the Europeans did (Fenn 2001). The exchange of diseases that began with this process has not ended, as the 2003 SARS outbreak showed. In this case, a single Chinese doctor facilitated a global outbreak after he moved into a room in the Metropole Hotel in Hong Kong while feverish and sick with SARS: "Although the doctor had little contact with others in the hotel, twelve guests staying on the same floor were ultimately diagnosed with SARS. Among them were a Chinese businessman who traveled to Hanoi to become the index case of the outbreak there, a Singaporean woman who was hospitalized soon after her return to her native city, an elderly woman from Toronto who went home to expose her large family in Canada, and a group of others who were admitted to Hong

Kong hospitals, where they spread the disease to many of the hospital staff to whom they were exposed" (Murray 2006, 19). SARS could be thought of like a product in a commodity chain that stretched from Guandong in China to the Scarborough Grace Hospital in Ontario, Canada, which became a symbol of the epidemic's danger.

SARS is not unique. North America has suffered from the introduction of West Nile virus, an African disease likely brought to the New World as part of the pet trade. In some areas, we have seen outbreaks of what has been termed "airport malaria" near airports, as mosquitoes fly off jets from exotic destinations and start local epidemics that have to be quickly stamped out. The pet trade has brought exotic diseases, such as monkey pox, to the United States. In Canada, Cryptococcus gatti, a fungal infection native to New Guinea, emerged on Vancouver Island in 1999. It has since spread into the Northwest and is now killing other species, such as a harbor porpoise that washed on the shore of Vancouver Island in 2012. Globalization continues to introduce "new" diseases.

These connections are particularly worrisome in a planet that is now mainly urban and where vast populations in the developing world live in squalor without adequate medical care. As Mike Davis's (2005) work illustrates, the world's continued population growth is largely taking place in slum areas of megacities in the developing world, where sewage, water, and health services are lacking. There is a clear connection between global health and development, as the work of Paul Farmer (2007) has shown. A doctor passionately dedicated to the issue of global health, Farmer has dedicated his life to providing health care in the poorest parts of Haiti, as well as Peru and Russia. Diseases such as tuberculosis and cholera thrive in areas of social misery, which in turn can be linked to global processes. The spread of AIDS in the Amazon among indigenous peoples is driven by a frontier environment in which poor young men flood areas claimed by native peoples in order to mine gold for the global market. Social conditions and health are linked. Attempts to alleviate or manage particular diseases are consistently compromised when the structural conditions that allowed them to develop are not ultimately addressed. This was clearly demonstrated in Russia after the collapse of the Soviet Union, as a country that long prided itself on its health system underwent what can only be described as a social collapse. Vaccinations stopped, childhood diseases returned, intravenous drug use skyrocketed, HIV spread rapidly, suicides climbed, alcoholism took off, and life expectancy plummeted. It was not until 2012 that Russia's demographic decline was fully reversed.

The association of development with health is not only a national issue. Structural adjustment programs and intellectual property provisions impact health programs and outcomes on a global level. To understand global health, one must talk about the roles of the World Bank and the World Trade Organization (WTO), in particular its Agreement on Trade-Related Aspects of Intellectual Property Rights (TRIPS) provision in facilitating or impeding policy creation and implementation. The links between global health and international organizations can be illustrated through the example of HIV. As we have already discussed, HIV is caused by a virus that has a remarkably long latency period, perhaps ten years on average from infection to the development of AIDS. One of the terrible aspects of this latency period is that it provides a lengthy period in which people can unknowingly spread the virus, or in which they must wrestle with the implications of being HIV positive. Globally, tens of millions of people are infected with the virus, and the number continues to climb. The region most impacted by the virus has been sub-Saharan Africa. In Botswana and Swaziland, it has been estimated that more than 40 percent of all adults are HIV positive. The educated, urban class—teachers, nurses, doctors, government officials, and other professionals—have been heavily impacted, which not only undermined the region's economies but also its ability to address the crisis. No part of southern African society has escaped the disease's impact, which ranges from the growing number of AIDS orphans to the falling rates of school attendance as families spend money on medications and not tuition. While southern Africa has been most affected, the disease has also spread broadly in the former Soviet Union, Eastern Europe, and Southeast Asia. AIDS is a truly global crisis. Sadly, despite long-term and well-funded efforts, the fact that HIV has many different clades (strains) complicates the drive to develop a vaccine. For the time being, we must manage this pandemic without a vaccine.

There is also reason for hope. In 1996 David Ho and other scientists announced that a combination of antiretroviral medications could suppress the level of the virus in the blood to a level so low that it could not be detected. This was not a cure. If the treatment was stopped, the virus returned. And failure to comply with therapy quickly led to drug resistance. But no longer did being HIV positive mean death. Instead, the disease began to change into a chronic condition for many people—though only if they could afford the treatment. In the early years, triple therapy might cost $10,000 to $15,000 annually. Such costs were heavy but perhaps manageable.

"When you have communities living in abject poverty, exposed to all the diseases, the diseases are going to recur and they'll keep on recurring, and we have to turn our attention to that. At this point, I put my money on the bugs" (Dr. William Close in Bienstock, Halpern, and Jacobovici, *Ebola* [2007]). If you were in charge of health policy decisions for your country, how would you balance budget allocations for infectious-disease prevention with budget allocations for general poverty reduction?

In the developing world, however, prevention appeared to be the only hope. The nations of the Global South refused to accept this discrepancy. The cost of these medications might be more than $10,000 a year if a pharmaceutical company produced them. But laboratories in Brazil or India could make the same drugs at a cost of $150 to $300 a year. Was it reasonable that tens of millions of people would die when treatments existed that could save them? Beginning in 1996, Brazil moved to make these medications available to everyone who needed them. This program proved to be effective: people wanted to know their status to receive treatment, so they were more likely to be tested for HIV. Mortality rates fell sharply. And the Brazilian government saved money because people did not enter public hospitals for expensive end-of-life care but rather remained employed and paid taxes (Marins 2002; Anonymous 2001, 331–37). The success of the Brazilian effort promised to change the terms of the debate about fighting AIDS in the developing world.

Pharmaceutical companies, however, argued that this policy was dangerous because it would discourage the research needed to produce new HIV/AIDS medications. The U.S. government initially supported this argument and tried to block the production of generic HIV medications using the TRIPS provisions of the WTO. Nonprofit organizations rallied to support the efforts of the developing countries by pointing out that many medications are produced with public funds. Few drugs had been produced for tropical diseases over the course of decades. Extracting profits from the developing world would do little to address the diseases in this region, critics suggested. They cited statistics that showed that "90 percent of the global expenditure on medical research is on diseases causing 10 percent of the global burden of disease. Moreover, of 1,223 new drugs developed between 1975 and 1997, only 13 were for the treatment of tropical diseases" (Benatar, Daar, and Singer 2003, 110). The result was a heated battle that the United States gradually realized it could not win (Smallman 2007, 14–15, 92–96). A turning point was the 2001 anthrax attack in the United States, which killed five people and made seventeen ill. The U.S. government debated producing the expensive antibiotic ciprofloxacin as a generic so that it could afford to provide care to all those affected (Bayer has since lost the patent, and the drug is available generically). In this context, it became difficult to deny poor countries facing the death of millions access to the medications that could address the pandemic. With the resolution of this international debate, many developing countries are moving to expand their citizens' access to these medications. By 2012 there was a realization in the medical community that people living with HIV are much less infectious when receiving treatment, which suggested that treatment was part of prevention. At this moment, an old dichotomy disappeared. This knowledge seems likely to reshape all debates about the costs of HIV medications in the future. Global health is shaped not only by microbes but also by international organizations and beliefs.

International factors also shape the discovery of new drugs and the availability of medications to the poor. The majority of the world's medications have been developed from plants, and this remains true even in an era of synthetic chemistry. Much of the knowledge that has permitted the rise of modern medical treatments has roots in indigenous knowledge, such as the discovery of quinine by Peru's indigenous peoples, which created the first effective treatment for malaria, and the use of curare, from which a drug was created for use in anesthesia (W. Davis 1997, 209–15, 302, 377). Ethnobotanists are people who study the cultural aspects of plant life. One famous ethnobotanist, Wade Davis, has provided a rich description of the intricate knowledge of forest plants held by indigenous peoples in the Amazon. In his book *One River: Explorations and Discoveries in the Amazon Rain Forest*, he describes the use by Amazonian peoples of a liana called *ayahuasca* or *yagé*, which they combine with other plants to create a hallucinogenic drink (W. Davis 1997, 153). What is interesting about this product is that it represents the combination of two classes of plants. The second plant can only have its hallucinogenic effect if combined with yagé because its main agent, tryptamines, are "denatured by an enzyme, monoamine oxidase (MAO), found in the human gut. Tryptamines can be taken orally only if combined with a MAO inhibitor. Amazingly, the betacarbolines found in yagé are inhibitors of precisely this sort" (W. Davis 1997, 217). To be able to use these plants ritually, forest peoples had to develop a sophisticated understanding of how they interacted.

One has to wonder how the indigenous peoples could ever have acquired this knowledge. Their own answers to these questions are seldom useful to someone trained in biology, as the following conversation, recorded by Wade Davis, suggests:

> "*Ayahuasca*," Tim said softly. "*Yagé*." He looked at Pedro, who was smiling.
> "But I thought it was only found in the lowlands," I said.
> "So did I," said Tim.
> "*Banisteriopsis caapi*," Pedro said proudly. "I got tired of buying from those people."
> "But how did you get the plant to grow here?" Tim asked.
> "It wasn't easy. The Ingano say there are seven different kinds. To me, it's just one species. What do you think, Timoteo?"
> For the first time since I had known him, Tim was speechless.
> "How do you tell them apart?" I asked Pedro.
> "They say that you must prepare the plant at the right time of the month. Then, once you come under its influence, you can distinguish the varieties based on the tone of the songs that each one sings to you on the night of the full moon."
> "Do you think it's possible?" I looked at Tim.
> "I don't know."
> "I'm growing them all so that I can find out."
> "Should be a whole lot more interesting than counting stamens," Tim said. Pedro smiled and nodded in agreement. (W. Davis 1997, 176–77, 197)

The point of this story is that there is a rich store of knowledge about the medicinal uses of plants. The development of new medications is not only a one-way exchange, with new therapies flowing from the North to the South. But there are significant debates about how indigenous peoples should be compensated for this knowledge. This creates a moral link between indigenous knowledge and global financial structures. Sadly, however, there are almost no examples of indigenous people being paid for their knowledge, despite many court cases and public appeals.

Many communities in the Global South are worried that if they share their knowledge with pharmaceutical companies, the companies will patent the active ingredient in the plant and local producers will no longer be able to sell their products. For people in developing countries, this was an emotional issue. After the U.S. patent office gave a patent for turmeric to researchers at the University of Mississippi Medical Center in 2005, the Indian government had to fight to prove that Indians had long been aware of the medical benefits of turmeric. They succeeded after a decade-long legal battle (Philip 2010, 250). But with intellectual property law permitting the patenting of life forms, people in developing countries now feared that the TRIPS clause of the WTO could be used to enforce companies' claims to traditional knowledge.

Other issues can be seen through the case of a breakthrough treatment for malaria called *Artemisia annua*, or Sweet Wormwood. Malaria is one of three infectious diseases that have been responsible for the greatest loss of life in the tropics. Hundreds of millions of people are infected each year, and hundreds of thousands die. With global warming spreading the range of the mosquitoes that serve as the disease's vector and the malaria parasite's increasing resistance to most drugs used for treatment, the future appears dire. But there is some hope. Sometimes, travelers find effective treatments using local remedies. For example, one student suffered from repeated bouts of malaria while working on volunteer programs in Tanzania, even though she had taken the standard drugs for prophylaxis. It was then that a fellow traveler suggested that she try Sweet Wormwood, a plant long used by Chinese herbalists to treat diseases, including malaria. She was rapidly cured of her third bout with malaria (Thom 2006).

The student then began to research the history of artemisinin, the drug extracted from Sweet Wormwood; she soon learned that the plant had been adopted by Chinese doctors who were searching to find a treatment for malaria in the 1960s in order to treat North Vietnamese soldiers infected during the fight against the United States. They isolated the active component in the 1960s, but it took another decade for the medication to become commercially available (Thom 2008, 3). This drug has now become a standard treatment for malaria; the Global Fund for AIDS, Tuberculosis, and Malaria is giving major grants to poor countries to purchase this medication while asking these countries to move away from some older drugs. The World Health Organization (WHO) is encouraging countries to adopt this medication, particularly where drug-resistant malaria is a problem (Thom 2008, 4–5).

The discovery of artemisinin is a triumph that has had both medical and social benefits. It has helped to return malaria to its former status as a treatable disorder and to buy time for the production of other new-generation malaria drugs. But it has also created an industry, because large amounts of Sweet Wormwood are needed to produce the drug. Thom's research found that for this reason, companies made plans to grow large amounts of the plant in East Africa (Thom 2008, 5–6). But this form of production is threatened by efforts to create a synthetic version of the drug, which would eliminate demand for the natural product: "If efforts toward applying a new biotechnology formula to an ancient Chinese tincture succeed, the new form of the drug could be patented and sustainable efforts of cultivation in Africa would be challenged, yet again" (Thom 2008, 6). There would also be benefits to being able to produce artemisinin synthetically, one of which would be that the cost of its production could fall, thus making it easier for poor countries to provide the medicine to their people. Such examples raise difficult issues: How should indigenous peoples be compensated for their knowledge and the products they create? What obligations do pharmaceutical companies have either to share their profits or to develop drugs to treat diseases affecting the poor?

The point of this section is not to ascribe major health issues to globalization, which is a two-edged sword. On the one hand, globalization brings structural-adjustment plans that can undermine health-care systems, facilitate the rapid spread of new diseases, and permit multinationals to block the production of generic drugs. But globalization also brings the expertise of the WHO to fight disease outbreaks, the work of the United Nations to improve health standards, donations from wealthy nations to fight illness, and the efforts of international NGOs to address health inequities. Nowhere can this dual character of globalization be seen with greater clarity than in the case of HIV in Brazil. When Brazil tried to implement a comprehensive program to provide free treatment to those suffering from HIV, it faced a struggle with both the United States and major pharmaceutical companies because of intellectual property issues. Yet this program itself was also made possible by a series of loans from the World Bank. The irony is that the World Bank did not believe that the provision of treatment to people living with HIV was sustainable. But the World Bank's funds helped to create the infrastructure of testing facilities, laboratories, pharmacies, and clinics that made the Brazilian program possible (Smallman 2007, 88–91, 96–97). Health cannot be separated from questions of global governance. Indeed, in some cases, one must wonder whether the current nation-state system provides the best structure to address global health issues.

This issue can be explored through the case of influenza, which raises questions about global health governance and the best way to face an urgent threat to global health. The influenza virus is a very contagious agent that causes a respiratory disease. In the Northern Hemisphere, the flu season usually begins in October and peaks around February. (The Southern Hemisphere's flu season peaks in July or August.) We are all familiar with the flu: the rapid onset of exhaustion, aches, headache, and coughing and heaviness in our chest. For most people, after some time in bed and a little care, the flu quickly passes. But flu is a highly mutagenic (changeable) virus, which sometimes undergoes major changes, in particular when a form adapted to birds enters into humans or other animals. In this case, the world can see a devastating pandemic (see www.pandemicflu.gov). The worst pandemic of the twentieth century struck in 1918, when an avian form of the flu adapted to humans and began to spread rapidly, perhaps beginning in Haskell County, Kansas. By the time the disease had run its course, perhaps 40 million people had died, from the hills of northern India, the country most devastated by the disease, to the trenches of Western Europe during World War I (M. Davis 2005, 26, 32). Many famous people suffered from the disease, for which there was no effective treatment. The pandemic killed William Osler, the outstanding physician of the age (Barry 2005; Crosby 1990; Davies 2000; Kolata 1999). As Alfred Crosby (1990) and Arno Karlen (1995, 145) have pointed out, one of the most unusual aspects of the pandemic is that it has been largely forgotten.

There were also flu pandemics in 1957 and 1968, although neither proved as deadly as the 1918 outbreak. In some respects, little has changed in the intervening decades. We do have some treatments now for the flu. There are currently four drugs used to treat influenza, and they can only be obtained in most developing countries with a doctor's prescription. All must be taken shortly after developing symptoms, and none cures the illness. Instead, they shorten the course of the disease and alleviate suffering. Vaccines are also available, but they currently represent an imperfect means to address this threat. The flu virus mutates rapidly, and there are many different strains, each characterized by different proteins in their outer shell. Every year, scientists scour the planet looking for different forms of the virus. They then have to guess which forms will likely dominate epidemics in the coming winter (for each hemisphere). They come to a consensus on three different forms. It then takes months to grow the virus in chicken eggs, the main means to make most influenza vaccines. But this approach has limitations; sometimes a strain of virus will circulate widely that is not covered by that year's vaccine. Another risk is that a novel form will appear for which the vaccine developers are completely unprepared.

In 1997 an outbreak of bird flu in Hong Kong sickened eighteen people and killed six. The government killed more than a million chickens in a few days, which stamped out the outbreak (M. Davis 2005, 45–54). But this was not the only appearance of bird flu. In February 2004, an outbreak of a different strain of bird flu in the Fraser valley of British Columbia caused the Canadian Food Inspection Agency to order the destruction of nearly 20 million chickens. In 2003 and 2004, bird flu again appeared in Southeast Asia, particularly in Vietnam, and it has since spread to countries as geographically distant as Turkey and Indonesia. In 2009 a new form of influenza, novel H1N1 (the so-called swine flu), emerged in Mexico. This new strain put years of preparation to the test from a completely unexpected virus. In the end, the 2009 pandemic did not come close to resembling that of 1918. But then H7N9 began to circulate in eastern China in 2013 and again raised concerns about the pandemic potential of a new influenza strain.

While health authorities conducted surveillance and took steps to prepare for a possible pandemic, efforts to fight the flu also raised key moral questions about equity in global public health. European and North American governments collectively spent billions of dollars stockpiling medications, testing vaccines, and encouraging basic research on the flu. At the same time, developing nations struggling to contain bird flu found comparatively little aid forthcoming for tasks such as culling infected flocks. With the emergence of H1N1, developed countries were able to activate preexisting contracts with major vaccine manufacturers, which gave them first access to vaccines. The manufacturers would not take orders from poorer but more populous countries because the companies did not have the capacity. This inequality threatened the world's efforts to contain flu pandemics.

Even before the emergence of novel H1N1, developing nations were reluctant to collaborate with First World nations to develop possible vaccines because they knew they were unlikely to benefit from this research in the event of an outbreak. In some cases, developing countries may have sought access to vaccines in the event of an outbreak by offering individual companies access to emerging viral strains. Indonesia, for example, did not want to share strains of the bird flu collected from fatalities because the country wanted guaranteed access to any vaccine developed from this resource. As a result, in 2007 Indonesia briefly stopped sharing viral samples of avian influenza from human cases with the WHO. It also briefly considered making a proprietary arrangement with a pharmaceutical company, in which Indonesia would share viral samples in exchange for free vaccines. It quickly abandoned this idea after international criticism. But the result of this crisis was a lengthy political struggle that drew in pharmaceutical companies, the World Health Assembly, and the WHO (Smallman 2013). At issue were the terms under which developing countries would share viral samples with the WHO. The United States and other developed countries argued that frontline countries had to share samples as a matter of international law, as governed by the International Health Regulations (IHRs). The frontline states argued that this was an example of biopiracy, in which developed countries received material from the WHO without any benefits accruing to the countries that provided the samples. As a result, the WHO made significant changes to its policies, as reflected in its Pandemic Influenza Plan (PIP) of 2011.

This struggle reflects the deep frustration officials in some developing countries have felt about inequalities in access to health resources and their government's inability to protect its own people. This issue is not new, and the anger it generates has sometimes proved destructive. Under President Thabo Mbeki, South Africa's health minister Manto Tshabalala-Msimang questioned the value of Western medicines to treat HIV and recommended a dietary regime of garlic, lemon juice, and beet root to treat the virus—at a time when hundreds of thousands of South Africans were dying from the disease (Dugger 2008). South African skeptics doubted that HIV caused AIDS. They said that pharmaceutical companies promoted this idea so that they could sell toxic antiretrovirals to poor Africans for a profit. In this view, racist ideas of Africans' sexuality formed part of a conspiracy to present HIV as the cause of AIDS. One Harvard study found that this tragic argument resulted in the death of 375,000 South Africans who would have lived (or not become infected, in the case of babies) with appropriate medications during the period from 2000 to 2005 (Dugger 2008).

In Nigeria, Muslim elders rejected a vaccination campaign against polio—which meant that the disease could not be eradicated from their nation—because they believed that the vaccines were designed to sterilize Muslims. In July 2008 the WHO announced that an eight-month-old Pakistani baby had tested positive for polio in a region where "militants have opposed vaccination" (Associated Press 2008). In 2013 polio campaign workers were killed by members of the Taliban in Pakistan. Such fears are not tied to one region or religion. Globally, health campaigns become embedded in larger issues related to how people in developing nations view their position in the world.

India and other developing nations have seemed inclined to support an Indonesian ideal of "viral sovereignty," which states that a country's right to "control all information on locally discovered viruses should be protected through the same mechanisms that the U.N. Food and Agriculture Organization uses to guarantee poor countries' rights of ownership and patents on the seeds of its indigenous plants" (Holbrooke and Garrett 2008). Holbrooke and Garrett have argued that this idea of sovereignty, as applied to something as denationalized as viruses, could fundamentally undermine efforts to control diseases such as SARS and HIV. Yet the perspective of developing nations regarding influenza is shaped by a belief that the world's effort to fight the disease may not help them.

At its root, this conflict is part of a larger debate concerning what is called global disease governance. At issue are some key questions: Is the nation-state the best framework within which to address global health issues? What role should the WHO play in fighting disease? How can the issues of the Global North and South be reconciled to ensure a collaborative response to illnesses such as influenza? The emergence of new forms of influenza has required global health authorities to propose changes in everything from animal husbandry practices to disease reporting. To do this on a scale likely to be successful entails a truly global commitment.

George Rutherford—currently a professor, the head of the Division of Preventive Medicine and Public Health, and the director of the Institute for Global Health at the University of California, San Francisco—lectured at UCLA on the prevention of avian flu and SARS (http://www.you tube.com/watch?v=K3P2Aqp5Axs). He identified the following activities as relevant to controlling the length and severity of epidemics:

1 Expenditures on experimental vaccines

2 Stockpiling antivirals that may be outdated when put to use

3 Stockpiling supplies (just in case)

4 Identify the impact of social distancing (for example, school closures) on the overall economy

With a partner, discuss which of these activities you are familiar with in terms of the 2009 or 2013 experience worldwide with the H1N1 virus.

Although people can collaborate to block the spread of disease, their decisions and actions often have the opposite result. As Arno Karlen (1995, 59–60) and others have explained, there is a long association between war and disease that dates back to the disastrous experience of Athens during the Peloponnesian War, as Thucydides described. During the medieval period, armies were more likely to bring death by the diseases they carried, such as typhus, than by the sword (Karlen 1995, 114–15). Even during the U.S. Civil War, more troops died from disease than in combat. Disease can also be much more than an unanticipated consequence of warfare; people have used disease as an instrument of war for almost as long as history. During Pontiac's Rebellion in 1763, Lord Amherst sanctioned the deliberate infection of rebellious tribes by means of smallpox-contaminated blankets, although it is unknown whether his request was acted upon (Fenn 2001, 88–89). There are many other examples of biological warfare. With the development of medical science and humanity's ability to manipulate the genome of disease organisms, there has been growing concern that escalating work on biological warfare could lead to a global disaster. For this reason, the Soviet Union and the United States signed a treaty to ban offensive work with biological warfare agents in 1970 (Mangold and Goldberg 2000, 53–59).

While the United States appears to have lived up to its treaty agreements, we now know that the former Soviet Union did not. Instead, it developed an immense industrial and research capacity with the goal of weaponizing disease strains and developing new means to deliver them, including specially designed intercontinental ballistic missiles. With the defection of Ken Alibek, one of the Soviet scientists charged with developing this weaponry, the West learned the true scale of the Soviet threat (Alibek and Handelman 1999; Mangold and Goldbert 2000, 62–195).

This revelation was especially horrifying because the 1990s saw increasing concerns about the dangers that bioterrorism posed. Unlike nuclear weapons, which might take a large portion of a state's resources to develop, bioterrorism agents could be easily smuggled and dispersed. Of special concern was the collapse of the Soviet military's research apparatus. There were considerable fears that a disgruntled scientist, unpaid for months, might decide to stick a test tube with smallpox into a suitcase and shop it to rogue states or terrorist organizations. A number of examples heightened this concern (Mangold and Goldberg 2000, 335–51). In Oregon in 1984, for example, followers of Indian spiritualist Bhagwan Shree Rajneesh deliberately laced salad bars at restaurants in The Dalles with salmonella in an effort to sway local elections. The water supply was also infected, and over 700 people fell ill. After Rajneesh was deported, the cult collapsed, but there were many similar groups that worried security analysts. Information grew that different groups were striving to obtain this capability. In particular, the sarin nerve gas attacks in Japanese cities carried out by the Aum Shinrikyo cult served as a warning that there were groups willing to use such weapons to cause the mass deaths of civilians. Aum Shinrikyo also researched biological weapons and carried out an unsuccessful attack on U.S. naval forces with botulinum (Goldberg and Mangold 2000, 340–41). How long would it be before another group had greater success?

On September 11, 2001, the world changed for many Americans in the United States as they watched jets slam into the World Trade Center's twin towers. This attack revealed the depth of hatred held toward the country by Al-Qaida, a group that most U.S. citizens had never heard of. On September 25, 2001, the first of a number of letters containing anthrax was received at news outlets. While the total number of deaths was small, it caused immense disruption and showed how easily a biological agent could be dispersed (Rosner and Markowitz 2006, 16–19, 123–28). No suspect was ever arrested, and we still do not know the identity of the attacker, although there are allegations it was a U.S. scientist. In the months that followed, many public-health authorities in the United States mused about the dangers posed by smallpox. This disease had once killed millions before vaccination had eliminated it from the face of the earth. Both the United States and Russia, however, still contained frozen strains of the virus in two special repositories (Karlen 1995, 155). And suspicions existed that some other nations might have smallpox samples, which they had not declared to the WHO.

With the clear threat from bioterrorism, funds poured into basic research and preparedness in this area, which greatly benefited local health departments in many U.S. states (Rosner and Markowitz 2006, 56, 68–69, 73). Project Bioshield, which passed the U.S. Congress in 2004, represented a major investment in the United States' health capacity. At the same time, some public-health officials argued that this distracted from their efforts to deal with other pressing issues, such as the spread of West Nile virus or the fight against drug-resistant tuberculosis (Rosner and Markowitz 2006, 77, 81–92). Part of the challenge was that it proved difficult to evaluate priorities because measuring the threat from bioterrorism was very complicated. If smallpox were reintroduced into humanity, it would

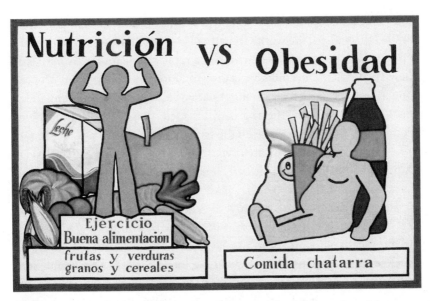

"Nutrition vs. Obesity" wall mural, Oaxaca, Mexico (Used with permission of the photographer, Margaret Everett)

represent a global calamity that could kill hundreds of millions of people before a successful medical response. At the same time, the threat was entirely theoretical, since there was not one person ill with smallpox anywhere on the planet (Rosner and Markowitz 2006, 98). Mike Davis has contrasted the funds spent on preparing for bioterrorism with those expended preparing for a flu pandemic (M. Davis 2005, 128). This contrast between the theoretical risks and the immediate costs undermined the federal government's efforts to vaccinate first responders in the United States against smallpox (Rosner and Markowitz 2006, 92–101). In the aftermath of the Iraq War, Americans learned that Iraq had not possessed the weapons of mass destruction that the Bush administration had referred to as a means to justify the invasion, raising questions about whether the administration had exaggerated or even lied about this threat.

There are certainly valid reasons to fear bioterrorism. But millions of people die every year because of the tobacco industry. How should these health challenges be evaluated? Is bioterrorism an ogre that frightens Western society now but will fade from the news in coming years? The global diabetes epidemic provides an example of another health threat that could also justify massive expenditures of money and funds. With changes in diet—in particular a rise in the consumption of sugar and processed food—combined with a decline in physical exercise, diabetes rates have climbed throughout the world. In particular, type 2 diabetes, which usually develops later in life, has been rising at a rapid rate (Zimmet, Alberti, and Shaw 2001, 783). The epidemic is growing most rapidly in non-European populations, in particular among Asians (Seidell 2000, 8). Many indigenous populations have been greatly affected, ranging from the Akimel O'odham in the United States to the native peoples of Oaxaca, Mexico. In some communities, the numbers are frightening: "In the Pacific island of Naura, where diabetes was virtually unknown 50 years ago, it is now present in approximately 40 percent of adults. The potential for increases in the number of cases is greatest in Asia" (Zimmet, Alberti, and Shaw 2001, 784). There are arguments within the scientific community about why these indigenous populations appear to be more vulnerable to diabetes. Some people argue that there may be a genetic basis, in that populations more exposed to famines conserved genes that in times of plenty proved disastrous (Zimmet, Alberti, and Shaw 2001, 785). But equally important must be the profound changes to traditional diets, the rise of high-fructose corn syrup, and the collapse of traditional lifeways.

The prevalence of diabetes in some of these communities is now approaching that of HIV in southern Africa. Such a high rate carries not only a human burden but also an economic burden, as the weight of managing the disease saps resources from other activities. For indigenous peoples already juggling multiple challenges, diabetes represents a major cost. But even for major states such as India and China, the expense entailed by the tens of millions of people affected by this disease is daunting (King, Aubert, and Herman 1998, 1416). Most new cases of diabetes will be in the developing world, where there is a strong dichotomy in the appearance of diabetes in that the prevalence is significantly higher in the cities (King, Aubert, and Herman 1998, 1415, 1417). In this sense, diabetes represents yet another urban health challenge in a developing world already overwhelmed by rapid urbanization. Type 2 diabetes is a largely avoidable disorder that is readily addressed by interventions in diet and exercise (Zimmet, Alberti, and Shaw, 2001, 785). How should the world respond to this "disease of development"?

The challenge of chronic disease can be so magnified by development that one might be tempted to question the benefit of economic growth at all. John Bodley captures this perspective well in a description of how "modernization" has impacted health in Pacific Island communities, beginning with the isolated island of Pukapuka.

Predictably, the population of Pukapuka was characterized by relatively low levels of imported sugar and salt intake, and a presumably
related low level of heart disease, high blood pressure, and diabetes.
In Rarotonga, where economic success was introducing town life,
imported food, and motorcycles, sugar and salt intake nearly tripled,
high blood pressure increased approximately ninefold, diabetes
increased two- to threefold, and heart disease doubled for men and
more than quadrupled for women. Meanwhile, the number of grossly
obese women increased more than tenfold. Among the New Zealand
Maori, sugar intake was nearly eight times that of the Pukapukans,
gout in men was nearly double its rate on Pukapuka, diabetes in men
was more than fivefold higher, and heart disease in women had increased more than sixfold. (Bodley 1999, 135)

Obviously, access to Western medicine has also brought great benefits, from childhood vaccines to the antibiotics that quickly cure otherwise
deadly infections. But there has been a trade-off.

This complexity makes all health-care decisions difficult. Laurie Garrett
(2007) has argued that the vast sums of money currently flowing into the
global fight against AIDS are stripping funding from more basic aspects
of public health. It is difficult to address one health-care issue without addressing others. Indeed, health care is a holistic topic, because it reflects
larger aspects of societal and environmental health. In the Arctic, northern
peoples who rely heavily on local game and fish are having serious problems with contamination from pesticides and mercury that come from developed regions. Similarly, the contamination of pet food with melamine, a
food additive used in China to boost protein readings, caused widespread
anxiety in North America in April 2007. The health of people in developed
countries is inextricably linked to economic and social issues in places that
they will never visit and of which they may not even be aware. Nowhere
is this clearer than with food-related issues, which are tightly intertwined
with health. Malnutrition increases a population's vulnerability to all diseases and can impact a child's health for life. Efforts to address the challenges of both infectious and chronic diseases entail engaging the food
issues discussed in the previous chapter.

Globalization and health issues also are intertwined, as one can see
by returning to the history of HIV. Undoubtedly, the movement of HIV
has been linked to the flows of people. In the case of South Africa in the
1990s, large numbers of men entered the country from neighboring states

to work in the gold and diamond mines, where they were separated from their families, had substantial income, and had ready access to a local population of sex workers. The result was the rapid amplification of HIV, which returned with the migrant laborers to their home countries, facilitating the spread of the disease. In South and Southeast Asia, it was less the voluntary migration of laborers than the human trafficking industry that drove the evolution of the virus, as young women from Nepal to Myanmar were entrapped and traded in a sex trade that stretched over thousands of miles (Beyrer 1998, 128–39). This was paralleled by a trade in opium that was so key to the epidemic's spread that it can be witnessed even on the fundamental level of viral biology by tracing the propagation of viral clades (forms) in the region (Smallman 2007, 213–16).

Mexico has long had a lower rate of HIV than its northern neighbor, but that may change as large numbers of migrant laborers from small, rural (and often indigenous) villages travel north. Young men, freed from the conservative strictures of their home communities, sometimes experiment with sex or drugs and then return home to their wives and families. Oaxaca is a poor state in southern Mexico where far more rural housewives than urban prostitutes are being infected with HIV. Ironically, HIV has also spread among Central American women, who may have entered Mexico on their way to the United States but then became entrapped in Oaxaca and enmeshed in the sex trade (Smallman 2007, 113–64). In other words, HIV itself feeds upon larger structural issues of gender inequality, labor mobility, and human trafficking. While the disease is a biological entity, the epidemic also is a social construct. Without a much-wished-for cure, HIV will have to be fought not only by medical means but also by addressing the social ills upon which the disease feeds globally. While this is true for HIV, the same can be said for many other diseases. Within the United States, for example, the documentation status of immigrants is a key variable for their health (McGuire and Georges 2003).

Conclusion

The key argument of this chapter has been that health cannot be narrowly defined in terms of access to Western biomedicine or the scientific knowledge that allows a professional class to treat patients. Instead, health is a complex topic that is intimately related to the most important issues in international studies, from development to the environment, global governance to security. For this reason, health-care decisions cannot be left to health-care professionals alone. Instead, health must be viewed in a social context. Technological developments will not save us from the dilemmas we face. Social and environmental change will continue to create new health issues that will in turn require political and social action to resolve. How do we weigh the potential threat of bioterrorism against the real damage caused by diabetes? How do we ensure that the interests of the Global North and the Global South are reconciled to permit indigenous knowledge to create new medicines or to combat bird flu? How do questions of food—its production, delivery, and quality—impact global health? How do global food and health issues impact you?

➤ VOCABULARY

ethnobotany	artemisinin
XDR	WHO
spongiform	SARS
encephalopathy	Kyasanur Forest Disease (KFD)
SIV	viral sovereignty
iatrogenic	TRIPS provisions

➤ DISCUSSION AND REFLECTION QUESTIONS

1 *Why might it be the case that health cannot be discussed outside of its social context?*

2 *What processes have contributed to the link between processed foods and disease?*

3 *How have globalization and the increase in border crossing and migration changed the shape of disease spread?*

4 *How is global climate/environmental change affecting the emergence of new diseases?*

5 *How does globalization introduce new diseases, and what is the most recent example?*

6 *How do structural adjustment programs and intellectual property provisions impact health programs and outcomes on a global level?*

7 *What is the relationship between NGOs, multinational drug companies, and local and regional infrastructures?*

8 *What are the conditions that can cause a public-health issue to become a security issue?*

9 *What are some ways to devise a more equitable resource distribution between "disease darlings" (HIV) and "old stalwarts" (malaria, tuberculosis, etc.)?*

10 *How would you decide how to fund bioterrorism research and relief versus pandemic research and relief?*

ACTIVITY 1 H1N1 (swine flu) emerged in 2009 as the newest potential pandemic to circle the globe. Reconstruct your personal calendar beginning in August 2009 and finishing in December 2009. What do you remember about how you became aware of H1N1? Were your daily routines changed, and if so, how? How were the routines of those close to you changed? Were your places of work and study affected by the pandemic? Were you aware of any international shifts that occurred? Did you receive a vaccine? Why or why not? What do you recall about the publicity regarding the vaccine and its availability? Talk with an individual close to you but outside your immediate family. Compare/contrast his or her H1N1 experience with your own.

ACTIVITY 2 Choose one of the diseases profiled in this chapter. See if you can find written information tracking its chronology and the location of particular disease outbreaks. Create a chart organized by time and location. Once your chart is complete, try and identify the degree to which Dr. George Rutherford's recommendations for epidemic/pandemic control (the third sidebar in this chapter) occurred in each of the outbreak locations. You may want to refer to the sample Ebola outbreak chart produced by the Centers for Disease Control in the United States, available at http://www.cdc.gov/vhf/ebola/resources/outbreak-table.html.

References

Aginam, O. 2005. *Global health governance: International law and public health in a divided world.* Toronto: University of Toronto Press.

Alchon, S. A. 2003. *A pest in the land: New World epidemics in a global perspective.* Albuquerque: University of New Mexico Press.

Alibek, K., and S. Handelman. 1999. *BioHazard: The chilling true story of the largest covert biological weapons program in the world—told from the inside by the man who ran it.* New York: Delta.

Altman, L. K. 2007. Rise of a deadly TB reveals a global system in crisis. *New York Times*. March 20. Retrieved March 21, 2007, from http://www.nytimes .com/2007/03/20/health/20docs.html?

Anonymous. 2001. Brazil fights for affordable drugs against HIV and AIDS. *Revista Panamericana de Salud Pública* 9 (May): 5, 331–37.

Associated Press. 2007. Indonesia won't share bird flu virus data. March 13. Retrieved March 21, 2007, from http://www.theglobeandmail.com/life /article745892.ece.

———. 2008. Pakistan: Polio found in baby. *New York Times*, A-9. July 18.

Barry, J. M. 2005. *The great influenza: The epic story of the deadliest plague in history*. New York: Penguin.

Benatar, S., A. Daar, and P. Singer. 2003. Global health ethics: The rationale for mutual caring. *International Affairs* 79 (1): 107–38.

Beyrer, C. 1998. *War in the blood: Sex, politics, and AIDS in Southeast Asia*. New York: Zed Books, Ltd.

Bienstock, R., E. Halpern, and S. Jacobovici. 2007. *Ebola: The plague fighters*. Documentary film. Boston: WGBH.

Bodley, J. H. 1999. *Victims of progress*. 4th ed. Toronto: Mayfield Publishing Company.

Boyd, R. 1999. *The coming of the spirit of pestilence: Introduced infectious diseases and population decline among northwest Indians, 1774–1874*. Vancouver: University of British Columbia Press.

Crosby, A. 1990. *America's forgotten pandemic: The influenza of 1918*. New York: Cambridge University Press.

Davies, P. 2000. *The devil's flu: The world's deadliest epidemic and the scientific hunt for the virus that caused it*. New York: Henry Holdt and Company.

Davis, M. 2005. *The monster at our door: The global threat of avian flu*. New York: The New Press.

Davis, W. 1997. *One river: Explorations and discoveries in the Amazon rain forest*. New York: Touchstone.

Dugger, C. W. 2008. Study cites toll of AIDS policy in South Africa. *New York Times*. November 26. Retrieved November 27, 2008, from www.nytimes .com/2008/11/26/world/Africa/26aids.html.

Eberstadt, N. 2002. The future of AIDS: Grim toll in Russia, China, and India. *Foreign Affairs* 81 (November/December): 22–45.

Elbe, S. 2002. HIV/AIDS and the changing landscape of war in Africa. *International Security* 27 (2): 159–77.

Farmer, P. 2004. *Pathologies of power: Health, human rights, and the new war on the poor*. Berkeley: University of California Press.

———. 2007. Aid, AIDS, and global health. *Foreign Affairs* 86 (March/April): 155–59.

Fenn, E. F. 2001. *Pox americana: The great smallpox epidemic of 1775–1782*. New York: Hill and Wang.

Garrett, L. 1994. *The coming plague: Newly emerging diseases in a world out of balance*. New York: Farrar, Straus and Giroux.

————. 2000. *Betrayal of trust: The collapse of global public health trust.* New York: Hyperion.

————. 2005. The lessons of HIV/AIDS. *Foreign Affairs* 84 (July/August): 51–65.

————. 2007. Do no harm: The global health challenge. *Foreign Affairs* 86 (January/February): 14–38.

Hackett, P. 2002. *"A very remarkable sickness": Epidemics in the Petit Nord, 1670–1846.* Winnipeg: University of Manitoba.

Holbrooke, R., and L. Garrett. 2008. "Sovereignty" that risks global health. *Washington Post.* August 10. Retrieved August 11, 2008, from www.cfr.org /publication/16927.

Hooper, E. 1999. *The river: A journey to the source of HIV and AIDS.* New York: Little, Brown and Company.

Karlen, A. 1995. *Plague's progress: A social history of man and disease.* London: Victor Gollancz.

————. 2000. *Biography of a germ.* New York: Pantheon.

Kidder, T. 2004. *Mountains beyond mountains: The quest of Dr. Paul Farmer, a man who would cure the world.* New York: Random House.

Kim, J. Y., J. Millen, A. Irwin, and J. Gershman, eds. 2000. *Dying for growth: Global inequality and the health of the poor.* Monroe, Maine: Common Courage Press.

King, H., R. E. Aubert, and W. H. Herman. 1998. Global burden of diabetes, 1995–2025. *Diabetes Care* 21 (9): 1414–30.

Kleinman, A., and J. Watson, eds. 2006. *SARS in China: Prelude to pandemic?* Stanford, Calif.: Stanford University Press.

Kolata, G. 1999. *Flu: The story of the great influenza pandemic.* New York: Touchstone.

Mangold, T., and J. Goldberg. 2000. *Plague wars: The terrifying reality of biological warfare.* New York: St. Martin's Griffin.

Marins, J. R. P. 2002. The Brazilian policy on free and universal access to antiretroviral treatment for people living with HIV and AIDS. February 20. PowerPoint presentation, Regional Forum of the Latin American and Caribbean Regional Health Sector Reform, Ocho Rios, S. Ann., Jamaica.

McGuire, S., and J. Georges. 2003. Undocumentedness and liminality as health variables. *Advances in Nursing Science* 26 (3): 185–95.

McKenna, M. 2010. *Superbug: The fatal menace of MRSA.* New York: Free Press.

McNeil, D. G., Jr. 2007. Indonesia to send bird flu samples, with restrictions. *New York Times.* March 28. Retrieved March 29, 2007, from http://www .nytimes.com/2007/03/28/world/asia/28birdflu.html?_r1&oref=slogin @page2.

————. 2008. Deal seeks to offer drug for malaria at low price. *New York Times,* A-9. July 18.

Miller, J. A. 1989. Diseases for our future: Global ecology and emerging viruses. *BioScience* 39 (8): 509–17.

Mock, N. B., S. Duale, L. F. Brown, and others. 2004. Conflict and HIV: A framework for risk assessment to prevent HIV in conflict-affected settings in Africa. *Emerging Themes in Epidemiology* 1 (October 29): 6. Retrieved October 30, 2008, from http://www.ete-online.com/content/1/1/6/.

Murray, M. 2006. The epidemiology of SARS. In *SARS in China: Prelude to pandemic?*, ed. A. Kleinman and J. Watson, 17–30. Stanford, Calif.: Stanford University Press.

Nichter, M. 1987. Kyasanur Forest Disease: An ethnography of a disease of development. *Medical Anthropology Quarterly* 1 (4): 406–23.

Osterholm, M. T. 2007. Unprepared for a pandemic. *Foreign Affairs* 86 (March/ April): 47–58.

Peters, C. J., and M. Olshaker. 1997. *Virus hunter: Thirty years of battling hot viruses around the world.* New York: Anchor Books/Doubleday.

Peterson, S. 2002. Epidemic disease and national security. *Security Studies* 12 (Winter): 43–81.

Philip, K. 2010. Producing transnational knowledge, neoliberal identities, and technoscientific practice in India. In *Tactical Biopolitics: art, activism and technoscience*, ed. B. da Costa and K. Philip, 243–67. Cambridge: MIT Press.

Price-Smith, A. 2002. *The health of nations: Infectious disease, environmental change, and their effects on national security and development.* Cambridge, Mass.: MIT Press.

Rosner, D., and G. Markowitz. 2006. *Are we ready? Public health since 9/11.* Berkeley: University of California Press.

Ryan, F. 1997. *Virus X: Tracking the new killer plagues.* New York: Little, Brown and Company.

Schnirrer, L. 2008. Supari accuses rich nations of creating viruses for profit. *CIDRAP News.* September 8. Available at www.umn.edu.

Schwartz, M. 2003. *How the cows turned mad.* Trans. E. Schneider. Berkeley: University of California Press.

Seidell, J. C. 2000. Obesity, insulin resistance, and diabetes—a worldwide epidemic. *British Journal of Nutrition* 83:5–8.

Smallman, S. 2007. *The AIDS pandemic in Latin America.* Chapel Hill: University of North Carolina Press.

———. 2013. Biopiracy and Vaccines: Indonesia and the World Health Organization's new Pandemic Influenza Plan. *Journal of International and Global Studies* 4 (2): 20–36. Retrieved December 28, 2013, from http:// www.lindenwood.edu/jigs/.

Smallman-Raynor, M. R., and A. Cliff. 2002. *War epidemics: An historical geography of infectious diseases in military conflict and civil strife, 1850–2000.* New York: Oxford University Press.

Thom, R. 2006. Artemesia Annua: A cure for Malaria. March 20. Unpublished student manuscript.

United Nations. 2006. World population prospects: The 2006 revision. Retrieved January 8, 2010, from www.un.org/esa/population/publications /wpp2006_Highlights_rev.pdf.

Velasquez-Manoff, M. 2007. Forests lure moose to Massachusetts. *Christian Science Monitor*. February 14. Retrieved July 21, 2013, from http:www .csmonitor.com/2007/0214/p13s02-sten.htm.

Wines, M. 2007. Virulent TB in South Africa may imperil millions. *New York Times*. January 8. Retrieved July 20, 2013, from http://www.nytimes .com/2007/01/28/world/africa/28tuberculosis?pagewanted=print.

Zimmet, P., K. G. Alberti, and J. Shaw. 2001. Global and societal implications of the diabetes epidemic. *Nature* 414 (December 13): 782–86.

TEN **Energy**

➤ **SYNOPSIS**

A few years ago, many observers believed that the world was about to reach its peak oil production, after which global oil reserves would taper away. With the development of hydraulic fracturing (fracking) and increased production of unconventional oil from sources such as Canada's Oil Sands, the global energy picture has changed dramatically. At the same time, the nuclear disaster at Fukushima in Japan has led nations such as Germany to abandon nuclear energy entirely, while the declining cost of both solar and wind have made coal and nuclear increasingly uncompetitive. As a result, the global energy supply is in a state of rapid change. Solutions to global energy needs in the emerging decades will call for flexibility and creativity—a difficult path within the confines of the nation-state.

➤ **SCAFFOLDING**

As you read through this chapter, think about how you would answer each of the questions below.

Besides the supply of oil now and in the future, what energy issues are things you think about on a weekly basis?

What global health issues are clearly linked to energy extraction?

What economic ideologies have governed much of the Global North's energy strategies in the twentieth and twenty-first centuries?

What incentives do multinational energy companies have to invest in alternative energy sources?

➤ **CORE CONCEPTS**

Why was Hubbert's concept of Peak Oil so central to global energy policies in the past three decades?

How has the rise of unconventional oil and fracking changed the global energy context?

What are advantages and disadvantages of using particular energy sources for our vehicles and for our daily use in other arenas?

The global energy picture is in a state of dramatic change. With the rise of fracking, North America has been able to rapidly increase its production of both oil and natural gas to such an extent that it may be able to achieve its energy independence. This change has geopolitical implications, as the Middle East becomes less critical to U.S. foreign policy than in the past. In other parts of the world, the Fukushima nuclear disaster has led countries to reconsider the potential benefits of nuclear power. Germany, for example, has decided to close nuclear plants, while at the same time investing heavily in renewable energy. The price of renewable energy has fallen sharply over the last five years (perhaps 50 percent); wind production has significantly increased, while solar is now approaching price parity with fossil fuels in some countries, such as Australia. The supply of coal is sufficient for centuries, but the industry is in decline because of both environmental concerns and market pressures (Randers 2012, 99; Cockerham 2013, A-3). In this context, energy markets are in a state of flux, with larger global changes taking place right now than at any time since the introduction of electricity in the early twentieth century. The one certainty is that many predictions for our energy future from a decade ago are now badly outdated.

While fracking as a technology dates back to the 1920s, it is relatively new as a large-scale practice in the energy industry. The term refers to the injection of fluids under high pressure into rocks that bear petroleum. When the rock fractures, its petroleum resources are released. By means of this technology, it is possibly to economically extract petroleum from otherwise inaccessible resources.

Peak Oil and Fracking

As late as 2010, an introduction to this chapter would have included dramatically different information. At the time, discussions of global energy issues were dominated by the so-called Peak Oil movement, which began as an academic community and morphed into a broad-based popular movement with its own website and conferences (see www.peakoil.com). Amazon.com and other booksellers were stocked with widely selling works on this topic, such as Kenneth Deffeyes's *Hubbert's Peak* (2001), David Goodstein's, *Out of Gas* (2005), and Richard Heinberg's, *The Party's Over* (2003). The movement was based on the 1956 prediction of petroleum geologist M. King Hubbert that U.S. oil production would peak in 1970. As it happened, his prediction was correct, although U.S. production briefly rebounded after Alaskan oil came online in the late 1970s (Bahgat 2003, 7; Heinberg 2003, 73, 87–92; Simmons 2005, 45). U.S. oil production then entered into a steady and long decline, despite deepwater discoveries in the Gulf of Mexico. Most Peak Oil authors predicted that the world's total production was about to peak (if it had not done so already) and would soon enter a decades-long slide. Their argument was not that there would be a sudden, dramatic falloff in the production of oil, but rather that global production of oil would show the same bell-shaped curve that we have seen from many oil-producing states.

The gradual fall in world production would take place at the same time that the emerging economic powers of India and China continued to demand increasing amounts of oil (Simmons 2005, 46). As evidence for this prediction, Peak Oil proponents pointed out that multinational oil companies were not discovering new reserves of oil as quickly as they were pumping petroleum out of the ground (Roberts 2004, 172–73). The future seemed bleak, as the developed nations of Europe, Asia, and North America entered into an intense competition for the remaining oil.

Today, oil is the most important global commodity. When people think of oil, they think of cars and gasoline, because those are the products through which the price of oil most directly and noticeably impacts us. But there are other uses of oil that are just as fundamental. Petroleum is used to create the nitrogen for fertilizers that are a key part of Western agriculture. In particular, corn is a key feedstock in the United States, and no other crop relies as much upon fertilizer. Our industrial economy relies on plastics for everything from children's toys to medicine bottles. These are almost entirely made from petroleum. Heating oil also remains an

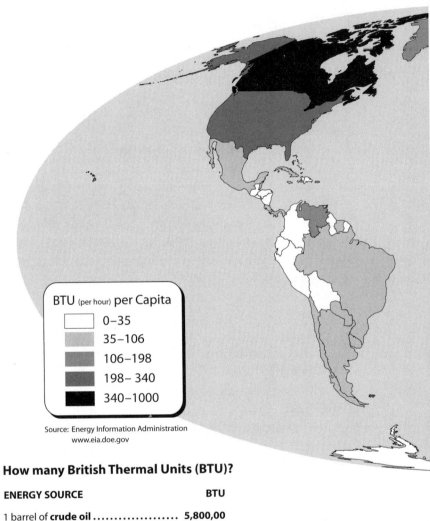

Source: Energy Information Administration
www.eia.doe.gov

How many British Thermal Units (BTU)?

ENERGY SOURCE	BTU
1 barrel of **crude oil**	5,800,00
1 gallon of **gasoline**	124,000
1 short ton of **coal**	20,754,000
1 kilowatt-hour of **electricity**	3,400

Map 8 World Energy Consumption (Steph Gaspers 2008)

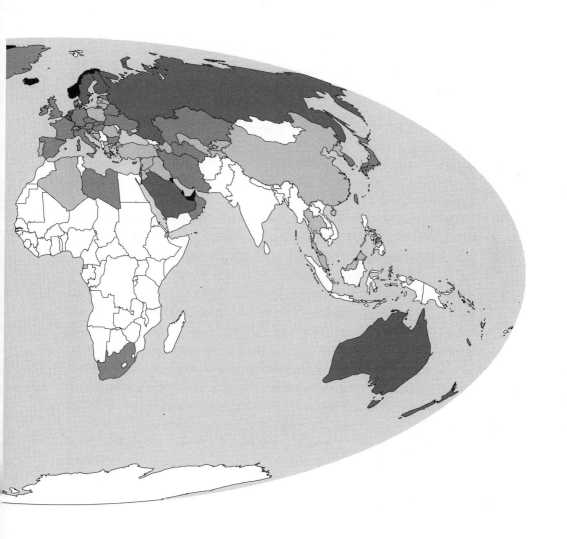

important energy source in many areas, such as southern Canada and the northeastern United States. Even if we could magically find an alternative source to oil to meet our transportation needs tomorrow, the problem of our dependency on petroleum would remain. This problem is acute in the United States, where it is commonplace to note that the country has 5 percent of the world's population but uses 25 percent (or more) of the world's petroleum. But this issue also worries Europe, as the North Sea fields enter into decline, and Japan, which is almost entirely dependent upon imported oil. For the emerging economies of Southeast Asia, the question is how they can develop without the energy resources that the West and Japan enjoyed during industrialization. Lastly, China, the world's emerging superpower, has relatively small oil reserves but is now the world's largest energy consumer.

Given the scale of this problem, as seen from a few years ago, the Peak Oil movement had an understandable tinge of hysteria. In the fall of 2005, Bryant Urstadt attended the second U.S. Conference on Peak Oil in Ohio, which he later described in an August 2006 article in *Harper's* magazine titled "Imagine There's No Oil: Scenes from a Liberal Apocalypse." The sad message that many members of the Peak Oil community seemed to purvey was not only that the world was running out of oil, but also that no good alternative would be found. Indeed, the movement's advocates seemed so determined to envision a future dystopia (the opposite of utopia) that Urstadt (2006, 36) found himself musing about the historical origins of the movement: "Americans seem born to love the apocalypse, although it jilts us every time. Peak Oil and *Left Behind* are mere froth on a sea of doom-saying that stretches back to the Puritans." But it would have been wrong to view the Peak Oil movement as a purely American group. Rather, it formed part of a larger discussion within the environmental movement, which argued that current practices in developing countries were unsustainable. Skeptics point out that there have been many predictions before that the world is about to run out of petroleum, as well as many other commodities. In almost every case, these items have not only continued to be found, but their price has also declined. From this perspective, the Peak Oil movement was a group of people united perhaps less by their fears than by their hopes.

The global energy picture has now changed so dramatically that the website the Oil Drum (www.theoildrum.com) announced in the summer of 2013 that it was closing. The site had provided a venue for the Peak Oil community to share information about the coming global collapse, driven by the shortfall of oil production. Many of its posters were people with substantial firsthand knowledge of the energy industry. But the website's editors announced that they could not find quality content any longer. Some influential posters had already left the website. After 2010 it proved increasingly difficult to believe in Peak Oil because U.S. oil production greatly increased with fracking. This term refers to a process by which fluid under high pressure is pumped into petroleum-bearing rocks, which creates fractures to release gas or petroleum. This technology has allowed energy companies to access petroleum resources that were completely inaccessible in the past. Such technological change means that we are unlikely to face any shortage of petroleum in the foreseeable future.

Fracking technology is not new. It was first attempted in 1947, but it became an economically viable technology in the space of a decade. This development has had a dramatic impact on natural gas production in the United States. In the eastern states, such as Pennsylvania, natural gas production has increased so rapidly that the price of natural gas has collapsed. According to some estimates, the nation may now have a century's supply of this fuel. The positive aspect of this change has been that natural gas releases less carbon than most other fossil fuels. In March 2012 the Obama administration announced new rules to limit carbon dioxide emissions from power plants. This will increase the costs for coal to compete with both natural gas and renewable energy, which could help fight climate change. But the new rules do not apply to existing power plants, which are grandfathered in. Energy companies are building very few new coal plants in the United States: "Coal still accounts for 37 percent of U.S. electricity generation, although its share has dwindled from 50 percent just a few years ago and natural gas is catching up" (Cockerham 2013, A-3). The declining cost of natural gas will also make it more difficult to build new nuclear plants. In the aftermath of the 2011 nuclear disaster at the Fukushima power plant in Japan, that country closed all fifty-four of its nuclear reactors, while Germany made a strategic decision to move away from nuclear power. So the nuclear energy industry was already under intense pressure globally, with China the only country in which large numbers of new nuclear plants are likely to be built. With the United States, however, the falling cost of natural gas has also made nuclear power seem increasingly uncompetitive.

The increase in natural gas production has also had an unexpected series of spin-off effects. Natural gas is the base element of petrochemicals, fertilizers, and other products. In the first decade of the millennium,

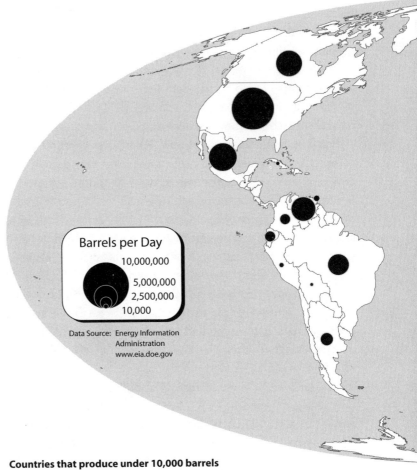

Barrels per Day

10,000,000

5,000,000
2,500,000
10,000

Data Source: Energy Information
Administration
www.eia.doe.gov

Countries that produce under 10,000 barrels
(in order from least to greatest): Ethiopia, Slovenia,
Madagascar, North Korea, Zambia, Tajikistan, Uruguay,
Barbados, Puerto Rico, Kyrgyzstan, Georgia, Sweden,
Aruba, Switzerland, Bulgaria, Morocco, Portugal, Greece,
Israel, Bangladesh, Estonia, Albania, Ghana, Belgium,
Finland, Suriname, Singapore

Map 9 World Oil Production (Steph Gaspers 2008)

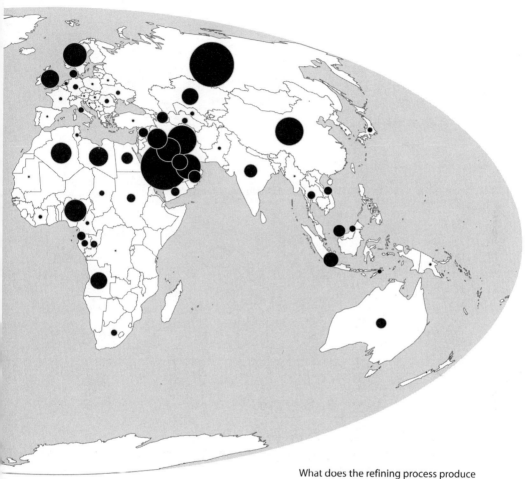

What does the refining process produce
from each barrel of crude oil?

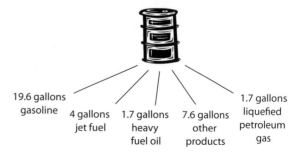

19.6 gallons
gasoline

4 gallons
jet fuel

1.7 gallons
heavy
fuel oil

7.6 gallons
other
products

1.7 gallons
liquefied
petroleum
gas

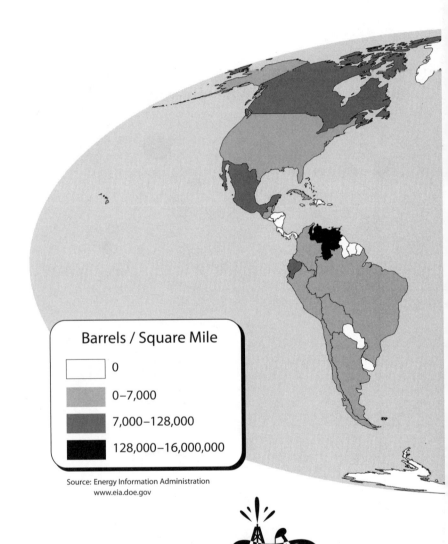

Source: Energy Information Administration
www.eia.doe.gov

Map 10 World Oil Reserves (Steph Gaspers 2008)

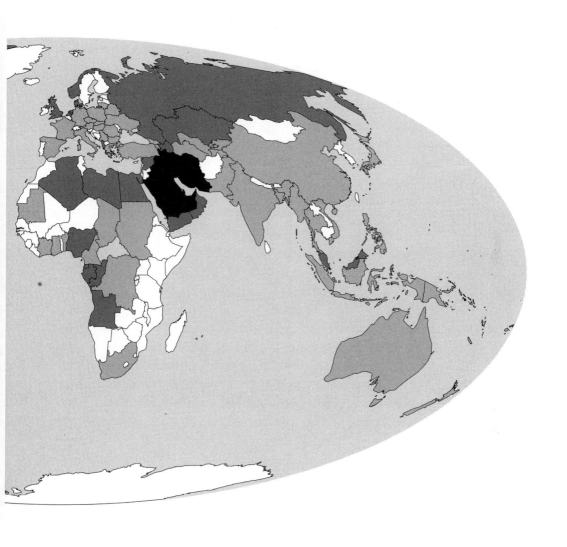

many U.S. manufacturers had moved overseas where energy was cheaper. With the falling cost of natural gas, many of these same companies are now moving production back to the United States, which has a huge price advantage over almost every country in the world. Steelmakers also use natural gas, which is helping that sector of the economy regain lost ground. This trend is leading to an increase in U.S. manufacturing, an area of the economy that had been in a long decline. It is also putting downward pressure on electricity costs and creating an alternative energy source for fleets of vehicles (such as garbage trucks and buses), which are often owned by municipalities. With the growing importance of natural gas in heavy vehicles and the emergence of electric cars, oil is no longer practically alone at the top of transportation fuels (Krauss 2013). U.S. energy companies that were building terminals to bring in liquefied natural gas (LNG) from abroad now want to build export terminals.

While much of the attention to fracking has focused on natural gas, the technology has also been used to release oil on a scale that would have been unimaginable around 2000: "Last year, U.S. production rose by about 800,000 barrels per day, the biggest annual increase since 1859. This year, it is expected to climb by another 600,000 barrels per day. And this has helped spur a huge increase in exports" (Bryce 2013). The main state for this production has been North Dakota, which now produces more oil than Alaska. The economic benefits for the state have been substantial, as it largely escaped the damage of the Great Recession. For the United States as a whole, domestic oil production is growing, and there are no signs that this increase will stop in the near future. Oil imports declined every year between 2005 and 2013, and by the end of the decade, the country may no longer rely on imported oil. The benefits stretch beyond the United States, having global implications: "Contrary to what most people believe, oil supply capacity is growing worldwide at such an unprecedented level that it might outpace consumption" (Maugeri 2012, 1). This expansion of production has been so large that it has had geopolitical significance. The United States relies less on the Middle East for oil, while globally, the power of OPEC has declined. Indeed, oil production in OPEC is languishing, and the economic power of key OPEC nations has decreased (Bryce 2013). The global economy is also now partly shielded from the danger of an oil shock plunging nations into a recession, as happened in 1973 (Krauss 2013). For nations such as Australia, Argentina, China, Mexico, and Russia, which have large holdings of shale oil, their economies may see significant increases in energy production (Krauss 2013).

These benefits have also come with significant environmental concerns. Energy companies place chemicals into the water that they push into the rocks. The companies don't like to release information on which chemicals they are using, arguing this is a trade secret and thus proprietary. But communities affected by fracking argue that they have a right to know and worry that these chemicals may be released into the watershed. While research has not yet shown that the chemicals migrate, the time frame to date has been relatively short. How long will these chemicals remain in place? Hundreds of different chemicals are being used, some of which (according to environmental groups) are known toxins or carcinogens. Some companies also have used radioactive tracers to help determine where cracks are moving. There is currently no technology that allows these companies to remove the chemicals or radioactive tracers from the rocks into which they have been injected. In 2005 the U.S. Congress exempted fracking from any regulation under the Safe Drinking Act in order to ensure that this industry could continue its rapid development. But environmental groups and some impacted communities argue that there is insufficient regulation of the industry.

There is another challenge with fracking, in that it can create earthquakes, although there is little research on this topic. Small earthquakes (4.0 or under on the Richter Scale) have been reported in Canada, Japan, and the United States. In this context, the economic benefits of fracking have been matched by significant environmental concerns. In October 2013 the European Union voted to tighten the environmental regulation of fracking by requiring an environmental audit before companies could work. Although the vote has not yet become law, it indicated Europe's concern with the environmental costs of new sources of oil (Kanter 2013). In October 2013 France's highest court upheld a ban on fracking (Jolly 2013). There are two major exceptions to Europe's general opposition to fracking. Britain views fracking as a possible means to replace its declining oil supply in the North Sea, while Poland views fracking as a possible means to end its energy reliance on Russia (Reed 2013). But environmental questions trouble all new sources of petroleum because of changes to the source of the global energy supply: "[I]n the aggregate, production capacity growth will occur almost everywhere, bringing about a 'deconventionalization' of oil supplies. During the next decades this will produce an expanding amount of what we define today as 'unconventional oils'—such as U.S. shale/tight oils, Canadian tar sands, Venezuela's extra-heavy oils, and Brazil's pre-salt oils" (Maugeri 2012, 2). Because much of the growth in the world's energy supply is taking place in North America, it is worth discussing trends in this region in detail.

Canada's Oil Sands

Ultimately, the real question may not be when will the world run out of petroleum, but rather, how dirty will oil have to become before nations abandon it (Randers 2012, 99)? Oil production from unconventional sources is increasing not only in the United States but also in Canada, the country that exports the most oil to the United States. Despite Canada's importance as an energy exporter to the United States, for many years it remained practically invisible in policy discussions surrounding petroleum. Canada's role did not attract attention because it was seen as a politically secure source of supply and also because most of its oil reserves are not in conventional oil, but rather in the Oil Sands. These deposits represent a vast petroleum resource. Although there are smaller deposits of Oil Sands in Australia and some other nations, major fields of Oil Sands exist in only two nations: Canada and Venezuela. This particular resource is so distinct that only relatively recently has the International Energy Agency (a Paris-based organization that helps developed states manage energy issues) included it when calculating Canada's reserves. To understand why this is the case, we need to first discuss the nature of the Oil Sands (Smallman 2003).

The oil resources in northern Alberta, Canada, seemed unlikely to create such a stir when they were first discovered. In the late 1700s, European explorers in northern Alberta began to find bitumen (a tarry material from which asphalt is made) along the Peace River. The Oil Sands are mostly sand, mixed together with smaller amounts of water, clay, and bitumen. The sands have an oily feel, and they smell of petroleum. This resource was buried beneath the boreal forest and muskeg over an immense area. People in the industry in Alberta commonly claim that the four main deposits cover an area greater than the state of Florida. The quantity of oil held in these lands is also staggering—by some estimates, more than a trillion barrels of oil. But this resource is produced in an unusual manner: it is not pumped but rather mined. What is distinctive about the process is that the challenge is not finding but rather releasing the oil in an environmentally sound (and fiscally feasible) manner. It is a capital-intensive product.

To compete with nations that can simply pump oil, companies in northern Alberta have turned to immense economies of scale. Outside of Fort McMurray, a boomtown north of Edmonton that houses most of this industry's workers, one can stand at the edge of a pit hundreds of feet deep and stretching almost to the horizon. Vast trucks, each weighing 320 tons, pass along the pit floor and receive the bitumen material dumped into them from gigantic bulldozers. From the pit's rim, despite their immense size, these trucks look like children's toys. Drivers work in shifts twenty-four hours a day throughout the year, despite the frigid Canadian winter. The drivers actually prefer the cold because it makes it easier to drive in the pit. Unless you have seen the scale of this undertaking, it is difficult to imagine. Two tons of sand must be mined in order to create one barrel of oil. The size of Canada's oil production from this industry can be measured in the face of the land and the quantities of earth moved to extract this resource.

The high cost of producing oil from the Oil Sands, and the technological challenges of producing oil in this manner, explain why for many years this resource was simply not included when calculating the size of oil reserves in Canada or Venezuela. Any estimate of the size of the reserves entailed predicting the future cost of oil. How much oil could be extracted depended upon its price and the technology available to extract it. How, then, could an accurate prediction be made? To create the necessary infrastructure to extract the oil entailed tens of billions of dollars in investment. What would happen if investors poured that money into the industry, only to find that the price of oil collapsed? No investor wanted to commit vast sums if the Saudis might decide to grab for market share and drop the bottom out of oil's price.

Estimates for the size of Alberta's oil recoverable reserves (based on what is economically recoverable, not the total size of the reserves) range from roughly 175 billion barrels to 300 billion barrels, which is larger than the total reserves for Saudi Arabia (if those estimates are to be believed, as Simmons [2005] points out). Two factors make it likely that a large proportion of this reserve will in fact be produced. First, the cost of producing oil from the Oil Sands has fallen sharply since the 1970s, when the price of a barrel of oil was roughly $30. As Larry Pratt (1976) describes in his book *The Tar Sands: Syncrude and the Politics of Oil*, only government subsidies allowed the industry to be created at that time. But with continued changes in technology, many companies now are targeting production costs of seven to eight Canadian dollars per barrel, although a current production cost of around thirteen Canadian dollars per barrel is more typical. At this price, oil produced in this manner is competitive on the world market.

Canada has enjoyed a financial windfall. Companies investing in the

Oil Sands, such as PetroCanada and Suncor, have seen record profits. Fort McMurray has attracted workers from as far away as Newfoundland and Labrador because it is a city where a truck driver can earn a six-figure income. Alberta's increasing wealth has brought the province greater power. The province has 10 percent of Canada's population but 15 percent of the country's GDP. Alberta also has the most rapid population growth of any province, as people have moved from declining manufacturing centers in Ontario and Quebec toward the west. Canada's entire economy has been buoyed by the Oil Sands production. The Canadian dollar is a petrocurrency, which appreciated sharply against the U.S. dollar to achieve parity. The United States will have access to a secure source of oil nearby to help meet its needs for many decades to come. And Canada will benefit from the wealth that this energy partnership will create. From energy-security and economic perspectives, the Oil Sands appear to be a blessing.

The Environmental Cost of Alternative Oil Sources

Economic questions aside, however, there are other serious problems with increasing production from the Oil Sands, which the Canadian government is reluctant to acknowledge or discuss. Environmental groups, however, are working hard to raise awareness about the massive problems associated with this resource. (To learn more, visit http://www.pembina.org/oil-sands; see also Heinberg 2003, 112; Burgess 2004; Cattaneo 2008, FP-1, 5; and Nikiforuk 2008.) In essence, mining this resource has a substantial impact on the land, air, and water. Some useful information has been produced by an environmental organization called the Pembina Institute, which has produced both a book, *Death by a Thousand Cuts* (2006), and an online documentary, *Oil Sands Fever*. According to the Pembina Institute and other critics, mining for the Oil Sands permanently changes the land. In order to gain access to the oil-bearing layer, roughly 75 to 100 feet of topsoil first has to be removed. The scale of this process is difficult to describe. Afterward, the tailings are returned to the land, and it is replanted. One oil company brings visitors to view land reclaimed in this manner, on which it keeps a Wood Buffalo herd managed by local native peoples. But critics say that it is impossible to restore the wetlands or muskeg to its previous condition. It may appear natural, but the land is not what it was in an area of boreal forest famous for its bird life. There are also by-products such as sulfur, vast piles of which accumulate near Fort McMurray. The support infrastructure for the Oil Sands also spreads out deep into the forest; water containment pits, sulphur piles, equipment staging, pipelines, and equipment storage extend beyond the boundaries of the mining areas.

Another problem with the Oil Sands development is its immense demand for water. A newer technology is now available for releasing the petroleum without mining called Steam-Assisted Gravity Drainage, or Sag-D. But this requires a steady supply of water, as does the process that extracts petroleum from the sands with conventional mining. According to Andre Plourde (2006) of the University of Alberta, in the latter case, it takes between "2.5 to 4 barrels of water" to extract one barrel of bitumen. The challenge is that after this process, the water is too contaminated with napthic acids and other toxic chemicals to be returned to the watershed. No one currently has a technology able to process contaminated water on an industrial scale. As a result, it is now dumped into tailing ponds that cover about fifty square kilometers, according to the Pembina Institute. Both fish and birds exposed to this water suffer serious harm.

In the spring of 2008, a flock of at least 500 ducks died after landing in one of the Mildred Lake Basin tailing ponds, which brought international attention to the issue of water pollution in the Oil Sands development (Witt 2008). Defenders of the Oil Sands argued that wind turbines "chop up thousands of birds each year with their massive blades" (Tait 2008b). But others pointed to the scale of the problem. The Mildred Lakes Basin is twenty-one kilometers in diameter, and there is no existing technology to clean the waters that it contains (Tait 2008a). As production from the Oil Sands increases, the need for large volumes of water will also grow. This may represent a fundamental physical limit on the ability of this resource to be developed, which no one in the industry or government wishes to face (Nikiforuk 2008, 57–92; for the industry view of the environmental issues related to the Oil Sands, see www.canadaoilsands.ca).

The most serious environmental problem with the Oil Sands is its potential impact upon global warming (Nikiforuk 2008, 117–28). It requires a great deal of energy to mine the sands, to separate the bitumen from the sand itself, and to convert the bitumen into oil. A portion of the oil produced is burned to produce the electricity that provides the steam that companies use to drive this process, or natural gas is employed. As a result, oil produced from the Oil Sands produces much more carbon dioxide (CO_2) than other sources: "Producing the steam requires burning enough natural gas each day to heat 3 million North American homes. The intensive burning of natural gas is particularly alarming to climatologists because it sends three times more climate-changing greenhouse gases into the atmosphere than drilling for conventional oil" (Witt 2008, A-21). To address this problem, Alberta's government has considered using nuclear energy to refine oil (Nikiforuk 2008, 129–38). This created excitement in the United States, where the nuclear industry has been in a prolonged slump since the accident at Three Mile Island. In the aftermath of September 11, however, nuclear reactors raised serious security concerns, and the problem of nuclear waste disposal remains unsolved. These challenges likely cannot be overcome in the near future.

Because of international concern about global warming, in 1997 countries negotiated the Kyoto protocol, which calls on nations to make cuts in their production of greenhouse gases—in particular, CO^2. In December 2011 Canada pulled out of the Kyoto protocol immediately after the 2011 UN Climate Change Conference, held in Durban, South Africa. Canada, which may have the world's second-largest oil reserves, clearly made the decision that the economic gains were too important to be sacrificed for environmental concerns. This decision had a global impact, as it gave impetus to other nations—such as Russia—that are also reluctant to see constraints on their omissions of greenhouse gases.

Pipelines

The tension between economic interests and environmental needs led to a major political contest over pipelines designed to bring petroleum from the Oil Sands to market in the United States. Companies have invested hundreds of billions of dollars in the Oil Sands, which is only valuable if a means exists to bring this oil to market. Without this ability to deliver the petroleum, the Oil Sands are a stranded resource. The energy industry would like to construct a pipeline from Alberta to the Texas coast, called the Keystone XL pipeline. But because this pipeline would have to cross the border, the U.S. State Department needed to approve it. This created a bitter political standoff between those who believed that the United States needed the oil and environmentalists who believed that there would be no hope of stopping climate change if all the petroleum in Alberta's Oil Sands were burned.

Frustrated, the Canadian government then turned to a planned pipeline called the "Northern Gateway," which would have carried oil 600 miles over the Rocky Mountains to the British Columbia coast. The challenge was that the pipeline would have to pass through the lands of nearly fifty different native peoples, not all of whom had existing land-claim settlements with the federal government. The pipeline also needed to pass through the Great Bear Rainforest, the world's largest remaining temperate rain forest—and the only home on the planet to the Spirit Bear (a white form of the black bear), as well as wolves that are accustomed to eating fish. Memories of the Exxon Valdez oil spill, and the difficult waters of the coast, led environmental groups to oppose this option as well. This factor, combined with opposition within the province of British Columbia, helped to kill the plan. At the time of this writing, the Canadian government faces a major challenge in bringing increasing levels of petroleum from the Oil Sands to global markets. While the struggle in Canada and the United States over pipelines receives the most attention, this is only one example of the transportation issues globally that are accompanying rapid increases in petroleum production. This challenge is not confined to oil, as other energy sources—such as natural gas—also require new infrastructure to support increased production. But the problem is most pressing with oil (Cardwell 2013). Because the energy revolution began in North America, events there presage similar debates from Australia to Argentina.

Throughout the planet, there are substantial reserves of unconventional or difficult-to-access oil. Currently, many European governments are debating the costs and benefits of fracking. Venezuela has the world's second-largest supply of unconventional petroleum in its Oil Sands. It currently produces about 400,000 barrels of oil a year from this resource, but this number could be greatly increased. Argentina may also have large reserves of shale gas. With global warming, the Arctic Ocean's ice cap is receding and thinning, which will open new undersea areas for oil exploration if the region becomes ice free during the summer in coming decades. Polar nations are now striving to assert their claim to the Arctic seabed in the hope that this region may contain significant oil reserves. Globally, the world would not appear to be on the verge of running out of oil, as the Peak Oil movement suggested. Rather, the question is how can the global economy move to more-sustainable resources, or at least to those that do not contribute to climate change?

In this context, recent shale oil discoveries in Australia seem like a parable. In the South Australia town of Coober Pedy, recent discoveries suggest that there may be over 200 billion barrels of oil, which would make Australia rival Saudi Arabia as an energy producer (CBC News 2013). There is still great uncertainty about the size of the reserve. But what is certain is that people in this remote Australian community live in a climate so hot that the town has houses and other buildings underground. People play golf on a grassless course with glowing balls at night because it is often too hot to play during the day. Will they drill water from declining aquifers to frack the wells, thereby making the community rely on imported water? What temperature might Coober Pedy ultimately reach if Australia develops all of the region's shale oil?

Nuclear Power

One global option for increasing energy resources without a parallel increase in CO^2 emissions is nuclear energy. Although it is a nonrenewable resource, there are substantial supplies of uranium in North America and other world regions to meet global demand. So this is one fuel in which there is no danger of a shortage in the near term. Yet there are substantial challenges for nuclear power, of which one of the most significant is the disposal of radioactive waste. This problem is a serious one, especially given the difficulties that have surrounded the nuclear-waste disposal facility at Yucca Mountain in Nevada. It now seems unlikely that this disposal site will ever be used. Internationally, Finland seems to have made the most progress toward the disposal of nuclear waste. Britain and France also have plans for underground disposal. Canada plans to place waste in a location deep underground near Lake Huron. Because any possible leak might contaminate the Great Lakes water system, however, there are concerns on the U.S. side of the border about this solution (McCarthy 2013). But no waste-disposal project has been fully implemented yet, so it remains difficult to assess the options.

Another possible idea would be to recycle the nuclear waste by using it as fuel for a new form of nuclear reactor called the TerraPower reactor. The most visible advocate for this approach has been Bill Gates, who is seeking to build a demonstration reactor, most likely in China. Supporters argue that this would eliminate nuclear material that might be used for weapons, and that there is now an 800-year supply of fuel in the form of nuclear waste. It is unclear, however, whether this approach is technically feasible, and advances in materials science need to occur given that the reactors would last thirty years and the neutrons produced would damage the metals of which the reactor would be made. In any case, it would likely be twenty years before such a reactor would become commercially available, so the TerraPower reactor (and similar new reactor designs) are not a solution to energy problems in the near term (Wald 2013a). At present, it seems that major nations will have to spend hundreds of billions of dollars to dispose of nuclear waste, even if no more is created.

Nuclear power also is associated with security issues, as well as the risk of a catastrophic accident. Nuclear reactors can create the plutonium for nuclear weaponry, which raises the fear of proliferation, such as is the case with Iran's nuclear program. After September 11, there were also real concerns about the possibility of a terrorist takeover of a reactor facility, as well as the theft of radioactive material to make a "dirty bomb" (Hertsgaard 1999, 151). Still, the major issue with nuclear power is the risk of a catastrophic accident, as happened in both the former Soviet Union at Chernobyl in 1986 and Japan's Fukushima plant after the 2011 earthquake and tsunami. In Japan, the nuclear accident magnified an already terrible crisis in which over 15,000 people died. Now Japan has to rethink its energy future while dealing with nuclear cleanup. At the time of this writing, vast amounts of contaminated water are overwhelming efforts to prevent nuclear waste from reaching the Pacific. It is not even clear if it will be possible to clean up this accident over a time frame of decades, or when people will be able to return to the local community. In the aftermath of the nuclear disaster, Japan closed its nuclear reactors—now the subject of great debate—plunging the entire country into efforts to conserve energy. Although rare, these events have devastating impacts that cross national borders.

It is difficult for national governments to have honest conversations with their people about the risks posed by nuclear energy. For example, as Wolf Richter (2013) has argued, the French government has sought to suppress information about the possible impact of a nuclear disaster in France:

> Catastrophic accidents, like Chernobyl in 1986 or Fukushima No. 1 in 2011, are very rare, we're incessantly told, and their probability of occurring infinitesimal. But when they do occur, they get costly. So costly that the French government, when it came up with cost estimates, kept them secret. But now the report was linked to a French magazine, *Le Journal de Dimanche*. Turns out, the upper end of the cost spectrum of an accident at a single reactor at the plant chosen for the study, the plant at Dampierre in the Department of Loiret in north-central France, would amount to over three times the country's GDP. Financially, France would cease to exist as we know it. Hence the need to keep it secret. The study was done in 2007 by the Institute for Radiological Protection and Nuclear Safety (IRSN), a govern-

ment agency under joint authority of the Ministry of Defense and the Ministry of Environment, Industry, Research, and Health.

Such an accident would also contaminate Belgium, England, Germany, the Netherlands, and Switzerland. In the aftermath of Fukushima, Germany committed to phasing out nuclear power. Given the risks that this energy supply poses, it is unlikely that any country will turn to nuclear power in a substantial manner in the future. Even China slowed its construction of nuclear power plants after Fukushima and recently canceled the construction of a uranium concentration plant in Guandong after popular protests (Bradsher 2012; Mullaney 2013). An additional strike against nuclear power is that it has proved to be a relatively expensive form and is having increasing difficulty competing not only with natural gas but also with wind and solar. Most energy forecasts predict a declining role for nuclear power in the future (Randers 2012, 114).

Coal

Coal also has a reputation as a "dirty" fuel. In England, when people think of coal, they think of the Industrial Revolution and the vast smokestacks that once covered the countryside. English literature from the Victorian era is filled with descriptions of the environmental damage done by coal—the grime that covered the cities and the yellow "fogs" of London. When an inversion layer covered the city in 1952, at least 4,000 people died from the trapped pollution (Christianson 1999, 150–51). This pushed the British to decide to move away from coal as a fuel source. In countries such as Germany, which has long relied on coal for much of its energy, people think of acid rain and the environmental damage suffered by the Black Forest (Morris 2006, 60–61; for more information on coal mining in Europe, see www.mbendi.com/indy/ming/coal/eu/p0005.htm). In coal-producing regions of the United States, people also think of the damage done to the land by the coal industry—the mountaintops leveled by strip mining and the tailings dumped down the hillside, where they leach pollutants into the watershed. In West Virginia, coal is more than a business; it is part of the culture. But it is reviled in literature and song, which often describe how miners have lost their lives or suffered. Miners working in the mines face serious risks, including lung damage from the exposure to coal dust. Whole towns have had to be moved to make way for coal. The same is true in Europe, as the experience of the German town of Horno illustrates

(Morris 2006, 65). Pollution from coal-fired energy plants in the U.S. Midwest plagues southern Canada and the New England states.

Coal is also a major source of greenhouse gases. Coal-powered plants generally run for more than fifty years. The coal industry often resists updating these plants because it is expensive, and once these plants pay for themselves, they are extremely profitable. For this reason, the industry has a poor environmental reputation, as it consistently has opposed stricter standards for its plants. Coal must be scrubbed in order to reduce pollutants as it is burned. The most serious pollutant is mercury, which contaminates the coal. When the coal is burned, mercury is released into the atmosphere and then returns to earth in rainwater. Chemically, mercury is an element, which means that it cannot be broken down into a safer substance. Once in the environment, it remains there and becomes increasingly concentrated as it moves up the food chain. Mercury causes serious health effects, particularly in prenatal children. It is for this reason that pregnant women are discouraged from eating too much fish: "Mercury acts on the central nervous system and can reduce mental ability, making kids shy, irritable, and slow to learn, and causing tremors and visual disturbances. Children under 7 should not eat more than a single 4-ounce portion of non-migrating fish every seven weeks, while women of childbearing age should eat no more than one 8-ounce portion a month" (Read 2006a). This food source has been contaminated by the coal industry, and all consumers of seafood carry this burden. The scale of the contamination is huge, not only in the inland waters of the United States or Europe but also in the vast waters of the world's oceans. The world will be paying the price of coal as an energy source for generations to come.

China is currently attracting global attention because of the rapid pace with which it is building coal power plants. China has a much larger population than the United States, but its petroleum resources are quite modest. As the nation struggles to join the developed world, it has turned to coal as a key domestic source of energy, a decision that has national global implications. As Mark Hertsgaard (1999, 164–70) eloquently describes in *Earth Odyssey*, Chinese cities such as Beijing already suffer from serious air pollution from existing power plants (see also Roberts 2004, 143–64). But as the *New York Times* noted in a 2006 editorial, China is building coal plants at a staggering pace: "Already, China uses more coal than the United States, the European Union, and Japan combined. Every week to 10 days, another coal-fired plant opens somewhere in China, with enough capacity to serve all of the households in Dallas or San Diego." With this pace of construction, China's energy development is creating pollution problems on a truly global scale, which undermines all efforts to limit global warming. In October 2013 the city of Harbin had pollution levels so severe that flights had to be cancelled, schools were closed, and monitoring stations recorded record levels of particulates. Of course, it is important to recognize that the United States, Britain, and other industrial powers also went through periods of great pollution early in their developmental history. These countries are also debating the role that coal plays in their energy mix.

In both Europe and the United States, the coal industry is attempting to market itself as an environmentally friendly business. The industry argues that new technology will permit coal to be much cleaner. In particular, coal proponents point to the opportunity coal presents for CO^2 sequestration. If this technology proves feasible, it would provide an opportunity to develop a widely available fuel source in a manner that would not drive global warming. In essence, the idea of carbon sequestration is to capture the CO^2 released from a fuel source such as coal and to inject it back into the earth, where it can be contained in geologically stable formations. Norway has already undertaken similar efforts with oil in the North Sea, with considerable success (Morris 2006, 63). But many questions remain about this approach with coal. Can coal be processed by this means in a financially viable manner? So far, most efforts at carbon sequestration have not proved to be sustainable: "Carbon capture and sequestration had been demonstrated in New Haven, W.Va., run by American Electric Power. But the utility shut down the project in 2011 because it could not sell the carbon dioxide or recover the extra cost from its electricity customers, and the equipment consumed so much energy that, at full scale, the project would have sharply cut into electricity production" (Wald 2013b). There are efforts globally to introduce a carbon tax. In North America, there is a shared market for carbon credits being created between California and the Canadian province of Quebec. Australia has also implanted a national carbon tax, but polls find that it is unpopular with the electorate. Such tax measures might finance carbon capture projects, but in the absence of such incentives, we see the number of carbon capture projects declining globally (Wald 2013b). The large supplies of coal make it a relatively attractive fuel source. But two factors undermine its future: global concerns about climate change and the falling costs of natural gas, wind, and solar. In the end, it is likely that economic factors will decrease the importance of coal, which is losing market share in the United States and globally with stunning speed (Wines 2013). If not oil and coal, what are the other choices for energy in the present day, and how realistic are they?

Biofuels: Ethanol and Biodiesel

One potential fuel source is ethanol, with which many drivers in the United States are already familiar. Ethanol can be stored in existing gas stations with minimal retrofitting. In theory, it also does not significantly contribute to global warming because—if you do not count the petroleum-based fertilizers used to help grow crops—it is made from plants that draw carbon dioxide out of the air as they grow. An equivalent amount is then released as the fuel is burned. These factors have made ethanol attractive as an alternative. The U.S. Midwest has a vast infrastructure now devoted to ethanol production, upon which both individuals and corporations have come to rely. The corn growers of the Midwest have formed a powerful political lobby. A key presidential primary is held in Iowa every four years. Across the country, politicians have found that supporting ethanol is an easy means to prove their environmental credentials. Biofuels now supply nearly 10 percent of the U.S. oil demand. This has helped to shield the United States from oil shocks (Krauss 2013).

Critics, however, argue that ethanol has been hyped beyond its real potential. Fundamental problems, they argue, limit its ability to replace oil as a fuel. First, only a small fraction of U.S. service stations carry ethanol, and they are mostly in the Midwest. Even supporters acknowledge (Lashinsky and Schwartz 2006, 78) that creating enough refineries and infrastructure to replace gasoline would take "hundreds of billions of dollars." Biofuels require a great deal of land, which means that increasing biofuel production increases the cost of other crops. When the price of corn rises globally to provide fuel, it increases the cost of food in poorer nations such as Mexico. There is a limited supply of farmland, and global population is increasing. Will wealthy people in developed countries obtain their fuel from farmland that otherwise would have produced food? One article (Harrison 2008, 19), reporting information provided by the aid agency Oxfam, claimed that "biofuels are responsible for a 30 percent increase in global food prices, pushing 30 million people worldwide into poverty." Other critics point out that most ethanol is currently produced using corn, which required huge amounts of fertilizer derived from petroleum. They suggest (and there is a large and passionate literature in this field) that it actually takes more than a gallon of gasoline to create a gallon of ethanol (Heinberg 2003,

156–57). From this perspective, ethanol does not solve the problem of fuel dependency but rather hides it. Defenders counter that only eight-tenths of a gallon of gasoline is required to produce a gallon of ethanol. But this small difference is not a powerful rallying cry. The reality is that ethanol production is entrenched but is unlikely to become a dominant component of the energy used for transportation.

In some markets—such as Brazil, which relies much more on sugar— biofuels provide a major part of the energy needed for transportation (Lashinsky and Schwartz 2006, 80–82; Rohter 2006). The Brazilians estimate that they obtain roughly six times as much ethanol per energy input as U.S. producers achieve with corn (Rohter 2006). According to Lashinsky and Schwartz (2006, 82), the result is that $69 billion that would have been sent to the Middle East has stayed in the country, where it is fueling a rural renaissance that has helped transform traditionally depressed areas. Perhaps if the United States turned to alternative crops to produce ethanol, it could do the same. One hope for ethanol's development in the United States and Europe lies in so-called cellulosic ethanol, which is attracting major investors. The goal of this technology is to produce ethanol from the waste products of agriculture, such as "cornstalks, grasses, [and] tree bark" (Lashinsky and Schwartz 2006, 87). Despite massive investments over the last decade, however, cellulosic ethanol has not yet become a major energy source, and it is unclear if it ever will.

Another major biofuel alternative is biodiesel. One of the attractions of this option is that individuals can adopt this fuel source without making a large investment of cash or having to wait for major corporations to take the lead. Over the last few years, students at U.S. universities have begun to adopt biodiesel on their own. They purchase inexpensive kits that enable them to convert their cars to biodiesel. Local biodiesel cooperatives help provide expertise and also serve as a location to purchase the fuel. An increasing number of service stations already carry this product. There is an aspect of folk populism, with a strong rural coloring, currently associated with this movement. One of the leading spokespersons for the biodiesel movement is country music performer Willie Nelson. He sells his own patented brand of biodiesel (20 percent biodiesel and the rest conventional diesel) at service stations, mostly in Texas (Sewer 2006). The great advantage to biodiesel is that it can be produced from a multitude of products, including turkeys, as one plant in Carthage, Missouri, has proven (Allen 2006; Lemley 2006). This case makes a point: biofuels can be made out of almost anything. This fact might make it possible to develop facilities on marginal lands without either deforesting Indonesia or Brazil to create biodiesel or taking cropland out of production in developing countries to produce ethanol. This is critical because there are concerns that biofuels fuel deforestation throughout the tropics. For example, soybeans have potential to become a major source of biodiesel. This crop effectively produces oil and is already in major production globally. At the same time, international demand for soybeans has sent Brazilian production of this crop skyrocketing, which drives the ongoing deforestation and species loss in Brazil's tropical savanna and the Amazon. Biofuels will have to be grown on land that either currently produces food or supports wildlife (Romm 2005, 169). It is feasible to reduce global petroleum demand using biofuels. But doing so will entail a complex trade-off, and informed people will disagree on whether this is a positive trend.

Wind and Solar

While fracking has led to dramatic and unexpected changes in the world's petroleum supply, the falling price of wind and solar is leading to equally dramatic changes in renewable energy production. For both resources, technology and cost have limited their adoption for so long that people became cynical that they would ever become viable alternatives. Over the last decade, however, the price of wind power has plummeted, which has meant that in the United States, it is now the single largest source of new electricity capacity: "Today, deployed wind power in the United States has the equivalent generation capacity of about 60 large nuclear reactors. Wind is the first non-hydro energy source to begin to approach the same scale as conventional energy forms like coal, gas and nuclear" (U.S. Department of Energy 2013, 2). The price of wind towers has fallen sharply, while the size of turbines has increased dramatically with new technology. The pace of this change has been breathtaking: "In 2012, the U.S. deployed almost twice as much wind as it did in 2011. In fact, wind accounted for 43 percent of new electrical generation capacity in the U.S.—more than any other source" (U.S. Department of Energy 2013, 3). Of course, not all parts of the United States have adopted wind power equally quickly. Texas has been the nation's leader in installed wind-power projects, but most of the southeastern states have lagged behind. Still, given the scale of wind as a resource—it could single-handedly supply all of the country's energy needs—wind has a bright future: "With continued technology improvements and policy support, the Department of Energy estimates that as much as 20 percent of U.S. electricity demand could be met by wind power by 2030" (U.S. Department of Energy 2013, 3). While Texas leads the United States, other nations are embracing wind as well. In Britain, there are vast supplies of wind offshore, which has led to the development of major wind projects in the ocean, such as the London Array. Denmark, Germany, Portugal, Spain, and Sweden lead Europe in total wind production, in which they are far ahead of the United States on a per capita basis. In the future, wind is likely to be the most cost-effective option for China and India, so these two countries will likely see rapid growth in this area.

While wind has increasingly come to be seen as a mainstream power supply, solar has only just reached a tipping point, which sets the stage for explosive growth. Of all energy resources, none can compare with solar power in terms of the total supply available: "In a strictly rational world with a long time horizon, people would have aimed directly for the ultimate energy solution, which is the sun. . . . The sun shines thousands of times more energy on planet Earth than we will ever use" (Randers 2012, 105). The price of solar photo-voltaic (PV) power has fallen with incredible speed, far more rapidly than the decline in the cost of wind (Randers 2012, 106). In some nations, such as Australia, solar power has already hit price parity with fossil-fuel generation. The cost of solar has fallen rapidly in parts of Europe, such as Germany, where its price is half that of the United States. Germany's feed-in tariff (which gives long-term contracts to companies producing renewable energy, while paying a higher price) has made it the world leader in solar power. Still, the price of solar is falling so quickly in the United States, too, that solar energy will soon be cheaper than other forms of power (U.S. Department of Energy 2013, 4). The great advantage of both wind and solar power is that once the plant is built, there is no expense for the purchase of fuel. This makes these plants financially predictable. As solar becomes less expensive than carbon-based fuels, there will likely be a rapid adoption of solar power by residential users, even in the absence of government subsidies (Randers 2012, 110). The future may have arrived early in Australia, where solar power is becoming so inexpensive that it is beginning to threaten the future of traditional utility companies.

It is important to note that as the supply of electricity from renewable energy increases, other technological changes are eliminating the problem posed by solar energy's variability. In Germany, Ontario, and Wales, companies are building large-scale energy-storage facilities that rely on pumping water from a reservoir to another location above it (pumped hydro-energy storage). This means that power can be released at night from solar energy captured during the day. Other companies have adopted solar technology that generates steam to create power. By storing energy in liquid salt, this heat can be converted into electricity hours after the sun has set. This is not a theoretical technology, but one that is now in use in places such as Arizona and California: "When it snowed in Flagstaff, Ariz., recently, thousands of people woke up and turned up their electric heating, and Arizona Public Service saw electricity demand reach a morning peak. To meet the demand, the company used the previous afternoon's sunshine" (Wald 2013c). In this case, the Solana project has a peak capacity of 280 megawatts, so this facility is not a small demonstration project.

At the same time, the rapid adoption of LED lights is reducing the demand for electricity for light, which is a major component of electrical use globally. Finally, electric vehicles (EV) have rapidly fallen in cost while improving in quality. Tesla, a new American car company, has created an electric car that has received rave reviews from car enthusiasts, while other electric vehicles have also received positive reviews: "For instance, for three years in a row the Chevy Volt has topped J.D. Power's *APEAL Study on Consumer Satisfaction for Compact Sedans*. And this spring, *Consumer Reports* said that the Tesla Model S was the best car they had ever tested" (U.S. Department of Energy 2013, 9). As the number of cars produced has increased, the costs have rapidly fallen: "Energy Department models for EV battery fabrication costs show that the cost of high volume EV batteries has fallen more than 50 percent in the last four years" (U.S. Department of Energy 2013, 8). In the near future, the costs of EV look likely to continue a significant decline. All of these changes have meant that many challenges to adopting solar energy have been diminished at the same time that its price has plummeted.

Conclusion

In the first edition of this book, this chapter was dominated by a discussion of oil and what could possibly replace this resource. It has now become clear that oil supplies will not collapse in the coming decades. At the same time, nations such as Germany and Denmark have managed to innovate and decrease their demand for traditional fuels. In this context, what is seen as a resource has changed. Solar energy and wind are now poised to dramatically remake the global energy market in a change that is perhaps driven more by their falling costs than global concerns about climate change. Some fuels, such as coal, that were historically important are declining not because of a diminished supply but rather because they are no longer needed. Since the nuclear disaster in Japan in 2011, most nations have been reluctant to build new nuclear power plants. But equally significant, the construction of such plants entails companies or nations committing to selling electricity for a certain minimum price for decades. However, if the price of wind and solar continues to decrease, there is a real risk that these plants would be uneconomical and would chain their owners to inflated costs for a long period. For this reason, some sources of energy that were important at the turn of the millennium may be much less significant in the future: "[T]he world's consumption of fossil fuels will be in steep decline by 2052. The contribution from nuclear will be declining. The real winner will be the new renewables—solar, wind, and biomass—which, along with hydro, will grow from 8 percent of energy use in 2010 to 37 percent in 2050" (Randers 2012, 105). While petroleum will likely remain a critical part of many nations' energy mix, it will no longer be the unique source of energy for transportation.

Obviously, it is difficult to predict the future because innovations—such as the development of fracking, and new technologies for the mass storage of electricity—can change global energy markets with astounding speed. From the perspective of 2050, it will be clear which energy sources will dominate, but we cannot know with certainty now. It is possible, however, to make more or less informed judgments, which accord with personal or national priorities. As you read articles in the press about energy, try to look for the underlying assumptions or beliefs that color their portrayal of the subject. What perspective colors each argument, and how does this influence the information that each author presents? How does an individual's argument embody the perspective of a larger group, either on a national or global level? And what voices and information are missing?

Energy consumers are tied to energy producers by complex commodity chains that have profound effects on local communities across the globe. It is true that we can all have an impact through our individual choices, from using public transportation and biking to purchasing vehicles that are fuel efficient or run on biodiesel. But the scale of the energy challenges that the globe faces are so large that any solution entails collective action. What steps should your nation take to address energy issues? What do you think are the solutions?

➤ **VOCABULARY**

Hubbert's Peak	International Energy Agency
Peak Oil	OPEC
petroleum	fracking
nationalism	carbon sequestration

➤ **DISCUSSION AND REFLECTION QUESTIONS**

1 *What is the Peak Oil movement?*

2 *Why is it the case that Canada's role as U.S. neighbor seems to have made her so invisible in policy discussions regarding petroleum?*

3 *Will there likely be a point in the future when people will decide that the environmental costs are too high to extract oil in areas like the Oil Sands?*

4 *Robert Jay Lifton uses the phrase "psychic numbing" to describe behavior on the part of citizens wherein they seem to ignore nuclear power plants in their midst, or fracking equipment next to their pastures, in order to go about their regular daily routine with a tolerable level of anxiety. Are you aware of any conversations among your friends and family that might be examples of this phenomenon?*

5 *If you had the opportunity to make a policy recommendation to a high-level federal administrator regarding energy policy for the next twenty-five years, what would it be and why?*

ACTIVITY 1 Look at the website from MBendi Information Services (http://www.mbendi.com/indy/ming/coal/eu/p0005.htm). It focuses on coal-use issues in Europe. Drawing from chapter information and this website, identify two issues that Europe and North America have in common as they make energy choices for the next fifty years.

ACTIVITY 2 The following countries are projected by the World Nuclear Association to become nuclear power users in the near future (http://www.world-nuclear.org/info/inf102.html; accessed February 20, 2010): Italy, Albania, Serbia, Portugal, Norway, Poland, Belarus, Estonia, Latvia, Ireland, and Turkey in Europe; Iran, the United Arab Emirates, Yemen, Israel, Syria, Jordan, Egypt, Tunisia, Libya, Algeria, and Morocco in the Middle East and North Africa; Nigeria, Ghana, Uganda, and Namibia in Africa; Chile, Ecuador, and Venezuela in South America; Azerbaijan, Georgia, Kazakhstan, Mongolia, and Bangladesh in Central and Southern Asia; and Indonesia, the Philippines, Vietnam, Thailand, Malaysia, Australia, and New Zealand in Southeast Asia and the Pacific Islands. Using a general world map, identify some geopolitical concerns that may arise in the particular countries listed. Can you identify two issues these newly emerging nuclear nations may face that contrast with those of nations that have had nuclear reactors for longer periods of time?

ACTIVITY 3 The website Cleantechnica (www.cleantechnica.com) is devoted to news articles that place a positive spin on renewable energy. Spend some time reading articles on the website. What picture do you have of global trends in renewable energy based on this website? What information is missing from this webpage?

ACTIVITY 4 Wind-farm developers in eastern Oregon have been forced to drop plans for several wind farms and scale down their plans for a remaining farm on Steens Mountain, which is famous for its natural beauty. Environmentalists oppose this placement because it will detract from the scenic splendor of the site, while wind-power advocates point out that it will bring jobs to an economically depressed area and produce clean, renewable power. If you were living in eastern Oregon—a rural, economically challenged part of the state—how would you respond to this issue?

References

Allen, G. 2006. Missouri town raising a stink over biofuel plant. Retrieved July 12, 2006, from www.npr.org/templates/story/story.php?storyID=528012.

Austen, I. 2006. Canada conservative gets aggressive with Big Oil. *New York Times*, C-1, C-9. June 14.

Bahgat, G. 2003. *American oil diplomacy in the Persian Gulf and the Caspian Sea*. Miami: University Press of Florida.

Barlow, M., and T. Clarke. 2002. *Blue gold*. New York: The New Press. New preface, 2004.

Bradsher, K. 2012. China slows development of nuclear power plants. New York Times. Retrieved October 25, 2013, from http://www.nytimes.com/2012/10/25/business/global/china-reduces-target-for-construction-nuclear-power-plants.html.

Bryce, R. 2013. How the U.S. became an energy superpower. *Oregonian*, A-5. October 20.

Burgess, P., director. 2004. *Extreme oil: The wilderness.* DVD. New York: Films for the Humanities.

Cardwell, D. 2013. Unplugging bottlenecks in oil and gas deliveries. *New York Times.* October 8. Retrieved October 25, 2013, from http://www.nytimes .com/2013/10/09/business/energy-environment/unplugging-bottlenecks-in-oil-and-gas-deliveries.html.

Cattaneo, C. 2008. An environmental quagmire. *National Post* (Canada), 1, FP-1, FP-4. May 17.

CBC News. 2013. Australian shale oil discovery could be larger than Canada's Oil Sands. January 24. Retrieved October 10, 2013, from http://www.cbc.ca/news /business/australian-shale-oil-discovery-could-be-larger-than-canada-s-oil sands-1.1320034

Christianson, G. E. 1999. *Greenhouse: The 200-year story of global warming.* New York: Walker and Company.

Clayton, M. 2006. Toyota moves to corner the "plug-in" market. *Christian Science Monitor.* July 20. Retrieved July 24, 2006, from www.csmonitor. com/2006/0720/p02s01-ussch.

Cockerham, S. 2013. EPA rule on emissions adds muscle but has a catch. *Oregonian,* A-3. September 21.

Cran, W., and R. John, directors. 2004. *Extreme oil: The oil curse.* DVD. New York: Films for the Humanities.

Deffeyes, K. S. 2001. *Hubbert's peak: The impending world oil shortage.* Princeton, N.J.: Princeton University Press.

Gerlach, A. 2003. *Indians, oil, and politics: A recent history of Ecuador.* New York: SR Books.

Goodstein, D. 2005. *Out of gas: The end of the age of oil.* New York: W. W. Norton and Company.

Harrison, P. 2008. Oxfam blames biofuel for rising poverty. *International Herald,* 19. June 26.

Heinberg, R. 2003. *The party's over: Oil, war, and the fate of industrial societies.* Gabriola Island, British Columbia: New Society Publishers.

Hertsgaard, M. 1999. *Earth odyssey.* New York: Broadway Books.

Jolly, D. 2013. France upholds ban on hydraulic fracturing. *New York Times.* October 11. Retrieved October 15, 2012, from http://www.nytimes.com/2013 /10/12/business/international/france-upholds-fracking-ban.html?_r=0.

Jones, J. 2008. Oil sands industry faces struggle reaching greens. *International Herald Tribune,* 19. June 26.

Kane, J. 1996. *Savages.* New York: Vintage.

Kanter, J. 2013. European lawmakers tighten rules on fracking. *New York Times.* October 9. Retrieved October 25, 2013, from http://www.nytimes.com/2013 /10/10/business/energy-environment/european-lawmakers-tighten-rules-on-fracking.html.

Krauss, C. 2013. Oil shocks ahead? Probably not. *New York Times.* October 8. Retrieved October 25, 2013, from http://www.nytimes.com/2013/10/09 /business/energy-environment/oil-shocks-ahead-probably-not.html.

Lashinsky, A., and N. D. Schwartz. 2006. How to beat the high cost of gasoline. *Fortune*, 74–87. February 6.

Lemley, B. 2006. Anything into oil. *Discover* 27 (April): 4. Retrieved July 3, 2006, from www.discover.com/issues/apr-06/features/anything-oil/.

Luft, G. 2008. Don't believe the energy naysayers. *Oregonian*, B-4. July 14.

Maugeri, L. 2012. Oil—the next revolution: The unprecedented upsurge in oil production and what it means. Discussion paper. Cambridge, Mass.: Harvard Kennedy School. June.

McCarthy, S. 2013. How to deal with tonnes of nuclear waste: bury the problem. *Globe and Mail*, A-8–9. September 13.

Morris, C. 2006. *Energy switch: Proven solutions for a renewable future.* Gabriola Island, Canada: New Society Publishers.

Mullaney, G. 2013. After protest, China cancels plans for petroleum plan. *New York Times*. July 13. Retrieved October 25, 2013, from http://www.nytimes.com/2013/07/14/world/asia/china-uranium-plant.html.

Nikiforuk, A. 2008. *Tar sands: Dirty oil and the future of a continent.* Vancouver: Greystone.

Plourde, A. 2006. Canada's oil sands: Potential and challenges. May 18. Presentation to the Detroit Association for Business Economics.

Pratt, L. 1976. *The tar sands: Syncrude and the politics of oil.* Edmonton: Hurtig.

Randers, J. 2012. *2052: A global forecast for the next forty years.* White River Junction, Vt.: Chelsea Green Publishing.

Read, R. 2006a. China's mercury flushes into Oregon's rivers. *Oregonian*, A-14. November 24.

———. 2006b. Our warmer world: China's dirty exports—mercury and soot. *Oregonian*, A-1. November 24.

Reed, S. 2013. Britain looks to fracking as North Sea oil dwindles. *New York Times*. October 18. Retrieved October 25, 2013, from http://www.nytimes.com/2013/10/19/business/energy-environment/britain-looks-to-fracking-as-north-sea-oil-dwindles.html?ref=business&_r=0.

Richter, W. 2013. France predict[s] cost of a nuclear disaster to be over three times their GDP. Blog post at http://oilprice.com/Alternative-Energy/Nuclear-Power/France-Predict-Cost-of-Nuclear-Disaster-to-be-Over-Three-Times-their-GDP.html. March 14.

Roberts, P. 2004. *The end of oil: On the edge of a perilous new world.* New York: Houghton Mifflin.

Rohter, L. 2006. With a big boost from sugarcane, Brazil is satisfying its fuel needs. *New York Times*, A-1. April 10.

Romm, J. J. 2005. *The hype about hydrogen: Fact and fiction in the race to save the climate.* Washington, D.C.: Island Press.

Salopek, P. 2006a. Oil: Feeding America's addiction. *Oregonian*, A-7. August 9.

———. 2006b. The world of oil: An ordinary tank of gas in a thirsty U.S. tracks back to shadowy global politics. *Oregonian*, A-6. August 8.

Sawyer, S. 1996. Indigenous initiatives and petroleum politics in the Ecuadorian Amazon. *Cultural Survival Quarterly* 20 (Spring): 26–30.

Schalch, K. Canadian dreams of ethanol distilled from grass. Retrieved July 24, 2006, from www.npr.org/templates/sforg/story.php?storyID+5407551.

Sewer, A. 2006. Fill 'er up, Willie. *Fortune*, 80. February 6.

Shelley, T. 2005. *Oil: Politics, poverty, and the planet*. New York: Zed Books.

Simmons, M. 2005. *Twilight in the desert: The coming Saudi oil shock and the world economy*. Hoboken, N.J.: John Wiley and Sons.

Smallman, S. 2003. Canada's new role in North America's energy security. *Security and Defense Review* 3 (2): 247–60.

Tait, C. 2008a. Fort McMurray feels duck glare "unfair." *National Post* (Canada): FP-5. May 17.

———. 2008b. Tailing ponds sticky dilemma. *National Post* (Canada), FP-5. May 17.

Taming king coal. 2006. Editorial. *New York Times*, A-14. November 25.

U.S. Department of Energy. 2013. Revolution now: The future arrives for four clean energy technologies. September 17. PDF accessed online.

Urstadt, B. 2006. Imagine there's no oil: Scenes from a liberal apocalypse. *Harper's Monthly*, 31–40. August.

Vaitheeswaran, V. V. 2003. *Power to the people*. New York: Farrar, Straus and Giroux.

Wald, M. 2013a. Atomic goal: 800 years of power from waste. *New York Times*. September 24. Accessed online at http://www.nytimes.com/2013/09/25/business/energy-environment/atomic-goal-800-years-of-power-from-waste.html.

———. 2013b. Despite climate concern, study finds fewer carbon capture projects. *New York Times*. October 10. Accessed online at http://www.nytimes.com/2013/10/11/science/earth/study-finds-setbacks-in-carbon-capture-projects.html.

———. 2013c. Arizona utility tries storing solar energy for use in the dark. *New York Times*. October 17. Accessed online at http://www.nytimes.com/2013/10/18/business/energy-environment/arizona-utility-tries-storing-solar-energy-for-use-in-the-dark.html?hpw.

Walker, C., director. 1996. *Trinkets and beads*. DVD. New York: First Run Icarus Films.

Ward, M. 2013. Study finds setbacks in carbon capture projects. *New York Times*. October 10. Accessed online.

Wines, M. 2013. A push away from burning coal as an energy source. *New York Times*. November 14. Accessed online.

Witt, H. 2008. Vast oil sands hide dirty environmental secret. *Oregonian*, A-21. November 27.

Yergin, D. 1991. *The prize: The epic quest for oil, money, and power*. New York: Free Press.

ELEVEN **Environment**

➤ **SYNOPSIS**

This chapter explores the beginning of the environmental movement, its tenets and contributions, and some important criticisms that have been leveled against it. Examples from the Brazilian rain forest and northern Arctic are presented. Atmosphere and climate issues—in particular, climate change's effects on biodiversity—are explored. An underlying current within the chapter is the notion that environmental issues reflect globalization perhaps more powerfully than any other thematic dimension presented in the text.

➤ **SCAFFOLDING**

As you read through this chapter, think about how you would answer each of the questions below.

How directly do media reports and news items about global warming affect you?

If you were countering general global warming arguments, what would you say?

Given the information in the previous chapter about energy sources and their environmental impact, what are key environmental issues you believe people should be familiar with?

Are there some geographic locations in the world that are impacted more than others by global warming?

> **CORE CONCEPTS**

What are the points and counterpoints in the general discourse between strong environmentalists and pragmatists such as Bjorn Lomborg regarding the environmental movement?

Why is the Amazon such an important case study in terms of environment and globalization?

What are some arguments from scholars and practitioners in the Global South regarding how the Global North uses environmental discourse to advance its interests?

How do species extinction and biodiversity loss impact your daily life?

How does this compare with the impacts on indigenous peoples throughout the world?

Perhaps the most surprising fact about the environmental movement is that it was established so recently. In the nineteenth century, there were authors and activists such as Henry David Thoreau and John Muir, but they were individuals more than a political bloc. Environmentalism only became a true movement in the early twentieth century, and it remained a relatively small subculture until the 1960s. By that time, the impact of DDT; the example of Love Canal; the mercury disaster at Minamata, Japan; the damage to the Great Lakes; the choking smog in cities; and growing worries about nuclear energy combined to create widespread concern about environmental issues in the developed world. From Al Gore's documentary *An Inconvenient Truth* (2006) to bestsellers such as *Fieldnotes from a Catastrophe* (Kolbert 2006), environmental issues are now visible politically. The power of the modern environmental movement reflects widespread fears about global warming, species loss, and deforestation. And people fear for the future of humanity. The nuclear disaster at Fukushima, Japan, in 2011, created an ongoing release of radioactive water into the North Pacific Ocean that now seems impossible to control. This disaster in particular has led people to think about the limits of technology.

At the same time, there is currently an intellectual backlash against the environmental movement, not only in the United States but also in Europe. Perhaps the best-known work is that of Bjorn Lomborg, the Danish author of *The Skeptical Environmentalist* (2001). Like a number of antienvironmentalist authors, he tries to make the case that the environmental movement has a long history of warning of disasters that never come to pass. In fact, these authors suggest, the world's environment is improving. Many of the environmentalists' arguments are based on flawed understandings of risk, simplistic models of climate, and plain bad science. In this characterization, environmentalism is a romanticized movement that harks back to an idealized past and downplays the benefits of economic growth. Lomborg and his supporters suggest that it fails to take into account human needs. Much environmental rhetoric is not only sensationalized but also reflects elitism. Many environmentalists border on misanthropy (the hatred of people), according to these critics.

Environmentalists could dismiss these arguments as the neoconservative ravings of groups closely associated with the U.S. position on globalization. Some multinational corporations are investing vast amounts of money to undermine efforts to fight global warming. Laurie David, one of the producers of *An Inconvenient Truth*, has described how the National Science Teachers Association (NSTA) turned down 50,000 free copies of the film because it threatened their fund-raising campaign. In particular, she suggests that the NSTA feared angering ExxonMobil: "In the past year alone, according to its website, ExxonMobil's foundation gave $42 million to key organizations that influence the way children learn about science, from kindergarten until they graduate from high school. And ExxonMobil isn't the only one getting in on the action. The oil industry, the coal industry, and the other corporate interests are exploiting shortfalls in education funding by using a small slice of their record profits to buy themselves a classroom soapbox through textbooks, classroom posters, and seminars" (David 2006; for parental protests against the film's screening, see Associated Press 2007). David believes that such materials form part of a larger industry strategy: "An API memo leaked to the media as long ago as 1998 succinctly explains why the association is angling to infiltrate the classroom. 'Informing teachers/students about uncertainties in climate science will begin to erect barriers against further efforts to impose Kyoto-like measures in the future'" (David 2006). Is this antienvironmentalist movement a smokescreen for the interests of major corporations, as David's article might suggest?

The reality is that antienvironmentalism is a complex ideology that draws on some unexpected sources (Spotts 2006). For example, a particularly powerful attack on the environmental movement comes from the Global South. One needs to look at the historical and political experience of southern countries in order to understand why their populations might not trust environmental rhetoric. One way of observing this reality is to examine the contested arguments about the future of the Amazon and how this issue is perceived in northern and southern nations. This perspective helps us to examine the interconnections between social and environmental issues in a manner that permits a more critical evaluation of environmental debates.

The Amazon

The Amazon is a powerful symbol for environmental destruction, given the issue of deforestation and species loss. Changes to the forest are so profound that they might have implications for planetary climate. Most works on the Amazon begin by describing the staggering size of the largest tropical rain forest on the planet and the river that gives it its name. If one end of the Amazon River were laid on the coast of Brazil, it would span the Atlantic Ocean and end in Africa. Or if the Amazon River Basin were overlaid upon the United States, it would cover most of the country (Hanson 1944, 4). It has "one-fifth of the freshwater flowing off the face of the earth" (N. Smith 1999, 4). Bolivia, Brazil, Colombia, Ecuador, French Guyana, Guyana, Peru, Suriname, and Venezuela all lay claim to parts of the river basin. Marajó Island, in the mouth of the Amazon, is the size of some small European nations. The Amazon has many tributaries that on their own would be major world rivers, such as the Negro. At its mouth, the river is farther across than the distance from France to England; that is, it is wider than the English Channel. But hearing such statistics, while impressive, is not the same as seeing it in person. Travelers can canoe through the Amazon and look down through crystal-clear waters to see trees beneath them. The trees have evolved to keep their leaves, and one can see fish flitting through the branches, feeding on the trees' fruit. Life seems to fill every imaginable niche in this environment.

The Amazon is tens of millions of years old and home to a vast number of species. From the air, you can fly for hours over green expanses of forest, which gives the land a surface impression of uniformity. But some geologists hypothesize that the forest has expanded and contracted through time, which has created pockets of forest with particular species called refugia (Leakey and Lewin 1996, 109); for scientists, these can be thought of as biological islands with plants and animals unlike those in other areas of the forest. The suggestion is that this geologic history may help to explain the immense richness of species that the Amazon possesses. From electric eels and bird-eating spiders to blue morpho butterflies and manatees, the Amazon is full of unexpected creatures. It is home, for instance, to the strangest of birds: the hoatzin. The national bird of Guyana, the hoatzin eats leaves, smells foul, has claws on its wings when young, and flies poorly. The capybara is the largest rodent on the planet and wanders the Amazonian forest looking like a guinea pig on growth hormones. Scientists are constantly discovering new species, such as the discovery of a new species of tamarin in the summer of 2009. It is perhaps telling that it was discovered only sixty-five miles from Manaus, the largest city in the Amazon. There is currently no good figure for the total number of species in the Amazon. The region is too vast, and the resources devoted to an inventory to date have been far too small. But from the trees that define the forest to the insects that live upon them, the Amazon is immensely rich in species.

The scale of the Amazon River Basin, which amazed early scientific explorers from Richard Spruce to Henry Walter Bates, long made it difficult to imagine that such a vast environment could be endangered. But far to the east, another forest's death has served as a warning. When the first Portuguese explorers arrived, they encountered the Atlantic Forest, which stretched from northern Argentina to northern Brazil. Despite its great length, it seldom reached over 200 miles in thickness, except in the very southern edge of its range, where it stretched into Paraguay. After discovery, the Portuguese first exploited the coastal region and then gradually moved to the interior, mostly settling in areas near the ocean so that they could export their main crop—sugarcane—to the mother country. Most of the country's major cities now lie in the region of the country that was once covered by the Atlantic Forest. Perhaps less than 7 percent of the original forest remains—a fraction of a forest that "once covered 466,000 square miles—an area larger than Texas and California combined—along the Atlantic coast of Brazil" (LaFranchi 1998, 12). Some of this forest is in unexpected patches. There are monkeys living on patches of forest at the edge of the Copacabana in Rio de Janeiro, and diminutive owls nest an hour outside of São Paulo, the largest city in South America.

Despite its shrunken area and the fact that many sections are now second growth, the Atlantic Forest remains astoundingly rich in species. For this reason, the Atlantic Forest is a World Biosphere Reserve. According to the Nature Conservancy, the Atlantic Forest is home to "around 20,000 species of plants, representing 8 percent of the earth's plants. In fact, in the 1990s researchers from the New York Botanical Garden counted 458 tree species in 2.5 acres—more than the number of tree species in the entire U.S. eastern seaboard" (Nature Conservancy 2006; see also LaFranchi 1998, 12). This wealth of plant diversity supports a corresponding diversity in other species. The forest has twenty-one species of primates found nowhere else in the world.

What is amazing about the Atlantic Forest is that patches of it are so accessible. One can take a path at Praia Vermelha at the base of Sugarloaf that winds around the base of this tourist attraction and holds a small remnant of the Atlantic Forest. Most of the people on the trail are Brazilians because few foreign tourists know of this site. They come to see the huge butterflies and small monkeys in the heart of Rio de Janeiro, one of South America's great cities. As Warren Dean (1995) has argued in his magisterial history of the Atlantic Forest, what remains is a ghost of an ecosystem. Yet "international interest in the Atlantic Forest is heightened by conservation biologists' growing attention to the world's remaining centers of biodiversity" (LaFranchi 1998, 12). The argument has been made that saving the Atlantic Forest is hopeless and that the remaining areas of the forest will not survive past the middle of this century. Attention should therefore be focused instead on the Amazon (LaFranchi 1998, 13). But the incredible biodiversity of the Atlantic Forest makes people reluctant to abandon it, and some surveys have found positive news about the biological health of the forest. The Brazilian government is placing renewed emphasis on protecting and restoring it. But challenges remain: there are now plans by ENRC, a British-Kazakh mining company, to build a railway right through one of the few remaining areas of virgin Atlantic rain forest: "ENRC's aim is to transport iron ore from a mine in the interior to the port of Ilheus, despite the region being named by Unesco as a priority region for conservation" (Lang 2013). The Atlantic Forest serves as a warning of what could happen to the Amazon. It is possible to kill an entire ecosystem.

The Amazon became an international environmental issue in the 1980s as people began to realize that if deforestation rates continued, this ecosystem could be destroyed. At the same time, a global tide of species loss made biodiversity a focus of popular attention. Geographically, the diversity of species increases sharply near the tropics. Most of the world's species exist in a band 30 degrees on either side of the equator. Some environments, such as the dry scrublands of northeastern Brazil, are surprisingly rich in species (Leakey and Lewin 1996, 103–4). But overall, the tropical rain forests are home to the most remarkable biodiversity on earth. As Richard Leakey notes, the result of this natural law is that much of earth's life lives in a surprisingly small space: "Termed the 'latitudinal species-diversity gradient,' this bold signature of nature has been known to biologists for many years. . . . Tropical rain forests are especially rich in biodiversity: they cover one-sixteenth of the world's land surface, yet are home to more than half its species" (Leakey and Lewin 1996, 103). As one might expect, tropical rain forests are central to current discussions surrounding biodiversity and species loss.

In a recent UNESCO publication, the authors concisely defined biodiversity as the "total variability among genes, plant and animal species, and ecosystems found in nature" (Skutnabb-Kangas, Maffi, and Harmon 2003, 53). In other words, biodiversity is a measure of the richness of life in an environment. It also seems to correlate with cultural and linguistic richness. Environments that foster a wealth of cultures and languages seem to be the same as those that create remarkable biodiversity (Skutnabb-Kangas, Maffi, and Harmon 2003, 9, 38–39). The Amazon and Papua New Guinea are rich in both languages and species; indeed, the island of New Guinea is the most linguistically diverse region on earth, with over a 1,000 languages (Skutnabb-Kangas, Maffi, and Harmon 2003, 26). But these biological hotspots are under mounting pressure at the same time that languages and cultures are being assimilated at a rapid rate. Deforestation, overhunting, and dams are rapidly changing the ecosystems in the Atlantic Forest, the Amazon, and the Congo River Basin, as well as Southeast Asia's forests.

One particular problem is that the areas of our planet with the greatest biodiversity are also those undergoing the most rapid population growth. One recent study found that biological "hotspots" cover 12 percent of the earth's surface, but the 20 percent of the earth's population that lives in these lands are growing at an annual rate of 1.8 percent rather than the 1.5 percent in other regions of the planet (Cincotta, Wisnewski, and Engelman 2000, 990). As the authors stated, this finding suggested that "substantial human-induced environmental changes are likely to continue in the hotspots and that demographic change remains an important factor in global biodiversity conservation" (Cincotta, Wisnewski, and Engelman 2000, 990). The authors also noted that the ongoing decline in human fertility globally provides hope for species preservation. Still, their finding highlighted the problem of human-caused extinction, as global population growth impacts entire ecosystems.

Extinction

Our world has endured mass extinction before. Over the multibillion-year history of life on our planet, there have been five great extinctions in which most life quickly disappeared: "This handful of major events, from oldest to the most recent, are: the end-Ordovician (440 million years ago), the late Devonian (365 million years ago), the end-Permian (225 million years ago), the end-Triassic (210 million years ago), and the end-Cretaceous (65 million years ago)" (Leakey and Lewin 1996, 45). For at least one of these extinctions, there is a clear explanation. Most scientists now agree that 65 million years ago, an asteroid or comet collided with the earth in the ocean off the coast of the Yucatán Peninsula, Mexico. This created a firestorm of energy, unleashed a massive tsunami, and heated the entire planet, which then slid into months of darkness. This event wiped out many life forms, of which the most famous were the non-avian dinosaurs.

Other events are more mysterious, such as the end-Permian extinction. There are many competing theories for this remarkable event, which came within a hair's breadth of wiping out all life on earth: in less than 100,000 years, more than 90 percent of all species disappeared from our planet. Perhaps because it was even more devastating than the end-Cretaceous extinction, this event has become a focus of popular attention. Two success-ful books, Peter Ward's *Gorgon* (2004) and M. J. Benton's *When Life Nearly Died* (2003), have attracted wide readership. Part of our fascination with this mystery may come from our understanding that life and environments are ephemeral. This can explain the thrill that came in 2005 with the (now doubtful) "rediscovery" in Louisiana of the ivory-billed woodpecker, long thought extinct. It also perhaps describes the almost personal sense of loss that people have when they hear that a species has vanished.

In December 2006 a team of scientists announced that a major survey of the Yangtze River had failed to find a single baiji, the Yangtze River dol-phin, which led them to declare it "functionally extinct" (Hutzler 2006). This did not mean that the last of these dolphins, once believed to embody a Chinese goddess, had died out. Rather, it meant that any survivors were now too isolated and too dispersed for the animal to have any hope of sur-vival (Hutlzer 2006). This white and nearly blind animal had survived in the Yangtze for perhaps 20 million years. Now it is irretrievably gone; the news received global coverage. In the case of the baiji, pollution, heavy ship traffic, and dams gradually undermined its ability to survive after World War II. But not all changes take decades.

Pollution, hunting, and deforestation can destroy ecosystems with astounding speed. Richard Leakey and Roger Lewin describe the experience of two scientists who discovered a ridge in western Ecuador called Centinela. It was an environment as rich as it was vulnerable: "Among the riot of diversity that is nurtured by this habitat, Gentry and Dodson discovered, were ninety unknown species, including herbaceous plants, orchids and epiphytes, which lived nowhere else. Centinela was an ecological island, which, being isolated, had developed a unique flora. Within eight years the ridge had been transformed into farmland, and its endemic species were no more" (Leakey and Lewin 1996, 243). Centinela is but one example of a larger process of extinction, which is not confined to western Ecuador but is taking place across the planet.

Scientists now argue that the current sweep of extinction is so dramatically different from that in the recent geological record that it should be recognized as something distinct. Some scientists argue that perhaps as many as 100,000 species a year go extinct (Leakey and Lewin 1996, 241). This devastation constitutes a "Sixth Extinction" comparable to the greatest mass extinctions in our earth's history (Leakey and Lewin 1996, 232–45). As Paul Martin has described, the damage inflicted by our industrialized society is only one part of a longer process in which humans have destroyed large mammal and bird species from North America to Australia (Martin 2005; Stone 2001, 111–20; Leakey and Lewin 1996, 170–94). Jared Diamond made the environmental damage of ancient cultures the major theme of his work *Collapse: How Societies Choose to Fail or Succeed* (2005); this book carefully described how past societies so thoroughly damaged their environments that civilizations or cultures suffered. The world lost dramatic species—from the moa, the largest bird that has ever lived, to the mammoth, which disappeared in North America shortly after the first humans arrived. Given humanity's dependence on its environment to survive, this destruction may seem difficult to understand. As Diamond's students asked him, what passed through the mind of the Easter Islander who cut down the last tree (Diamond 2005, 419)? But these extinctions were only a forerunner for the far broader damage now being done to our modern world.

No part of our planet seems to be safe from species loss. Frog species are going extinct at a rapid rate globally for reasons that are hard to understand but may have something to do with an invasive fungus spread by human activity. In the oceans, overfishing threatens multiple species. Even where species survive, commercial fisheries are collapsing under the pressure of mounting global demand for fish. The cod fishery in the North Atlantic, for example, was scientifically managed into oblivion (Kurlansky 1998, 144–233). This trend is a global phenomenon, but not all regions are equally affected. At the core of this process is the loss of tropical forest, which is taking place with stunning speed, as Diamond describes: "For example, destruction of accessible lowland tropical rain forest outside national parks is already virtually complete in peninsular Malaysia, will be complete at current rates within less than a decade in the Solomon Island, the Philippines, on Sumatra, and on Sulawesi, and will be complete around the world except perhaps for parts of the Amazon Basin and the Congo Basin within 25 years" (Diamond 2005, 498). Such forest loss will inevitably be accompanied by large-scale species loss. Leakey describes what scientists envision may happen if tropical forests continue to shrink at their current rates, according to current models. If only 10 percent of tropical forests remain, the "arithmetical relationship based on the theory predicts that 50 percent of species will go extinct—some immediately, some over a period of decades or even centuries" (Leakey and Lewin 1996, 240).

Such an immense catastrophe is difficult to fathom. In the past, there was little concern about preserving dying species. The last thylacines (Tasmanian tigers) died in Australian zoos because nobody bothered to breed them. Of course, saving even a single species can be an overwhelming task that requires an immense amount of resources; it can be very expensive, and there often is no margin for error. Yet the total scale of the extinctions is overwhelming: "[H]alf of the freshwater fish of peninsular Malaysia, ten bird species of Cebu in the Philippines, half of the forty-one tree snails in Oahu, forty-four of the sixty-eight shallow-water mussels of the Tennessee River shoals, and so on" (Leakey and Lewin 1996, 243). Some rare species, such as the Nepalese rhino, require both large amounts of territory and constant protection from poachers. There is no way that a global response to this problem could focus on individual species. Instead, any such effort must focus on the broader problems that many species face. (For a list of these challenges, see Diamond 2005, 486–96.)

There is no consensus, however, that the cost of doing so is worthwhile. (For a short list of the arguments used against environmentalists, see Diamond 2005, 503–14.) Popularly, most people agree that the loss of a species is a tragedy. But preserving species often comes with a cost, whether it be preserving old-growth forests to save the spotted owl in the U.S. Northwest or fighting the illegal ivory trade to preserve elephants in Kenya. This has led to a tension between people advocating for environmental preservation and people who argue that employment and development have to be equally valued. One example of this stress can be seen in the March 2010 vote at a UN wildlife meeting to continue to allow fishing of the Atlantic bluefin tuna even though its stock has been depleted almost 75 percent. Part of the reason for this decision, as described in an Associated Press account, is that "Japan won over scores of poorer nations with a campaign that played on fears that a ban would devastate their economies. Tokyo also raised doubts that such a radical move was scientifically sound. . . . 'Let's take science and throw it out the door,' Susan Lieberman of the Pew Environment Group said sarcastically" (Associated Press 2010). In spite of environmentalists' quantification of the economic value of biodiversity (Leakey and Lewin 1996, 124–25), there remains a larger antienvironmental critique.

The Antienvironmental Critique

The argument of the antienvironmental movement can be broadly summarized around several key points. The environmental movement has created a narrative of constant environmental decline, even though there has been significant progress. Its strong political agenda has also warped its use of science. Critics argue that environmentalists do not create a nuanced or qualified picture of environmental trends, which are often complex and contradictory. Instead, they tend to create a bleak vision of the future as a political tool to mobilize support. Historically, however, many of their predictions have proved to be wrong. The success of the movement owes as much to its political work, especially within the educational system, as it does to the power of their arguments.

These critics argue that the pendulum has swung so far in the environmental movement's direction that development and employment are often threatened. In this narrative, the environmental movement is elitist and disconnected from the concerns of the working majority of Europeans and Americans. Many of the policies that the environmentalists advocate are simply not practical. For example, renewable energy sources have been touted for decades as an alternative to fossil fuels. But there are serious obstacles to their adoption, which the environmental movement glosses over; instead, the movement tends to blame its failures on big business in revisionist historical accounts that rely heavily on conspiracy theories. At root, these critics argue that much of the environmental movement is antiscience and antigrowth—if not antihuman, as Fred Smith (2002,

295) describes: "Environmentalists see the world in 'terrible toos' terms: There are too many of us, we consume too much, and we rely too heavily on technology that we understand too little about." From Smith's perspective, the environmental movement has a clear political agenda: to increase government involvement in the economy.

Much of the criticism of the environmental movement has a strong free-market component. These authors argue that the solution to environmental problems is not more government regulation but rather privatization. For example, one of the most influential pieces of environmental writing was Garret Hardin's 1968 *Science* magazine article "The Tragedy of the Commons." In this work, Hardin argued that resources held in common, such as fisheries, tend toward disastrous overuse because individual actors can benefit from actions that are collectively disastrous. In response, Fred Smith has argued that this should not be seen as a market failure but rather a call for more privatization. This is true for many issues, including efforts to address species loss: "Note also that while many species of wildlife are threatened, domesticated species—pets as well as livestock—are prospering" (Smith 2002, 297). Smith argues that if people see economic benefits from endangered species, such as elephants, then they will work to preserve them (Smith 2002, 308). Of course, keeping track of wildlife can make efforts to privatize this resource difficult, but technology may be able to provide some of the answers: "'Beepers' or computer chip implants that would signal the location of larger wildlife (manatees, whales, Siberian tigers) might well have value" (Smith 2002, 310). Rather than being the problem, Smith suggests, the free market is ultimately the solution to most environmental problems. Habitats need private owners to serve as stewards: "By extending the institutions of markets and private property throughout the world, humanity will gain the proper incentives to save nature and better ability to do so. Ocean reefs in the South Pacific, Andean mountaintops, elephants in Africa, the shoreline of Lake Baikal—all deserve stewards, property owners, who can protect them from misuse" (Smith 2002, 316).

To most environmentalists, such a position is anathema. They would point to the many situations in which private property owners are making decisions that are profoundly destructive to the environment. In the 1980s, the poster child for environmental destruction might have been the cattle ranchers of the Amazon. Today, it might be the major soy farmers, who are also replacing the forest, partly to produce biodiesel. There are larger philosophical issues involved: does biodiversity only have value if it provides economic benefit? What are the economic benefits of the species that provide oxygen, purify water, and pollinate the plants we eat—in short, what is the value of the ecosystems that make the earth a livable planet? Leakey and Lewin (1996, 124–44) have described this debate in detail. Yet it would be a mistake to characterize the antienvironmentalists' arguments as uniformly naive.

Bjorn Lomborg

One of the most influential critics of the environmental movement has been the Danish author Bjorn Lomborg. A statistics professor at the University of Aarhus in Denmark, Lomborg is a former member of Greenpeace who is profoundly critical of the widely held viewpoint that the world's environment is consistently worsening. In particular, he attacks the statistics that the environmental movement uses to advance its arguments regarding everything from deforestation to biodiversity loss. His arguments have drawn a powerful backlash from within the environmental community. Because Lomborg is an academic published by Cambridge University Press, his work posed a serious intellectual challenge. There are numerous websites and articles that examine Lomborg's arguments (Nisbet 2003). Much of the criticism directed upon him has come from scientists, who allege that his work is sloppy and does not properly draw on peer-reviewed works. But his arguments have been influential and widely read, and they are worth considering in detail.

Lomborg harshly criticizes biologists and ecologists who argue that the earth may be losing 40,000 to 100,000 species a year. From his perspective, there are no careful studies to support this assertion, which is largely driven by the political goals of the environmental movement: "Although these assertions of massive extinctions of species have been repeated everywhere you look, they simply do not equate with the environmental evidence. The story is important, because it shows how figures regarding the extinction of 25–100 percent of all the species on Earth within our lifetime provide the political punch to put conservation of endangered species high on the agenda. Punch which the more realistic figure of 0.7 percent over the next 50 years would not achieve to the same degree" (Lomborg 2001, 249; for a description of similar arguments, see Leakey and Lewin 1996, 235–36). Part of Lomborg's argument is that not all biodiversity may be equal. The biodiversity of wild cousins of domestic crops may be more valuable than that of nonfood plants. Biologists tend to focus attention on large animals, while the majority of animals that probably go extinct are small and uncharismatic (Lomborg 2001, 250–51).

Lomborg admits that it is true that extinctions have been increasing in the historical period. But there is no good evidence for the widely used figure of 40,000 species a year going extinct. In fact, this figure was arrived at in the 1960s using very crude guesswork from then-predominant theories about diversity (Lomborg 2001, 250–52). Lomborg argues that this data has not been supported by careful surveys since this period by groups such as "World Conservation, which maintains the official Red List of threatened animals" (Lomborg 2001, 254). Part of the reason for this discrepancy is that rain forest loss has been nowhere as large as widely predicted. In contravention of older theories about habitat and species loss, patches of rain forest have proved to be unexpectedly robust at preserving species. The best example of this is the Atlantic Forest, which is one of the most degraded tropical rain forests in the world. Yet extinctions have not taken place in this rain forest at anything near the rates that would be expected (Lomborg 2001, 255). Lomborg does not deny that extinction is a problem but proposes that environmentalists exaggerate it:

> An extinction rate of 0.7 percent over the next 50 years is not trivial. It is a rate about 1,500 times higher than natural background extinction. However, it is a much smaller figure than the typically advanced 10–100 percent over the next 50 years (equal to some 20,000 to 200,000 times the background rate). Moreover, to assess the long-term impact, we must ask ourselves whether it is likely that this extinction rate will continue for many hundreds of years (accumulating serious damage) or more likely will be alleviated as population growth decelerates and the developing world gets rich enough to afford to help the environment, reforest and set aside parks. (Lomborg 2001, 255–56)

From Lomborg's perspective, one of the reasons for hope is the fact that economic growth can create the wealth that will permit environmental stewardship.

Lomborg has similar views about the issue of tropical deforestation. He contrasts the dramatic warnings about forests' destruction with his perspective that the planet's total forest cover is remarkably constant (Lomborg 2001, 111). He does state that some countries, such as China, have had significant losses of their forests. But he suggests that focusing on individual countries can be misleading: "Countries such as Nigeria and Madagascar have admittedly lost well over half their original rain forest, and Central America may have lost 50–70 percent. But overall, they are only home to about 5 percent of the world's tropical forest" (Lomborg 2001, 114). He sees a clear dichotomy between trends in northern latitudes and in the south: "The temperate forests, most of which are in North America, Europe, and Russia, have expanded over the last forty years. On the other hand, quite a lot of tropical forest is disappearing" (Lomborg 2001, 113). Still, Lomborg says, predictions about the decline of the tropical forests are badly exaggerated. The rates of forest loss are low enough that as people's incomes rise, nations will have the resources to address the problem. Private land management can also reduce the pressure on tropical forests, such as the use of plantations to meet the world's demand for paper. Lomborg argues that the future is not one of gloom but optimism (Lomborg 2001, 117).

Southern Critiques of Environmentalism

The ideas that Lomborg articulates are clearly coming from the perspective of an author in the developed world. But there are also significant objections to the environmental movement in the developing world. One can clearly see these arguments around the Amazon, the largest remaining tropical rain forest in the world. As mentioned earlier in the chapter, the Amazon came to prominence as an international cause in the 1980s, driven by rising concerns about global warming and the publicity associated with the death of Chico Mendes, an environmental and union activist in Brazil's Amazon. At this time, there was a great deal of media attention devoted to the Amazon, which attracted the support of public figures such as the rock star Sting. In environmental publications, the Amazon was described as being "the lungs of the Earth"; this was the region that generated oxygen for our planet.

In response to these concerns, there were thoughtful efforts to see how developed nations could help South American nations address the issue of deforestation. One popular answer that policy makers suggested was "debt-for-nature" swaps. Under these agreements, wealthier nations would forgive the debt of poor countries, which did not have the capacity to repay their debt in any case. In return, these nations would set aside certain areas as nature reserves. It seemed to be a win-win situation for all.

Within developing countries, however, such efforts were sometimes viewed as being very threatening. To understand why, you have to consider the historical and cultural context that shaped South American governments at the time. This is not to deny the serious damage that was being done to the Amazon. In 1990 documentary filmmaker Adrian Cowell released five videos that formed the *Decade of Destruction* series. Watching these videos, it is as if someone had gone into the Wild West of the United States in the 1870s with a video camera in hand. Cowell's work documented the environmental and human costs of Brazil's Amazon policy. Viewers have been moved to tears watching the tragic encounters between native peoples and settlers, or gunmen and squatters.

Yet the beliefs and attitudes held by people in Brazil and other Amazonian countries are not invalid. If one were to summarize the views of many Brazilians and combine them with the writing of various authors on the Amazon, a skeptic's viewpoint might be described as follows: Europeans have long imposed their views of an exoticized nature onto the Amazon, beginning with the first ideas of El Dorado, who led the first Spaniards to descend the Amazon. Europeans and North Americans continue to impose these images upon the Amazon, in part because it is a politically safe way for them to address environmental issues (Nugent 1994, 15–21, 214–15; Slater 2003a, 41–68).

Nobody in the United States, Germany, or Japan has to lose a job to fight deforestation in the Amazon. Mark Hertsgaard has described how one cartoonist portrayed this attitude:

> Life without a car is literally unthinkable for most Americans, an assumption comically skewered by cartoonist Tom Toles. His cartoon opens with four people agreeing that the greenhouse effect threatens global catastrophe and that carbon dioxide production therefore has to be reduced. But when one person says, "The biggest problem is automobiles," a silence falls over the group. "Somehow," the narrator dryly observes, "the discussion always stops at this point." The solution the four finally hit upon is to tell South Americans to stop burning down their rain forests. "Yeah," one character says with relief, "the South Americans." (Hertsgaard 1999, 105)

This cynical viewpoint captures the widespread attitude of many people within South America toward both Europeans and North Americans (Christianson 1999, 189–91). From their perspective, northern countries have largely deforested their nations as part of the developmental trajectory (Nugent 1994, 19; Christianson 1999, 182). But now that Brazil or Peru wants to follow in their path, northern countries are telling them that they cannot do so. The governments of Amazonian nations argue that they are preserving far more of their old-growth forest than the United States or Europe has (Stewart 1994, 23). Moreover, these nations owe immense sums to these rich countries. There is no realistic hope that they can repay these debts unless resources such as the Amazon are developed. In the United States, the federal government is fighting to preserve a small fraction of its original forest cover that is old growth. While the Amazon is being developed, nations like Brazil have set aside large areas as nature reserves.

South American governments also argue that the Amazon is not as vulnerable to development as environmentalists have proposed. One of the reasons that the Amazon is so species rich is that, historically, the forest has waxed and waned, with periods when much of the Amazon Basin looked more like a savanna with divided patches of forest (Leakey and Lewin 1996, 109). Nor is the forest in some primeval state. The indigenous people have modified this forest for thousands of years. Some authors use the term "cultured forest" to capture the extent to which the forest's composition has changed. Native peoples burned extensive areas of forest. They created plantations of their favorite fruit-bearing crops, some of which have endured for centuries (N. Smith 1999, 32). They even created canals to connect different branches of rivers together, as have more-recent settlers (Raffles 2002, 26–27, 34). After disease and slave raids caused the Amazon's population to collapse, the forest reclaimed many of these fields and plantations. But the impact on the soil and plant composition was profound, so that local peoples can readily identify areas where native peoples once lived even centuries after they have left (N. Smith 1999, 24–28). The Amazon is not an untouched wilderness that is easily destroyed by human contact. Rather, what Europeans took to be wilderness had been emptied of people by European diseases and slave raiders after contact. Many government officials and businessmen in Brazil believe that the people who have seized upon the Amazon as an environmental issue have only a vague idea of the region's nature and history.

In a 2007 article for *National Geographic*, Scott Wallace interviewed Blair Maggi, a soybean "king." Maggi's attitudes probably represent those of many Amazonian elites:

> To Maggi, deforestation is an overblown issue, a "phobia" that plagues people who can't grasp the enormity of the Amazon. "All of Europe could fit inside the Amazon," he says, "and we'd still have room for two Englands." What does he think of [Sister] Dorothy Stang's vision of small growers carrying out sustainable projects in complete har-

mony with the land? "Totalmente errado—completely wrong," Maggi
says, adding that without heavy subsidies such projects run counter
to the march of history and are doomed to failure. "All business tends
toward concentration. . . . Unit prices fall, and you need huge volumes to survive." (Wallace 2007, 64)

Of course, many of the poor squatters might have a different vision of
the future. But that view, too, might not necessarily be defined by environmental concerns.

For South American critics, the current effort to impose the environmental values of the developed world upon South American nations represents a modern form of imperialism. It is true that developed countries
are no longer using military means to impose their control. Now, they
implement their will by threatening to deny World Bank loans or funding
for packages that serve key national interests. The idea of debt-for-nature
swaps is particularly disturbing, because it represents a threat to national
sovereignty. The United States has a long and sad history of interventions
in Latin America, ranging from Haiti to Nicaragua and Colombia, and European nations have no greater legitimacy among southern governments
and populations. How, then, do these northern nations have the authority
to tell South America how to use land within its own territory?

We do not personally subscribe to the South American viewpoint described here—quite the opposite. But it is important to hear these voices.
Many of the feelings surrounding this topic are raw. South Americans
surely know how they are being portrayed abroad, and it angers them.
There are clear cases when the people are articulating simplistic arguments, such as the man who successfully ran for governor in one of Brazil's Amazon states with the slogan: "For every peasant, a chain saw." But
more thoughtful arguments are also voiced by Brazilians and Peruvians,
as well as by some North American experts. Environmental issues must
be discussed in a social context if they are to persuade the people involved.

As Adrian Cowell's work makes clear, the people responsible for much
of the environmental damage in the Amazon are the poor and the dispos-
sessed, who act not from malice but from need. Simplistic narratives of
the Amazon's destruction ignore the larger social and economic factors
that drive deforestation. Without more nuanced views, it is difficult to gain
the support of people who actually live in the Amazon, many of whom
are now urban dwellers. The advocates for the forest need to understand
different perspectives in order to craft broad alliances. It is true that there

are "pro-growth" or "antienvironmental" sentiments in many developing nations. But dramatic growth can come with an equally dramatic cost, as China is now learning. Environmental perspectives do not break down on a clean north/south line, and environmental concerns are becoming more powerful in the developing world.

Atmosphere and Climate

It is possible to bring together all of the world's nations to address environmental issues, which is necessary if humanity is to combat the pollution of the planet's atmosphere. One positive example is provided by the global effort to eliminate chlorofluorocarbons (CFCs), which were used in everything from refrigerators to Styrofoam cups (Kolbert 2006, 182–83). In the 1980s, researchers realized that in the upper atmosphere, CFCs broke down into chlorine, which served as a catalyst in reactions involving ozone. Although ozone is a poisonous gas at ground level and commonly thought of as a pollutant, in the upper atmosphere it serves to protect the planet from dangerous levels of ultraviolet radiation. In the mid-1980s, scientists documented significant holes in the earth's ozone at the poles. In 1987 the world came to together with the Montreal protocol, which began the phased elimination of CFCs, despite significant opposition from industry. The result has been that the global release of CFCs has plummeted. It will take probably more than half a century for the hole in the ozone to heal, given the level of damage that was done and the length of time it takes for the chlorine to break down. But there is evidence that the holes have stopped growing and are beginning to shrink (Arctic Climate Impact Assessment 2004, 98–107). In this case, a global coalition was able to prevent an environmental disaster.

A similar effort will be needed to prevent the worst possibilities of global warming, which is widely perceived to be humanity's greatest challenge. Global warming is the heating of the planet driven by rising levels of carbon dioxide (CO_2) and other greenhouse gases in our atmosphere. Atmospheric gases trap heat, without which it is unlikely that our planet could support life:

> The greenhouse gas effect is indispensible for life on the Earth; it is the weakness or excessive strength of the effect that is a matter for concern. The effective radiative (blackbody) temperature of a planet without an atmosphere is simply a function of its albedo (the share

of incoming radiation that is directly reflected into space) and its orbital distance. The Earth (albedo 30 percent) would radiate at −18 degrees Celsius, compared to −57 C for Mars and −44 C for Venus, and all these planets would have permanently frozen surfaces. A planet ceases to be a perfect radiator as soon as it has an atmosphere some of whose gases . . . can selectively absorb part of the outgoing infrared radiation and reradiate it both downward and upward. (Smil 2008, 172)

In other words, greenhouse gases are essential to life on our planet because they capture sufficient heat to maintain the planet's temperature sufficient for liquid water to exist.

The problem is that humanity is changing the balance of these gases in our atmosphere by increasing the level of CO_2. This chemical is released through the burning of fossil fuels, as well as by deforestation. The loss of forests is particularly serious because it not only releases carbon but also changes the planet's reflectivity, or albedo (Smil 2008, 178). At the same time, methane is a potent greenhouse gas released by our farming practices, in particular our reliance upon cattle. CFCs and nitrogen dioxide are also greenhouse gases (Smil 2008, 177). Combined, these chemicals are increasing the quantity of the sun's energy that our atmosphere retains.

People have known that humanity was impacting the atmosphere for a long time. Swedish chemist Svante August Arrhenius described the basic mechanism for global warming in the nineteenth century (Kolbert 2006, 39–42). Scientists can measure the level of CO_2 in the atmosphere over a large span of time, even in the absence of modern measuring machines: "Atmospheric CO_2 levels are now known for the past 650,000 years thanks to the ingenious analyses of air bubbles from ice cores retrieved in Antarctica and in Greenland. During that period CO_2 levels never dipped below 180 ppm [parts per million] and never rose above 300" (Smil 2008, 175). In 1850 the CO_2 level had been roughly 280 ppm. In 1959, as Elizabeth Kolbert describes, the level was perhaps 316 ppm, and it is now rising and may reach 500 ppm by the mid-twenty-first century (Kolbert 2006, 44). A graph of CO_2 levels called the Keeling Curve provides dramatic evidence that greenhouse gases are rising at a dramatic rate (Christianson 1999, 167). This matches with careful calculations of temperature rise over time: "Consequently, it can be stated with a high degree of confidence that the mean temperatures during the closing decades of the twentieth century were higher than at any time during the preceding four centuries, and it is very likely that they were the highest in the past 13 centuries" (Smil 2008, 177). (Temperature reconstructions are controversial; see Monastersky 2006.)

As Gale Christianson and Jared Diamond have documented, even small changes in climate historically have had dramatic impacts on cultures as varied as the Maya, the Greenland Vikings, the Anasazi, and the inhabitants of the U.S. Great Plains during the dust bowl years (Christianson 1999; Diamond 2005). There is now mounting evidence for global warming from multiple measures, including the northward shift of species ranges, the rising elevations at which species are typically found, the bleaching of coral reefs, the pattern of record warm years, the thawing of permafrost, and the retreat of glaciers. With global warming comes particularly dramatic possibilities. Ocean levels will rise, in part because of the melting of glaciers (particularly in Antarctica) as well as the Greenland ice cap. Recent data suggests that Greenland's ice sheet is melting far faster than scientists had predicted: "It is the acceleration that stuns scientists. Greenland's glaciers are adding up to 58 trillion gallons of water a year to the oceans, more than twice as much as a decade ago and enough to supply more than 250 cities the size of Los Angeles, NASA research shows" (Milstein 2007, A-1).

Warmer water also fills a greater volume. Scientists can already measure the warming of the oceans: "The strength of this warming signal varies by ocean and depth. North and South Atlantic warming, by as much as 0.3 C, reaches as deep as 700 m, whereas Pacific and Indian Ocean warming is mostly limited to the top 100 m" (Smil 2008, 182). The impact for some places, such as the Netherlands, Louisiana, Florida, and Bangladesh, is ominous (Arctic Climate Impact Assessment 2004, 40–43). In 2012 Hurricane Sandy caused $65 billion in storm damage—most of which was the result of flooding—in New York and New Jersey. This raised questions about how these states should prepare for higher ocean levels. India is constructing a high-tech fence that is 2,100 miles long, in part because it fears that 15 million Bangladeshis might flee their country for India as rising waters flood coastal areas (Friedman 2009). It is a common observation to say that many of the countries that will suffer the most (such as the Pacific Island nations of the Maldives and Tuvalu) are those that have contributed the least to global warming (Flannery 2005, 287; for a description of island loss in the Pacific, see Pearce 2007, 55–62).

Many effects of global warming may seem counterintuitive. One factor that particularly worries scientists is that vast amounts of freshwater flooding off of Greenland's ice cap could change current flows in the North

The Arctic is warming far faster than other regions of the globe. A large portion of Arctic peoples are indigenous. How do you think these two facts will affect the ability of Arctic peoples to shape debates about global warming? What duty do people living in the Southern Hemisphere have toward their neighbors to the North? It is also true that international migration will likely challenge major powers. How should a nation respond when a climate catastrophe sends waves of refugees across its borders?

Atlantic. They argue that Greenland's climate has undergone dramatic changes in very short periods of time in the past, based on information taken from ice cores on the island. Over 12,000 years ago, Greenland's "average annual temperatures shot up by nearly twenty degrees in a single decade" (Kolbert 2006, 51). In other words, our planet may have more than one stable climate state, much as a canoe has two stable states—one upright, one capsized. Another possible impact of global warming is that the Gulf Stream, which transports heat from the equator to the North Atlantic, could be shut down by vast amounts of freshwater. If that were to happen, a strange trend could occur in which the world gradually becomes warmer at the same time that Europe is suddenly plunged into a dramatically colder environment. We know that this has happened before (Arctic Climate Impact Assessment 2004, 36–37; Flannery 2005, 60–61, 190–96).

The impact of global warming is likely to be particularly dramatic at the earth's poles. While all parts of the world will be affected, not all parts will heat up equally. For a number of reasons, the impact in the Arctic will likely be especially severe, and it is now in places like Alaska that the impact of global warming is becoming most apparent. The ice cap that has covered the North Pole for "at least 1 million years" is fading and will likely disappear this century (Davis 2005). Some predictions suggest that it could be gone by as early as 2040, while other models predict that it will have declined by roughly half by the end of this century (Revkin 2006; Arctic Climate Impact Assessment 2004, 24–25, 35, 82–83; Flannery 2005, 144). Ice melting in the Antarctic also has the potential for disastrous rises in sea level (Flannery 2005, 147–49). There is no question, however, that the ice cap is shrinking, and that the ice cover itself is becoming thinner. In the past, it had long been thought that the area under the ice was largely sterile. Recent biological investigations have revealed, however, that there is a diverse ecological system under the ice. How will the plants and animals that have evolved over geologic time to live with the ice adapt to its disappearance? Some seals will likely go extinct: "Adapting to life on land in the absence of summer sea ice seems highly unlikely for the ringed seal as they rarely, if ever, come onto land. Hauling themselves out on land would expose newborns to a much higher risk of being killed by predators. Other ice-dependent seals that are likely to suffer as sea ice declines include the spotted seal, which breeds exclusively at the ice edge in the Bering Sea in spring, and the harp seal, which lives associated with sea ice all year long" (Arctic Climate Impact Assessment 2004, 59).

Other animals that live on the ice will likely disappear as well, from the walrus to seabirds (Arctic Climate Impact Assessment 2004, 59). A primary example is the polar bear. In December 2006, U.S. interior secretary Dirk Kempthorne proposed "listing polar bears as a 'threatened' species on the government listing of imperiled species. . . . 'Polar bears are one of nature's ultimate survivors, able to live and thrive in one of the world's harshest environments,' Kempthorne said. 'But we are concerned that the polar bear's habitat may literally be melting'" (Heilprin 2006). In recent years, polar bears on the southern edge of their range are thinner in the spring; they are also having fewer cubs, and fewer of these are surviving (Arctic Climate Impact Assessment 2004, 58). Polar bears are unquestionably smaller now then they were a century ago, perhaps because they now face greater stress. The future is uncertain. One of the unexpected impacts of global warming is that as oceans warm, they release more vapor, which leads to more Arctic snow. This means that at the same time that temperatures rise, total snowfall in some areas may increase dramatically, which will also change polar environments (Arctic Climate Impact Assessment 2004, 29; Smil 2008, 182–83). The impacts of global warming are complex and will likely include many surprises.

Some nations are already planning how to respond to global warming. For example, the Netherlands is preparing to abandon some land for use as a flood plain while redesigning homes that float in key areas; and Kiribati, Tokelau, Tuvalu, and the Marshall Islands are considering building sea walls around their respective island nations. To what extent are such plans positive? Could they also be considered problematic because they undermine efforts to fight global warming.

Many of the changes that global warming will set into effect will lead to a cascade of further trends, which may also contribute to the planet's warming. As forests spread northward, for example, they will absorb more carbon, but they will also absorb more sunlight than the snow-covered tundra. The overall effect will contribute to planetary warming. Equally important, as the Arctic Ocean is uncovered, it will also be transformed from an environment that reflects most sunlight to one that absorbs most of it. Finally, much of the northern land is made up of permafrost, which is soil that has remained frozen for at least two years. As this melts, it may release large amounts of methane (a potent greenhouse gas) into the atmosphere, especially from vast reserves in Siberia (Arctic Climate Impact Assessment 2004, 38; Pearce 2007, 90–100). There are also concerns that methane hydrates in the ocean could be released: "The release of methane from this source is a less certain outcome of climate change than the other emissions discussed here because it would probably require greater warming and take longer to occur. If such releases did occur, however, the climate impacts could be very large" (Arctic Climate Impact Assessment 2004, 38–39). Indeed, just such a phenomenon is one of the hypotheses (the clathrate gun hypothesis) used to explain the Permian Extinction, the greatest mass dying in the Earth's geologic history—the time when life itself nearly ended (Flannery 2005, 199–201). Recent scientific publications raise the possibility of sudden and catastrophic global warming as a result (Sergienko et al. 2012).

Events in the Arctic have implications for the entire planet (Arctic Climate Impact Assessment 2004, 34–35). They also raise geopolitical questions. Canada, Denmark, Russia, and the United States are currently arguing over travel rights through the newly opening sea lanes, as well as maritime borders, as each nation strives to lay claim to the resources of the Arctic seabed (Funk 2007, 45–55). These environmental and political changes will have complex and enduring impacts on indigenous peoples, who make up "roughly 10% of the current population of the Arctic" (Arctic Climate Impact Assessment 2004, 7). One of the most famous examples of this process is in Shishmaref, Alaska, which lies on an island off the Alaskan coast. With the waning of ice cover, powerful waves from major storms now are causing rapid coastal erosion. The entire community will likely be forced to evacuate, given the ocean's advances (Kolbert 2006, 7–10). This community is not unique. As a people heavily dependent upon food from the ocean, many Eskimo/Inuit communities have long lived on the shorelines and hunted out on the ice. Now, communities from Nelson

Lagoon in Alaska to Tuktoyaktuk in Canada are threatened (Arctic Climate Impact Assessment 2004, 78–81). Other changes are also serious. Migration patterns for some animals are changing. Hunters notice that animals arrive at different times of the year or use new routes. This impacts the hunters' ability to feed their communities, as many northern peoples still rely on game in their diet (Arctic Climate Impact Assessment 2004, 16–17, 61, 71–72). Indigenous peoples are also seeing the arrival of new bird species such as the robin, which they have never seen in their communities before (Arctic Climate Impact Assessment 2004, 45).

Global warming presents a serious challenge to the culture and folkways of northern peoples from Siberia to Greenland. For example, the Sami people of northern Scandinavia find that their reindeer herds are also threatened by climate change (Arctic Climate Impact Assessment 2004, 106, 108–9). Because native communities have long traditions in an area and often depend upon the land for their livelihood, they have a rich store of indigenous knowledge that can complement scientific observations about global warming. Their reports contribute to our understanding of the changes that global warming is already making in the north (Arctic Climate Impact Assessment 2004, 92–97).

Arctic peoples are some of the first to be able to observe global warming's effects, but its effects are now becoming manifest globally. In Tuvalu in the Pacific, the groundwater levels are rising, and salinization (salt) is destroying crops. In the Maldives, tides and ocean waves are now overtopping areas never before touched. In the South Atlantic, the first hurricane in 500 years of recorded history reached Brazil (Flannery 2005, 136). It used to be thought that hurricanes could not form in this part of the Atlantic, in part because the waters are too cool. But with Hurricane Catarina (also known as Cyclone Catarina) in March 2004, this no longer seems to be true (M. Davis 2005). And in the United States, Central America, and the Caribbean, there is rising concern that hurricanes may be growing more powerful because ocean waters are warming. If this proves to be true, even developed countries will have difficulty adapting to these changes. Hurricane Katrina flooded New Orleans on August 29, 2005, because the levees failed. The subsequent disaster laid bare the multiple institutional, financial, engineering, and leadership failures that made the city vulnerable. But if hurricanes are strengthening, we will have less room for error.

No place will escape global warming's impact. One issue embodies this fact. In the long term, as the acidity (pH) of the oceans increases, the lime in shells may begin to dissolve (Flannery 2005, 186). One study in the United States in 2008 reported that the "acidity is much higher than expected in the ocean just off the West Coast, hitting the relatively shallow waters of the fruitful continental shelf during spring and summer" (Learn 2008, A-1). There is no doubt that the CO_2 responsible for the acidity came from manmade sources. "The chemical signature of the carbon dioxide makes clear it is from fossil fuel combustions, and not natural sources such as volcanoes," the researchers said (Learn 2008, A-12). Once the pH reaches 7.5, the shells of sea life will "dissolve faster than their hosts can create them" (Learn 2008, A-12). How will such a profound change ripple throughout the marine ecosystem as the base of the food chain dissolves into the acidic oceans?

In December 1997 the world's industrialized nations negotiated the Kyoto accord, which was designed to prevent future increases in CO_2 emissions. This would not stop global warming, but it would help to keep the process from accelerating. The United States had deep concerns about the agreement because it exempted developing economies such as that of China and India (Kolbert 2006, 153–57). European countries argued that the developed world had to show leadership and develop new technologies if it was to ask similar sacrifices of emerging economies. In the end, President George W. Bush decided not to uphold Kyoto, although he had supported it during his campaign (Kolbert 2006, 157–58).

There are numerous and vocal critics who argue that global warming is not taking place, that it is a natural process, or that it will not necessarily have negative impacts (Kolbert 2006, 158–59; Flannery 2005, 156; for the best critique of global warming as a phenomenon, see Michaels 2004; for a rebuttal, see Pearce 2007, 10–17). But most of these publications are not by scientists, and they are not published in peer-reviewed journals or by academic presses (that is, presses associated with an institution of higher education). In academia, rigor is ensured by a process of peer review in which articles are sent out to experts in the field. Scholars carefully read the work and respond to the editor with a detailed evaluation of its strengths and weaknesses. Of course, many times, reviewers do not agree. They may have political or personal interests that cause them to oppose publications. But good works survive this process and are published having met a high academic standard. Books published by academic presses pass through a similar process. There is still a debate over global warming, but it is distinctive in that it no longer takes place within an academic or scientific framework.

The scientific consensus is so strong that most publications critiquing global warming are published by conservative think tanks or with the support of industry backers. Michael Crichton's novel *State of Fear* (2004) also contains an attack on the scientific argument for global warming, which attracted media attention. But articles and books like these no longer generally survive the peer-review process, although critics point to bias within the process itself. The November 2009 scandal at East Anglia University that suggested that climate scholars manipulated data and strove to keep contradictory information from their peers raised serious questions. Critics also suggest that there is evidence that Ragendra Pachauri, the head of the UN's Intergovernmental Panel on Climate Change, made catastrophic predictions about the disappearance of Himalayan glaciers to gain funding even though he knew the predictions were false (Leake 2010). These are important problems. Still, the shift in the discussion outside the peer-review process marks an important moment in any debate. Overall, the work on global warming that is recognized for its rigor and sophistication now takes place on the side of those scientists who believe that it is happening. (For the ongoing debate over global warming, see Kolbert 2006, 162–70.)

Global warming will be difficult to address because of our demographic reality. As demographers Mary Kent and Carl Haub (2005) have argued, our planet's population grew from 1.6 billion people in 1900 to 6.1 billion in 2000. And it will add perhaps an additional 3 billion people by 2050. It is true that fertility rates are dramatically declining in some areas, such as Japan, Russia, and most of Europe. This will lessen the pressure on resources in these nations, permit forests to expand, and decrease the human footprint. But even as global fertility rates decline, there is so much momentum behind population growth that the planet will still see a substantial increase in Asia, Africa, and Latin America for decades to come. In the long run, demographers predict that the population for the entire planet will likely decline after reaching a peak around midcentury. This means that there is reason to be hopeful about those species that make it through this bottleneck. But in the meantime, humanity will face a difficult challenge as it strives to preserve the natural environment in a world with more people than at any time in history. (For a detailed look at demographic trends globally, see Kent and Haub 2005.) In this sense, the current generation will make choices that will be of unique and lasting importance.

While global warming is perhaps the greatest environmental threat facing the planet, it is only one of many forms of atmospheric pollution, which impacts not only other species but also people. This is particularly true for Asia in general, and China particular:

The symptoms of industrial pollution are everywhere in Asia, where pedestrians wear surgical masks to filter the air and urban smog is sometimes so thick that Beijing's Forbidden City is rendered nearly invisible behind a cloud of soot. Just this month, Chinese authorities canceled flights at Beijing's main airport amid especially heavy pollution, and shuttered highways in and out of the city. The implications for human health are obvious: studies show pollution is shortening life spans in northern China by five years or more. Intel engineers in Oregon are now discovering that rotten air is also taking a toll on electronics in China and India, with sulfur corroding the copper circuitry that provides neural networks for PCs and servers and wrecking the motherboards that run whole systems. (Rogoway 2013)

Intel Corporation has responded by setting up a special testing facility that exposes computer motherboards to high levels of pollution. The goal is to ensure that computers built in Asia will not be damaged by the corrosive effects of air pollution (Rogoway 2013). But what does it mean for human health when the pollution is so severe that it corrodes the copper in computers? The problem of climate change is so immense that it can overshadow other issues that impact human health, from the release of nuclear radiation into the Pacific Ocean from the damaged Fukiyama power plant to the spread of plastic particulates throughout all the world's oceans. All life on our planet, including human life, is challenged by global pollution, of which CO^2 is only the most dangerous element.

Conclusion

In many respects, environmental issues are the ultimate international problem. Pollution does not recognize borders. The costs of inaction are high. It takes comprehensive agreements and global cooperation to address issues such as ozone depletion and global warming. At the same time, local actors can have significant effects. While the United States as a nation has not taken the lead in the fight to stop global warming, the state of California has. Even small nations such as Denmark, which is making a dramatic shift to renewable energy, can have a powerful impact through their example. On many environmental issues, cities have also taken the lead. Curitiba, Brazil, has become famous for its example as a sustainable urban area. People are not powerless, as Tim Flannery argues: "Climate change is very different from other environmental issues, such as biodiversity loss and the ozone hole. The best evidence suggests that we need to reduce our CO^2 emissions by 70 percent by 2050. If you own a four-wheel-drive and replace it with a hybrid fuel car, you can achieve a cut of that magnitude in a day rather than half a century. If your electricity provider offers a green option, for the cost of a daily cup of coffee you will be able to make equally major cuts in your household emissions" (Flannery 2005, 6). If current predictions are correct, almost everyone who reads these words will live to see dramatic changes brought about by global warming and global population growth. But it is possible to shape this future with political will and to avoid the bleak visions that are now forecast.

➤ VOCABULARY

biodiversity	biological islands
Global South	Keeling Curve
CFCs	latitudinal species-diversity
DDT	gradient
Montreal protocol	debt-for-nature swaps
Kyoto accord	World Biosphere Reserve
five great extinctions	

➤ DISCUSSION AND REFLECTION QUESTIONS

1 *What are three flaws in environmentalists' arguments?*

2 *What is meant by the notion that many environmentalists have been elitists?*

3 *What are some factors that account for differing environmental perceptions on the part of the Global South?*

4 *Why are the tropics so important in terms of biodiversity?*

5 *Identify two or three dimensions of the antienvironmental critique.*

6 *Who is Bjorn Lomborg and why is it important to be familiar with his work?*

7 *How does a debt-for-nature swap work?*

8 *Why might it be the case that "for South American critics, the current effort to impose the environmental values of the developed world upon South American nations represents a modern form of imperialism"?*

9 *Why is it likely that nations that have not contributed in any major way toward global warming may suffer the most, particularly in the Pacific?*

10 *Why might it be the case that "events in the Arctic have implications for the entire planet"?*

ACTIVITY 1 What is your personal take on global warming? Is there a connection between theoretical information you have and your daily activities? Make a diagram that looks like a wheel with a center and spokes radiating out. Identify five people who are important to you in your life. Can you describe their attitudes toward global warming? Are you aware of connections between this attitude and their daily activities?

ACTIVITY 2 Go to Bjorn Lomborg's website and read some of the news articles that he has posted there, and the arguments that he makes on the site. Write a one-page reflection on the portrayal of environmental issues on this website and the strengths and weaknesses of the arguments that Lomborg is highlighting. Have your personal views changed as a result of your introduction to multiple perspectives? Why or why not?

ACTIVITY 3 A climate forum was held in Denmark in the summer of 2009. A concurrent Children's Climate Forum was also held in which a fifteen-year-old from the Pacific Island community of the Maldives spoke eloquently of the real possibility that his island home could be under water within thirty years. Mohamed Axam Maumoon asked listeners in an interview with Amy Goodman, "How would you feel if someone wanted to murder you?" Read through the transcript (available at http://www.democracynow.org/2009/12/8/would_you_commit_murder_15_year) or explore the concept of "climate refugees" via an electronic search. Prepare a one-paragraph response to Maumoon's question listed above or to the question, "How may climate refugees impact your life in the next thirty years?"

ACTIVITY 4 Conduct an Internet search for a map of future sea-level rise as a result of global warming. What nations will be affected the most? How many are Global North nations, and how many are Global South nations? How does this reality affect how both groups of nations view the issue of sea-level rise?

References

Arctic Climate Impact Assessment. 2004. *Impacts of a warming Arctic*. New York: Cambridge University Press.

Associated Press. 2007. Schools restrict showings of "Inconvenient Truth." *Oregonian*, D-5. January 27.

———. 2010. UN rejects ban on tuna export, global sale of polar bear skins. *Oregonian*. March 19. Retrieved March 20, 2010, from http://www.oregonlive.com/newsflash/index.ssf?/base/international-27/1268929733151470.xml&storylist= international.

Bailey, R., ed. 2002. *Global warming and other eco-myths: How the environmental movement uses false science to scare us to death*. Washington, D.C.: Forum.

Barlow, M., and T. Clarke. 2002; new preface, 2004. *Blue gold*. New York: The New Press.

Benton, M. J. 2003. *When life nearly died: The greatest mass extinction of all time*. New York: Thames and Hudson.

Bodard, L. 1971. *Green hell: Massacre of the Brazilian Indians*. Trans. J. Monaghan. New York: Ballantine Books.

Campbell, D. 2005. *Land of ghosts: The braided lives of people and the forest in far western Amazonia*. New York: Houghton Mifflin.

Crichton, M. 2004. *State of fear*. New York: Harper Collins.

Christianson, G. E. 1999. *Greenhouse: The 200-year story of global warming*. New York: Walker and Company.

Cincotta, R., J. Wisnewski, and R. Engelman. 2000. Human population in the biodiversity hotspots. *Nature* 404 (April): 990–92.

Cowell, A. 1990. *Decade of destruction*. Four-part documentary series. Oley, Pa.: Bullfrog Films.

David, L. 2006. Science a la Joe Camel: Deep-pocketed corporate interests are targeting the kids in our classrooms with junk science. *Oregonian*, E-4. December 2.

Davis, M. 2005. Melting away. *Nation*. October 7. Retrieved December 16, 2007, from www.thenation.com/doc/20051024/davis.

Dean, W. 1995. *With broadaxe and firebrand: The destruction of the Brazilian Atlantic Forest*. Los Angeles: University of California Press.

Diamond, J. 2005. *Collapse: How societies choose to fail or succeed*. New York: Penguin.

Flannery, T. 2005. *The weather makers: How man is changing the climate and what it means for life on earth*. New York: Grove Press.

Friedman, L. 2009. How will climate refugees impact global security? *Scientific American*. March 23. Retrieved March 3, 2010, from http://www.scientificamerican.com/article.cfm?id=climage-refugees-national-security.

Funk, M. 2007. Cold rush: The coming fight for the melting North. *Harper's*, 45–55. March 23.

Guggenheim, D., director. 2006. *An inconvenient truth*. Documentary film. Distributed by Paramount Classics.

Hanson, E. P. 1944. *The Amazon: A new frontier*. March. New York: Headline Series, Foreign Policy Association, 45.

Hardin, G. 1968. The tragedy of the commons. *Science* 162 (December): 1243–48.

Hecht, S., and A. Cockburn. 1990. *The fate of the forest: Developers, destroyers, and defenders of the Amazon*. New York: Harper Perennial.

Heilprin, J. 2006. Polar bears' lives rest on thinning ice. *Oregonian*, A-1, A-4. December 28.

Hertsgaard, M. 1999. *Earth odyssey: Around the world in search of our environmental future*. New York: Broadway Books.

Hutzler, C. 2006. Rare white dolphin declared as extinct. *Washington Post*. December 13. Retrieved December 16, 2007, from www.washingtonpost.com /wp-dyn/content/article/2006/12/13/AR2006121300304.html.

Jacquot, J. 2008. Come on, bubble, light my fire. *Discover* 14 (February).

Kent, M., and C. Haub. 2005. *Global demographic divide*. Population Reference Bureau. *Population Bulletin* 60 (4): 3–25.

Kolbert, E. 2006. *Fieldnotes from a catastrophe: Man, nature, and climate change*. New York: Bloomsbury.

Kurlansky, M. 1998. *Cod: A biography of the fish that changed the world*. New York: Penguin.

LaFranchi, H. 1998. Bye-bye to Brazil's bio-paradise. *Christian Science Monitor*, 12–13. December 7.

Lang, K. 2013. Trying to save the heat-seeking Atlantic bushmaster. *BBC News Magazine*, October 5. Retrieved October 10, 2013, from http://www.bbc.co.uk /news/magazine-24396013.

Leake, J. 2010. U.N. climate chief "got grants through bogus claims." *Sunday Times* (London). January 24. Retrieved March 3, 2010, from http://www .timesonline.co.uk/tol/news/environment/article6999975.ece.

Leakey, R., and R. Lewin. 1996. *The sixth extinction: Patterns of life and the future of humankind*. New York: Anchor Books/Doubleday.

Learn, S. 2008. Gases tipping ocean's balance. *Oregonian*, A-1, A-12. May 23.

Lomborg, B. 2001. *The skeptical environmentalist: Measuring the real state of the world*. New York: Cambridge University Press.

Martin, P. S. 2005. *Twilight of the mammoths: Ice Age extinctions and the rewilding of America*. Berkeley: University of California Press.

Meunier, J., and A. M. Savarin. 1991. *Amazonian chronicles*. Trans. Carol Christenson. San Francisco: Mercury House.

Michaels, P. J. 2004. *Meltdown: The predictable distortion of global warming by scientists, politicians, and the media*. Washington, D.C.: Cato Institute.

Milstein, M. 2007. Greenland ice melt shocks scientists. *Oregonian*, A-1, A-10. September 9.

Monastersky, R. 2006. Climate science on trial. *Chronicle of Higher Education*, A-10–A-15. September 8.

Nature Conservancy. 2006. The Atlantic Forest of Brazil. Retrieved November 15, 2008, from http://www.nature.org/wherewework/southamerica/brazil/work /art5080.html.

Nisbet, M. 2003. The skeptical environmentalist: A case study in the manufacture of the news. January 23. Retrieved November 14, 2008, from http://www.csicop.org/scienceandmedia/environmentalist/.

Nugent, S. 1994. *Big mouth: The Amazon speaks.* San Francisco: Brown Trout Publishers, Inc.

O'Connor, G. 1998. *Amazon journal: Dispatches from a vanishing frontier.* New York: Plume.

Pearce, F. 2007. *With speed and violence: Why scientists fear tipping points in climate change.* Boston: Beacon Press.

Perlin, J. 1989. *A forest journey: The role of wood in the development of civilization.* New York: Norton.

Raffles, H. 2002. *In Amazonia: A natural history.* Princeton, N.J.: Princeton University Press.

Revkin, A. 1990. *The burning season: The murder of Chico Mendes and the fight for the Amazon rain forest.* Boston: Houghton Mifflin.

———. 2006. Open Arctic Sea likely by 2040, study says. *Oregonian*, A-7. December 12.

Rogoway, M. 2013. The gunk in the machine: Intel is trying to make circuitry less vulnerable to the pollution that's pervasive in the developing world. *Oregonian.* D-1, D-6. October 13.

Sergienko, V., et al. 2012. The degradation of submarine permafrost and the destruction of hydrates on the shelf of the East Arctic seas as a potential cause of the "methane catastrophe": Some results of integrated studies in 2011. *Doklady Earth Sciences* 446 (1): 1132–37.

Skutnabb-Kangas, T., L. Maffi, and D. Harmon. 2003. *Sharing a world of difference: The world's linguistic, cultural, and biological diversity.* Paris: UNESCO/WWF/Terralingua.

Slater, C. 2003a. Fire in El Dorado, or images of tropical nature and their practical effects. In *In search of the rain forest*, ed. C. Slater, 41–68. Durham: Duke University Press.

———, ed. 2003b. *In search of the rain forest.* Durham: Duke University Press.

Smil, V. 2008. *Global catastrophes and trends: The next fifty years.* Cambridge, Mass.: MIT Press.

Smith, F. 2002. Enclosing the environmental commons. In *Global warming and other eco-myths*, ed. R. Bailey, 293–318. Washington, D.C.: Forum.

Smith, N. 1999. *The Amazon River forest: A natural history of plants, animals, and people.* New York: Oxford University Press.

Spotts, P. N. 2006. Global warming: a few skeptics still ask why it's happening. *Christian Science Monitor.* December 8. Retrieved December 16, 2007, from http://www.csmonitor.com/2006/1208/p01s03-usgn.html.

Stewart, D. I. 1994. *After the trees: Living on the TransAmazon highway.* Austin: University of Texas Press.

Stone, R. 2001. *Mammoth: The resurrection of an Ice Age giant.* London: Fourth Estate.

Wallace, S. 2007. Farming the Amazon. *National Geographic*, 40–71. January.

Ward, P. 2004. *Gorgon: Paleontology, obsession, and the greatest catastrophe in earth's history.* New York: Penguin Books.

Williams, M. 2003. *Deforesting the Earth: From prehistory to global crisis.* Chicago: University of Chicago Press.

World Conservation Monitoring Center. 2006. The red lists of threatened plants and threatened animals. Retrieved December 17, 2007, from www.wcmc .org.uk/species/plants/plant_redlist.html and www.wcmc.org.uk/species /animals.

TWELVE **Where to Go Next?**

As you work your way through your undergraduate curriculum,
it is important to look toward potential careers that an international
studies major may lead to. This chapter lays out a variety of options
for career development, including jobs in government, business,
the military, higher education, and nongovernmental organizations
(NGOs). An annotated set of references at the end of the chapter
further frames your prospective job search.

► SCAFFOLDING

As you read through this chapter, think about how you would answer
each of the questions below.

*Are you completely familiar with required coursework and sequencing for
your major?*

Have you always dreamed of a particular type of international job?

*What do you know about requirements and skill sets for entry-level posi-
tions in this area?*

*Who are the individuals on your campus best able to assist you in your
search?*

► CORE CONCEPTS

*Your interest in international events and situations may take you
into job spaces that you never imagined.*

*Both human resources and electronic resources can serve to give
you the most accurate sense of how to proceed in your job search.*

You can be engaged internationally in activities that are not linked to your career.

As an international studies major, you would probably like to know more about the different career opportunities that are available to you. There are four main paths that most graduates follow: government, business, NGOs and international organizations (IOs), or jobs for which further education may be required. The last category includes a wide range of different opportunities, such as Teaching English to Speakers of Other Languages (TESOL in the United States and TEAL in Canada), study abroad advising, international student advising, international admissions at universities and colleges, and teaching international studies at the postsecondary level. This chapter describes how to find a career in each of these paths and gives information on everything from preparing for the State Department exam to finding internships in consulates. It also discusses the advantages and disadvantages of master's and other graduate programs and how to decide which program best meets your needs. Throughout, we have tried to give information on career paths that is relevant for students in both the United States and Canada.

Government Career Paths

United States

There are a variety of ways to use your international studies background to enter government service. Perhaps the best known of these is to join the Foreign Service, now a division of the Department of State. Foreign Service officers work in one of five areas: Consular Affairs, Economics, Management, Political Affairs, and Public Diplomacy. On the U.S. government website, there is a questionnaire you can fill out that will help you decide which of these tracks is appropriate for you and your interests (http://careers.state.gov/officer/career-track.html). General information about the exam can be found at the State Department website (http://www.state.gov/careers). This site contains a great deal of information about this career path.

In addition to serving as a Foreign Service officer, there are many other career possibilities in government service. Almost all branches of the government have some international responsibilities, from Homeland Secu-

Mosaic door in Morocco (Used with permission of the photographer, Aomar Boum)

rity to the Department of Agriculture. But there are several key institutions or positions that you might consider, which include roles as a civil service officer, Foreign Service specialist, or an attorney. You could also work in diplomatic security, the Peace Corps, the U.S. intelligence community, or the U.S. Agency for International Development (USAID). The latter organization might be particularly attractive for students who are also interested in working with NGOs. Some colleges either provide symposia or training sessions for the Foreign Service exam through their career centers or specific departments like international studies or political science. Some professional test centers like Kaplan also provide workshops. At the end of this chapter, under resources, we list a variety of Foreign Service exam preparatory materials.

Another possible career path is to join the armed services, mostly likely as an officer candidate. If you choose this path, there is a language aptitude test you will take. If you score well, you may be sent for advanced language training in one of several sites. Perhaps the best known is the Defense Language Institute. The U.S. Department of Defense maintains an extensive list of strategic languages for U.S. national security. The Defense Language Institute has tracked exactly how many weeks it takes to achieve a particular skill level in each language. No matter which language you study, you will spend more than forty hours per week for up to a year and a half working only to develop your language skills. With this background, it is possible for you to apply to be a Foreign Area Officer (FAO) within the armed services.

Once you have completed a strong base of training as a regular branch officer (such as infantry, artillery, or signal), you will begin training as an FAO. When possible, you will be kept within your area of regional and language expertise. If, however, nonlanguage skills are in higher demand or the need is great, it is possible that you would serve in a geographic or language area outside of your primary area of expertise. This occurs more often among those who are not officers but rather enlisted personnel in

Well before you finish your studies, you should become familiar with the resources available to you in your campus career center. Visit your career center and ask to see what resources they have available with respect to international employment. Find information about two possible international careers that interest you. Write up this information to bring to your class to share with two fellow students.

areas like interrogation. Ultimately, you could end up serving as an inter-preter, working in specific areas of language and culture program design, or working at one of the service academies teaching language and culture. Keep in mind that if you are interested in using your language capabilities, you should also develop other skill sets; simple proficiency in a particular language, even one with important security implications for the United States or Canada, is not highly regarded by itself. In contrast, if you have public policy training plus language capability, or technology skills with language skills, you would be a very attractive candidate.

Canada

In Canada, the career paths open within the government in many ways par-allel those in the United States. Because of globalization, there are very few government departments that do not have international issues as part of their portfolio. The Department of Justice performs significant work with international questions, while Environment Canada has people working on global climate change. The Canadian International Development Agency (CIDA) disburses all of Canada's foreign aid and plays a role much like that of USAID in the United States. There are some differences; in Canada, for example, there is no equivalent to the Peace Corps. But in Canada, most people interested in an international career enter the Foreign Service. As in the United States, this entails sitting for the Foreign Service Exam. It is offered only once a year in Canada, usually in late October or November. In a typical year, 6,000 to 10,000 people might take the exam to try for 50 to 100 jobs. The requirements to take the exam have changed over time, but generally a bachelor's degree is required, and there is a strong prefer-ence for people with knowledge of a key language. In addition, all Foreign Service officers will be expected to be bilingual in both of Canada's official languages, French and English. People who are not bilingual are hired at a reduced rate (roughly 80 percent of the bilingual salary) while they undergo a year of training in the other language. They then must pass a language exam in order to remain in the service.

Canada is somewhat different from the United States in that the Foreign Service places less emphasis upon international knowledge in selecting applicants. Of course, having that background will be helpful to doing the work and will advance your career. But you do not have to come from a specific educational background related to international affairs to find a job. Lawyers can apply, for example, who have never practiced or studied international law. The Foreign Service places great emphasis upon judgment. Flexibility is also important. Most people will rotate between different jobs, so that they may work on trade issues for a period of time before being reassigned to human rights issues. This is good for people who enjoy new challenges, but it can be challenging for others who might be frustrated that they do not get to see projects through to the finish. People must also be prepared to rotate through different postings abroad, which can be both an attraction and a challenge of the job. Every rotation places a demand on families that must relocate, and if your spouse or partner has his or her own career, this can be difficult. There is no firm number for how many postings most people will have. Although most Foreign Service officers might have four or five postings in a career, others may have only two. You generally have some say in where you are posted, in particular if you have strong skills related to one language area or region. Despite the challenges they bring, these positions are highly sought after, and morale in the Canadian Foreign Service generally is good. The government's official website for these positions is www.international.gc.ca.

Business

Business careers offer graduates a broad range of opportunities, from teaching English as a second language to working in a multinational corporation in the United States or being stationed in another country. Among the many advantages of international business careers is that they can prepare you well for work in NGOs or even the government. You will have options later. In addition, it may be possible to live very well in developing countries if your salary is matched to that of your home country. But these jobs also come with some risks. You may find yourself stationed in successive countries over time, which can be hard if you have a spouse or partner. It can be challenging to raise a family abroad if you know that you are going to return to your home country someday. For these reasons, as people progress in their careers, they often choose to return to their home countries while still working with international issues. You should be mindful of these constraints as you make your choice, even though the opportunities are exciting.

Students considering an international career should think about the particular skills that companies want. Employers generally look to hire people who can work in a multicultural setting, not only to interact in a culturally sensitive manner but also to help frame the marketing of the corporation. They want to identify people who can tolerate ambiguity and have strong social skills. A facility with language and knowledge of a major world tongue are desirable. It is perhaps less important which language is chosen (Chinese, German, Japanese, Spanish) than the ability to master that language. But you should not assume that you will necessarily be hired to work in an area directly tied to your language knowledge; you will have to be flexible. Remember, too, that cultural skills are often as important as language ability.

Corporations need people who can help them avoid making cultural mistakes, such as when one major shoe manufacturer developed a shoe with flames on the back that had an unfortunate resemblance to a word in Arabic script. For this reason, a background in anthropology or other academic disciplines can be as helpful as one in business itself. Choose a major that has an international component, whether it is international studies, political science, history, anthropology, or another international discipline. Even if you may wish to work for NGOs or for government agencies, you might want to consider a minor in business. The skills learned in these programs are valued in many different areas. If possible, a study abroad program may be a valuable way to develop not only language ability but also multicultural skills. Consider studying in a country that is not traditionally a focus for study abroad; the vast majority of U.S. students still study in Europe. There are also many opportunities in Korea, Japan, China, Latin America, South Asia, and elsewhere. Your family or loved ones may need some reassurance, but be persistent. Most professionals in your school's study abroad office are quite willing to talk one-on-one with parents and guardians who are nervous about their children studying outside of their home country, particularly in regard to safety and security.

For many students, the financial and life commitments entailed by a semester or year abroad are simply not realistic. But many schools are also developing short-term study abroad programs that often last for two weeks. Some schools also have international capstone experiences in which senior students work on a project to help communities abroad. You should meet with a study abroad advisor if this interests you, because he or she can help to explain such issues as how your credits will transfer and how you can use your financial aid. Some programs may also have scholarships, or you may even receive funds for foreign study from governments abroad. Finally, the Rotary Club and many similar organizations have some scholarships. There are many books available on this topic to explore these possibilities, and your study abroad advisor can point you in the right direction.

It also makes sense to consider internships. Most universities have internship programs. You can generally also arrange your own internships with the support of a faculty member, who can do an independent study course with you. These classes are created by an agreement between a faculty member and a student, both in the subject of study and in the requirements to complete the course. There are many different areas in which you might intern. If you are in a large urban area, there may be a consulate nearby that would appreciate an intern. Even some small urban areas may have an honorary consulate that might appreciate support. You do not have to be a citizen of that particular nation in order to work at the consulate. Do not worry about working with a consulate in your particular region of interest. The experience itself is what matters—as well as the letter of reference that you can get afterward.

Most major U.S. cities also have a branch of the World Affairs Council, which is an excellent place to develop skills. There are likely also NGOs in your area working with international populations, whether it be supporting refugees or helping arts organizations. In cities, look for international trade centers or research institutes for businesses. A call to your local chamber of commerce can help you to identify these. Even rural areas often have local businesses that do international trade or organizations with an international aspect. An internship in one of these areas can help you to build your résumé, develop important experience, and learn more about the business world.

There are other ways to develop multicultural experiences. If you live at home, see if your family might be willing to host a foreign student for a year. Attend international events on your campus. If you are attending a residential campus, see if your university has an international hall or floor; most colleges and universities do. Explore the possibility of tutoring someone learning English in exchange for having them tutor you in their language. Listen to world music. Read novels set in other countries or written by foreign authors. Watch foreign films. When you can afford to dine out, have your meal at a restaurant from a region you know little about. Experiment with Ethiopian food. Avoid even minor infractions of the law (such as obtaining or making a fake I.D.) that could give you a criminal record. This will restrict your choices later. For all international travel, you need to have appropriate credentials to enter a new country and return to your home country; passports are the most broadly used credentials. Even if you do not have immediate plans to travel, get a passport now. You probably won't need to look very hard for opportunities for international experiences; they will come up.

Even before your senior year, you should visit the campus career center. Follow the job postings. Work on a draft of your résumé and have someone at the career center critique it. When you have a class with a faculty member with whom you have a good relationship, ask them for a letter of recommendation at the end of the class. Do not wait until two years later, when the faculty member may be on sabbatical or has left for another institution. Do informational interviews with people in fields that you find interesting; that is, meet with people not to apply for a job but only to learn about their work. These interactions take some courage to arrange, as you need to pick up the phone and make the call. But most people are willing to take a half hour to speak to someone considering their career path. Be flexible. Many colleges and universities have a career day when they bring employers to campus to do interviews. Attend these well before your senior year. Dress professionally, bring copies of your résumé, and talk with as many corporations as possible. It is good to do interviews even if you are not certain you are interested in a job; just getting the experience is important. Both the career center and the international studies program likely have books for those considering an international career. Read them. If they are not available on campus, go to your local public library.

If you wish to work abroad for a short period of time, you should consider the TESOL track (described more fully later in the chapter). Most certificate programs at universities are at least one year long, and master's programs range from two to three years. There are also shorter certificate programs through what is termed the Cambridge certificate program, or CELTA. They range from one month to six weeks and typically cost in the range of $1,500 to $2,500. They exist all over the world; you could be in a place like Thailand and be teaching and studying at the same time. To learn more, do a Web search for CELTA programs.

For many people interested in a career in international business, a master's degree, a master's in business administration (MBA), or a master's in international management will be necessary. There are many schools with strong programs, and a Web search will quickly find many of these. But a visit to your school's business school advisor or faculty member is probably a more useful way to gain information. If you are interested in a particular school, phone and ask if you can speak with an advisor at the institution. One question to pose is if they would give you the names and phone numbers of some students in the program. You should be careful not to make your decision primarily based on what these students say (you may catch them on a bad day), but they can give you a different perspective. Carefully research the institution online. Does the school discuss its placement record and the resources it makes available to its graduates? Does it have opportunities for internships or study abroad? Can you speak with alumni in your area? It's worth taking the time to do careful research. If you do not want to do an MBA, a master's in a clearly international discipline (such as international studies) may also be a good path for you. Finally, consider completing your MBA or other master's program in another country so that you have the chance to complete a truly international experience. There are many websites and books that can help you to make these choices, but it is also best to speak with an advisor or faculty member. Actually, speak to more than one, because each will have his or her own perspective. Be courageous.

Working for Nongovernmental Organizations and International Organizations

Nongovernmental organizations are primarily outreach programs providing service or assistance, often in the form of development aid, crisis management, education, and health. Many NGOs have both domestic and international programs. They are sometimes restricted to one country, but most often they have missions expanding beyond one nation-state. Individuals directing programs can be in-country nationals or expatriates. The programs may be international in scope—their boards of directors and organization headquarters may be outside of the country where they deliver assistance. Or their leadership and organization may lie within the country where they work. Sometimes NGOs work side by side with governmental organizations, and sometimes they are actually at odds with the government of the country they are located in. Aid workers have frequently developed their skill sets on the job, but many have completed graduate or undergraduate work in a field related to international development. Most students in the United States are familiar with the Peace Corps. But there are many other options. One resource for identifying these opportunities is Caitlin Hachmyer's *Alternatives to the Peace Corps* (2008). In terms of further education, there are more than ninety-five graduate programs in development listed within the United States.

Go to the e-jobsite for the Riley Guide (http://www.rileyguide.com/ internat.html) and identify NGO positions outside of the United States and Canada. See if you can find other NGO job sites and identify at least four skills that you would need to get one of these jobs.

You should know that your career working for an NGO will probably give you less monetary rewards than other career pathways related to international studies. In Canada, the NGO community is somewhat smaller and less well funded than in the United States, but that certainly does not mean that there are not large and sophisticated NGOs. When preparing to apply to an NGO, keep in mind that they often like to see the same business and organizational skills that are attractive to other employers. These jobs also tend to be highly competitive. Even if you wish to work for an NGO, you may need to pay your dues by first working for the government or in business. This does not mean that students never walk into wonderful NGO jobs right after they graduate. We have alumni who have worked everywhere from Asia, where they helped to manage nature preserves, to an immigrant-rights center in Chicago. Nonetheless, you may need to develop a stronger résumé before you are ready to apply to a major nonprofit.

To find descriptions of graduate programs in international development, several search engines may be helpful. The website GradSchools. com (http://www.gradschools.com/ListingFunctions/FindAProgram.aspx) allows you to search for specific United States–based programs in international development under the main areas of either international studies or business with the subfield "international development." If you are in Canada, two main centers are the Comparative, International and Development Education Centre (CIDEC) at the University of Toronto and International Development Studies at McGill University in Montreal.

Many NGOs also do work in the field of international conflict resolution, human rights, global public health, peace studies, and gender and global change. Graduate work in any of these areas would also provide the combination of academic studies, grant-writing experience, internships, and project-based learning necessary to be a competitive applicant for an NGO position.

International organizations are another possible career pathway. These bodies are created by multiple countries to achieve a particular goal. Some examples of IOs include the United Nations, the Organization of American States, the World Bank, the International Monetary Fund, the International Committee of the Red Cross, and the Organization for Economic Cooperation and Development. This is a very brief list. These jobs tend to be very competitive, and the hiring procedures vary widely among them. In particular, the United Nations has a reputation for having an extremely slow and bureaucratic hiring process. But these jobs can also be very rewarding, giving people the opportunity to work in areas that can bring meaningful changes. Some jobs also come with substantial perks, such as the relatively high pay at the International Monetary Fund and World Bank. Each of these organizations has a Web page that contains information on the organization and its hiring procedures.

Jobs for Which Further Education May Be Required

An international studies major provides a solid undergraduate background to enter a master's-level professional program. Of particular relevance are four jobs in higher education: international student advising, study abroad advising, international admissions and credentials evaluation, and Teaching English to Speakers of Other Languages (TESOL).

International Student Advising

International student advisors are part of the international education team at all institutions of higher education that admit students from outside their home countries. Most U.S. and Canadian universities and community colleges employ these advisors, who monitor students at their institutions to ensure that the students are in compliance with relevant immigration rules, monitor their successful completion of programs of study, communicate as necessary with the education advisor at the students' respective embassies, and ensure that the students receive all assistance necessary to succeed in their academic programs. To work at this level, a master's degree is required. Many international student advisors have completed degrees in student affairs and/or counseling. Some have completed degrees in TESOL (discussed below). Very few universities have dedicated preparatory programs for individuals interested in these positions. Lesley University in Boston, Massachusetts, offers a master's program in this area titled International Higher Education and Intercultural Studies. Another possibility is to complete a master's degree in international studies. If you are interested in such a position, we suggest that you interview one of the international student advisors at your institution and ask them about their career path.

It is not necessary for you to be from the country where you wish to work. Some of the most successful advisors are individuals who have actually been international students themselves. In all cases, though, individuals who wish to serve as international student advisors will need to put in service time—either via a paid or unpaid internship—at one or more institutions prior to applying for a position.

To find out more about these positions, please consult either NAFSA: Association of International Educators (www.nafsa.org) or the Canadian Bureau for International Education (www.cbie.ca/). Both organizations sponsor annual conferences, as well as regional conferences with presentations relevant to international student advising. It is possible to volunteer at these conferences and receive reduced rates for attending them.

Study Abroad Advising

As with international student advising, a master's-level degree is required for most positions in study abroad. Study abroad advisors typically manage all study-away activities for their universities. This includes term- and year-length study programs, various types of internships, and short-term study-away opportunities varying from two to six weeks. Advisors are expected to have completed some type of overseas study program themselves prior to advising others. Both NAFSA and CBIE have professional development workshops at their annual conferences for individuals just joining the field. A typical master's degree program could be in the same fields as discussed for international student advising, with the addition of region-specific area studies programs, such as Latin American studies.

International Admissions

Most individuals working in international admissions have moved from regular admissions appointments into the international arena. That is, the skill set they first develop is related to domestic student recruitment and retention. It is useful to be a detail-oriented person in this field, particularly because of the range of education, grading, and transcript systems you will come in contact with. Some level of experience in the general admissions office as a work-study student or student worker will give you a sense of the hectic nature of this position. Because international education systems vary so widely in the United States and Canada, individuals interested in things such as international grade equivalencies or whether credentials are real or fraudulent may find this a fascinating field. While a master's degree is not essential for an entry-level position, degrees in either student personnel or business affairs would be helpful for promotion to leadership positions.

TESOL

Teaching English to Speakers of Other Languages (TESOL or TESL in the United States; TESL or TEAL in Canada) is another field that is linked quite logically to an interest in other countries and cultures. While there are certificate-level programs that can be completed at the undergraduate or post-baccalaureate level, a master's degree in TESOL would allow you to teach English to speakers of other languages at the university level both in your home country and abroad. The international professional organization TESOL (www.tesol.org) can assist you with your investigation of various programs, as can the American Association of Applied Linguistics (aaal.org) and the Linguistic Society of America (linguisticsociety.org). You may wish to investigate how long the programs last and whether a thesis is required or optional.

Teaching International Studies at the Graduate or Undergraduate Level

To teach at the community college level, a master's degree is essential, while a Ph.D. is necessary for the university level. Because our field is interdisciplinary, you could complete an advanced degree in almost any social science field and be a strong candidate for a teaching position in international studies. Questions you may wish to ask yourself before you apply to a program include whether you are most interested in being a generalist or have a particular regional or thematic area of focus. Are you particularly interested in the Middle East, Africa, or the Caribbean? Are you most interested in international development, women and gender, international health, or language and area studies? Do you wish to attend a program with a particular reputation or one with a strong alumni and career network? Are you bound by geographic location? The more you know about where you would like to teach and exactly what you would like to teach, the easier it will be for you to choose your graduate program. All social science disciplines have professional organizations, such as the International Studies Association, the American Association of Geographers, or the American Anthropological Association. Frequently, these associations publish directories of graduate programs in the United States and Canada. These programs are ranked. You can also find out what types of financial aid are available. Do not hesitate to talk with your professors about their recommendations for particular programs that best suit your needs.

For many of you with university teaching and research goals, a Ph.D. will ultimately be required. You may choose to complete a master's degree at one time and then subsequently complete your Ph.D., or you may attend a school that allows you complete your master's in a seamless manner as you complete your doctoral requirements. There are significant advantages to the latter path. Most master's programs provide less financial aid than doctoral programs do. They also generally require two years to complete, as well as possibly a thesis. On the other hand, as a student admitted to a Ph.D. program (at a school with an integrated master's/Ph.D. program), you can sometimes apply for a master's after a single year of coursework, and you are much more likely to receive a strong financial aid package. While it can take time to locate schools with these programs (Yale is one example), it is worth considering them.

It is also the reality that traveling to attend a school of choice in the field is worth the effort, inconvenience, or expense. It is generally not wise to receive your graduate degree from the same school where you went for your undergraduate education; people may think that you went to graduate school there because you were place-bound or could not get into other schools. It is also generally believed that you will have a greater diversity in your education if you attend more than one institution. That said, there may be an exception if your university is particularly well known in an area that is important to you.

When applying to universities, think hard about the location of the school. A Ph.D. program generally takes six or seven years to complete (although people sometimes finish in five years or less). You want to be somewhere you will be happy. Pick a limited number of schools to apply to; four to five is usually a good number. At least one school should be a backup that you are more confident will accept you. Give the faculty member (or members) that you ask for a reference at least three weeks to write it; a month is even better. Give them a copy of your personal statement and let them know things about yourself that you'd like the admissions office to know.

When working on your application, spend a lot of time on your personal statement. This matters a great deal in the admissions process. Rewrite and proofread it until you are sick of it, then have others whom you trust read it. You should look at the school's website to find if there is someone there that you are interested in working with. There is no point in attending a great university if the only possible advisor is not someone with interests that match yours. It is best to choose a department where you can work with more than one lead advisor; if you have a difficult work relationship with one, you can turn to the other. Refer to the faculty member's work in your application. Suggest that you have a particular area/topic that you would like to investigate for your Ph.D. (you will not be held to this). Research carefully the particular requirements for your program. What is the language requirement, and when does it have to be fulfilled? It is often a good idea to pick up the phone and try to call some of the faculty members and the departmental registrar. Ask if they will give you the name of a graduate student to talk to. Then call them. Check to make sure that the people you want as advisors will not be on sabbatical the year that you arrive. Look at the course offerings and make sure that it has enough depth that you will have the choices you want. Do not be shy about talking to the departmental registrar concerning teaching assistantships and financial aid. But be positive: you are selling yourself. Do not get too personal, and do not come across as needy.

In order to apply to many graduate schools, you must sit for the Graduate Record Exams (GREs). These are multiple-choice tests that examine your ability in logic, mathematics, and language. For students with test anxiety, the GREs can be a formidable obstacle. One academic secret to keep in mind: some universities take the GREs very seriously, others do not require them at all, and others require them but place little emphasis on them unless they are unsure about a particular student. There are books about preparing for the GREs, and some testing services provide training. Some preparation helps, but after a couple of weekends, you will probably hit a saturation point. Do not cram the night before; you want to walk into the test rested. You can retake the test, but it is offered a limited number of times per year. There is also a charge each time you take it, just as there are application fees for each graduate application. Your acceptance and rejection letters from the universities may seem quite random: you could receive a full offer from one school, with tuition assistance and a stipend, only to be turned down by others. It is important to try not to put your ego on the line (this is hard to avoid) and to have a backup plan. The process can be time-consuming, exhausting, and difficult. But there are few things more exciting in life than a letter of admission to graduate school. After I (Shawn Smallman) received mine, I had to walk to the grocery store to buy food for dinner for my housemates. I took the letter in my pocket so that I could stop and reread it over and over as I went down the aisles—it just seemed impossible.

Final Thoughts

While your career is important, it is only one part of your life. If you do not follow an international career path, we hope that this book and your college course have interested you enough that you will want to remain internationally engaged. That can take many forms, from travel plans and music choices to personal friendships. Many international studies courses begin by showing you how international factors affect your life, including security problems, financial investments, and the immense reach of globalization. You will be a more informed citizen, and it may open new life opportunities to you. All of these are important factors. But an international perspective also makes for a richer perspective in the best tradition of liberal education. We hope that whatever path you take, you choose to remain interested in, and curious about, global affairs.

➤ **VOCABULARY**

Department of Homeland Security
International Organizations (IOs)
Canadian International Development Agency (CIDA) Foreign Service
TESOL, TESL, and TEAL
Foreign Area Officer (FAO)
U.S. Agency for International Development (USAID)

ACTIVITY 1 Based on your area of interest, identify a potential graduate program that would suit your professional needs. See what kinds of materials you are required to submit. If there is an essay, try and do some brainstorming as if you were going to respond. Write down your ideas.

ACTIVITY 2 If you are living in the United States, go to the NAFSA: Association of International Educators website (www.nafsa.org) to identify what regional conference is in your area. These programs generally occur in the fall. Look over a conference program and think about whether there are sessions you would like to attend. If you volunteer at the next conference, you can attend sessions without paying a registration fee. If you live in Canada, go to the Canadian Bureau for International Education (CBIE) website (http://www.cbie.ca/events/events-calendar/) to investigate upcoming conference information.

References

Foreign Service Resources (Canada)
Bartelman, J. 2004. *On six continents: Life in Canada's Foreign Service, 1966–2002.* Toronto: Douglas Gibson Books (a division of McLelland).
Freifeld, S. 1990. *Tales from the Canadian Foreign Service.* Lancaster, UK: Gazelle Book Services, Ltd.
Hantel-Fraser, C. 1993. *No fixed address: Life in the Foreign Service.* Toronto: University of Toronto Press.
Weiers, M. 1996. *Envoys extraordinary: Women of the Canadian Foreign Service.* Toronto: Dundurn Press.

Foreign Service Resources (United States)
Dorman, S. 2003. *Inside a U.S. embassy: How the Foreign Service works for America.* Washington, D.C.: American Foreign Service Association.
Grayson, F. N. 2006. *Foreign Service officer exam: Preparation for the written exam and the oral assessment.* Hoboken, N.J.: Wiley (Cliffs Test Prep).
Krasowski, J., ed. 2005. *American Foreign Service officer exam.* 4th ed. Laurenceville, N.J.: Thomson/Peterson's.
Linderman, P., and M. Brayer-Hess. 2002. *Realities of Foreign Service life: True stories of rescued golden retrievers and the people who love them.* Lincoln, Neb.: iUniverse, Inc. (Associates of the American Foreign Service Worldwide).

Intercultural Education Preparation
Leeds-Hurwitz, W. 1990. Notes in the history of intercultural communication: The Foreign Service institute and the mandate for intercultural training. *Quarterly Journal of Speech* 76 (3): 262–81. DOI:10.1080/00335639009383919.
Paige, R. M., A. Cohen, B. Kappler, J. Chi, and J. Lassegard. 2004. *Maximizing study abroad: A student's guide to strategies for language and culture learning and use.* Minneapolis: University of Minnesota.

International Development Careers
Hachmyer, C. 2008. *Alternatives to the Peace Corps: A guide to volunteer opportunities.* 12th ed. Oakland, Calif.: Food First Books.
Mueller, S. L., and M. Overman. 2008. *Working world: Careers in international education, exchange, and development.* Washington, D.C.: Georgetown University Press.

Russell, D. 2013. *Choosing a career in international development: A practical guide to working in the professions of international development.* College Station, Tex.: Virtualbookworm.com.

Social Change Graduate Programs
Powell, J., ed. 2001. *Education for action: Undergraduate and graduate programs that focus on social change.* 4th ed. Oakland, Calif.: Food First Books.

THIRTEEN **Conclusion**

As we asserted in the introduction, globalization is the dominant force of our time, with profound social, political, and cultural consequences for all of us. Here, we will explore what the future may look like for our planet. Predicting the future is always a dangerous task, and many scholars have made predictions—such as the end of the United States' unique position of power—only to be proved wrong over time. While nothing is determined, some demographic, environmental, and political trends are clear, and it would be difficult to change these without great political will. An overview of these trends will allow you to reflect on how they will impact your life and your local community. After looking to the future, we will return to the question of global citizenship. Given that globalization affects every individual and community, how should we think of our role and allegiances? What are our responsibilities in this international order? Finally, we will look to the lives of some key individuals who have made the connection from the local to the global through civic engagement in order to address major global problems.

Imagining the Future

In terms of security, some trends are complex. One of the more serious issues will be the international community's inability to prevent nuclear weapons proliferation. While individual nations may make the choice to abandon their nuclear development efforts—as has happened in the past in Brazil and South Africa, for example—the fact remains that the international community does not appear capable of stopping nations that are determined to acquire nuclear weapons. In the future, therefore, we are likely to see more nations with nuclear weapons, some of which obtain them as a response to their neighbor's development of nuclear capability in a so-called domino effect. Over the long term, it is likely that the danger from Islamic terrorism will decrease because, historically, few terrorist threats have endured for extended periods, and there is no clear reason why this threat would be different. But other groups will likely arise, as technology enables smaller groups of people to create dangerous weapons, especially with the further development of biological and chemical technologies. Sadly, the end of Al-Qaida will not end the danger of terrorism.

The increased complexity of security threats will lead to the rising influence of human security as an ideal. But traditional security concerns will remain paramount, particularly in Asia, where many nations will have to adapt to the rapid rise in the power of China and India and the relative decline of Japan. The power of nationalism, unresolved border issues, and the changing balance of power among states in the region means that, globally, a major war is most likely to take place on this continent in the decades to come. In contrast, Europe will continue to benefit from the peace brought by the European Union at the same time that its military and diplomatic influence fades globally.

In terms of economic globalization, we will see both the declining power of neoliberalism in the wake of the economic downturn of 2008 and continuing tensions around the world—particularly in the European Union between those who seek a workforce-based set of solutions to economic problems and those who seek a traditional market-based set of solutions. We will see the rising power of states as economic actors and creative problem solvers that draw on their nation-state contexts to solve their financial woes instead of depending on multinational, one-size-fits-all remedies. Iceland is perhaps the best example of this phenomenon. This may mean that economic globalization may continue, but multinational corporations may lose some of their relative influence. It is also true that the world will continue to see its economic center of gravity shift toward Asia, although the United States will not suffer an absolute decline in economic power.

Regarding political globalization, the international order will have to adapt to the relative rise in the power of Africa, Latin America, and Asia as these three world regions gain in population, with the most dramatic increase to come in Africa. The major European states—Germany, France, and Britain—will fall in most measurements of power. In their place, we will likely see Brazil, Russia, India, China, and South Africa (the so-called BRICS) act as major powers. They will be augmented by other nations that may acquire new political influence to reflect their economic rise, such as Turkey, and possibly Mexico if it is able to resolve its political problems.

This will increase the pressure to reform the United Nations to create a new global architecture that will reflect this modern-day power balance rather than the one prevalent in 1945. Overall, the two great world powers will be China and the United States. Historically, many wars between Great Powers were caused by the rapid rise of one power, which threatened the power of another. If China's rise is to avoid conflict, it will take not only skillful diplomacy but also greater power on the part of regional associations and international bodies. At the same time, democracy is likely to retain its political attraction, and many authoritarian states are likely to see regime changes. This is the greatest challenge facing China, which currently relies on economic growth and nationalism for legitimacy. Should the nation face difficult times, these are unlikely to prove sufficient.

In terms of cultural globalization, the world is likely to see significant migration because of broad differences in birth rates among world regions, as well as political and economic instability resulting in pressures that pull the workforce from one space to another. Despite Europe's efforts to maintain its identity, it will become increasingly pluralistic in terms of religion and will face great pressure from migration from North Africa. Japan will find it hard to avoid some increases in immigration, which will lead to difficult political choices. And the United States will continue to see the rising power of its Latino population. These trends all mean cultural globalization will deepen as populations become increasingly diverse. Linguistically, we will continue to see the waning of small languages, while globally, the dominance of English will be challenged at the regional level by the rise of Chinese, Spanish, Hindi, Russian, Bahasa Malaysia, and Arabic (Graddol 1997).

In the area of development, an increasing number of countries will make the transition from developing to developed status. This has already happened in South Korea and will happen in the next two decades in Chile, barring some unexpected trends. China, India, and Brazil will also achieve developed status in this century. This will lead to a more complex world in terms of development aid, as these nations become increasingly important donors. At the same time, the World Bank may be weakened, given the declining influence of neoliberalism. This is unlikely to change in the near future. At the micro level, lending institutions such as the Grameen Bank will permit local development to occur, regardless of what is happening on state, regional, and international levels.

Patterns of food distribution, production, and consumption will continue to change. The number of countries deemed "food insufficient" will increase. In like manner, as the water we consume becomes regulated and commodified (Barlow and Clarke 2003), both global and local tensions will increase. Nation-states will become more possessive of their resources, even as the WTO and TRIPS strive to maintain global control. Countries dependent on single foodstuffs (monocropping) for export will continue to be buffeted by the winds of political instability, weather changes, and market demands.

The world will continue to face health concerns such as the danger of epidemic disease, as the influenza pandemic of 2009 illustrated. The increasing density of human populations, the development of antibiotic resistance, and the spread of insect vectors with global warming will mean that "plagues" are not only a legacy of our past. In the end, the urban civilizations of the classical world were devastated by both malaria and Justinian's plague. It will take great investments and wise public-health policy—not to mention luck—if we are to avoid a similar health disaster in our age. At the same time, as many public-health specialists note, we may face a double burden as chronic diseases such as diabetes increase. While increasing wealth creates the opportunity to respond to these challenges, the optimism of the 1950s seems naive today.

With regard to energy, petroleum will continue its slow decline for the next half century. The Arab world will very likely have greater power because it holds most of the world's proven reserves. While new oil will be found in the deep ocean—bringing wealth and influence to Brazil and Angola—this will not be enough to stem the decline. As the 2010 leak in the Gulf of Mexico also shows, such deepwater oil also comes with great risks. Unconventional sources of oil will remain an alternative, but as the Oil Sands of Canada prove, they come with a high environmental cost. The question will ultimately be: how dirty does oil have to become before we abandon it? And in terms of alternative energy sources, what future damage to the environment are we willing to risk to release underground sources of natural gas? How will nation-states and regions resolve questions regarding nuclear power and nuclear waste? Ultimately, over the next decade, environmental concerns and technological breakthroughs—such as new battery technologies or the development of synthetic gasoline from algae—will lead to a move away from petroleum and expanded choices for energy.

The environmental future is one filled with challenges. It seems clear that the world will not be able to prevent global warming in the near term. Even with breakthroughs in fuels for transportation, the sustained use of coal and natural gas for electricity will continue this trend. With the diminishment of the earth's polar ice cap in the north, the globe's albedo will change (that is, the region will reflect less sunlight), which will cause a positive feedback loop in which the ocean will absorb more of the sun's energy. The result is that rather than resolving the issue, the international community instead will be trying to prevent catastrophic change and manage living in a warming world. There will be clear losers in this effort— Bangladesh and the Netherlands, Florida and Louisiana. Some Pacific Island nations will disappear. The future for coral reefs and the species that live under or on the Arctic ice appear bleak. But there may be some winners, too, such as Canada, Denmark, and Russia, as new areas open to agriculture or transportation from Greenland to the Northwest Passage (Easterbrook 2007). For animal species, however, there will only be loss, which will be exacerbated by the looming peak in the planet's global population in the mid-twenty-first century. Environmentalists will struggle to ensure the survival of key species, with the hope that the declining human populations after midcentury will lead to better natural conditions for the very long term. This will be a hard period in the earth's history.

Global Citizenship

Given the scale of these changes and the impact they will have upon all of us, what are your responsibilities? At the start of this text, we introduced you to the idea of global citizenship. Global citizens view themselves as actors in relation to all of humanity, with particular rights and responsibilities apart from any owed to one's nation-state (Pike 2008). This idea is widely debated, with some people questioning whether global citizenship exists. From the viewpoints of the critics, the international order above the scale of the nation-state is largely defined by anarchy. You cannot have a passport as a global citizen. Any obligations that you have are those that pertain to your nation alone. Within this framework, the ideal of global citizenship is idealistic and unrealistic (Dower 2000, 555–57). Still others question whether it is again the Global North that is defining for the rest of the world how we should behave in various contexts.

Other authors say that with contemporary globalization, it is inevitable that we begin to think of ourselves in a global context. From this perspective, there are two ideals of global citizenship (Falk 1994, 39). The first vision is that of global business elites who view globalization from a financial perspective. One can see concrete examples of this perspective in human resource journals that deal with identifying outstanding managers (Osland, Bird, Mendenhall, and Osland 2006; Jokinen 2005). These works look at the challenges that managers face on a global scale and the particular skills that they need. The literature on "global leadership" is extensive because corporations believe that a chief executive with the right mindset can define a successful global strategy (Osland, Bird, Mendenhall, and Osland 2006, 199–202).

While some critics of global citizenship ask whether the term is meaningful, in a business context, having a global mindset is perceived as a precious commodity with a measurable value. Many of the skills that global leaders are supposed to have—resilience, optimism, social judgment, empathy, motivation to work in an international environment, acceptance of complexity and its contradictions, and social skills—are qualities that would also be advocated by people who favor an opposing construction of global engagement (Siebert 2005; Jokinen 2005, 206–9).

Robert Falk (1994, 39) argues that if the first vision is that of "globalization from above," the second vision is that of "globalization from below" defined by a commitment to "environmental concerns, human rights, hostility to patriarchy, and a vision of human community based on the unity of diverse cultures seeking an end to poverty, oppression, humiliation, and collective violence." From this perspective, global citizenship is a vision that is largely defined by a sense of empathy with people of vastly different backgrounds. The language that surrounds it differs sharply from that adopted in the human-resource journals, as the following quote from Peggy McIntosh (2005, 23) suggests: "What would it take to be global citizens? I can answer only from my own experience and perceptions. I associate the idea of a global citizen with habits of mind, heart, body, and soul that have to do with working for and preserving a network of relationship and connection across lines of difference and distinctness, while keeping and deepening a sense of one's own identity and integrity."

While this concept may seem rather vague, Nigel Dower (2000, 553) and others have made the point that this vision of global citizenship has deep historical roots that reach back to classical civilization. Many authors stress that the scale of global problems requires people to redefine their sense of self and to demand institutions that will "exercise global responsibility" (Dower 2000, 553). Dower emphasizes, however, that belief in global citizenship does not entail belief in global government; rather, it entails a shift in perspective, such that people and populations are concerned with the needs of humanity on a global scale (Dower 2000, 553). Within this second perspective, we see a strong ethical component to this concept of global citizenship.

John Urry (2000) argues that globalization arose at the same time that people internationally began to rethink the meaning of citizenship. As a result of this process, there are multiple meanings and ideals of global citizenship, most of which are contested (Urry 2000 62–63, 69). One concern with global citizenship is that if we perceive ourselves to have obligations that lie above those that we owe to the nation-state, we might in some sense be disloyal to the entity to which we owe our primary allegiance. This is particularly troubling in an era defined by war and terrorism. Yet we all have multiple allegiances, some of which are below the state (such as to our local community) and some of which may lie above it (humanity's need to fight global warming). In reality, many global processes are undermining traditional ideals of national citizenship, and these challenges are likely to increase (Urry 2000, 68–74).

As authors, we also share an ideology that includes a commitment to the belief in the value of global citizenship, in the sense that our actions have implications for others. We want to be explicit about our own perspective. We are all global actors, whether it be because of the commodity chains in which we are embedded, the votes that we cast, or the beliefs that we advocate. This reality carries a moral obligation with it. We recognize that in practical terms, the idea of global citizenship is complicated. There are many challenges to the idea of global citizenship, and the duties that it entails can be interpreted in widely differing ways. This may mean thinking of yourself as a global citizen, or perhaps in a slightly different manner: as a globally minded citizen. Whether you agree with our argument or not, however, what is important is the reality that we are embedded in a web of connections that stretches to unexpected parts of the planet.

Biographies

At this time, we want to introduce you to three individuals who personify some or all of the dimensions of global citizens described above. In the first chapter, you were introduced to McIntosh's (2005, 23) six capacities of mind: "(1) the ability to observe oneself and the world around one; (2) the ability to make comparisons and contrasts; (3) the ability to 'see' plurally as a result; (4) the ability to understand that both 'reality' and language come in versions; (5) the ability to see power relations and understand them systemically; and (6) the ability to balance awareness of one's own realities with the realities of entities outside of the perceived self."

As you read these people's stories, try and identify which of McIntosh's descriptors apply to each of them. In a way, these life stories are a kind of portrait of global leaders. Perhaps you will recognize some of your own traits in theirs. None of these individuals set out to become model global citizens. Most never expected to cross disciplines and regions or become engaged in international issues. Yet their lives took them from one continent to another, from their local environment to a global environment. As you reflect upon their stories, think about the common threads in their experience—how these individuals planned for their futures, only to take a different course. Were there hints that someday they would become actors on a global stage? Are there parallels between their lives and your own?

Chico Mendes

Francisco Alves Mendes Filho was one of seventeen siblings born to a family of poor rubber tappers in the Brazilian state of Acre. Only six of the original seventeen survived childhood. One reason may have been their father's clubfeet, which made it hard for him to walk great distances through the forests to tap rubber trees and thus less able to provide for his family (Revkin 1990). From a young age, Francisco worked hard, like millions of forest people living in Amazonia, a region with little government aid, widespread malaria, and chronic violence. Plagued by weak land titles, peasants and rubber tappers in this region often find themselves forced off of their land by hired guns. While still a teenager, however, Francisco, who came to be called Chico Mendes, befriended an escaped political prisoner from an elite family. During many long nights in his friend's hut, Chico learned about politics and listened to world events broadcast on the former prisoner's shortwave radio.

As major landowners increasingly threatened the lives of people in his community, Chico Mendes organized the rubber tappers to block the illegal deforestation of their land and press the government for schools, hospitals, and justice. Chico Mendes might have remained in obscurity, but in 1978 Mary Allegretti, a Brazilian anthropologist, brought him to national and global attention. At the time, the international environmental movement needed local allies to raise awareness of the Amazon's deforestation. Chico Mendes knew nothing of this movement, but he agreed to travel to the United States, where he lobbied congressmen, helped impact terms for World Bank loans, and influenced the policies used by the Inter-American Development Bank (Revkin 1990, 208–30). A documentary filmmaker, Adrian Cowell, followed Chico Mendes's work and made him an international icon.

Chico Mendes probably thought his international profile would protect him from violence. It did not. Local ranchers hated him, especially Darly Alves da Silva, a powerful patriarch with thirty children and a bad reputation. On December 22, 1988, Chico Mendes stepped out of the back of his house to cool off with water. When he opened the door, a shotgun blast ended his life. As a consequence, the international media flooded into Xapuri, and the police arrested Alves da Silva and his son (Revkin 1990, 283). The ranchers were shocked. How could millions of people in Europe or the United States view a common rubber tapper as the symbol of a worldwide movement? Although the violence continued in the years that followed, the rubber tappers acquired new power, and the extractive reserves advocated by Chico Mendes now cover millions of acres and provide for thousands throughout the region.

Hernando de Soto Polar

A famed Peruvian economist, Hernando de Soto Polar has challenged prevalent ideas about why many people in Latin America—and in other developing nations—are poor. He was born in the city of Arequipa, Peru, in 1941, but his family was soon exiled, and he was raised and went to graduate school in Switzerland. He then returned to Peru, where he worked as an economist for both the private sector and the government. What brought him to global attention, however, was his publication of a book in 1989 titled *The Other Path: The Invisible Revolution in the Third World*, the first of three influential works. In his first book, de Soto argued that poverty existed in Latin America and other areas not because capitalism had failed but rather because it had never been truly tried. From his perspective, Latin American governments had warped the market so severely that the poor were in effect permanently excluded from the formal market, no matter how entrepreneurial or intelligent they might be. *The Other Path* looked at the bureaucratic obstacles that kept many poor Peruvians confined to an "informal economy" because they could not navigate the regulations and bureaucracy to access credit, receive permits, and collect sales taxes.

De Soto's work had an impact, both because this was a time when neo-liberalism was rising as an economic ideology and because of his detailed descriptions of the problems faced by the poor. This work also gave him political influence in Peru, where he founded the Institute for Liberty and Democracy (ILD; see www.ild.org.pe) in 1983. He is now president of this think tank, which has helped to shape public policy in Peru and spread his views abroad.

At the core of de Soto's work has been his concern with the challenges that the poor face in gaining title to their own land. Many people cannot afford to legally purchase their land, so they buy their property informally, build their property without permits, and then expand it without notifying city authorities. Because of this situation, Latin America's cities are ringed by slums, within which live people who do not have title to their own homes. This means that they cannot receive a mortgage to purchase property, they do not have security of title to what they do have, and they cannot receive loans to improve their property or to start a business. In effect, these communities exist outside the reach of the state. There is an immense economic cost to this, as hundreds of billions of dollars of property is undercapitalized and unprotected. The ILD, therefore, has helped more than a million Peruvians gain title to their own homes and hundreds of thousands of businesspeople enter the marketplace legally.

While de Soto's work has had the greatest influence within Latin America, he has also helped to implement similar programs in both Africa and the Middle East. His model has not succeeded everywhere, and it has vocal critics. With the rise of the Left in Latin America and the serious recession of 2009, neoliberalism has lost favor internationally. But Hernando de Soto Polar's work continues to command respect because of the grassroots empowerment that lies at the core of his philosophy and his emphasis on the experience of the poor.

Vandana Shiva

Vandana Shiva was born in Uttarakhand, India, in 1952. She received an undergraduate degree in physics and a master's in philosophy from the University of Guelph in Ontario, Canada, before completing a Ph.D. in quantum physics at the University of Western Ontario. Shiva became an active participant in the Chipko movement in India in the 1970s, when followers of the environmentalist Sunderlal Bahuguna fought to protest logging in India by encircling and hugging the trees that loggers wished to cut (Chipko Movement 2009).

Shiva refined her passion for the environment over time as she pursued her academic work and her activism. A prolific author of more than 300 books and papers, she is perhaps best known for her work on biopiracy and intellectual property rights. In 1993 she won the Right Livelihood Award (sometimes called the "alternative Nobel Prize"). She founded the Research Foundation for Science, Technology, and Ecology, as well as Navdanya, a seed bank in Uttaranchal (now Uttarakhand) in northern India. The seed bank and the organization Navdanya, a term signifying "nine crops that represent India's source of food security" (www.navdanya.org), work to promote biodiversity by protecting heritage seeds. In her chronicle on the Navdanya website, Shiva tells of founding the organization in 1984 to respond in a positive way to violence in the Punjab region of northern India and to the terrible industrial accident in Bhopal that claimed the lives of roughly 5,000 people. She speaks of four passions that have guided her: "the search for knowledge, a longing for freedom, a concern for justice, and a deep love and reverence for nature" (Vandana Shiva Right Livelihood Acceptance Speech 2007).

Shiva discovered that she could best reach her goals by leaving the field of academia. In her acceptance speech for the Right Livelihood award, she stated:

> [T]he combination of the urge for free enquiry and my concern for nature and people . . . made me leave the narrow confines of academia where disciplines are fragmented from each other, where knowledge is separated from action but linked intimately to power. In 1982, I left an academic career with a dream to build an independent research initiative for generating a different kind of knowledge, which would serve the powerless not the powerful, which would not get all its cues from Western Universities and international institutions, but would also be open to learn from the indigenous knowledge of local communities, which would break down the artificial divide between experts and non-experts and subject and object. (Vandana Shiva Right Livelihood Acceptance Speech 2007)

A member of the International Forum on Globalization, Shiva is strongly opposed to the genetic modification of food and to large-scale "technofarms." Her work is not without criticism, however, as this passage by ecologist David Wood of the Center for Global Food Issues shows:

> It's decision time for Shiva. She must now choose between being a patriotic supporter of Indian food and fibre production, or being a future tool of foreign agricultural export interests (interests cloaked in anti-GMO, pro-organic rhetoric, and a complex web of NGO funding). She must ask herself if her success on the international lecture circuit is in India's interest. She should calculate the cost to India's farmers of all her foreign "free lunches," and ask who really picks up the tab. India cannot yet afford the luxury of organic farming. Faced with intense global competition to dominate trade in staple crops, India also cannot afford the luxury of having foreign activists trying to damage national crop production. For cotton alone, this is a billion-dollar issue. (Wood 2007)

Wood's comments focus as much on Shiva's personal choices as her academic and activist work. Her critics at the Center for Global Food Issues hold very different notions of how to resolve food issues than do those working at Shiva's Research Foundation for Science, Technology, and Ecology. No matter how much individuals agree or disagree with her ideologies and policy recommendations, Shiva remains a political force shaping debates about environmental issues globally as well as within India.

Hope and the Future

We have chosen to end the book with these examples because they make the point that global citizenship entails the idea of civic engagement. You may not agree with what each of these people fought for, but what is important is that they each chose to act on their beliefs to help other people on a scale that ultimately had global implications. Each of these people first looked beyond their local communities for different reasons. Chico Mendes first reached outside the Amazon because he saw national and international resources to help in a local struggle. Hernando de Soto Polar looked to the slums that ringed Lima and Cusco and dreamed of a better future for the poor, not only in Latin America but also throughout the developing world. Vandana Shiva grew disillusioned with what she perceived as the sterility of academia and was inspired by the Chipko movement to work on behalf of others. All three then made the leap from the local to the global. They were not victims of change. They all came to believe that it was not enough to be aware of global trends; they also had to become leaders.

One of the challenges with a book such as this is that it can quickly become a litany of global problems. Some of these issues—from global warming to population growth—are unlikely to be entirely solved in our lifetimes. But that does not mean that these problems cannot be mitigated through civic engagement, new ideas, and public policy. Through this work, we have sought to make you aware of the major economic, political, social, and biological trends that are accompanying globalization and will impact everyone's lives. You have been exposed to different views and should now be able to think critically about these perspectives, to decide which arguments appear persuasive to you, and to reflect on what information you may be missing. Ultimately, we want you to think about the idea of global citizenship in a way that does not leave you feeling overwhelmed by our planet's problems but rather instilled with a sense of responsibility for addressing humanity's concerns through means that are both possible and necessary.

References

Bacon, N. 2003. Redefining citizenship for our multicultural world. *New Horizons for Learning*. March. Retrieved January 25, 2009, from http://www.newhorizons.org/strategies/multicultural/bacon.htm.

Barlow, M., and T. Clarke. 2003. *Blue gold: The fight to stop the corporate theft of the world's water.* New York: W. W. Norton.

Biography of Vandana Shiva. Retrieved September 16, 2007, from http://www.bio.davidson.edu/people/kabernd/seminar/2004/GMbios/LH.html.

Chipko Movement. Retrieved January 25, 2009, from http://healthy-india.org/saveearth6.asp/.

De Soto Polar, H. 1989. *The other path: Redefining citizenship in the Third World.* New York: Harper Collins.

———. 2000. *The mystery of capital: Why capitalism triumphs in the West and fails everywhere else.* New York: Perseus.

Dower, N. 2000. The idea of global citizenship—a sympathetic assessment. *Global Society* 14 (4): 543–67.

Easterbrook, G. 2007. Global warming: Who wins—and who loses? *Atlantic Monthly*. April. Retrieved January 8, 2010, from www.theatlantic.com/doc/200704/global-warming.

Falk, R. 1994. The making of global citizenship. In *The conditions of citizenship*, ed. B. Van Steenbergen, 39–50. London: Sage.

Graddol, D. 1997. *The future of English*. British Council. Digital edition created by the English Company (UK) Ltd. Retrieved January 16, 2010, from www.officiallanguages.gc.ca/docs/f/Future_of_English.pdf.

Hanvey, R. 1982. An attainable global perspective. *Theory into Practice (Global Education)* 21 (3): 162–67.

Jokinen, T. 2005. Global leadership competencies: A review and discussion. *Journal of European Industrial Training* 29 (3): 199–216.

McIntosh, P. 2005. Gender perspectives on educating for global awareness. In *Educating citizens for global awareness*, ed. N. Noddings, 22–39. New York: Teachers College.

Michelfelder, D. 2008. Global citizenship and responsibility. *Macalester civic forum: Meditations on global citizenship* 1 (Spring). Minnesota: Macalester College.

Navdanya. Retrieved January 1, 2008, from www.navdanya.org/.

Osland, J. S., A. Bird, M. Mendenhall, and A. Osland. 2006. Developing global leadership capabilities and global mindset. In *Handbook of international human resource management research*, ed. G. Stahl and I. Bjorkman, 197–222. London: Edward Elgar Publishers, Ltd.

Pike, G. 2008. Reconstructing the legend: Educating for global citizenship. In *Educating for human rights and global citizenship*, ed. A. Abdi and L. Shultz, 223–38. Albany, N.Y.: SUNY Press.

Pratt, M. L. 1996. Arts of the contact zone. In *Resources for teaching ways of reading: An anthology for writers*, ed. D. Bartholomae and A. Petrosky, 440–60. Boston: Bedford Books.

Revkin, A. 1990. *The burning season: The murder of Chico Mendes and the fight for the Amazon rain forest*. Boston: Houghton Mifflin.

Siebert, A. 2005. *The resiliency advantage*. San Francisco: Barrett-Koehler Press.

Thurow, R., and S. Kilman. 2009. *Enough: Why the world's poorest starve in an age of plenty*. New York: PBS Public Affairs.

Urry, J. 2000. Global flows and global citizenship. In *Democracy, citizenship, and the global city*, ed. E. F. Isin, 62–78. New York: Routledge.

Vandana Shiva Right Livelihood Acceptance Speech. Retrieved September 16, 2007, from http://www.rightlivelihood.org/shiva_speech.html.

Wood, D. 2007. One hand clapping: Organic farming in India. Center for Global Issues. Retrieved September 20, 2007, from http://www.cgfi.org/materials/articles/2002/dec_12_02_wood.htm.

Acknowledgments

A large number of people worked to make this book possible. Patrice Hudson, Robert Halstead, and Cara Clark Martinez carefully edited drafts of these chapters. Janice Smith, in particular, has served as not only a superb copyeditor but also a reflective mentor to both of us in terms of process and text organization. Nathan Houtz did research for this text—in particular for the security chapter, where his work was invaluable. Tasia-Jana Tanginoa proved to be an expert on the United Nations; her research greatly improved the political globalization chapter. Michael Bonham and Jamie Biesanz did work on Antarctica that was also key to the political globalization chapter. Steph Gaspers, with help from David Banis, designed the maps that are used in the text. Margaret Everett, Aomar Boum, and Christina Caponi have allowed us to use their photos. We also want to recognize our Portland State students who have read different drafts of this work and provided important feedback. We are grateful to our current and former international studies colleagues who have brainstormed extensively with us: Aomar Boum, Stephen Frenkel, Tugrul Keskin, Leopoldo Rodriguez, and Birol Yesilada. We have derived inspiration from published work by the Institute for Global Citizenship at Macalester College. Elaine Maisner and the editorial and marketing teams at UNC Press proved to be outstanding partners. Finally, we would both like to thank our families, who supported us through the process.

Index